ACCLA

"Masterful. A powerful and fascinating ~~story~~ thoroughly researched, brilliantly organized, and written in a sharp, riveting style . . . most chilling when it probes the dark relationship between a son who kills and a mother who covers for him."
—John Philpin, author of Beyond Murder

"Pienciak has done a remarkable job of treating a complex case." —Publisher's Weekly

"If this were a perfect world and justice were served, she would be serving a long time in jail."
—William J. Purdy, prosecutor, in New York Newsday

"This account of a dangerously dysfunctional relationship will interest true crime buffs."
—Library Journal

"The story is bizarre, and the players uniquely evil . . . the book tells us concretely about these hideous lives."
—Kirkus Reviews

RICHARD T. PIENCIAK

Mama's Boy

THE TRUE STORY
OF A SERIAL KILLER
AND HIS MOTHER

AN ONYX BOOK

ONYX
Published by New American Library, a division of
Penguin Group (USA) Inc., 375 Hudson Street,
New York, New York 10014, U.S.A.
Penguin Books Ltd, 80 Strand,
London WC2R 0RL, England
Penguin Books Australia Ltd, 250 Camberwell Road,
Camberwell, Victoria 3124, Australia
Penguin Books Canada Ltd, 10 Alcorn Avenue,
Toronto, Ontario, Canada M4V 3B2
Penguin Books (N.Z.) Ltd, Cnr Rosedale and Airborne Roads,
Albany, Auckland 1310, New Zealand

Penguin Books Ltd, Registered Offices:
80 Strand, London WC2R 0RL, England

Published by Onyx, an imprint of New American Library, a division of Penguin Group (USA) Inc. Previously appeared in a Dutton edition.

First Onyx Printing, April 1997
20 19 18 17 16

 REGISTERED TRADEMARK—MARCA REGISTRADA

Printed in the United States of America

To My Mother and Father

For always being there to nurture and support, and because this tragedy demonstrates the important role that caring and loving parents play in a child's development.

Acknowledgments

As always, many thanks are in order for a research project of this magnitude. First and foremost, special thanks to my wife, Cheryl, for all of her hard work with transcripts, taped interviews, editorial advice, positive encouragement, and perhaps most important, her prodding during my periods of distraction.

An extraspecial thanks to my two extraspecial sons, Adam and Ryan, for their patience in allowing me to disrupt their lives with yet another book.

I am particularly grateful to Michael Vinciguerra for pitching the Napoletano story to me as a fascinating topic for a book during many rounds of golf. I also wish to thank those who gave freely of their time—some for many, many hours—but who, for whatever reasons, wish to remain anonymous. Their assistance was invaluable and I am deeply appreciative.

Heartfelt thanks to two dear friends from the world of professional journalism, Timothy D. Harper and Sharon Rosenhause, for taking a great deal of time to help me when I needed their editorial and emotional advice the most. I also appreciate the yeoman efforts of my sister-in-law, Edie Pienciak, for her work on interview transcripts, and friend Diane Cristantiello for providing valuable insight during my early plodding on how to keep the story moving. Thanks to Bob Gearty, another friend from the world of journalism, and to Eddie McCarthy, from his life of leisure in Florida, for sharing their acumen on the life and times of the Bronx and other New York City institutions.

Thank you to Clifton Police Chief Frank J. LoGioco and the entire Clifton Police Department, a most dedicated group of women and men; to FBI Special Agent Thomas A. Cottone, Jr., and to the many cooperative FBI agents and officials in Washington, D.C., New York, Newark and West Paterson, New Jersey, and Albuquerque, New Mexico.

From the Passaic County Prosecutor's Office, I am particularly grateful to Senior Assistant Prosecutor William J. Purdy, Jr., Assistant Prosecutor Walter R. Dewey, Jr., and Senior Investigator Peter T. Talarico, Jr.

On the defense side, I would like to thank attorneys Ernest M. Caposela, Louis Acevedo, and Susan McCoy, and investigator Francis R. Murphy.

Also, thanks to the staff at the Official Court Reporters' Office at the Passaic County Courthouse, the county court clerk's office, Assignment Judge Nicholas G. Mandak, Judge Vincent E. Hull, Jr., his various clerks and staff, and to Sheriff's Deputy Archie Vogel and his courtroom assistants.

At *The Record*, thanks to Editor Glenn Ritt, Director of Photography Rich Gigli, Teri Auchard in the Photo Department, and to the newspaper's photography and news staffs. At the *North Jersey Herald & News*, thanks to Editor Diane Haines, photographer Bill Hillermier, and the photo and news staffs. Thanks also to Michael Lipack, Eric Meskauskas, and Angela Troisi in the Photo Department at the *New York Daily News* as well as Scotty Browne and the rest of the news library staff. A debt of gratitude also is in order on the photo side for Jeff Langendorf of Manhattan Color, Inc., for solving my technological nightmare regarding a critical photograph.

On the business front, a profound thanks to Stuart Krichevsky, my literary agent, for service above and beyond the norm; and to Jody Hotchkiss, my film agent at Sterling Lord Literistic, for once again negotiating turbulent waters.

At Dutton Signet, I owe a special thanks to Associate Publisher Michaela Hamilton for her guidance, vision, and patience, and to Senior Manuscript Editor John Paine, once again a gentle master with the machete. A note of thanks also to Jory Des Jardins and Neil Stuart.

As always, a deep feeling of gratitude to my mentor, Willard E. Lally, for his original direction more than twenty years ago, and for his wise and sage advice in more recent times.

Finally, a sincere thanks to the various victims' family members who assisted in the project. To all of the victims' families, I send a prayer that the grief will lessen with each morning's sunrise.

Author's Note

The separate chapters of italicized discourse entitled "In Her Words," as well as the italicized quotations at the beginning of each section, were drawn from in-depth interviews with Carolyn Napoletano, the mother of Eric Napoletano, the main defendant in the case. In order to keep the text flowing smoothly, author's questions, improper grammar, and extraneous matter were eliminated. There also were occasions where two or more discussions about the same topic were combined and presented in accurate chronological order. The italicized copy is otherwise as Carolyn Napoletano spoke it.

In agreeing to be interviewed at length, Carolyn Napoletano said she wanted to explain "the other side" of the complicated events that are documented in this book, both on her own behalf and on behalf of her son. The result is a greater body of information for the reader to rely on in deciding, as any juror must do in a trial relying on circumstantial evidence, whether the defendants' stories make sense, whether they follow logical progression, and whether the events could have possibly occurred in the coincidental manner that Carolyn Napoletano claims. If there is no logic, there can be no credibility.

I believe the answer is in her words.

—Richard T. Pienciak

PROLOGUE

By the time Alexander William Nyce pulled into the Arrow
Island Overlook that Saturday, June 2, 1984, he had spent a
good portion of the morning hopping from one scenic viewing
station to another. The pristine landscape of the Delaware
Water Gap and the nearby Appalachian Trail offered a glo-
rious vista of peaceful picture-postcard views. But this was
not to be a day of tranquillity for the twenty-year-old tourist.
As Nyce looked down the steep embankment, his gaze focused on a distinctive multicolored comforter resting against
a small tree in heavy brush, just twenty feet below. Protruding from one end of the orange, brown, and tan bedspread
was the upper body of a lifeless woman. The blanket and its
contents were bound with a strong white cotton cord. The victim's feet also were bound, and covered with a green plastic
garbage bag.

Nyce, visiting the Pocono region from Springfield, Virginia, ran back to the car and raced down the rural highway,
Route 611. He pulled into the Slateford Inn, where he called
the Pennsylvania State Police. Within half an hour the area
was swarming with law-enforcement personnel, some of
whom would spend the next decade trying to solve the gruesome homicide.

Down the embankment, the investigators determined that
the body was that of a teenager or young adult. She
appeared to be Latina. The victim was clad in a blood-
stained bra and jeans with five-inch zippers on the leg bot-
toms. Inside the jeans' pockets, the investigators found a
cigarette lighter, a pack of matches, and a tube of lipstick—
but no identification.

The body was savagely mutilated. The victim's throat had
been slit by at least five stab and slash wounds. She had
dozens of additional stab wounds across her face and body,
and a massive hole between her eyes. In some places, the

weapon had penetrated right to the bone. Both of her hands were riddled with defensive wounds deep enough to cut through muscle. Her breasts had been poked, most likely with a pencil, perhaps while she was still alive. A wound on one of her arms appeared to have been made by a lighted cigarette. The body's cardiovascular system was devoid of blood, suggesting that the victim had been murdered while suspended upside down, thereby allowing her blood to drain through the deepest gashes.

The area surrounding the scenic overlook was relatively remote, within the confines of the Delaware Water Gap National Recreation Area, more than 70,000 acres spanning both sides of the river gorge. The body probably had been thrown over the embankment within the previous twenty-four hours, most likely a "quick dump" from a populated urban center, either from New York City, seventy-five miles to the east, or Philadelphia, to the south.

The murderer had no doubt expected the corpse to roll considerably farther down the precipice. But in fact, the body would not have remained hidden even then, because several hundred yards down the cliff—well before the river-bank—the land flattened out to accommodate a railroad track and a hiking trail. This suggested that the body had been dumped at night.

The county coroner was summoned, and the body was removed for an autopsy. Crime-scene experts searched for forensic evidence. The area between the 76 Truck Stop off Interstate Route 80 and the nearest truck stop across the river in New Jersey was canvassed to determine if the victim had been observed in any of the motels, bars, and restaurants. The survey came up empty.

It was obvious that the victim had not gone quietly. But the autopsy, as performed by Doctor Isidore Mihalakis, a forensic pathologist at Lehigh Valley Hospital Center in Allentown, Pennsylvania, suggested the fatal attack had been a drawn-out torture, as if the murderer had enjoyed the victim's attempts to fight back.

The assault had also probably proved to be an erotic experience for the murderer. The frenzy had been so ferocious that the killer's rage could have been directed at another woman in his life—perhaps his mother. That would help explain the vicious overkill.

Detailing the wounds became a nauseating exercise,

going on for pages in the autopsy report. The number and variety of the slashes and cuts and punches were astonishing. The multitude of wounds was so extensive that Dr. Mihalakis found himself explaining how one slash crossed paths with several others, how this incision merged with that slit. Documentation of the injuries was organized by section of the body.

The cutting wounds of the throat transected the trachea and esophagus. The major neck wound measured six inches "from side to side." Multiple blood vessels were severed. The right external carotid artery was perforated. The larynx was totally bisected. The rear of the esophagus was the only structure visible when the back of the throat was viewed through the gaping open wound.

There were stab wounds in the face, neck, and chest. The thyrohyoid ligament was totally cut. Cartilage was slashed. There was a slicing cut across the bridge of the nose, another across her forehead. There were defensive cutting wounds on both the victim's hands. And there were multiple bruises on her arms, face, and scalp. The right eyebrow and cheek area was peppered with severe abrasions and lacerations. There was a stab wound in the base of the chin, as well as cuts along the right jawline. There was a stab wound in the left cheek, a stab wound in the right base of the neck, a puncture wound in the middle of the chest, and a jab wound in the sternum. Several fresh contusions littered the victim's left arm. The murderer's fingernails had dug into the victim's face. Her breasts also had sustained numerous scratches. There were bloodstains, some of them crusted, literally from head to toe.

Of special note were three bruises on the right side of the victim's face, just in front of the ear, "resembling knuckle marks." Additional knuckle marks were found on the right chin, and a series of similar marks on the victim's right and left arms. These wounds suggested that the murderer had punched out the victim's face and upper body prior to the stabbings and slashings.

But an even more startling discovery was made: The woman had been pregnant, making this, some would say, a double homicide.

News of the unidentified corpse received passing mention in the next morning's local newspaper, whereupon the investigation fell into a disappointing pattern of unproductive tips and clues. An enormous amount of energy was expended investigating a brown-and-white school bus seen near where the body was discovered. An elderly woman who worked at a Pocono mountain resort said she had seen the bus and a late-model blue car parked in the scenic overlook just four hours before the wrapped-up body was discovered. To add to the intrigue, she said she had seen a well-dressed Latino man get out of the car and walk over to another well-dressed Latino, whom she believed was the bus driver.

When the school-bus angle was publicized, purported sightings poured into the state police barracks. A Pocono Mountain High School bus driver remembered seeing such a vehicle on Route 611, with New Jersey plates. There was a rack on the roof, made of old galvanized pipe. A heavyset man with long blond hair and wire-rim glasses had been driving. But troopers eventually tracked down the bus operator in western New Jersey, and concluded that he had nothing to do with the Arrow Island Overlook corpse.

And so it went, bum lead after bum lead. Try as they might, Pennsylvania State Police investigators were unable to identify the victim. Missing-persons reports on the National Crime Information Center (NCIC) computer network shared by police departments across the country were frequently checked, especially reports concerning disappearances from the New York metropolitan area. A composite sketch was prepared by an expert from the Delaware State Police and broadcast on television in Philadelphia. A dental examination of the cadaver revealed portions of brace work in place. And scrapings were taken from beneath the victim's fingernails.

But the investigators had nothing to compare the samples against. No one matching the corpse's physical characteristics had been reported missing.

Weeks turned to months. The case file worked its way to the bottom of the pile. In the meantime, the mystery corpse was buried under a gravestone reading MS. JUNE ARROW ISLAND OVERLOOK, to mark the month and location of the tourist's grisly find.

PART 1

Myra's Disappearance

We were more friends than son and mother because Eric and I were always like brother and sister.

—Carolyn Napoletano

-1-

The front doors to city hall swung open wildly that Friday evening, shortly before midnight. The date was June 22, 1990, six long years after the discovery of the body in the Delaware Water Gap. A jittery man of twenty-five led the way. He was sandy haired and wiry—about six feet tall and 150 pounds. He had weirdly darting hazel eyes. Entering the Clifton, New Jersey, Police Department's reception area, he identified himself as Eric Napoletano of 25 East Sixth Street, Apartment 3. The woman at his side—short, with glasses and long, flowing red hair—was his mother, Carolyn. In her midfifties, she was a bit on the heavy side—frumpy-looking, really—and had two frightened-looking toddlers in tow, her grandsons.

Highly agitated, Eric Napoletano demanded that someone explain to him why the police had been snooping around his apartment.

Officer Thomas Burrows overheard the commotion at the front desk. He knew exactly what the man was talking about; he had just returned from that address. He had been sent there to look for someone with the very same name, Napoletano, but had turned up nothing during his canvass of the two-story building and surrounding neighborhood. Burrows had been dispatched to the Napoletano home after a relative of Eric Napoletano's wife, Myra, called headquarters to express concern that her cousin had not been heard from for more than two days. The caller, a woman named Nereida Flick, had made it sound as if Myra Napoletano had disappeared off the face of the earth.

Burrows walked down the hallway to summon his supervisor, Sergeant John Zipf, who at that moment happened to be on the phone with Flick, informing her of Burrows's unproductive search. When told that Myra's husband had just appeared at the front desk with his two sons, Flick's concern about her missing cousin increased considerably.

Zipf told the woman he would have to call her back, then walked out to the reception area to meet the husband.

Eric Napoletano again identified himself, then demanded, "Why did you send someone to my house?"

Zipf explained to Napoletano that his wife's cousin had called to express concern about Myra's whereabouts. The police had gone to the apartment simply to take a look.

The answer was not good enough for Eric Napoletano, though. "But why did you send someone there?"

There was an arrogance to his tone. It was clear he had not come to headquarters to report his wife missing. He and his mother were more upset that the police had been nosing around his residence. Nothing Zipf said appeased them. Eric said he could not fathom why the sergeant would dispatch anyone, anywhere, simply on the inquiry of Nereida Flick. He suggested that his wife's whereabouts was none of the woman's business. "Why is she so concerned anyway? They're not even that close."

Eric then sought to assure Zipf that his wife was not missing. He said she had walked out on him, and was probably staying in New York City, fifteen miles to the east, with her half sister in the Bronx or other relatives. He said he had last seen Myra only two days earlier, on Wednesday. It was no big deal; he would call over to her relatives to track her down. With that, Eric, his mother, and the two youngsters headed for the door.

The sergeant returned to the back office to call Nereida Flick. He told her of Eric's suggestion that Myra was staying with her half sister.

"No, that can't be," Flick replied. "That would be Miriam. I just talked to Miriam. Myra's not there."

Flick also assured Zipf that her family was certain Myra was not staying with any other relatives. They had checked everywhere. She insisted that Myra would have never gone off without telling her family. Something had to be done.

Zipf, whose shift was about to end, told Flick she could not file a missing-persons report on the phone. A family member would have to come to Clifton headquarters. Flick, who lived in the adjacent community of Nutley, said she would drive over immediately.

When she arrived less than a half hour later, she was

greeted by Patrolman Phil Bradley. She again detailed her
cousin's disappearance, and added that Myra had just
learned that her husband was having an affair. Flick said
Myra was thinking about leaving him to return to a house
she owned in Puerto Rico near her parents' residence. She
filled in the official forms, describing Myra as five-foot-
three, 105 pounds, brown eyes, brown hair, and twenty-two
years old.

Of course, as Flick explained, there was more to Myra
Acevedo Napoletano than mere statistics. A fun-loving
person who often wore a bandanna in her hair, Myra liked to
sing and dance and dress up. When she turned seventeen,
she had joined the New York City Police Department's auxiliary police force. For a time she had wanted to become a
cop, but her husband had made her abandon that dream; he
said the job was too dangerous. Very close to her mother
and father, the respectful and deeply religious young
woman frequently sought their advice, no matter how sensitive the problem. Myra Acevedo Napoletano sounded like a
very nice person.

After finishing with Bradley, Flick returned home, where
she called Myra's half sister in the Bronx, Miriam Colon.
The two women took stock of the situation: how long since
Myra had last been heard from, Eric's indifference to her
disappearance, his bizarre visit to the police station, and,
most important, the fact that the kids were with him and his
mother, Carolyn. It made no sense that Eric had the children; Myra would never have left the boys behind. Angelo
was only eighteen months old, and Eric Junior would be
four in September.

Flick told her cousin that the police needed a couple of
photographs of Myra. Miriam decided to drive across the
George Washington Bridge at once. She did not care that it
was now the middle of the night.

Arriving in Clifton at 3:20 A.M., Miriam told Officer
Bradley that she too had last spoken with Myra that
Wednesday. Myra had told her she was waiting for plane
tickets for a flight to San Juan. Miriam recalled being told
by Myra that Eric had strongly objected to her plans to take
the children and leave.

Miriam said the family was so concerned about Myra's
disappearance that their father, Pablo, was flying up from
Puerto Rico in the morning.

Bradley looked at the photographs. They showed a pretty, smiling mother surrounded by her adorable children. The officer attached the snapshots to the paperwork. There was nothing else he could do. He left the file for the Detective Bureau. Someone would be coming on duty there in a couple of hours.

Many miles away in the western hills of Puerto Rico, Pablo Acevedo was very worried that Friday evening. He could not sleep, troubled by the disappearance of his oldest daughter. No one in the family had spoken with Myra for more than two days, and Pablo sensed that something was gravely wrong. Myra was extremely conscientious when it came to family matters. Pablo knew that she would never have left without telling anyone or without taking her two children with her.

Pablo Acevedo was a dedicated family man. He and his wife, Carmen, had five children: Myra, Paul, Eric, Elizabeth, and Lizzette. When he married Carmen, she already had two children from a previous marriage, four-year-old Miriam and three-year-old Jeanette, known as Janet. As a result of Pablo's nurturing devotion to their development, the two stepdaughters—now in their twenties—had grown to consider him their father, too.

The Acevedos were rock solid: responsible, respectable, and hardworking people. A strong Catholic belief was the linchpin of family unity. The girls were not allowed on dates unescorted; two siblings generally drew the supervision assignment.

Short in stature but strong of heart, Pablo was a tender man, soft-spoken and easygoing. When his children had been infants, it was not uncommon for him to bring out his guitar to sing them a lullaby. When he'd had spare time, he spent it playing with them.

The Acevedos resided in Moca, a small rural community in Puerto Rico's interior blessed with lush, gorgeous mountains as a backyard backdrop. The family home was beautifully appointed, complete with a spacious *marquesina*, a roofed patio with casual, outdoor furniture and hanging, tropical plants. The large property was dotted with orange trees. The stillness of any given afternoon was broken by the hum of passing sugarcane trucks.

The Acevedos had come a long way since living in a

small apartment on Southern Boulevard in the Bronx. They had spent seven years in their native Puerto Rico during Myra's childhood, returned to New York for several more years, then returned permanently to their homeland to establish a small candy factory with Pablo's brothers. Over the years Pablo often worked two jobs, and a third on weekends. He wanted his children to have fulfilling lives.

Pablo's present problem, one he had been preoccupied with for five days now, was dealing with Myra's latest marital crisis. She had been on the phone with him and other relatives constantly since learning that her husband had a mistress. The last time she spoke with her father, on Wednesday evening, she had promised to call the following day to continue discussing her plans to move back to Puerto Rico with her two boys.

But Myra had failed to call back. And repeated calls to her apartment Thursday afternoon and evening had all gone unanswered.

At Pablo's request, Myra's cousin, Nereida Flick, had first contacted the Clifton police Thursday evening. An officer dispatched to the Napoletano apartment failed to find anyone home. When Flick was told of the unsuccessful visit, she confided that her cousin had been having marital problems. She insisted that the police return to her cousin's home and actually enter the apartment to search it. The police had returned later Thursday night and, after using bolt cutters to break a chain lock across the door, searched the apartment without finding anyone or any indication that a struggle had taken place.

Pablo had spent all day Friday on the phone, trying again and again to reach Myra and discussing his growing concerns with various family members. By that point the relatives were talking among themselves, too. It turned out that Myra had spoken to many of them about her latest troubles with Eric. In the Acevedo family, everyone shared their joys and sorrows.

That evening, as Pablo packed his suitcases and received long-distance updates from Myra's distraught sisters and cousins, the Acevedo family's fears over their loved one's disappearance were in stark contrast to the indifference being exhibited at that very moment by Eric and Carolyn Napoletano at the Clifton police station.

As Pablo conferred on a three-way hookup with his two

stepdaughters, Miriam and Janet began crying. Janet observed how strange it was for Myra not to be available to help solve a family crisis. They talked on the phone all the time.

It was difficult for Pablo to keep from crying, too. But he had to be strong. He knew he had to find Myra, even if she was dead.

- 2 -

Detective Nicholas Donato was not thrilled to hear the jarring buzz of the alarm clock. Through the fog, he deduced that this was going to be a blurry, slow-motion kind of Saturday. Donato would have loved to roll over and grab another hour of sleep, but he knew he had to get out of bed and make his way to headquarters.

A short, muscular man who enjoyed tae kwon do, jogging, and lifting weights, Nick Donato was a very personable guy. He was a product of a Catholic grammar school—Franciscan nuns—and Clifton High School. His father was in construction work, his mother a housewife. The youngest of three brothers, he had been fascinated by police work since he could remember, influenced by TV shows such as *Police Story* and books such as Joseph Wambaugh's *The New Centurions*.

After graduating from high school, Donato worked in a machine shop but quickly decided that the job was not for him. Following a stint in the army, he earned a degree in police science at a local community college while working part-time for the college as a veteran's adviser. After spending several years on a waiting list, he joined the Clifton Police Department in 1982.

Nick Donato was a stickler for details, and he took pride in his work. Over time, he wanted more from his job. The idea of following a case from beginning to end appealed to him, so he set his sights on becoming a detective. In January 1989, after seven years in the Patrol Division, Donato began working upstairs in the Detective Bureau, filling in for a veteran on temporary medical leave.

He made an impression as a solid, intelligent worker who put in the hours. Six months later, he was allowed to stay on to await another detective's retirement. By the end of the year, he was permanently assigned to the Detective Bureau.

"I put my heart and soul into this job," Donato said of his approach to police work. "But I'm not out to 'screw' someone. I want to get who is responsible."

Donato pulled into the Clifton municipal complex parking lot about 8:30 that Saturday, June 23, 1990. The police department was housed within the modern, two-story city hall. He climbed the steps to the Detective Bureau, a large office area on the second floor. There, he greeted his partner for the day, George O'Brien, a veteran with more than twenty years on the force.

Like detectives everywhere, Donato and O'Brien had no idea how busy their day would be. In Clifton, though, slow days were becoming obsolete. The seventh largest municipality in New Jersey, Clifton is an aging, urbanized suburb of 72,000 residents. The city's ethnic mix—for decades dominated by hardworking Italians, Irish, Poles, and Germans—had begun to rupture from the growing influences of its low-income and high-crime neighbors, most notably the bordering cities of Passaic and Paterson. Clifton was experiencing a rapid influx of minorities and immigrants, many of whom did not speak English, and the new population mix brought with it an increase in crime.

Still, even with the increased workload, the law-enforcement mission in Clifton more resembled that of a small town. Murders, as well as other major felonies, were still a big deal. Homicides were rare, no more than a half dozen in a bad year. And each one was high priority, worked on until solved.

Nick Donato had yet to catch a big case of his own; the infrequent murders—most recently, the death of a man pushed off the balcony of a high-rise apartment by his homosexual lover from Hawaii, and the murder of three deaf-mutes—went to the more experienced investigators. But Donato had spent a great deal of time working the fringes of those murders, learning from the experts. He especially liked working with O'Brien, a lead investigator on the deaf-mute case. O'Brien had graciously taken him under his wing.

As the senior man on duty that Saturday, O'Brien reviewed the incident reports from the previous evening, instinctively being drawn to Nereida Flick's missing-persons report and the accompanying paperwork about the police visits to the Napoletano apartment. He was intrigued by several facts: The wife had planned to take the children and leave; the husband did not want her to leave; the husband had a mistress; the children were with the husband when he visited headquarters two days after the disappearance; and the missing-persons report had been filed by the wife's relatives, not the husband.

Scheduled for vacation the following week, O'Brien decided to let Donato start the investigation, since there was no sense starting something he might not be able to finish. "Here," O'Brien instructed. "You might have to make a couple of phone calls on this one."

Donato read through the file, designated Central Complaint Number 90-9260, and agreed with O'Brien's assessment that something was strange here. He was especially struck by the level of apprehension exhibited by Myra's relatives. From reading the reports, he could tell that their concern was genuine.

After failing to find any leads in the overnight Teletype reports, he called Nereida Flick. She explained that her cousin Myra was very religious and was devoted to her children. She never would have left the kids behind. Flick said every family member had been contacted, and not one had heard from Myra. She said they also had tried repeatedly to reach Eric at the apartment, without success.

Donato then contacted Myra's half sister, Miriam Colon, at her home in the Bronx. She also emphasized that Myra never would have left her children behind, then added that Eric was frequently abusive to Myra, speaking negatively about her Puerto Rican heritage. Miriam said Myra had told her Eric threatened to kill her if she ever left. She also recounted a recent incident where Eric had tried to poison himself. But as far as Miriam knew, he had spit out the substance before it could take effect.

To Donato, Eric sounded like a control freak desperate for attention. He asked for the names of Eric's closest friends. Miriam said she knew Eric was very close to his mother, Carolyn, who lived somewhere in Manhattan, and to a man named Albert Jiovine, whose apartment in Queens she had visited the day before, looking for Myra. Miriam explained that Jiovine, often referred to as "Uncle Al," was a husky, bald man in his fifties, variously described as Eric's father, stepfather, or uncle.

She said she had gone to the Jiovine residence because Myra and Eric sometimes stayed there overnight, but when she got there the only occupants were a young Latino man named Greg Velez, a teenage female, and an infant. While Miriam was talking to Velez, the phone rang. Since it was Jiovine, she had grabbed the receiver to talk to him. "What the heck are you doing at *my* house? You have no right to come into my house," Jiovine had told her.

Miriam said Jiovine claimed that Myra was supposed to be with her. That comment had made no sense to Miriam. If Myra was with her, why had she driven out to Queens? At that point, Miriam recalled, Al Jiovine ended the conversation, saying, "I can't talk to you. I don't want to talk to you. I don't know nothin' about your sister."

Donato recognized he had his work cut out. Eric Napoletano, his mother, and this Uncle Al character all sounded very strange. Jiovine's comments to Miriam Colon were inexplicable. Why didn't any of them care about Myra's whereabouts? Why were they so defensive? Why would a husband object to the police inquiring about his missing wife?

The detective called the local hospitals and crisis units in case Myra had been a victim of domestic violence or a drug overdose or amnesia. If she was despondent about her marriage, she could have committed suicide. All the checks, however, were fruitless. Using the police department's computers, he determined that neither Eric nor Myra had criminal records in New Jersey. He searched the state motor-vehicle database in hopes of finding another useful address for either of them, an inquiry that also came up negative.

Unable to reach anyone by phone at the Napoletano apartment, located near the Paterson border in an older, poorer section of Clifton, Donato headed to the residence with Detective Mike Kotora from the Juvenile Bureau.

There was no answer at Apartment 3 on the second floor, the Napoletano residence. No one was home in Apartments 2 and 4, either. At Apartment 1, however, Donato found Theresa Maltese, who said she had last seen Myra on Wednesday afternoon about five o'clock, when a moving man came to the building lobby looking for her.

Mrs. Maltese said that she and her husband, Tony, had gone upstairs with the man, then banged on the Napoletanos' door for some time before Myra answered. According to

Mrs. Maltese, a giant of a woman known as the neighborhood busybody, Myra seemed quite upset, but had let the moving man in. She said that when she asked if everything was all right, Myra had slammed the door in her face.

The woman explained that she had talked with Eric's mother, Carolyn, and the two boys outside about two hours later, sitting in a burgundy Toyota. She said that while she was chatting with Carolyn, Eric hurriedly left the building looking very angry. Mrs. Maltese said that Myra had been nowhere in sight.

Donato returned to headquarters. It struck him as odd that Eric's mother was being described as one of her son's closest friends. Miriam Colon and Nereida Flick also had said there was considerable tension between Myra's immediate family and Eric's mother. From their descriptions, Carolyn Napoletano came across as overprotective, to the point of coddling her son. Myra's relatives also contended that Carolyn Napoletano was very prejudiced against Latins and blacks. For example, she had refused to attend Myra's wedding; no one was good enough for her son, especially some Puerto Rican girl.

The detective conducted several computer checks on Carolyn Napoletano. But the inquiries were all a washout. He did uncover the fact that she had an unlisted phone in Manhattan.

Donato decided he had heard enough about the Napoletano family to warrant an increase in concern. He typed out a brief nationwide police Teletype message. He made sure his tone was neutral and objective, but he also wanted an early-warning notice for all law-enforcement personnel reading the message. In addition to the standard information— Myra's description, her last known whereabouts, her plans to take her children and leave—Donato included several "read-between-the-lines" observations about his missing-persons case: Myra's relatives had reported her missing; she had been having marital problems; her husband had been seen with their two children; and the husband claimed his wife had vanished without telling anyone.

With each passing hour, Myra's relatives grew more distressed and more willing to point an accusatory finger at Eric. Shortly after three o'clock that Saturday afternoon, Donato received a call from Martha Morales, another of

Myra's cousins. She said several family members had gathered at Miriam Colon's apartment in the Bronx to discuss
the situation, including Janet Mendez, Myra's other half
sister, who had traveled with her husband from their home in
Sunbury, Pennsylvania, and Pablo Acevedo, Myra's father,
who had just flown in from the family home in Puerto Rico.
Once again, there was no mistaking the Acevedo family's
sincerity.

Pablo Acevedo recalled that he had spoken with his
daughter several times that week. His most troubling conversation had taken place on the evening of her disappearance, when they discussed her intentions to return to Puerto
Rico with her children to live in the house she owned with
Eric. He said his daughter sounded very nervous, and he
recalled that at one point during the call she informed him
she had changed her mind about moving. Pablo was quite
certain that he had heard Eric in the background, forcing
Myra to change her plans. Pablo said that in response to his
protests, Myra had promised she would call him the next
day to continue their discussion, but the return call never
came. Pablo said he had not spoken with his daughter since.

Donato thanked the family members for their time and
assured them he would do his best to find Myra. Heading
home for two days off, he pondered the situation. After listening to the relatives' grief, he was prepared to rule out the
possibility that Myra was hiding from her family. Here was
a stable and sensible woman who had burned up the phone
lines all week complaining about her husband and their
failing marriage. Her family was right; it made no sense that
none of them had heard from her. Why was this woman not
with her children, especially since everyone who knew her
insisted that she would never abandon them? With Eric
gone all day at work, she would have had ample opportunity
to escape with them when Eric was not home. And why,
unless harm had befallen her, had she not found the time to
make a single phone call to let her family know she was
okay and to check on her boys?

Equally troubling to Donato was the cold apathy being
exhibited by Eric Napoletano and his mother. First, they
stormed into police headquarters to complain about the cops
checking up on Myra, then vanished without any apparent
concern for her whereabouts and well-being. And why was

the husband not staying around the family residence, the last place his wife was seen?

Donato had come across an additional curious fact that increased his uneasiness: While discussing how Myra and Eric had met, her relatives related how husband and wife, as well as Eric's mother, had been auxiliary police officers in New York City.

Nick Donato didn't know it yet, but he had just caught his first really big case, the kind of investigation most detectives never come across during thirty-year careers.

- 3 -

Myra Napoletano had been missing nearly a week now, and Donato's investigation had become complicated. Judging from events that had unfolded during his days off, it was evident that Eric and Carolyn Napoletano were putting a great deal of effort into laying down a coordinated alibi about the night Myra vanished. The Napoletanos were streetwise as well as schooled in the way police investigators operate. The mother-son team was going to be considerably more to handle than Donato had first imagined.

The detective had left word with his colleagues late Saturday to look for Myra's elusive husband. As it turned out, Eric and his mother made their presence known twice in Clifton during his absence. When Donato read the official reports about the incidents, it only magnified his anxiety about Myra's safety.

Detectives William Cooke and Ed Snack had encountered the Napoletanos first, when they stopped by the East Sixth Street apartment that Saturday evening to look for Eric. He cordially invited the investigators into his living room for a chat, but son and mother both acted nervous. Almost every time Cooke asked a question, one or the other interrupted to demand why he needed to know that particular piece of information.

Eric explained that he was no longer living in the Clifton apartment. Pointing at his mother, he said he was now living with her. The detectives asked Carolyn for her home address and phone number. "I don't like to give that out to anyone," she answered sternly. When the detectives pointed out that they had no way to make contact if Myra was located, though, Carolyn revealed that she lived at 354 East Eighty-third Street in Manhattan, between First and Second Avenues on the Upper East Side.

Eric explained that he and Myra had engaged in many

discussions the previous week about whether to separate. He said Myra ultimately decided to fly to Puerto Rico with the children that Friday, two days after she was last heard from. "They've been having problems," Carolyn interjected.

Asked to explain his actions the evening of Myra's disappearance, Eric stated that he had departed the Clifton apartment with his sons that Wednesday about 7:00 P.M. to drive into Manhattan to pick up his mother. He said he wanted to give Myra some space because she had had a rough day.

He said he tried to call Myra from his mother's apartment to ask if she wanted to join them for dinner, but got no answer. He said he continued calling throughout the evening without success, then returned to Clifton. He contended that when he arrived with his mother and the boys about 3:00 A.M., Myra was gone, along with her purse and birth-control pills.

Keeping to the version he had given during his stormy visit to Clifton headquarters the previous evening, Eric said he believed Myra was staying with her sister, Miriam, in the Bronx. Carolyn Napoletano heartily nodded her head in agreement.

The evasiveness was to continue. When basic pedigree information was solicited, Eric claimed he did not know his Social Security number. He had left the card in his wallet, and his wallet was at his mother's. When asked where he was employed, he hesitated at first, then said that he worked in New York City.

Cooke pointed out that the police needed to know precisely where he was employed so that they could contact him with any news. Eric hesitated again, then stated that he was a traffic enforcement officer for the City of New York's Department of Sanitation. He said he was presently enrolled in the agency's training academy.

Asked if he owned a vehicle, Eric answered that he did not. Well, then, who owned the Toyota he had just gotten out of? Eric said it belonged to his uncle.

Eric Napoletano played the game well. He presented himself as cooperative, yet gave ambiguous, if any, information. His vague answers would be difficult to disprove or confirm. As the detectives prepared to depart, Cooke gave Eric a business card with Donato's phone number and advised him to call for an interview. Eric promised he would.

Outside the building, the detectives recorded the Toyota's

New Jersey license plate. The car would turn out to be registered to Albert Jiovine—the "Uncle Al" described by Myra's relatives.

Unbeknownst to Cooke and Snack, Eric watched them check out the car from the upstairs window. He would later claim that their actions had put him on the defensive, leading him to conclude that the police believed he was responsible for Myra's disappearance.

The next police encounter with the Napoletano family occurred Monday evening after Detective Paul Ogden took a call at headquarters from Jeanette Konuklu, one of Myra and Eric's neighbors. The woman said Eric was at his apartment removing clothing. Ogden, who had been briefed on the case when Donato stopped by the office Sunday morning, rushed over to the Napoletano residence, where he found Konuklu and Eric chatting away at the curb.

The detective introduced himself. Eric responded with a strong handshake that did not fit his skinny form. It was clear, though, that the Clifton Police Department had worn out its welcome. There would be no invitation to come inside; this time the interview would take place in the street. Sensing that she should leave the two men alone, Konuklu excused herself. "I'm going to go say hello to your mother," she announced.

Ogden explained that Detective Donato had been trying to reach him to talk about Myra. Eric said he had been busy—going to school, running back and forth, you know, the usual kind of stuff. He assured Ogden that he still had Donato's number and would call first chance he got.

Ogden asked Eric if he had any ideas about his wife's whereabouts. "She took off," he replied matter-of-factly. As he told his story for the night of Myra's disappearance, it differed in one key detail from the scenario given to Cooke and Snack: When he last saw Myra that Wednesday evening, his mother had been with him. He specifically told Ogden he had gone into New York to get her, then returned to New Jersey to discuss dinner plans with Myra. Perhaps Eric and Carolyn had realized that neighbor Theresa Maltese would remember speaking with Carolyn at about seven o'clock that evening.

Eric's latest version also contained a few more details. Now he said that when he returned to Clifton and found Myra gone, he discovered that two suitcases and an equivalent amount of clothing were also missing with her pocketbook and birth-control pills. Eric put extra emphasis on the pills, as if their absence would project a picture of a promiscuous wife.

Ogden encountered the same cocksure vagueness that Cooke and Snack had found. Where had they gone to eat? Actually, they never did, Eric said. They had gone back to his mother's place in Manhattan. What about Myra's plans to leave? She was supposed to have taken a 10:00 P.M. flight that Friday out of Kennedy Airport. In fact, he had made the arrangements himself with American Airlines.

Eric tried to make the dissolution of his marriage sound amicable, claiming that he and Myra had talked things through during a Chinese dinner the evening before her disappearance. But when pressed for details, Eric claimed he could not remember the name of the restaurant or where it was located.

"Aren't you concerned something happened to her?" Ogden wondered.

"Naaaah," Eric insisted. "She's all right." He again stated that as far as he knew, Myra was with her sister, Miriam, in the Bronx.

Eric admitted that he felt bad about the situation but volunteered that he at least had his girlfriend to talk things over with. In the next breath, however, he proclaimed that if Myra returned, he would gladly take her back. "I still love her," he said.

As Eric continued to weave his tale, his new story differed in one other regard. He now claimed he was enrolled at the New York City Traffic Enforcement Academy, not the previously mentioned New York City Sanitation Department.

Eric told Ogden that his neighbors were under the impression that he still drove a truck. He said he used his mother's Manhattan address because of the City of New York's residency requirements for his civil-service job. He said he did not want his Clifton neighbors knowing his living arrangements for fear one of them would report him and jeopardize his job.

As Eric spoke with increased confidence, he announced that he had a question. Now that Myra had left him, would he be able to keep his children legally?

Ogden was taken aback by the query. "It's a little premature for that," the detective explained. "That's something only a court of law can decide."

Just then, as if on cue, a shrieky voice from behind the screen in one of the second-story windows pierced the night air. "Errrr-rick! Errrr-rick! Get up here, Eric." It was Carolyn Napoletano summoning her son.

With that, the interview ended. Eric stopped talking and immediately did as he was told; he ran back to his mother.

Ogden participated in another important development during Donato's absence: He met with Myra's father; sister, Miriam Colon; a cousin, Martha Morales; and brother-in-law Sammy Mendez when they visited Clifton police headquarters. The family again emphasized that they were not about to take Myra's disappearance passively. Morales reiterated that Myra would never have left her children behind; it was because of her love for Eric Junior and Angelo that she had stayed with Eric so long.

Pablo said he had double-checked with every relative in New York and Puerto Rico. No one had heard from his daughter. He looked like a man already in mourning, saying he suspected that Myra was dead, "or else we would have heard from her."

There was a good reason for Pablo's belief. Saying he had something important to reveal, he assured Ogden he had no independent proof of what he was about to say, but felt that under the circumstances the police should know everything about his son-in-law. But first, Pablo insisted, he wanted Ogden to assure him that Eric would never learn of the conversation. In case he was wrong, Pablo did not want to incur Eric's wrath.

After receiving a guarantee of confidentiality, Pablo revealed that shortly after Myra and Eric were married in 1985, Eric began moving from residence to residence throughout New York City. According to Pablo, Eric explained that he had to stay on the move to hide from the police. They wanted to talk to him about a former girlfriend who had been found dead in western New Jersey. In telling his story to Ogden, Pablo emphasized that when Eric explained the police interest in him, Carolyn Napoletano had kept butting in to offer explanations, excuses, and observations.

Pablo said Eric had assured him he had not been involved in the girl's disappearance or death. Myra's father added with a tinge of regret that he had found Eric's explanations plausible and had therefore given him the benefit of the

doubt. It was a generosity Pablo was no longer willing to
extend.

On Tuesday afternoon, the day of his return to headquarters, Donato finally received the promised phone call
from Eric. The chat was brief, however. Eric insisted he was
very busy, but offered to drive over to Clifton for a personal
interview.

"Can you come in this afternoon?" Donato asked.

"No, I can't. I'm on lunch at the academy," Eric replied.

"Well, how about this evening?" the detective suggested.
Again, Eric said he was tied up.

"How about tomorrow?" Donato asked.

"No," Eric said. "I can't make it during the daytime."

"Well, tomorrow night, then," Donato insisted. Eric hesitated. He said he would try.

"Eric, come on. We have to get this done; it's your wife."

Finally Eric relented, telling Donato he would try to be
there the next evening between seven and eight.

Donato asked Eric about his Social Security number. Was
he at least able to provide that information now? Eric apologized; he still did not have the card on him.

Well, what about his place of residence? Where did he
live? Why was he never at his apartment? "I don't really
live in Clifton," Eric repeated. "I live with my mother in
New York." To hear Eric tell it, he had never lived in
Clifton, he had only "stayed there with Myra a couple of
days a week."

After confirming that he did have a New York State
driver's license, Eric said he had to go. He assured Donato
they would talk the next evening.

Donato was steamed. Eric Napoletano's behavior was reprehensible. He acted as if he did not give a damn about his
wife. Based on the information provided by Pablo Acevedo,
Donato prepared a Teletype to police agencies in New Jersey
outlining the possibility that Eric had been a suspect in a previous homicide. He also drafted a message to be distributed
on the National Crime Information Center computer system;
Myra was now officially missing across the country.

Entering Myra's disappearance on the NCIC system represented a significant escalation of the investigation. In
today's transient society, the NCIC network represents an

essential law-enforcement tool. With it, police agencies large and small unmask the secrets of young runaways as well as unidentified corpses murdered in one jurisdiction, then dumped in another. Donato was still not prepared to say that Myra had been murdered, but the other possibilities now looked very improbable.

Later that afternoon, Myra's father, Miriam, and cousin Martha again visited Clifton headquarters. They wanted to keep up the pressure on the police. Pablo indicated that he had finally spoken with Eric. While he was certainly worried more than ever about his missing daughter, Pablo said he had also asked Eric about his grandsons. If Eric had harmed Myra, there was no telling what he might do to the children. Pablo said that when he questioned Eric about the boys' whereabouts, his son-in-law told him only that they were staying with a friend. He would not reveal where they were staying or allow Pablo to see them. Instead, Pablo added, Eric had changed the subject, asking whether there would be hard feelings if Myra suddenly reappeared.

Donato said he needed more details about Eric's dead ex-girlfriend to help him track down the incident. Pablo said that all he ever heard was that the girl had lived with Eric for a while, her body may have been found in New Jersey, she might have been an auxiliary cop in New York City, and Eric would have been questioned by police sometime between 1983 and 1985.

Pablo's information would have made good fodder for Donato's interview with Eric. But the talk was not to be. That evening, Sergeant William DeVos took a call from Lawrence M. Fagenson, who identified himself as Eric Napoletano's New York lawyer. The attorney explained that Eric would not be speaking to Detective Donato or anyone else from the Clifton Police Department. "If you've got something to charge my client with, charge him. Otherwise, he's got nothing to say to you. Leave him alone."

When the news reached Donato, he was floored by the fact that Eric had retained an attorney and by the "Get outta my face" message. But Eric's attitude only spurred Donato on. He set out on a new round of interviews.

Neighbor Jeanette Konuklu recalled that Myra had been secretly saving money for airline tickets for her move. When she went inside to chat with Carolyn Napoletano Monday night, though, she got a quick chance to look for

Myra's wallet, which she knew Myra kept hidden on top of a bedroom dresser. The wallet was not there.

Downstairs neighbor Theresa Maltese said she now remembered speaking with Eric in the hallway the day after Myra disappeared. She said Eric told her Myra had received a call from a boyfriend the night she disappeared. Mrs. Maltese quoted Eric as saying that he believed Myra had run off with the guy.

While Eric concocted exculpating scenarios at a dizzying pace, his mother conducted her own campaign of obstruction. On the evening of June 28, eight days after Myra's disappearance, the Clifton dispatch desk received a call regarding "suspicious activity" at the Napoletano residence. Officer Joseph Klein was dispatched to the Sixth Street address. He had no idea of the ongoing investigation, being instructed simply to make a report on the people who were inside the apartment.

Klein's knock at Apartment 3 was answered by a heavy-set, red-haired woman. He identified himself and explained his assignment. "Who are you?" he asked the woman.

She identified herself as Carolyn Napoletano. The man with her identified himself as Albert Jiovine. "I'm just the taxi service. I just gave her a ride, that's all," Uncle Al claimed.

Eric's mother explained that she had come to the apartment to pick up some clothing. "I'm Myra Napoletano's mother-in-law."

"Who is Myra Napoletano?" Klein asked.

"She lives here."

"Well, where is she?"

"That's for you to find out!" Carolyn snapped back.

Klein wondered what he had gotten himself into. He requested basic information from the woman, such as where she lived, her date of birth, her phone number, and where she worked.

Carolyn Napoletano declined to answer any of Klein's questions. She wasn't about to tell any of the Clifton cops where she worked.

- 4 -

With several ominous leads pointing eastward to New York City, Donato realized he needed help with his mushrooming investigation. He and his new partner, Lieutenant John Burke, could never have imagined the sordid history of tangled lives and bungled investigations they would soon learn about.

The Clifton Detective Bureau was squeezed to the limit, complicated by summer vacations. Having two investigators looking for Myra Napoletano full-time was out of the question, so Burke, a supervisor in the bureau, agreed to shelve his administrative duties temporarily to assist. A native of the Bronx and a former postal worker, Burke had joined the Clifton force in 1974. Since his background was in patrol, he had less investigative experience than Donato. But Burke was a capable guy and a hard worker. They would work well as a team.

The two men figured that the only way to track down the leads across the Hudson River properly was to work them in person. They realized things could get dicey. Cops are never comfortable with outsiders. This was especially true within NYPD. They hoped Burke's title would smooth over the intrusions.

Gradually, the long hours began to pay off. During one of their trips to New York, they confirmed that Eric, in fact, was employed by the New York City Department of Transportation as a traffic-enforcement agent in training.

"While you're at it, does your computer show anything for a Carolyn Napoletano?" Donato asked the helpful official.

"Yes," the woman replied. "She works for NYPD, the police department."

"Yeah, we know that. She's an auxiliary, right?"

No, the bureaucrat replied. She was not referring to the auxiliary police; her records did not contain information about the volunteer corps. "This is her regular job. She works for the New York City Police Department."

Donato looked at Burke. They were stunned. "Getoutta-here!" said Donato. "She works for what?"

"The police department," the woman confirmed.

Additional details were tough to come by. But the investigators did manage to learn that Carolyn had a civilian job. At least she wasn't a cop.

Fascinated by the links to NYPD, Donato and Burke were determined to work their way through the bureaucracy. Ultimately, they located police officials who confirmed that Eric, Myra, and Carolyn indeed had all been auxiliaries. They also ascertained that Carolyn worked full-time at One Police Plaza, the storied NYPD headquarters in downtown Manhattan. She was assigned to the chief's office in the Organized Crime Control Bureau, the ultrasensitive division responsible for enforcement of narcotics, gambling, and undercover Mafia operations.

The auxiliary records indicated that Myra had been a uniformed member from February 1985 through 1986, assigned to the Forty-first Precinct in the Bronx. Carolyn Napoletano had been an auxiliary in the Central Park Precinct for years and, in fact, was still an active member.

Eric had been an auxiliary cop from 1982 to 1986, also assigned to the Central Park Precinct. His personnel file indicated that he had lost his badge and identification card on two occasions. Records also showed that from 1984 to 1986 Eric had frequently changed residences, just as Pablo Acevedo had claimed. However, the NYPD records—or at least those shared with Donato and Burke—offered no hint of explanation for Eric's nomadic existence during those years. The information also was devoid of any reference to a murder or mysterious death linked to Eric, in New Jersey or elsewhere.

Myra had been missing for two weeks now. The prospects for finding her alive were virtually nil. As sources of information, Eric and his mother were worthless. Any additional "cooperation" from them would no doubt be misleading and self-serving. Desperate to penetrate the Napoletano inner circle somehow, Donato turned his focus on Albert "Uncle Al" Jiovine.

The man did not have a law-enforcement connection, but

he did seem to be on the fringe of so many things involving Eric, Carolyn, and Myra's disappearance. Donato determined that Jiovine was employed by Y.G.M., Inc., an import-export firm located at 3 East Fifty-forth Street, near Fifth Avenue in Manhattan. He handled the paperwork for shipments of shirts, pants, sweaters, and designer jeans from the Far East.

The New Jersey Division of Motor Vehicles computer showed that the Toyota Eric drove was registered to Jiovine at a Dumont, New Jersey, address. But when Donato and Burke visited Jiovine's "home," they discovered that it was really his mother's residence. In fact, Uncle Al lived in Queens, at the apartment where Miriam Colon had gone looking for Myra. He used the New Jersey address only to register his several cars and save on insurance.

Through one of Jiovine's half sisters at the home in Dumont, Donato managed a phone conversation with Jiovine. He admitted that he let Eric drive his burgundy Toyota now and then. When asked what he thought had happened to Myra, Jiovine said that, like Eric and Carolyn, he believed she was staying with her sister. As for Eric, Carolyn, and the kids, he claimed, "I've been keeping away from those people."

Donato was struck by the contradiction in Jiovine's statements: He had guessed Myra was staying with relatives, but at the same time he had inexplicably asserted a defensive, hands-off attitude about the Napoletanos. The detective guessed that Al Jiovine knew more than he was saying.

It so happened that Donato and Burke were scheduled to work on July Fourth. As the morning progressed, routine matters appeared to be under control, so the two investigators headed for Queens. If Al had the day off, perhaps they could catch him off guard.

Al's next-door neighbor buzzed the detectives into the high-rise lobby. Taking advantage of the situation, they showed her several photographs. She easily picked out Myra and Eric. She had even baby-sat for one of the boys so Myra could take the other to the doctor's office. Matter-of-factly, the woman identified Eric as Al Jiovine's son. She said Myra and Eric had lived with Al for a time, but that he now had a young male roommate.

While Donato and Burke spoke with the neighbor down

the hall from the Jiovine residence, a loud voice inside the apartment cried out, "Hurry up! They're on their way!"

A few minutes later, Eric appeared in the hallway with his mother and the two boys. As Al opened the door, Burke and Donato approached from behind, displaying their badges. Carolyn arrogantly demanded to know what the detectives were doing there.

"We're looking for Myra," Burke explained.

Carolyn became defensive. Of course Myra was not there, she bellowed. Furthermore, they had no idea where she was.

Visibly annoyed, Eric stepped into the conversation. "I told the detectives already!"

As Carolyn began to speak again, Eric told her to shut up. He was in no mood to discuss his missing wife. He was in a hurry to get to Mafia kingpin John Gotti's annual Independence Day block party in another section of Queens. Eric considered himself to be a friend of the don and did not want to be late.

Donato told Eric that he and Burke realized they could not talk to him because he had an attorney. They had come to see Jiovine.

Eric stared at the detectives, unimpressed with their explanations. Carolyn would later claim that her phone must have been bugged: How else would Donato and Burke have known to show up at Jiovine's, on a holiday, at the same time she and Eric arrived?

Ignoring Donato completely, Carolyn explained to Burke that she had already provided the essential information to the Clifton police.

In a flash, Eric became extremely angry. Boisterous and vulgar, he emphatically told his mother to keep quiet. But she would not listen. She was determined to provide her version of events leading up to Myra's disappearance.

Carolyn said that she had been at her apartment in Manhattan the evening in question, June 20, 1990, when Eric called to say he was coming with the kids to pick her up. She said they later tried to get Myra to go out with them, but she declined.

"Shut the fuck up!" Eric screamed. The tall, lanky young man towered over his short, pudgy mother, his Adam's apple protruding, his face turning red with anger.

But Carolyn kept talking. She said that when she, Eric,

and the boys had returned to Clifton that evening, Myra and her two navy blue, zippered airline bags were gone.

Eric was in a rage. The more his mother talked, the angrier he became. He forcibly grabbed her and tried to push her through Jiovine's doorway. "Shut the hell up!" he shouted. "Don't talk to them!"

Trying to keep things calm, Carolyn told Burke that she did not understand all the questions, reiterating that they had already provided all the necessary information.

Eric interrupted again, thundering at his mother to remain silent. He claimed he had previously told Detectives Cooke and Snack at the Clifton apartment that he had purchased a ticket for Myra's trip to Puerto Rico. "I also told them what airline. You guys should be talking to Myra's family. I think she's in Puerto Rico with her sister."

Oh, thought Burke. Now it wasn't "Myra is with her sister" *or* "Myra is in Puerto Rico"; it was "Myra's with her sister *in* Puerto Rico."

Carolyn could not refrain from rejoining the conversation, claiming that she vividly remembered telling Detectives Cooke and Snack about Myra's blue airline bags being gone. "Cooke and Snack. You know, you cook to eat. You cook a snack. Ha, ha, Cooke and Snack. That's good."

Carolyn had a good laugh. The stupid comments had come out of nowhere. But Donato did not stop. Instead, he asked her about the airline bags. Could she provide more details?

Her response was quite dramatic. "Oh, yes. The bags. Yeah, the bags." Carolyn struck a pensive pose, hand on chin, rubbing it in to show that she was giving the matter a lot of thought. "They were her two bags. You know, they were those navy blue airliner types. Yeah, those were the ones she took, the navy blue ones."

Following the emerging pattern, she sought to present herself as a pillar of cooperation, describing the bags down to their tiniest detail, gesturing with her hands, speaking firmly, all the while avoiding the more important issues.

As Carolyn continued to wallow in minutiae about the airline bags, Eric continued to rebuke her. "Shut up! Shut the fuck up!"

"No!" Carolyn retorted. "I want to get this taken care of."

Back and forth they went, mother and son.

Playing good cop to Donato's more aggressive stance,

Burke decided to attempt a separate inroad with Carolyn. He assured her they meant no harm and took her aside to give her one of his business cards. He explained that perhaps they could meet to talk under better circumstances. "Give me a call," he said in as friendly a tone as he could muster.

Abruptly, Carolyn broke off, as if a warning buzzer had suddenly gone on inside her head. She took possession of the card, but began to shake her head. "I've got nothing more to say!" she replied curtly.

Running out of options, the detectives zeroed in on the person they had driven out to Queens to see in the first place, Uncle Al. Like Carolyn, he presented a cooperative façade. "All the family wants is for Myra to return safely," Al said solemnly.

Instantly, Eric redirected his fury. "You'd better shut up if you want me to work on your car!" He ordered Al to get out of the hallway and return to his apartment. Like an obedient pet, Al scooted back in.

Now Carolyn started talking again. Desperate to cut her off for good, Eric gave the detectives a phone number. He said it was for the home he "owned" with his mother in Manhattan. Just as quickly, though, he belligerently warned them not to follow him or talk to his friends or visit his job.

"Yeah! And that goes for me, too!" Carolyn interjected. "If you show up at my job, I'll have you escorted out."

Biting their tongues, the detectives departed the building. Driving away, they spotted a burgundy Toyota. Donato jumped out for a closer look. The license plate was New Jersey, FHD-80R, registered to Albert Jiovine.

As Donato moved in for a closer look, Burke noticed Eric and Al rapidly approaching. Eric was carrying a large red mechanic's tool chest. As Burke warned Donato, Eric hollered out, "Don't be fucking with my car!"

The detectives drove off as Eric continued his diatribe. "Don't be fucking with my car!"

Eric began inspecting the vehicle for a listening device he was certain the detectives had planted.

Riding back to New Jersey, Donato and Burke took stock. It was obvious that Eric and his mother had no intention of assisting in the search for Myra. The officers were offended and insulted by Carolyn's demeanor. Here was an NYPD employee telling members of another police jurisdiction she would have them thrown out of One Police Plaza if they had the nerve to show up at her desk.

The only positive development the detectives could discern from their trip was that the Napoletano boys—Eric Junior and Angelo—appeared to be in good shape. But even that assessment was relative, as neither officer had been able to talk with the youngsters. All that could be stated with any certainty was that the children were alive; on the downside, they were still with their father.

Uncle Al represented the best chance for a breakthrough. If he was not prepared to give up everything he knew just yet, Donato and Burke hoped they could uncover something that would push him along. They decided to visit his mother's house in Dumont again.

Rose Dugan explained that Al was her son from a previous marriage. She said that her family had met Eric through Al years ago, when Eric was still a boy. She said that one of her three daughters, Marilyn, knew Eric and Myra best. She suggested the detectives talk with her.

Donato and Burke found Marilyn Knoepfler at a card store in Dumont, which she owned with her husband, Larry. As the investigation into Myra Napoletano's disappearance continued to unfold in the coming months, Donato would often wonder about the sincerity of both Knoepflers— how much they really knew, whom they were protecting. Although Marilyn would provide useful information on sev-* eral occasions, Donato never shook the feeling that she and her husband were holding something back.

Marilyn Knoepfler outlined a version of events for the evening of Myra's disappearance that differed markedly from the one given by Eric and Carolyn. She stated that she had first heard, from Al, that Myra had not stayed in Clifton but had gone to New York City with Eric and the two boys, then departed Carolyn's apartment to visit her sister in the Bronx. When Eric eventually arrived home in Clifton, he discovered that Myra had failed to return from her visit as expected.

Knoepfler also recalled that Al had called their mother, Rose, about six o'clock the morning after Myra's disappearance to ask if she would baby-sit Angelo and Eric Junior because Myra was gone. Knoepfler said her mother had refused because she was scheduled to undergo eye surgery that very day. She could not have watched the kids even if she had wanted to. Also, Knoepfler recalled her mother telling her that as Al and Eric were preparing to leave her home to head for the Clifton apartment on the Saturday after Myra's disappearance, she overheard a worried Eric ask Al, "What do we do if the cops are there?"

Knoepfler also was helpful in providing insight about the Napoletano inner circle. But in doing so, she made it sound as if no one in her immediate family had ever questioned the propriety of Al's close relationship with Eric. Knoepfler said she had no idea how they had actually met, but remembered Al first bringing Eric around when he was about twelve years old, in what had been described to her as "a Big Brother type of situation." She recalled that Al had been a Big Brother to a different young man for several years prior to his meeting Eric, but that man had been killed in a car accident.

She was not finished. Her best information—vague but chilling nonetheless—was yet to come. She said that in the spring of 1983 or 1984 Eric had brought a girlfriend around, a Puerto Rican named Marilyn. She said the girl, only fifteen or sixteen years old, had later been found dead in Pennsylvania, wrapped in a blanket and bound by rope. Knoepfler also recalled that both Al and Eric had been questioned about the death, but not until several years later.

Hearing mention of Pennsylvania, Donato realized why he had been unable to track down details about the dead girlfriend Pablo Acevedo had mentioned: Eric had told Pablo the girl's body had been found in New Jersey.

Knoepfler said she had more to tell. Although her information was again vague, she said she had heard that before Eric met Myra, he had been married to a Puerto Rican teenager named Wanda. Somewhere around Christmas 1984, Eric had told Knoepfler that he was no longer living with the girl. At first, Knoepfler said, Eric had told her that his wife was missing; then he claimed she had moved back to Puerto Rico—after her mother was shot and killed on a New York City street.

Donato had little to go on, but back at the office he prepared another missing-persons Teletype about Myra, marked with special attention to Pennsylvania and New York authorities. He included the fact that one of Eric's previous girlfriends

might have been found dead in Pennsylvania and that Eric and
Uncle Al Jiovine would have been questioned in the matter. It
took less than forty-eight hours for the Teletype to work.
Events then unfolded rapidly.

He and Burke started out July 9, 1990, making several
stops in Brooklyn. While heading back toward New Jersey,
they heard a crackle on their police radio. Detective Richard
Onorevole was trying to get a message to them from headquarters in Clifton, but it was impossible to make out what
he was saying. As luck would have it, they had just passed
the Seventy-eighth Precinct. Rather than look for a working
pay phone, Burke pulled over and they entered the station
house.

Displaying their badges at the front desk, Donato and
Burke were buzzed upstairs to the Detective Squad. Donato
asked the only detective in the office, Julio Martinez, if he
could use the phone. Donato called Clifton headquarters,
where he was told to contact James Leidy, a detective from
NYPD's Missing Persons Bureau, with whom he had
spoken several times about Myra's case. Leidy had noticed
a possible lead regarding the last Teletype and told Donato
to contact a Sergeant Donald Goode at the Pennsylvania
State Police.

Goode disclosed that on June 2, 1984, the body of a teenage female had been found dumped off a sight-seeing cliff in
the Delaware Water Gap, just across the river from New
Jersey. However, not until July 1986 had authorities matched
the victim with a missing-persons report for a girl named
Marilyn Coludro from New York City. Goode said that once
the body had been identified, the girl's boyfriend, one Eric
Napoletano, became the main suspect. But, he added, the
homicide remained officially unsolved. No one had ever been
arrested.

While Donato was on the phone, Burke provided Detective Martinez with details of their missing-persons case:
Myra's name, then Eric's name, and finally, Eric's mother's
name. Upon hearing the names, Martinez jumped out of his
chair and shouted, "Time out!"

Before his most recent promotion, to detective sergeant,
Martinez had been assigned to the Internal Affairs Division.
While in that post he had worked on a complaint filed by
Eric's mother against a New York City police detective,
James Fazzini, of the Forty-third Precinct in the Bronx.

Back in 1985, Eric's first mother-in-law had been murdered, just as Marilyn Knoepfler said. The woman had been gunned down shortly after she convinced her daughter to leave Eric and go into hiding. Eric had been the only suspect in that homicide, too.

Martinez explained that Fazzini's aggressive questioning of Eric and Carolyn Napoletano had angered them, prompting Carolyn to file a spurious complaint against Fazzini. Martinez advised Burke that he and Donato should contact Fazzini.

When Donato finished his call with Sergeant Goode in Pennsylvania, he was excited to tell Burke what he had learned. Burke, meanwhile, could not wait to reveal his news about the murder in the Bronx. This was one hell of an afternoon. The luck of running into Detective Martinez while simply looking for an available phone was remarkable.

Donato quickly dialed the Detective Squad at the Forty-third Precinct. Fazzini was off, but his superiors reached him at home. A few minutes later, he called the Seventy-eighth Precinct for Donato. Even the preliminary outline of Fazzini's story was incredible. He explained that he had indeed investigated the 1985 shooting death of one Gladys Matos, the mother of Eric Napoletano's wife Wanda. He had also worked on the murder of the girl found in Pennsylvania; she had been Eric's lover and roommate.

Donato attempted to provide a rundown on his missing-persons case, but Fazzini cut him off. The seasoned New York detective wanted to be polite, but he had little patience when it came to Eric and Carolyn Napoletano, especially Carolyn. He had spent countless hours on the two homicides, but his efforts had gone for naught. Instead, he had been forced to defend himself against Carolyn Napoletano's ridiculous accusations of harassment.

Fazzini insisted that Donato come to see him in person. There was only so much they could discuss on the phone.

The following morning, Donato and Burke headed across the George Washington Bridge for the Forty-third Precinct, where Fazzini was waiting with a pot of coffee and an emotional tale of murder, manipulation, obsession, domestic violence, and a big-city criminal justice system that had failed miserably.

Frustration was etched into Fazzini's face as he provided an overview of the unsuccessful investigations into the murders of Eric's girlfriend and mother-in-law. In his heart, Fazzini knew who was responsible for those homicides. His voice resonated with disappointment while he explained how Eric had gone unpunished all those years. He became even more outraged as he described the paradox of Carolyn Napoletano's NYPD job and her persistent interference with official police investigations. Her behavior was an affront to law enforcement personnel everywhere.

When Fazzini finally allowed Donato to relate the key details of the New Jersey investigation—how Myra had been planning to leave Eric when she disappeared, how her relatives had reported her missing, and how Eric's mother had played such an active role in protecting him—the New York detective exploded.

"I knew it! I knew it!" Fazzini yelled, banging his fist on the desk in anger. "I can't believe it. He did it again."

Donato and Burke exchanged glances. How could Fazzini be so certain? The veteran investigator assured them he knew what he was saying. "Let me tell you something about that girl you're looking for: She's not missing; she's dead!"

The finality of Fazzini's words stung like a slap on the face. The way he saw things, Myra Napoletano's decision to take the kids and leave her abusive husband had represented her death sentence.

Donato's mind was racing. It sounded as if Eric Napoletano was a serial killer. Only the victims did not fit the stereotype of strangers, prostitutes, or children. If Eric had killed all of these women, he had killed women he knew quite well.

Donato was having a hard time understanding what had gone wrong. Why hadn't Eric been arrested and prosecuted years ago? Why had the criminal justice system failed to stop him even after he had been so clearly identified as the only suspect in both homicides? How in God's name had Carolyn Napoletano kept her job with NYPD? Surely if something had been done to stop this madman and his mother years ago, everyone would not be worrying now about Myra's whereabouts and safety.

Nick Donato knew what he had to do. He had to learn everything he possibly could about Eric Napoletano—and stop him before he killed again.

PART 2

Eric and His Women

They are shaking in their boots about me. This has been the worst thing possible— a "serial killer's" mother working for the police department.

—Carolyn Napoletano

- 5 -

IN HER WORDS

My name is Carolyn—one word, one name. I don't like Carol. At work I'm Carolyn, and if people call me Carol, I don't answer until they come up in my face and say it.

Eric is a lot like me. He is an extension of me. He likes the last word. When he's mad at me he calls me Carol. If he wants to impress something on me, he calls me Mother.

I don't look my age and I don't act my age. My sister and I are silly. They used to call us the Goonie Girls. I used to go to professional wrestling matches with her. We liked Buddy Rogers, Johnny Valentine, the Chiropractor—and Bruno Sanmartino. He was, like, so big. But I don't like that stuff now.

I've been in Gracie Mansion. I worked for Nelson Rockefeller, and John Lindsay when he was mayor. I was a volunteer. Always a volunteer. I volunteered for the hospital and the auxiliary police. That's it, no more. I've done enough.

I'm a loner. I grew up reading. Reading is my hobby, my pastime, my everything when I'm not doing anything. I like any kind of book. I go to museums, but I don't like them. I've been to the opera. I don't like it. I've been to the ballet I've been to Broadway plays because I used to get free tickets. I used to go to the car shows. I used to get tickets. I used to take my mother to the boat show. Some things I like to try because it's a night to dress up. I do like the movies. But now with Home Box and Showtime, I don't go. Or, if I do go, I prefer to go alone. I do not like some chatterbox talking to me.

I learned a long, long time ago that you can't trust people. So never tell anybody what you wouldn't want said out in a room or on a loudspeaker. I was never really friendly with anybody because everybody was jealous of me. Don't ask me why. I don't know.

I am *nasty, but I'm not nasty to everybody. I never bother with any of my neighbors. And I don't tell people where I work. It's nobody's business. I never have ever said to anybody, "I work in the police department."*

Eric and I got along good. Eric don't drink; I don't drink either because I take medicine. We don't even smoke. We always talk about people wasting their money on cigarettes.

When he was a baby, and I would be doing the crossword puzzle in the paper and not paying attention to him, he would come and crumble it up. But as he got older, he understood; he would hunt for puzzles for me to do.

Yes, he calls me Anal. Eric's a great tease. You know what he used to do? We would be standing on the curb waiting to cross the street; he'd hold on to my arm and say to people, "I don't want you to be afraid of her, but they let her out on a weekend pass from the nuthouse." He's so funny. We're in the mall in Paramus and I tell Eric, "I have to go to the bathroom," or "I want to look at this," he starts, "Okay, Anal. Okay, Anal." While we're walking by people he'll say, "You know why I call her Anal? She's a proctologist." He don't mean anything by it. What you don't think is funny, we'll be on the floor. All we have to do is look at each other and we laugh.

When he was younger he was like a brat. He wasn't a bad kid to get in trouble; he was just a fresh kid. He was like me with outbursts. Oh, he tried to boss me, because he was the male. But, no. He was okay. I didn't take any crap from Eric. I was not intimidated by him. I used to punch and hit him. He never hit me. Maybe you could say he was a lonely kid. But he always got a lot of toys and stuff at Christmas. When he got older, we became friends.

You have to remember, it was the city. We lived on East Eighty-eighth Street. There was nothing to do in the city. It is hard for a kid to grow up in the city, in an apartment, and you have to play outside on the street. It is very difficult.

He always went to school. He could have gotten all As, but he didn't. Was he a B student? Maybe. Yeah. Eric didn't play hookey. Eric did his homework. Eric was a good boy. And he didn't get in any trouble with the police, nothing with the law. He did not want to go to college. He decided he would go in the Marines. I was so happy. He wanted to be an MP. He figured when he was older, he could come out and join the police department.

- 6 -

Carolyn Margaret Napoletano wanted to be the only woman who ever really mattered to Eric. She was the measuring stick for every other female he fell in love with. Their relationship was subject to wild swings. One moment their synergy was violent, the next it radiated warmth and tenderness. But even with the bumpy emotional ride, Carolyn dedicated her life to making things right for her only child. She would do virtually anything to protect and defend him; her subterfuge knew no bounds.

Eric was all Carolyn had. She could never let go. Eric never met his father, and Carolyn was abnormally attached to her son. They were inseparable; they were best buddies. Whenever possible, they traveled to work together, ate meals together. They served as each other's most trusted adviser. Without hesitation, she lied for him and offered convoluted excuses for his failures.

Yet at the same time, Carolyn and Eric could be the worst of enemies, screaming, cursing, and threatening each other. She hated blacks and Latinos—the women Eric fell in love with. Perhaps her dislike prompted his attraction. Worse, just as Eric reached the vulnerable age of puberty, Carolyn practically gave him away—to a man she barely knew.

One of two daughters of Norman and Florence Hankinson, Carolyn was born in New Brunswick, New Jersey, on April 21, 1940. Seeking a degree in communications, she took college courses in public speaking, writing, psychology, and political science but never completed her formal studies. Still, she considered herself highly educated and well informed. She watched the TV news religiously and regularly read a wide selection of current nonfiction books, three New York City newspapers, and dozens of magazines. Carolyn did not always buy her reading material, though: When her neighbors left for the weekend, Carolyn often "borrowed" and read their Sunday *New York Times,* then returned it to their doormat.

She told people she did not have a happy childhood, that her family moved a lot. On her own, Carolyn Hankinson had ended up living in Queens, the New York City borough adjacent to Long Island. One night at a bar, she dumped her blind date and ended up with a guy named Eric Ernest Napoletano. She fell in love. Soon after, she was pregnant.

To hear Carolyn tell it, Eric Ernest was also very attached to her, and they became engaged in the summer of 1964. While waiting for her wedding day, she moved to a nice section of the Bronx, into an apartment that would be the couple's home.

But the union was not to be. In Carolyn's version, the man's family offered her money to go away. After she declined and his family threw a gala engagement party, Carolyn claimed that "the bitch"—her future mother-in-law—kept all the money given as gifts. Finally, as Carolyn's due date approached, young Eric Ernest went off and joined the military.

Carolyn said she never questioned that she would go through with the pregnancy. On May 2, 1965, she gave birth to Eric Ernest Napoletano, Jr., whom she would immediately take to calling Ricky. Even though she never saw the older Eric Ernest again, Carolyn assumed his last name, going to court to make the change official. When Eric was old enough to understand, Carolyn explained that his father had died in a car accident. Over the years, she delighted in telling people that "it killed the father's family to no end" that she had taken the name Napoletano and given it to Eric.

There were differences between Carolyn's story and the version provided by Eric Ernest Napoletano. He said Carolyn had told him she wanted to get married because she was pregnant. He challenged her to prove that he was the father, even offering to take a blood test for confirmation. He said Carolyn told him to go to hell, and he never heard from her again. More than twenty years later, living in Connecticut, he said he was unaware that Carolyn had given birth and even claimed surprise that she had really been pregnant.

Carolyn never got over the rejection. Her memories were filled with bitterness, to the point that she claimed—without any supporting evidence—that the Napoletanos were "all in the Mafia."

Scurrilous remarks about Eric Ernest's family notwithstanding, Carolyn and young Eric developed an infatuation with organized crime. She became fascinated with godfathers and Mafia capos. Books about organized crime were among her favorites. Her self-described Mafioso idol was John Gotti, the head of all New York organized-crime families. She said there was nothing specific about her empathy for Gotti, that it was just a curiosity. At the same time, though, she admitted that she planned to write a book about him, had already started collecting research material, and had attended several sessions of one of his federal racketeering trials.

To Carolyn, there was no paradox between her personal life and her NYPD job. She was utterly unconcerned about having been spotted in the Gotti trial courtroom by several of her Organized Crime Control Bureau colleagues. "I took a vacation day. I am entitled to do what I want. I wasn't hiding it." She believed that her aggressive, know-it-all attitude was the only way to live. Carolyn was convinced that she was smarter than anyone she ever dealt with. She had an answer for everything. No one could tell her a story she could not top.

One telling yarn early on featured a female neighbor who accused Eric of tampering with her locks. Carolyn called the woman an asshole and threatened to sue. She complained that the woman had been running around telling tenants in their Manhattan high-rise that Eric was crazy. Lying, Carolyn angrily informed the woman that Eric had earned all As in school, and that crazy people did not succeed as he had. She promised that before she was through, every resident would know that the complaining neighbor was the crazy one.

To be sure, Carolyn and Eric had a rough go of it during Eric's early years. Shortly after his birth, Carolyn moved out of the Bronx to East Eighty-eighth Street in Manhattan, near Gracie Mansion, the home of New York City's mayor. She felt safe there with her windows nailed shut and an assortment of locks on her doors.

But troubles came from within the apartment walls. Mother and son fought constantly. Carolyn felt sorry for herself, lamenting how Eric's father had deserted them. Over time, Eric acquired one of his mother's persistent traits: He

disliked taking orders and following rules. Eric expected to
get what he wanted, when he wanted it. Furious domestic
clashes were inevitable. Most often Eric emerged as the
winner.

He was not an emotionally healthy child. He briefly
attended third grade in Saint Joseph's Grammar School at
420 East Eighty-seventh Street but rebelled at the religious
discipline. Too much to handle, his mother checked him
into Bellevue Hospital in early 1974. At the age of eight, he
spent three months in the facility. Eric then spent his fourth-
and fifth-grade years at Green Chimneys, a "residential
treatment center" in Brewster, New York. Records indicate
that Eric was discharged on June 6, 1976. Hospitalized
again for nearly two months while in the sixth grade, Eric
would later claim that his mother had sent him away so she
could have more time to herself.

It was against that backdrop, during the summer between
seventh and eighth grades, that Eric met Albert Jiovine, a
middle-aged import manager. "Uncle Al" had a history of
living with young males.

The intimate involvement of Al Jiovine in Eric's life
would have a profound effect on the Napoletano mother-son
alliance. At times, Al would be the glue that kept Carolyn
and Eric together. On many other occasions, however, he
would instigate violent arguments within the household. On
yet other occasions, a jealous Al Jiovine would meddle in
Eric's relationships with the various women who competed
with Carolyn for her son's affections.

Born November 15, 1930, in Brooklyn, Albert Joseph
Jiovine was five-foot-nine and 175 pounds. Bald, slouchy,
and shifty-eyed, he was animated when talking. While in the
company of other adults, he often acted visibly nervous, and
he was uncomfortable around little children.

Jiovine told acquaintances that he had been out of contact
with his father for more than thirty years. Hard of hearing,
he had a volume enhancer attached to his home phone. He
loved cars, frequently bought jalopies, and was beset with
what an insurance agent would call "an above-average
claims history." Like Carolyn Napoletano, Jiovine often
tried to pass himself off as an expert on everything. He
deceived people as a matter of course, even friends and
members of his immediate family. When caught in a lie, he

usually revealed only enough to get out of trouble. Uncle Al Jiovine never came totally clean; he probably did not know how.

He managed only two years of high school, then lied about his age to join the army. After a four-year hitch, he joined the Marines. Years later, he told Eric he had been a Marine drill instructor, but his records showed he had been a bus driver. Not only that, Jiovine's Marine record was rife with "offenses and punishments," from being AWOL, to being out of uniform, to failing to cover a sentry post. Not recommended for reenlistment, he was discharged in 1956 and returned to his mother in New Jersey.

The story of Eric and Al's relationship was bizarre, starting with how they met. One afternoon in 1978, while Eric was riding his bike in Central Park, he befriended a boy his age named Wally. The youngster told Eric that he lived nearby with an older businessman named Bob. Eric brought Wally home to meet Carolyn, gave her Wally's phone number, and told her he was going over to his new friend's home to play. Days later, Bob called Carolyn out of the blue to ask if Eric could join him, young Wally, and an adult friend named Al on a trip to the Bronx Zoo. Bob vouched for his chum, Al Jiovine. Although she still had not met Bob, Carolyn approved the trip.

When subsequently pressed to defend her decision, Carolyn explained that Bob the businessman had "sounded nice on the phone." Besides, she met him soon after the trip and eventually spoke with Al Jiovine on the phone, then met him several months later. But by that time, Bob had faded from the picture; Eric and Al were already close friends.

A bachelor in his forties, Jiovine had abruptly found himself in need of companionship, driven into a deep depression by the death of his twenty-year-old roommate, Marshall "Mitch" Mastrangelo.

As with so much of Al Jiovine's life, details of his relationship with Mastrangelo were murky. The young man had died when the car he was driving, owned by Jiovine, inexplicably slammed into the metal supports of the Queensboro Bridge. One of Jiovine's friends told police that Mastrangelo, Jiovine, and a third man had been involved in a lovers' quarrel just prior to the fatal incident. Another associate quoted Jiovine as boasting that he had done whatever was necessary to please Mastrangelo while he was alive, including murdering a third male who had been involved in a triangle with them.

Carolyn Napoletano said that when she finally met Jiovine, he gave her the impression that he had been active in the organizations Catholic Charities and Big Brothers for years and had spent considerable time volunteering to help young boys without fathers. She figured Eric could benefit from an adult male presence, so she was pleased that he and Jiovine had bonded. "Eric started staying over his house, staying a little longer, and a little longer, and a little longer," she said. "This was like a buddy to him, too. I thought it was okay; here was someone for Eric."

She rejected any suggestion that she had essentially given her son away, insisting that Eric "did not live with Al; he just stayed with him from time to time. Eric still lived with me." But Eric effectively did live with Jiovine in the Jackson Heights section of Queens for most of his high school years. Together, they cared for a succession of pet birds: Junior, Bonnie and Clyde, Polly and Candy. On most weekends, Jiovine drove out to visit his mother in New Jersey with Eric in tow. They spent entire summers together.

Eric generally referred to Jiovine as "Uncle Al" or as a family friend. But there were many times where he left the impression, or flatly asserted, that Al Jiovine was his biological father.

Jiovine at times claimed fatherhood himself. At one point, he requested that Eric be transferred to a school in Queens, but Board of Education officials denied the request on the grounds that he did not have legal custody. As a result, Eric continued to attend school in Manhattan, taking the subway back to his mother's Yorkville neighborhood to attend Robert F. Wagner Junior High on East Seventy-sixth Street, then Julia Richman High School on East Sixty-seventh Street and Second Avenue.

Jiovine catered to Eric's every whim, spoiling the teenager even more. Eric also grew meaner, nastier, and more obnoxious. But to Carolyn, her son was just fine. "When I saw Eric, it seemed everything was okay. They seemed to get along together." She said she sensed that Eric and Jiovine both obtained emotional satisfaction from the relationship.

But hadn't she ever doubted the sincerity of Al Jiovine's interest in her son? Hadn't she ever feared that Al might like boys in a sexual way? Carolyn claimed she had asked herself those questions about Jiovine but had been assured by Eric that his relationship was totally nonsexual.

In fact, Uncle Al *was* homosexual. He was in the company of young men often. Sometimes he picked them up at gay bars or the Port Authority Bus Terminal for one-nighters. Other times they lived with him. But he acknowledged his sexual orientation to a trusted few, never to his family in New Jersey.

When confronted about his lifestyle, Jiovine always sought to dodge the age issue, wanting to avoid being tagged as a pedophile. The liaisons he acknowledged involved older teens or young adults. Also, he admitted to long-term sexual relationships with males prior to the time he lived with Eric and afterward. But for as long as he could, Al insisted that his relationship with Eric had been strictly platonic. Eventually, though, Jiovine would admit to police what logic dictated he could not deny: Eric, too, had been one of his sexual partners.

Growing up, Eric fixated on one career ambition: to become a New York City cop. While still in high school he was accepted as a member of NYPD's volunteer auxiliary police force. Eric felt powerful playing cop. He especially enjoyed "going on patrol" with his nightstick, even when off duty.

There was little his mother would not do to help him achieve his goal, so she also joined the auxiliary police force. "When I went to sign up Eric, they said, 'Why don't you sign up too, because it would be a nice mother-and-son team?' So I did," Carolyn recalled. "If you want to become a cop, being an auxiliary helps. You are using a police radio. You are confronting. And you get to learn the law. You have everything the same as the cops, the entire uniform from head to toe. Handcuffs, everything—except a gun."

Eric and Carolyn were soon working together out of the Central Park Precinct. Uncle Al lent a hand by buying Eric a police scanner for recreational use.

Eric also began the arduous preparation for becoming a regular police officer, even lifting weights to build up his skinny frame. Over time, he passed the written tests and the physical, and was placed on a list of approved applicants.

But the hiring process would remain frozen for Eric and thousands of others because of acute budget constraints.

Carolyn's membership on the auxiliary force fueled an interest in law enforcement. With her son's encouragement, she began working full-time for the New York City Police Department in 1983 as a civilian police administrative aide. She began wearing clothing adorned with the NYPD insignia—jackets, sweatshirts, windbreakers, T-shirts. "I knew a lot of cops being an auxiliary police officer," Carolyn later explained. "So the cops who knew me would tell the cops who didn't, 'Hey, she's A-OK. Don't worry, she won't tell your wife where you are, and she'll make sure you get the calls from the girlfriends.' "

At first, she was assigned to the same Central Park Precinct where she performed her auxiliary duties. "I knew the captain there very, very well. He's a deputy inspector now." But life at the precinct was difficult. "Everybody was against me because they thought I was filling the captain's ears. Nobody trusted me. The civilians were all black or Spanish—mostly black. They thought that because I was friendly with the captain I was going to get their job."

Before long, Carolyn was transferred to the Communications Division at One Police Plaza, located behind City Hall in the shadow of the Brooklyn Bridge. Bored with shuffling paperwork, she was granted her request to be assigned to a computer terminal.

During her career, Carolyn would come in contact with countless officers, detectives, sergeants, lieutenants, deputy chiefs, and chiefs. She met good ones and bad ones. She had social relationships, even dates, with some of them. They did favors for her, she did favors for them. Sometimes, when they called her apartment to sweet-talk her, she recorded the conversations. She once told her son of a friend who used to conduct electronic surveillance for the commissioner's office; he had warned her to be careful when talking on the phone since there was no telling who could be eavesdropping. Over time, several close friends were promoted to ranking positions. Carolyn hoped that her friendships would help Eric get on the force, then advance up the ladder.

* * *

Carolyn had a distorted view of her son's teenage years, from his performance in school to his involvement with the military.

She often described Eric as a genius who earned As and Bs in school. But, in fact, he fared poorly. A classic under-achiever, Eric's tenth-grade average at Julia Richman was 48. He failed two courses in the first semester, six courses in the second. In typical New York City fashion, he was pro-moted anyway.

Eric did develop an interest in macabre creative writing. In one story he titled "The Rope," the husband viewed his wife as a demanding, nagging bore. She was angry because they were poor and she thought he was fooling around. Instead of bringing her a cup of coffee as promised, he put a rope around her neck. In explaining his characters, Eric observed that people in love frequently fight about silly things.

For another assignment, Eric reviewed a book about a killer and a con man who deceived his friends. He said there were two lessons from that story: One, if anyone does some-thing wrong to you, pay them back; two, never trust anyone you have harmed because they will retaliate. He added the word *revenge* in parentheses.

In another insightful, creative undertaking, Eric provided thumbnail parodies for then-popular soap operas, dramas, and sitcoms: "Nights of Our Lives," a typical evening of hate and hope, love and fear, and terror in Midtown; "Bad Times," criminals saddened because they have no one to use their guns and knives on; "68th Street Blues," love and pas-sion in an East Side park, where rich people lure the less for-tunate into perverse misconduct; "The Guiding Class," the story of stupid people pulling down the smart ones; "Hate Boat," a gathering spot to meet those you hate most; and "All My Friends," the story of a gay man trapped in a train with fifty males.

Bad grades and all, Eric graduated from Julia Richman on schedule in June 1983, and that summer he began working at a Fayva shoe store on Third Avenue, several blocks from his mother's apartment. But Eric had grander ambitions. Idolizing Jiovine, he wanted to become a Marine drill instructor. He and his mother assumed that the enlistment would help him become a cop, too.

These were big steps for Eric: joining the Marines, leaving

his mother and Al, going out on his own. Carolyn decided it was time Eric knew the truth about his father. She confessed that she had concocted the car-accident story to spare him the emotional pain of knowing he was a bastard. She then launched into a diatribe about "what *he* did to us."

Eric took the news hard. Bitter and angry, he filed papers in civil court to change his name. Instead of Eric Ernest Napoletano, Jr., he became simply Eric Napoletano.

A month later, Carolyn mysteriously broke her arm, causing her to go on disability at NYPD. This injury was at least the second time she had sustained broken bones under mysterious circumstances. Years later, Al Jiovine would allege that Eric had been responsible for the injuries, but Carolyn vehemently denied those claims. Regardless, Eric began acting out in other ways, engaging in frequent and heated arguments with one of his mother's neighbors.

Ten days before Christmas 1983, Eric was assigned to the Marine Corps Recruit Depot on Parris Island, South Carolina. Before his five-man contingent departed Fort Hamilton in Brooklyn, he was appointed "group leader."

Unwilling to let go, Carolyn began writing letters constantly. She tried to be supportive, but could not help but play her son's emotions like a yo-yo. One day she would be happy and encouraging, the next day caustic, feeling sorry for herself, or in pain from one physical ailment or another.

In one note she assured Eric that he was so tough and intelligent he was destined to finish number one in boot camp. But in her next note, she told Eric she was lost without him and lamented that she no longer had anyone to play cards with. At times, her words sounded as if she were writing to a lover rather than her child: She had cried several times since he left, had been unable to get a good night's sleep, and could not wait to hear his voice on the phone. She ended one typewritten letter, "LOVE YOU, LOVE & KISSES RICKY, Love Mommy," with nine Xs underneath.

Eric's enlistment drew Carolyn and Al closer together. They spoke on the phone three or four times each day, usually at great length. All they could talk about was Eric. Although their boy wonder had barely unpacked, they were already making plans to fly down for graduation, which was more than two months away. Al was so excited about the prospect of Eric graduating first in his class that he decided to rent a Lincoln Town Car for the day.

Carolyn figured that Jiovine liked his frequent phone chats with her because she was an extension of her son. At the same time, though, for a woman who had sent her son off to live with Jiovine for so many years, she was now jealous that she had to share Eric with him. In one note, she curtly informed Eric that she had been heartbroken to learn that he had called Al instead of her, and scolded him for signing his letters "Eric." To her, he would always be "Ricky."

As a sidelight, Carolyn kept Eric up to date on NYPD news, especially the department's plans to hire more cops eventually. She laced her letters with references to pals at various station houses and "downtown" at One Police Plaza. To hear Carolyn tell it, by the time Eric got out of the Marines, the different bosses would be fighting to get his talents.

Eric reciprocated with lengthy letters to Carolyn and Jiovine. To Al, he made unconditional declarations of love, thanking him for saying he would always consider him his son. Eric added that in his eyes, Jiovine was his father.

His most touching prose, however, was reserved for his mother. Eric informed her that he was using their time apart to reflect on their relationship. He said he loved her and missed her dearly. He suggested that their family get together more often, since everyone was getting older and life had no guarantees. Eric averred that he did not want to fight with her anymore.

Carolyn cried over her son's poignant remarks, observing that she had always assumed he had not cared about her. She vowed to keep her New Year's resolution to be nice to him, too. But at the same time, she was unable to resist telling her son that she had never been the source of their problems. She said they never would have fought if only he had learned to accept what she had to say.

It did not take long for Eric's world at Parris Island to fall apart. First he feared that someone was reading his letters. Then he began to pepper his notes with comments about how much he missed his mother and Jiovine.

As his homesickness deepened, Eric's letters turned darker. He wrote of recruits who had gone "nuts," threatened to commit suicide, or been sent home. He wrote Jiovine that he was beginning to wonder if Parris Island was "a crazy place."

With each day Eric's confidence ebbed. He broke the news that he was not going to graduate number one as everyone had assumed. He said the worst part about boot camp was the verbal harassment, the way the sergeants called him "Boy!" or yelled "Move!" or treated him "like a nothing."

Initially, Carolyn and Jiovine both offered encouragement. Al told Eric he would be proud regardless of where he placed in the graduating class. Carolyn suggested he was homesick because he had never been separated from her under circumstances where he could not see her. She promised he could always live with her and assured him that being number one was not that important; finishing in the top ten would be just fine with her! Anyway, before long he would be joining NYPD; that's when she would really be proud. He needed to look at the Marines simply as a prerequisite.

More than ever, Eric's future as a New York City cop was all that mattered to Carolyn. But much more was at stake for Eric. He had already decided that he was going to win himself a discharge from boot camp. He missed his mother and Al so much he could not live without them.

Officially, Eric laid claim to a more legitimate reason for needing a discharge: "My nuts," he explained bluntly. He had had an operation earlier that summer on his left testicle and had been complaining since his arrival at the Marine depot that the pain in that area had resurfaced. He claimed the symptoms had worsened as the intensity of training increased.

On New Year's Day, Eric reported for sick call. Assigned to limited duty, he reasoned that the Marines would have to discharge him because it would cost too much money for them to let him hang around. He minimized the impact an early discharge would have on his dream of becoming a cop. Down the road he would simply explain that his condition had fully healed. *You know how I work. Not meaning nothing wrong by it, but I usually get what I want when I play my cards right,* he wrote home one day.

At first Eric was afraid to give his mother the bad news. He asked Al to explain the situation, then get her to convince Marine officials in New York to intervene. He assured Jiovine that Carolyn always knew how to handle sticky situations. She could always threaten to complain to the highest levels.

When Eric finally talked with his mother about his plans to bail out, she harangued him. Eric was not about to listen to her, though; he told her he had to get off the phone, and hung up.

Carolyn was not so easily deterred and promptly typed a vicious letter. She accused her son of being a fake and a quitter hiding behind minor medical problems. She warned that he was going to wind up "a nothing," that he would never be able to become a cop if he didn't make it through boot camp, that he was going to ruin his future just because he was homesick. She said he had made her real proud when he joined up, but now she felt like he had kicked her in the ass.

Al weighed in with several critical notes, reminding Eric that the Marine Corps was a far cry from the Boy Scouts. Even Carolyn's mother joined in, asking her grandson to reconsider.

Prompted by Carolyn, Eric's Marine recruiter, Staff Sergeant C. J. Kelley, wrote, "There's no future back in New York as a policeman if you give up now, and I know you don't want to sell shoes forever." Kelley advised Eric that many boot-camp attendees became homesick because they were young men who had "never left Momma's apron strings."

But none of the encouragement worked. Eric continued to feed his mother and Al tales of woe.

Carolyn lashed back, promising she would never accept his mutiny. She referred to him as "a spineless, weakling creature" who would never amount to anything. She said he was upsetting her terribly. She'd been sick all week. Her broken arm hurt. She couldn't do her exercises. He'd never handle the police academy training. Her life would continue to be rotten. She warned him not to look for any more letters. In a final salvo, she replaced her usual complement of handwritten love Xs with a stern warning in giant block letters: "CHANGE YOUR MIND BEFORE IT'S TOO LATE!!"

But it *was* too late.

Eric was shipped off to the urology clinic at the Naval Regional Medical Center in Charleston, where a medical consultant concluded that his condition would not improve on active duty. Discharge was recommended.

Eric had been at boot camp for only a month. He had spent more than half that time thinking about getting out.

Two weeks later, he was given an "entry-level separation" due to a preenlistment physical disability.

If the doctors thought Eric was faking, they did not say. It really did not matter. The Marines would not have him either way.

Carolyn's little Ricky was on his way home, still looking for a way to prove he was a man.

And the killings were about to begin.

If Eric was depressed about his failure in the military, it did not take him long to regain his cocksure confidence. He moved back in with Uncle Al in Queens and resumed planning to become a cop. On his second day home, he met Marilyn Coludro, a troubled fifteen-year-old Puerto Rican from his former school, Wagner Junior High in Manhattan. An eighth-grader who had been left back twice, Marilyn was impressed that Eric had been in the Marines; he was exactly the kind of "white boy" she always wanted. She was exactly what Eric needed, someone who would see him for the great guy he really was. The problem with this scenario was that Eric immediately began mistreating her in the same love-hate fashion that had marked his relationship with his mother.

Marilyn Coludro came from a broken home and lived with her mother, Marta Rivera, and a younger brother in a nice apartment in a city housing project several blocks north of the Napoletano residence. Marilyn spent a great deal of her childhood behind a closed bedroom door, writing to an imaginary friend, Winnie, but she also had a close bond with her mother and often watched TV in bed with her. "She used to say, 'Mom, just come next to me and caress my hair.' She liked me to caress her hair and blow into her ears softly," said Marta Rivera.

Marilyn liked to paint, draw, and design dresses. She wanted to attend the High School of Fashion Industries to study fashion design. She also liked to smoke marijuana.

At thirteen, she became severely depressed when her parents divorced. "Marilyn had serious emotional problems. She was emotionally disturbed," said Rivera. "She was a very difficult girl at the time. She was getting worse and worse. Her behavior was out of control." The youngster got into fights. She cut classes. Her grades turned bad. She

stopped eating. Many nights she woke up screaming that
she was seeing demons.

Rivera sent her daughter for a psychiatric evaluation at
Metropolitan Hospital, where she was admitted. "They
found that she was a schizophrenic. They insisted on keeping
her in the hospital for six months."

Against doctors' orders, however, Rivera signed for her
daughter's release on June 26, 1983, Marilyn's fifteenth
birthday. Back home, Marilyn said the medication was
working. She returned to school that fall, and appeared to be
progressing. But then she met Eric, on Groundhog Day 1984.

Marilyn was an easy target, mesmerized by the attention
Eric showered on her. At five-foot-seven and 155 pounds,
she went on a diet and lost twenty pounds. She did not want
Eric comparing her unfavorably to other girls. Since Eric
did not smoke or drink, she gave up smoking dope.

Eric and Marilyn had several things in common: rebel-
lion, violent temper, and disrespect for elders. Marilyn took
to wearing her naturally curly black hair in a red punk cut.
She thought Eric's military close-crop looked punk, too. On
occasion, when she was angry, she punched holes in her
bedroom walls. Her relationship with her mother was far
from tranquil. Discipline was a subject of frequent discord.
Marilyn also resented her mother for having put her in the
hospital.

Two weeks after they began dating, Marilyn and Eric
moved into Uncle Al Jiovine's apartment. Already there
was talk of marriage. None of the adults involved was
happy with the relationship or the living arrangements.

Still smarting from her son's Marine Corps debacle, Carolyn thought Eric could do better. She still fancied him as an
up-and-comer who needed someone intelligent and savvy,
someone from a better social circle, especially for when he
joined NYPD.

Marta Rivera was concerned because of her daughter's
age and vulnerability. She also had a very uncomfortable
feeling about Eric. Here was this skinny, gawky guy from
another ethnic background hypnotizing her daughter with
promises of everlasting love. "There was something in the
way he looked, in his eyes. It didn't click to me. I saw
emptiness," she said. "One thing that really got my attention
was the way he would say, 'Yes, ma'am, yes, ma'am, yes,

ma'am. Oh, yes, ma'am. Beg your pardon, ma'am.' He was always trying to be so polite just to gain my confidence."

As Rivera saw it, Eric turned Marilyn even more against her. "He brainwashed her into believing that I put her away for six months because I wanted to get rid of her, because I was not a fit mother. So she started to hate me. She stopped believing what I told her, because now Eric was her savior."

Out of the blue, Marilyn called home to tell her mother how much she hated her. "Mama, I don't want to hear from you. Stop bugging me. Stop following me," Marilyn ordered. "I'm with Eric. We're going to get married."

Rivera had other reasons to be gravely concerned about her daughter's safety. Marilyn passed on several bizarre statements she attributed to Eric regarding his relationship with his mother, Carolyn: that she had sexually abused him as a child; that he had tied her up in her apartment, handcuffed her, and beaten her; that he had abused her to the point where he broke her arm; and that she had sent him to Bellevue Hospital during his elementary school years because she wanted to be by herself.

"That's why he hates his mother and punishes her," Rivera said. She told Marilyn she could not understand why she stayed with him. "You can see that this guy is no good if he's doing all of this to his own mother."

"Mom, you have no idea what a bitch she is," Marilyn replied. "Don't worry. He won't do it to me." She insisted that Eric was treating her well, helping with her schoolwork and teaching her to stand up to those who sought to take advantage of her.

Of all the adults involved, Uncle Al had the most to say about the relationship; after all, they were living in his home. He harangued Eric about Marilyn's presence, complaining that she was a disruptive influence on the household. Jiovine did not mind Eric's presence. In fact, he made it clear he wanted Eric to stay, just without Marilyn.

On March 8, 1984, Jiovine left Eric an ominous note, ordering him to remove Marilyn from the apartment within a week. Sounding jealous, Al told Eric that if he and Marilyn had decided on marriage that was fine, but she still had to get out of his apartment: *She by no means belongs here, and you know it. You have taken on her responsibility, and used me. She is here against my wishes. You are wrong to take her from her mother, and then bring her here.*

He left two postscripts: *Eric, she is very, very dangerous. Mark my word. I feel hell in her,* and *I think you have taken on much more than you can chew. Pls get her out of here. She is going to ruin you and me. Pls keep alert.*

Marilyn and Eric failed to meet Al's deadline. Instead, on March 27, 1984, less than two months after they met, they became engaged. Eric proposed on Al's rooftop about seven o'clock that evening, presenting Marilyn with a diamond ring.

By accepting, Marilyn set herself up for a nasty roller-coaster relationship of highs and lows. Although he had already let snippets of his evil personality surface, Marilyn's commitment triggered an intense release of Eric's vicious inner self. From that point on, he would not only dominate and control; he would do so in the cruelest ways imaginable. He would go out of his way to beat down Marilyn's already low self-esteem. Eric was the master, Marilyn the slave.

Just *one hour* after Eric's rooftop proposal, Marilyn found herself so upset that she felt like killing herself. The reason? After professing his love, Eric called Marilyn "a slut." He suggested that she was sexually active with schoolmates at lunchtime because she was lonely and could not wait until she saw him again.

Day two of the engagement brought worse. Eric found Marilyn's diary and handcuffed her while reading the previous day's entry. She lashed back, calling him "a motherfucker," "an asshole," "a slut," and "a cocksucker." A few minutes later, however, she forgave him. Marilyn's emotions were putty in Eric's hands.

The bewitching effects of Eric's powerful love-hate spell was a complex matter. His allure could not possibly be explained as charm or grace or charisma. Part of his appeal was no doubt grounded in the fact that he offered Marilyn Coludro an alternative to her unhappy home life. She convinced herself that he had changed her life for the better. She was willing to take his mistreatment in return for his adulation. In each instance where Eric abused her, she calmed down, then forgave him. He, in turn, always promised to keep his emotions in check, then renewed his vow of undying love.

With all that "love" came sex, and lots of it. Marilyn shared Eric's obsession with intercourse. If they felt like spending all day in bed, they did. Marilyn would cut classes, and Eric would be absent from the messenger and chauffeur job Jiovine had helped him get. Marilyn said she was so committed to Eric that she would kill anyone who tried to take him away.

Bowing to Jiovine's continued pressure, Eric and Marilyn found their own place, a modest apartment in the Bronx. Eric instructed her not to bring anyone over, especially relatives. But Marilyn allowed her brother to visit one afternoon. When her disobedience tugged at her, she told Eric what she had done.

Eric stormed out of the apartment to call Uncle Al. When he returned, a sobbing Marilyn asked him if he was going to eat the canned soup she had heated for dinner. Eric said he was not, so she dumped it in the kitchen sink—only to spend the rest of the evening worrying whether her true love was hungry. In the end, abusive Eric always won out.

The strain of dealing with Eric's mood swings gradually began to wear on Marilyn. Alternating between fits of anger and bouts of silence—sometimes by the hour—he told Marilyn he wanted her all to himself.

Marilyn wondered if some of Eric's tantrums were expressions of jealousy, say, when she invited her mother over for a visit. She really loved Eric, but she still had feelings for her mother. She asked him to refrain from his insults; she had made sure to refrain from insulting his mother, even though she couldn't stand the "white bitch cocksucker." Marilyn warned Eric that he was lucky Carolyn Napoletano was his mother; otherwise, she might have killed her by now.

Eric wanted to make sure his outbursts kept their sting, so he increased his nastiness. Marilyn could not understand why, if Eric loved her as much as he claimed, he felt compelled to call her names like "a fat slob" or "slut." Eric's barrage of disparaging comments made Marilyn cry frequently. She began to feel so bad about herself that she wished she had never been born.

Despite her pleas, Eric continued with the verbal abuse. Instead of extricating herself, though, Marilyn dug in, more committed than ever to marrying him. She began to acquire many of Eric's views on life—for example, his hatred for blacks and certain types of Puerto Ricans, the "low-class people" she used to be friends with. She agreed with Eric's assessment that their new Bronx neighborhood was nice because only white people lived there. She did not need her old friends anymore.

Determined to please him at every opportunity, Marilyn began making arrangements for a surprise party for Eric's nineteenth birthday. But as events unfolded, Marta Rivera learned that there was very little to celebrate. Her maternal instincts had been right all along. While visiting to assist with the festivities, Rivera managed to read some of her daughter's diary entries. In between the comments about sex and love, there were passages detailing severe physical abuse.

Marilyn had written of being handcuffed, tortured, and beaten with a belt. She quoted Eric as having threatened to kill her and himself if she left him.

Outraged, Rivera examined her daughter's body and found bruises and scars on her wrists, neck, and arms. Rivera feared that if she did not act immediately, her daughter would end up dead. She insisted that Marilyn return home.

Marilyn agreed, but not without a fight. Rivera realized that the reconciliation would be a fragile one but rationalized that her most immediate concern was to get Marilyn away from Eric.

The next morning, May 3, 1984, Rivera filed a formal complaint, charging Eric with unlawful imprisonment, assault, sexual abuse, and harassment. She alleged that Eric had unlawfully kept her daughter "with intent to cause physical injury," specifically, striking her with a belt, punching and slapping her, and causing contusions and lacerations on her entire body. Rivera also alleged that Eric had threatened to kill her and Marilyn.

Even in this emergency situation, the justice system moved slowly and deliberately. The judge, Stanley B. Katz, issued a temporary order of protection, prohibiting Eric from contacting Marilyn or her mother pending a hearing.

Rivera thought of sending her daughter away to Puerto Rico. But Eric got wind of the plan and confronted them one afternoon on the corner of Eighty-sixth Street and Third Avenue. "You know what he did, this crazy psychopath? He knelt down in front of me, begging me. 'I want Marilyn back. Please don't send her away from me. She's my love. Please, don't do that, Marta.' Then he started to kiss my hands and my feet—right there on the street, in front of everybody. He was acting so crazy, I stood there paralyzed. I didn't know what to do."

Eric camped out on Ninety-second Street, twenty-three stories below Rivera's apartment. When Marilyn came to the window, Eric ran back and forth, blowing her kisses. "It was like Romeo and Juliet," Rivera recalled. "He'd yell, 'Marilyn, Marilyn, I love you, I love you.' "

On another occasion, Eric sneaked up on them as they were walking to a therapy session with Marilyn's psychiatrist and psychologist. As he blocked their path on the busy Manhattan sidewalk, Marilyn started shaking. "Please, Eric. Don't hurt my mother. Please, don't hurt Mommy."

Eric stood his ground, his eyes darting from one woman to the other.

Rivera tried to play it cool. "You're very welcome to come with us," she said. "If you really love Marilyn, come with us to the session."

"No, no," Eric replied. "I don't want to go there because they might think I'm crazy."

Rivera and her daughter went on their way. Several days later, however, Eric changed his mind and decided that he did want to participate in a counseling session. As Rivera recalled the incident, "As soon as the psychiatrist saw him, she said, 'This man is a sociopath.' "

The two therapists told Eric they thought it was best to stop seeing Marilyn. He reacted by exploding at them. "He was furious, screaming at the doctors, 'You're not going to take Marilyn away from me!' " The frightened therapists summoned hospital security, and Eric was escorted out.

But he was far from finished. He was determined to work his bizarre charm. Marilyn made it easier for him; she was still attracted. And, as nice as her mother tried to be, the girl did not like living at home. So, when Eric came looking for her several days later, the easily impressed Marilyn succumbed and left with him.

Rivera was furious and reported the incident to the police. The following evening, Eric was arrested at Uncle Al's apartment by Housing Authority police for violating the order of protection. Jiovine said he had not seen Marilyn, but, curiously, he turned her in several hours later.

Eric spent the night in jail and was released in the morning to his mother. He was extremely agitated at Marilyn and her mother, contending that he was unaware of any order of protection, insisting that no one had ever served him with a copy.

Back with her mother again, Marilyn signed a "misdemeanor information," accusing Eric of disobeying the judge's order of protection. She showed her bruises to a Bronx assistant DA. But the system again would do nothing to protect her. "He wrote it all down. But they didn't do anything," Rivera asserted. The new charges were assigned a court file separate from the first set of charges. Each case carried a different, and incorrect, spelling for Eric's last name—Napolital and Napolitano—as well as different home addresses. It would be weeks before any of the charges were brought before a judge.

In the meantime, Marilyn ended up back with Eric. Although they were seen by several friends, the two lived underground, sleeping most nights in the basement of the building where Eric's old high school buddy Marcelino Cotto lived in the Bronx. They also spent time at Uncle Al's. Marilyn was expelled from junior high for absenteeism, and Eric was fired from his job.

Frustrated, Marta Rivera filed an official missing-persons report with the New York City Police Department. She told the officer at the local precinct that she believed her daughter was in the company of a boyfriend named Eric Napoletano. Being honest, Rivera mentioned that Marilyn had run away before with Eric and had been seeing a psychiatrist. "They laughed at me. They told me, 'She'll be sixteen pretty soon, and if she wants to go off with her boyfriend, we have no power to make her come back home.' " Marta Rivera felt she had been treated with disrespect because of her economic and ethnic background.

After hearing nothing for several weeks, Rivera journeyed downtown to the main NYPD Missing Persons Bureau at One Police Plaza. She told an investigator that she feared Marilyn had been kidnapped by Eric; her daughter had never said she planned to run away with him, just get married. There was no reason for her to disappear completely. And there was no acceptable explanation for her having left behind all of her makeup and clothing. "There's something wrong," Rivera insisted.

"Marta, we have cases like this by the dozens in New York City. This is not a special one," the investigator told her.

"Well, this is special to me," Rivera replied. "I know my daughter. I'm begging you to find out if she is doing all right."

Rivera said the cop told her they would see what they could do. But, she continued, she never heard from anyone at NYPD again.

Marilyn Coludro became an insignificant statistic, no doubt categorized as an unsteady kid who had probably run away from home. The officers assigned to the case conducted the required preliminary investigation, and when they failed to locate her, they moved on to the next batch of reports.

On the first of the court dates scheduled for the abuse charges, Marilyn and Eric, who had dyed his sandy hair black, both failed to appear in court. The hearing was postponed for two weeks, to coincide with a proceeding regarding Eric's arrest for violating the order of protection. In the interim, to protect Marilyn and her mother, the judge extended the unenforced order of protection until the next court date. As usual, Eric suffered no consequence; he was getting his way, just as he had so many times in the past.

Several days after the postponement, Marta Rivera received a letter, purportedly from her daughter, stating that she hated her mother because she had caused Eric to be arrested and spend a night in jail. She accused her mother of being crazy and of viewing all men in a negative light simply because her own marriage had failed. Marilyn promised that she was going to marry Eric even if it was the last thing she did.

Shortly before the rescheduled hearing, the clerk's office at the Bronx County Courthouse received a notarized letter, also purportedly from Marilyn, in which the girl insisted she was "in good health and fully aware and accountable" for her actions. "I wish to withdraw all charges against Eric Napoletano," the letter stated. Marilyn asserted that the allegations contained in the criminal complaint had never occurred and had been leveled while she was suffering from "extreme emotional disturbance." She said the order of protection should be dropped, too, because there was no need for it. She contended that she had signed the charges against Eric "while under extreme pressure from my mother. . . .

She made me say that all of the above charges were true, telling me that Eric Napoletano, who is my fiancé, was no good for me."

The letter said Marilyn would not appear in court, explaining that she had run away from her last residence because of her mother's refusal to allow her to be with Eric, "who I love very much and want to marry." The letter said she wanted the court to know how good a person he was, assisting her with her homework, teaching her right from wrong. "Eric Napoletano is a definite necessity in my life, for my well-being, and for strengthening my mental health."

In language considerably beyond the level expected from an eighth-grader left back twice—and beyond the writing skills previously displayed by Eric Napoletano—the letter went on to cruelly question Marta Rivera's parenting skills, mental competency, and sex life. "This is not a proper example for her children to follow. I hope the court will see the unsuitability and unfitness of Marta Rivera and allow justice to be served by dropping all charges, warrants, and legal actions arising from this unfortunate case, which Eric Napoletano was wrongfully subjected to."

The letter made a point of assuring the court that Marilyn was making the statement of her own free will, without any pressure or duress. And, as if to prove that Eric had nothing to do with the correspondence, its author informed the court that Eric also had been sent a copy.

When the next court date rolled around, Marilyn Coludro again failed to appear. Both sets of charges were again postponed, with the judge indicating that if Marilyn failed to appear the next time, all charges would be dismissed.

Marta Rivera was crestfallen but figured that, based on the letters from her daughter, there was little she could do. If Marilyn was hell-bent on marrying Eric, she would just have to live with it.

Still, Rivera was determined to make sure that her daughter was all right. She began staking out Carolyn Napoletano's apartment on East Eighty-eighth Street in the hopes she would see Marilyn visiting, but she failed to spot even Carolyn. She left messages on Carolyn's answering machine, but the calls were never returned. Abruptly, Carolyn changed her phone number. She wasn't about to answer to anybody, especially some Puerto Rican.

In fact, Carolyn Napoletano had moved from her residence of eleven years, to resurface in an apartment on East Eighty-third Street. But Marilyn Coludro was never to be heard from again.

- 8 -

IN HER WORDS

I told Eric, "Puerto Ricans are nothing but trouble." I said that. And now I got to say, "I told you so."

You might say I'm prejudiced. I'm not really. It's only when people irritate me, then I say, you know, "spic" or "nigger." I told Eric there are a lot of white girls around. You do not have to bother with black girls or Puerto Ricans.

But Eric has always liked them. He did have a nice Italian girl, but he didn't like her. I liked her, and he had another one, she was Jewish and Spanish. But he didn't like them.

I don't know what it is about black or Spanish girls, but Eric says they are more down to earth. Eric doesn't like phonies. You have to remember Eric went to school with all black people and Spanish people. They were always his friends, not white people. Eric does not like white people. He does not like white girls.

I had so many conversations with black parents calling me to tell me, "It's just not right that the two of them see each other. If we have to send our daughter down South to live, we'll take her out of school here." Of course, I agreed with them.

It all started with Marilyn Coludro. Then it started with her mother. Then it started with the order of protection. And then Marilyn disappeared.

I was sitting in the precinct in Central Park working midnight when I heard the missing persons come over the police radio. I was working TSB, the telephone switchboard. I did not know Marilyn was missing until I heard it. When I heard the police report come over, I woke Eric up. I told him the report just came over that Marilyn was missing, with a

*description of her. We were all upset. But I had nothing to
do with that.*

*I also had nothing to do with Eric seeing Marilyn. He
helped her with her schoolwork. He was very nice to her. I
told Eric to stay away from her after he told me the kind of
family she had. Marilyn was a neglected child. She had psychiatric problems before she ever met Eric. Her mother
used to drag her to the clinic. Eric had even gone to the
clinic with her and her mother.*

*Marilyn loved Eric and someday she hoped to marry him.
But she was no angel. She had other boyfriends. She had
one black guy that she showed me a picture of. No one can
say that Eric was the last to see her. Marilyn ran away.
Marilyn went off on her own. She said in her letter to the
court that her mother was a slut and that she didn't run
away with Eric. She had it notarized. That is why they didn't
arrest him. They had nothing.*

*She also wrote me a letter. I immediately called the detec-
tive in Missing Persons and read it to him. He had given me
his number and said, "If you hear anything, call me." When
I got the letter, I called him. He asked me to put it in the
mail or bring it down. Because I was already in the department, I took it to him in person. Eric and I even had lunch
with him. He met Eric. They talked on the phone.*

*The detective had an Italian name. He and I were friends.
He always wanted me to go out with him, but I wouldn't go.
Anyway, we were good friends. He did a couple of favors for
me, and I did a couple of favors for him. He was good.
When he was transferred out of headquarters, he told the
next person about Marilyn's mother—how she lied—and to
shelve it.*

*Marilyn's letter was brought into court when Eric went,
and the judge said, "This is not the record of a schizophrenic. This is a person who knows what she is saying."
Marilyn never showed up. Her mother and brother were
there. As soon as they saw us with a lawyer, they left. They
were in there until they saw us. The judge threw the case out
of court. They never arrested him, because they never had
any evidence. So how can you say he's a serial killer?*

- *9* -

To the few who asked, Eric said he had no idea where Marilyn Coludro had run off to but was certain she would show up sooner or later. When his two court cases were finally convened on June 15, 1984—thirteen days after the grotesquely mangled body was found in the Delaware Water Gap—the charges of false imprisonment, torture, sexual abuse, and violation of an order of protection were dismissed on motions from the Bronx DA's office. Prosecutors felt the charges could not stand up without the victim's testimony. Ebullient, Eric restored his hair to its natural light brown color, moved back in with his mother, got a job through Uncle Al's connections at a Kennedy Airport messenger service—and set his romantic sights on another young Latina woman.

Seventeen-year-old Wanda Matos was five-foot-four, medium build, dark-golden complexion, with a broad nose and frizzy, pulled-back black hair. She had met Eric in passing the year before, introduced by his high school friend Marcelino Cotto, who had also introduced Marilyn Coludro to Eric. As the pressure surrounding Coludro's disappearance dissipated, Eric told Cotto he wanted to look up Matos, and so a meeting was arranged.

More mature than Marilyn, Wanda was nonetheless impressionable. She did not care that Eric had been prematurely discharged from the Marines because of "something about his penis." It mattered only that he had been a leatherneck.

Eric's initial treatment of Wanda mirrored his behavior during the first stage of his relationship with Marilyn Coludro. He smothered Wanda with obsessive love letters, flowers, and candy; they talked for hours while sharing banana splits and long walks. He promised never to disappoint her, always to love her, to do anything she wanted, to make her the happiest girl in the world.

Stuck in an unglamorous job at McDonald's, Wanda loved Eric's attention. No one had ever treated her like a princess. She fell in love.

Again mirroring the Coludro relationship, it did not take long for Eric's dark side to emerge, albeit more slowly. The more enraptured Wanda became with Eric, the more he filled his expressions of love with desperation. He *had* to have someone to love. Always! He had to make sure she understood that he loved her "so, so much, and deeply." He promised Wanda anything she wanted, except sharing her with her family. The relatives would surely interfere with the great thing they had going, especially her mother, and he wasn't about to let anyone get in the way.

The courtship was less than a week old when the couple became engaged. They scheduled the ceremony for that December, four months away. Eric said he wanted to get married as soon as possible so they could stay out late without their mothers complaining. He promised Wanda a quaint middle-class existence. First, there would be a nice apartment, perhaps in his mother's neighborhood in Manhattan. And once he became a cop, they would have kids and buy a house.

The marriage plans were received with chagrin on all familial fronts. Carolyn was extremely displeased with the situation for two reasons: She had been spending more leisure time than ever with her son since Marilyn Coludro's disappearance, and she *knew* that her Ricky could do better, a point of view she discussed with her future daughter-in-law. "He deserves better," Carolyn chided Wanda, ridiculing her as "inexperienced" and insufficiently schooled in the ways of the world. She also criticized Wanda for not having enough formal education or a well-paying career, as if her son were an Ivy League graduate turned corporate executive.

"Wanda was a mess," Carolyn later contended. "That girl was stupid. I don't know how Eric could have even liked her. She was slow and stupid. It took her an hour to tie her shoelaces. She has a child by Eric. So now I have three grandchildren.

"Once I went home with him, and I will never, ever, ever forget that. There was nothing to drink except water! There was nothing in the refrigerator. She made him that macaroni and cheese from a package. Their lights were very dim; you couldn't do anything. They really didn't have much. It was just awful. I felt so sorry for him. Wanda was so jealous, too. She didn't want him seeing me, but we were very close. We always have been. Hey, I'm his mother."

Like Marta Rivera before her, Wanda's mother, Gladys, disliked Eric with a passion. Wanda's father lived in Florida, but Eric received negative evaluations from Wanda's brother, Luis, and her mother's brother, Jesus Flores, who often helped out with family matters. The relatives hated Eric so much they argued about him in his presence. They all *knew* that Wanda could do better.

But she would have none of it. She assured Eric that no one could stop them, not even her mother. Like Marilyn Coludro, Wanda had come to view Eric as an exciting escape from stern maternal discipline.

Obsessively, Eric moved firmly to isolate Wanda from her mother and uncle. He explained that he had to have her to himself, that he could not do without her. He was quick to explain that no one understood him, especially her relatives. He warned that they should trust no one, watch whom they talked to, realize that others were out to "get" them.

While Eric told Wanda that his past was difficult to forget, he revealed very little to her about his life with Marilyn Coludro, only that her family had not liked him, he and Marilyn had lived together, she left him out of the blue without even taking her clothing, and he had spent countless hours looking for her.

Within days of their engagement, Eric and Wanda moved up the wedding to Halloween week. Several days later, they rescheduled for the beginning of October. They would live with Uncle Al while searching for an apartment.

Then they could not wait another day. On September 6, 1984, Eric married Wanda Ibelis Matos in her mother's Bronx apartment. Eric had moved fast. He and Wanda had been dating less than three weeks. Marilyn Coludro had been missing for only three months.

The Christian ceremony was witnessed by Wanda's mother and two friends. Carolyn Napoletano was absent, angry because she *knew* her son could do better. She also was annoyed that he had not discussed his marriage plans with her beforehand. "I was very crushed. He told Al. I remember Al calling me all upset, saying Eric was going off marrying a spic. I told Eric that it was the first time I ever really was just beside myself with him."

Upon the newlyweds' return from a weeklong honeymoon in Cape May, New Jersey, Wanda's brother, Luis, told her he had heard a terrible story about Eric—that he had once kept a girl named Marilyn prisoner in Marcelino Cotto's basement. Wanda confronted Eric, but he denied the allegations. From that time on, however, whenever Wanda questioned Eric about Marilyn, he either changed the subject or observed that he could not bear to think about what Marilyn had put him through.

While Wanda heard about Marilyn Coludro, Marilyn's mother indirectly heard about Wanda. Marta Rivera began to doubt her assumption that Marilyn had gone off and married Eric. Her pessimism increased when she was told by an acquaintance that Marilyn could not possibly be with Eric Napoletano because he was involved with another woman.

This made absolutely no sense to Rivera, but she nonetheless passed the information on to NYPD's Missing Persons Bureau. Sure enough, when an investigator talked to Eric— on the phone—Eric confirmed his relationship with Wanda.

Inside and out of NYPD, Eric and Carolyn told anyone who would listen that Marilyn Coludro was just a troubled teen who had run away from her mother. They suggested that the time had come for Marta Rivera to give it up.

Wanda and Eric moved into an apartment in the Bronx. Again with Uncle Al Jiovine's help, Eric switched jobs to become a file clerk in an office near One Police Plaza, while continuing to pursue an appointment to the police force.

Wanda was to find married life physically onerous. Eric demanded sex nonstop, night and day, to the point where she felt tired and weak. "Every day, the same thing, over and over again," she explained. "He just wanted sexual intercourse."

That wasn't Wanda's only problem, though. Sticking to his pattern, Eric began displaying the hateful side of his unique brand of "love." He became so obsessed with exclusivity that he would not allow Wanda to leave the apartment to visit with her family. He especially abhorred being around Wanda's maternal relatives because most of them

generally spoke Spanish, leading him to assume they were
talking about him.

With her family, he began to treat her disrespectfully. He
publicly degraded her, cursed at her, and criticized her for
being Puerto Rican. When they visited her Uncle Jesus's
house, Eric declined to join the family at the dinner table.
He also began calling Wanda the same names he had used
against Marilyn: whore, prostitute, and bitch.

Wanda begged Eric to stop telling lies about her. But Eric
did not stop.

Less than a month into the marriage, the arguing turned
violent. "If you say I'm a bitch and I'm a prostitute, then
that's what I am," Wanda announced. Eric clenched his fists
and began pummeling Wanda about the face, head, and
back. The beating was so severe that she fainted.

For the next few weeks Wanda remained hidden, to allow
the wounds to heal in private. She threatened to leave, but
Eric cried that he could not live without her. He promised to
change his ways and never mistreat her again. Wanda chose
to believe him.

The truce lasted less than two weeks, though, shattered
after the *New York Daily News* published an article about the
missing Marilyn Coludro under the headline HAVE YOU SEEN
THESE PEOPLE? It had taken five months for her disappearance to receive public notice. Originated through NYPD's
Missing Persons Bureau, the brief story reported Marilyn's
physical attributes accurately, but the rest of the information was deficient. Her last name was spelled incorrectly—
Colurdo. No mention was made of the fact that she had spent
several weeks living with Eric in the Bronx, or the court
order of protection against Eric, or the abuse. Instead, the
police were quoted as saying that Marilyn "suffers from
emotional problems."

Wanda listened with interest as Carolyn tried to discuss
the article with Eric. He angrily cut his mother off and
changed the subject, but Wanda became inquisitive. Eric
told her he was not going to discuss the matter. But she kept
asking. Later that week, Wanda asked once too often, and
Eric punched her in the nose.

Upon learning of the latest incident of abuse, Gladys
Matos beseeched her daughter to get out while she could.
"When a man hits a woman, when he beats a woman, he
won't stop. He'll keep doing it and doing it," she said. "If

you stay with him, he will beat you up again, again, and again—until he kills you."

Wanda told Eric she was going to leave the next time he beat her. Again, Eric promised to behave. But on January 21, 1985, he administered another severe beating, then stormed out of the apartment.

Wanda sat down to write a good-bye letter. It was easier, and safer, than having another face-to-face confrontation. She told Eric she now realized she had made a terrible mistake marrying him. He was selfish, immature, disrespectful, and abusive. She said it was obvious that he was never going to change. His promises meant nothing. She said she was too young to spend the rest of her life with someone so evil. No one had ever mistreated her as he had—the yelling and screaming, the cursing, the degrading comments.

She warned Eric not to try to find her. Her decision was irrevocable. In fact, Wanda said, she never wanted to see him again. She needed to get on with her life and suggested that he do the same, that he stop blaming others for his failures.

Having said all that, Wanda revealed that Eric still had a compelling power over her. She ended her letter by telling Eric she would never forget him and would always love him.

Wanda packed a few essentials into an overnight bag and fled. She sought refuge with her mother, who gladly took her in. Later that day, a suspicious fire occurred in the Napoletano apartment. Firefighters found Wanda's remaining clothes burned in the kitchen sink.

Gladys Matos kept her daughter from public view. There was no way she was going to let crazy Eric get at her. "From now on, you only go out when I go out," Gladys instructed.

Wanda was a bundle of nerves. Over the course of the next few weeks she threw up blood, vomited often, and always felt tired. Her mother took her to Lincoln Hospital, where doctors determined that she was pregnant. Wanda made sure that Eric would not learn this news.

Eric, meanwhile, was livid about Wanda's rejection and tried every ruse possible to get someone in her family to tell him where she was living. He said he wanted her back and promised that he was a changed man.

But the Matos family, led by Wanda's mother and her uncle, Jesus Flores, stood firm. Gladys told Eric that the entire family wanted him out of their lives. A reconciliation was out of the question.

Every time Eric asked about his wife, he was rebuffed. With each refusal he grew more agitated. During a two-week span Uncle Jesus's car windshield was smashed twice, once while he was visiting Gladys and Wanda, a second time in front of his own home. Flores told police he believed Eric was responsible and gave them the license plate of a car registered to Al Jiovine, which had been seen in the area by an eyewitness.

Eric also took to stalking his mother-in-law, waiting for her every morning at the same street corner as she walked to work. Most of the time he just intimidated her, content with making sure she knew he was there. On several occasions, though, he ran up and screamed in her face, demanding to know where Wanda was hiding.

But Gladys stood her ground. Wanda was going to stay hidden.

The repeated rebuffs only stiffened Eric's resolve. One morning he assured Gladys that he would find Wanda and kill her. He promised she would "not feel a thing." He told Gladys to make sure she told Wanda what he had said.

Terribly frightened, Gladys began carrying a folding pocket knife for protection. But she was not about to tell Eric where Wanda was staying, especially in light of his threats.

Eric's stalking became more aggressive. And with each encounter he directed his anger more at Gladys Matos. Determined to extract his revenge in any way possible, he confided to Michael Sanchez, a drugstore clerk and one of his auxiliary police colleagues, that he was going to use his mother-in-law as a substitute target for his retribution.

Eric asked Sanchez to get a gun for him, but the man declined. They discussed various types of weapons that could be used, the best location, and the best time of day to carry out an attack. After considering several scenarios, Eric decided he would shoot Gladys with a .38-caliber revolver early in the morning, as she walked to work.

Several days later, Eric and his mother went to visit Sanchez. While Carolyn waited in the car, the two men talked on the nearby sidewalk. Eric explained that he and his mother were going to Harlem to purchase a gun for about $200. With that, Eric spun away from his friend, walked back to his car, and drove off with his mother

Sanchez did not know what to think. For sure, Eric was a loudmouth and a big talker. But Sanchez also recognized that, for once in his life, Eric might actually do what he promised.

10

The morning of her death, Gladys Matos rose before five o'clock, as she did every weekday. Within the hour she began walking to work, clutching her pocket knife while keeping a worried eye out for her son-in-law. She lived in terror these days. Only the night before, Wanda had begged her not to go out anymore, even for work. But Gladys had insisted she was not going to let Eric Napoletano control her life.

Gunfire rang out without warning: six bullets from a .38-caliber revolver. Gladys Matos died exactly the way Eric had said she would.

Police converged on the scene that April 29, 1985, but were unable to recover the gun or any other physical evidence. Worse, they failed to locate a single eyewitness, despite an extensive canvass of the apartment houses in the Bronx neighborhood.

The killer had inflicted terrible damage. Each shot had been fired at point-blank range. The victim sustained injuries to the face, throat, and chest. Her trusty knife remained folded shut in her hand. Less than thirty-six hours had passed since Eric had told his friend Sanchez that he and Carolyn were on their way to buy a gun.

The body bore identification cards in the name of Gladys Matos. Detective James Fazzini, a veteran investigator who caught the case from the Forty-third Detective Squad, and one of his colleagues, Detective Donald Schappert, headed over to the Matos home at 1050 Soundview Avenue, just one block from the murder site.

The door to Apartment 4E was answered by Wanda Matos Napoletano. Told of her mother's death, she screamed, "I knew something like this was going to happen!" She told Fazzini that as far as she was concerned, her estranged husband was responsible. Over and over she cried out that it was her fault, that she should have listened when her mother told her not to marry Eric.

The detectives questioned Wanda about Eric's friends and the history of her relationship with him. She said she had been introduced to Eric by Marcelino Cotto, who lived just down the block from the murder site. She said Eric also spoke of a man she knew only as "Mike," meaning Mike Sanchez.

The detectives headed over to Cotto's and brought him back to the precinct. The man conceded he had heard gunshots that morning, but claimed he had not been curious enough to get out of bed to take a look. He admitted to being aware that a woman had been killed in the shooting, but insisted he did not know that his friend Eric's mother-in-law had been the victim. Cotto also maintained he had not seen Eric for more than a week, when he had come around with his mother. He said they had not discussed anything special, certainly not any plans for murder.

Fazzini and Schappert next visited Jesus Flores, Wanda's uncle. He immediately blamed Eric for his sister's murder. Contending that Eric had mental problems, Flores detailed the vandalism done to his car and related how Eric had been stalking Gladys every morning on the corner precisely where she had been gunned down.

During the course of her interview, Wanda had revealed that Eric's mother worked for NYPD. Detective Schappert called down to the Department of Personnel, and confirmed that Carolyn was an administrative aide assigned to the Communications Division.

Throughout the day Fazzini tried reaching the woman, visiting her apartment and leaving a message on her answering machine. When Carolyn Napoletano finally phoned the precinct that evening, fourteen hours had passed since the shooting. Fazzini told her he wanted Eric to come to the Forty-third because his mother-in-law had been shot and killed that morning.

As Carolyn explained that it was rather late for a drive to the Bronx, a male voice picked up the extension and identified himself as Eric Napoletano. Fazzini again emphasized that their cooperation was essential; they had to come up for an interview. Reluctantly, the Napoletanos agreed.

When Carolyn and Eric arrived just before eleven, Fazzini thought the mother and son looked familiar, but he could not immediately place them. In fact, the Napoletanos had stormed into the Forty-third Precinct several weeks earlier to complain that Wanda's uncle had threatened them regarding his broken windshield. When Eric made a point of reminding Fazzini about the prior visit, it all came back to the detective, especially the arrogance Eric and his mother had displayed.

Fazzini turned the discussion to the matter at hand; he specifically asked Eric if he had killed Gladys Matos. That was impossible, Eric said; he had been sleeping at the time. Besides, there was no way he would be so stupid as to jeopardize becoming a police officer in less than two months. Eric explained that he would soon be going to the NYPD Police Academy. That comment caught Fazzini's attention. The mother worked as a civilian downtown. Now the son was claiming he was about to become a uniformed officer.

Taking the offense, Eric said he was annoyed at being summoned at such a late hour, to be questioned about a shooting he knew nothing about, involving someone he clearly did not like. He said he had been out of contact with his wife and her family since she left him in January. He alleged that Wanda had set the fire in their apartment the day she left. Therefore, Eric continued, he was not really concerned what happened to either woman; no one in that family liked him, so why should he care about them?

Carolyn also stated that she was not concerned about Gladys's death; she had only met the woman once. She went on to explain that she had not approved of her son's marriage, mainly because he and Wanda came from "such different backgrounds." She confessed that she was much happier since Eric and Wanda had split.

The detectives sought to establish Eric's whereabouts for the time of Gladys Matos's murder. Eric explained that, like every morning, he'd risen at about 5:15 A.M., and departed his mother's apartment at 5:35. Together, they drove to the Park Row Gourmet, just south of City Hall, where they had breakfast. He claimed he then drove his mother to One Police Plaza, stopped by the post office to grab his company's mail, then reported to his clerk's job at a nearby customs broker.

Separately, Carolyn corroborated Eric's story, then added several details that, if true, represented an ironclad alibi.

She said her alarm clock woke her at 4:15, and when she
passed from her bedroom through the living room, she saw
Eric sleeping on the sofa bed. She also insisted that she had
the only set of keys to the apartment door; if Eric had
opened it, the alarm would have sounded. Carolyn said she
woke Eric about 5:15, he dressed, and they departed at 5:35,
on schedule. Carolyn made it very clear that she would
never lie about something like this to the police, even if it
did involve her son.

Eric handled himself well, too. He gave up Cotto's
address, but claimed he did not know the last name, address,
or phone number of the "Mike" whom Wanda had mentioned. Mother and son both claimed they had not seen
"Mike" in ages.

It was clear that Carolyn and Eric were not going to be of
any help, so the detectives allowed them to leave. But even
though the Napoletanos had to get up for work in several
hours, they did not go to bed immediately. As soon as they
could, they placed a crucial call—to Mike Sanchez.

Sanchez was beside himself when told of the murder.
Carolyn and Eric both warned him that the police were
trying to locate him; they instructed him to "lay low" and
ordered him never to call their apartment again. They feared
that the phone had been bugged in the hours since the
shooting.

Concerned for his family's safety, a terrified Mike
Sanchez initially did not know what to do. It took the drugstore clerk a week to muster the courage, but he finally contacted the police. At first he had a friend call the Forty-third
Precinct anonymously to report that a guy named "Mike"
knew the identity and motive of the killer. After a bit of
coaxing by Detective Robert Sodine, Sanchez got on the
phone.

Continuing to identify himself only as "Mike," Sanchez
explained that he was a longtime friend of Eric Napoletano's. He said Eric lived with his mother, and offered that
they "did not behave as mother and son, but acted more like
close friends." He said he had seen Eric violently disagree
with Carolyn a number of times, throwing temper tantrums
and spewing vile language at her. "Mike" said he knew that
Eric was responsible for Gladys Matos's murder the
moment he heard about it; Eric had told him he had been

stalking his mother-in-law and had sought his advice on the
best method of killing her.

Sodine told "Mike" that it was imperative he speak with
Detective Fazzini, the lead investigator on the case. He
agreed to report to the precinct the following afternoon,
when Fazzini would be back on duty.

When he appeared the next day, Sanchez told Fazzini that
Eric had talked with him about killing the woman in two
lengthy conversations prior to the actual attack. Generally,
he continued, he did not believe anything Eric told him.
That was why his heart sank when Eric and Carolyn called
him the night of the murder to tell him that Gladys had, in
fact, been killed.

Feeling more comfortable, "Mike" revealed his full name.
He said he had known Eric for several years, since they
worked together at a hot-dog stand in Queens. Sanchez said
he and Eric had remained very good friends, keeping in
touch on a regular basis, sharing the camaraderie of their
police auxiliary membership.

In his mind, Eric and Wanda's marital problems were the
catalyst for Gladys Matos's murder. From the day Wanda
moved out, Eric had been obsessed with killing her for
revenge. When he could not find her, he had selected his
interfering mother-in-law as a substitute.

Turning to the premurder planning sessions, Sanchez
confessed that he had discussed key details with Eric: using
a .38-caliber weapon because it would not jam as easily as a
nine-millimeter, and shooting Gladys in the early morning
when fewer witnesses were likely.

Finally, Sanchez detailed a visit the Napoletanos had paid
him the night after the Matos shooting, when Eric told him
that if he was ever arrested for the murder, he would blame
it on Wanda's uncle, Jesus Flores, and make up a story
about the man being involved with drugs.

At the behest of Fazzini, Sanchez continued to let Eric
and Carolyn believe that the police had not yet found him.
This was a splendid ploy, as the Napoletanos continued to
cover up. Eric again warned Sanchez never to call the apartment on Eighty-third Street. "The phone company is monitoring all incoming calls," he said, now attributing the
supposed monitoring to efforts to catch an obscene caller.
Sanchez was also warned that if the police ever determined

who he was, he had better not mention that Eric had said he
wanted to kill his mother-in-law.

On the morning of May 10, 1985—eleven days after the
murder—Eric called Fazzini at the precinct. During the
twenty-five-minute conversation, which Fazzini taped, Eric
again insisted that he did not know the last name, phone
number, or address of his friend, "Mike," and had not seen
the man for several weeks, meaning prior to Gladys Matos's
murder.

The conversation prompted Fazzini to pursue Sanchez
again. This time Sanchez assigned a much more active role
in the cover-up conspiracy to Carolyn Napoletano. In fact,
Sanchez now said, Carolyn had been the one who called to
break the news to him about Gladys's murder and to instruct
him on the precautions he should take. Only later had Eric
gotten on the phone to proclaim, "The bitch got killed, and
they think I did it." Most startling of all, Sanchez told
Fazzini that when he asked Carolyn where Gladys Matos
had been shot, she had replied, "The head, the chest, and the
stomach."

Fazzini was stunned. At no time had he mentioned to
Eric, Carolyn, or Sanchez the location of the injuries to
Gladys Matos. The Napoletanos knew intimate details about
the homicide.

Professionally insulted, Fazzini had reached his limit.
The Napoletano family's behavior was a disgrace, especially given Carolyn's employer and Eric's career goals. In
the aftermath of the Matos murder, Eric had not only filed
an application to become a police officer; he had also
passed several qualifying tests.

Fazzini felt compelled to take action within the department. He had previously mentioned the possibility of Eric's
involvement in a homicide to NYPD's Applicant Investigation Section and the psychologist assigned to review Eric's
application. But that notification had been a cursory preliminary one. Fazzini decided to increase the pressure. He personally visited the Applicant Investigation Section offices
to document his growing circumstantial case. Eric was no
longer merely a possible suspect; he was now officially *the*
suspect.

Fazzini also contacted NYPD's Internal Affairs. He
briefed the sergeant on duty about the evidence he had collected, emphasizing the possible involvement of three auxil-

iary police officers in Gladys Matos's murder: Eric Napoletano, whom he additionally described as "a future member
of the department"; civilian employee Carolyn Napoletano;
and Michael Sanchez. An official Internal Affairs file was
opened.

When Carolyn was notified that Fazzini had reported her
and Eric, she turned around and filed a complaint against
him, alleging harassment. From that point on, the Napoletano investigation was very personal to Jim Fazzini.

The detective convinced Sanchez to wear a concealed
recording device in an attempt to trap Carolyn into making
an incriminating statement. Sanchez arranged to meet her
just outside the front door of One Police Plaza at four
o'clock on July 22, 1985. As far as Carolyn knew, the detectives still had not identified Sanchez.

As the tape rolled, the conversation removed any lingering doubt about the closeness of Sanchez's relationship
with both Napoletanos. Carolyn admitted that she had lied
to Fazzini when he asked her if she knew the full identity of
"Mike." She also made it clear that she and Eric had been in
frequent contact with him during the weeks immediately
preceding the Matos homicide. Carolyn also confirmed that
her intradepartmental complaints against Fazzini were spe-
cious, lodged in the hopes of thwarting the detective's
investigation of the Matos murder.

At that point, Carolyn began coaching Sanchez on how to
answer questions in the event the police learned his full
name and tracked him down. The important thing, Carolyn
explained, was to convince everyone that his relationship
with her and Eric was casual and distant.

In the midst of the coaching, Eric arrived to drive his
mother home. He, too, began dispensing advice to Sanchez
on how he should handle himself with Detective Fazzini.

Sanchez took Eric out of his mother's earshot at one
point, telling him softly, "Between me and you, I know you
killed this fucking woman!" Eric just laughed.

"What do you want me to tell these people?" Sanchez
demanded.

Calmly, Eric resumed coaching. He specifically insisted
that Sanchez deny they had ever discussed the possibility of
his killing Gladys Matos. But Sanchez protested; they *had*
discussed murder plans. Eric blew him off, instructing him
to deny, deny, deny. "Tell them to fuck off."

Eric, Carolyn, and Sanchez agreed that if they ever needed to meet again, they would do so only in the police department courtyard, when Carolyn got off duty. They agreed never to talk again on the phone. As they parted company, Sanchez pretended he was going into hiding. Of course, he reported back to his police handlers.

The next day, Carolyn called the Forty-third. She emphatically stated that she did not wish to speak with Fazzini. Detective Robert Sodine, the investigator who had first talked to Sanchez, got on the line. Carolyn claimed she had important information to provide about the Matos homicide: She had reason to believe that the shooting had been carried out by a "hit man named Mike." It sounded as if Carolyn feared that the police would eventually find Sanchez, so she wanted to point a finger at him the same way she and Eric had cast aspersions on Wanda's uncle, Jesus Flores.

Later that day, after discussing the matter with Fazzini, Sodine called Carolyn back at One Police Plaza under the guise of needing more information about the supposed assassin. Before dialing, the detective connected a tape recorder to his phone line. The Forty-third Precinct was now tapping headquarters.

Weaving her dangerous web, Carolyn told Sodine that when she and Eric had appeared at the Forty-third to discuss the dispute about Jesus Flores's broken windows, a man who called himself "Mike" had accompanied them. She insisted that she did not *really* know this "Mike," so had not lied when she said she did not know anyone by that name. She went on to say that she had found the man's speech and demeanor to be suspicious, and had been told he intended to flee to avoid being questioned by the police.

That evening, just prior to the end of Carolyn's shift, Eric entered One Police Plaza. A few minutes later, he and his mother departed the building through an exit they did not normally use, effectively eluding Mike Sanchez.

Twenty-four hours later, Sanchez stationed himself at another exit. Still wired for sound, he encountered the Napoletanos on their way out. Eric told Sanchez that he and his mother had dodged him the night before because he was being followed. He assured Sanchez he had avoided making contact to protect him from getting involved.

Sanchez played along, intent on getting Eric to incriminate himself on tape. But Eric was too slick. When Sanchez reviewed their premurder chats and pointed out that the killing had been committed exactly the way they had discussed, Eric just laughed, then warned, "Sssssshh. The place could be bugged." Eric advised Sanchez to relax. He insisted that the police had no evidence. "There's nothing to worry about."

Then, just as Carolyn had slipped when revealing that she knew where the bullets had struck Gladys Matos, Eric divulged that he knew the exact number of times she had been shot—six times. He also told Sanchez he knew that the police had failed to find any witnesses to the shooting.

Once again Fazzini was outraged. He was certain he had not given Eric or his mother any such confidential information about the investigation. He was convinced that the only logical explanation was that Eric was gaining access to confidential police department records through his mother.

When details of the troubling situation ultimately made the rounds within NYPD, high-ranking superiors agreed. The commanding officer of all detectives in the Bronx, Deputy Chief Emil A. Ciccotelli, dispatched a seven-page memo to the chief of detectives, downtown at headquarters. The confidential document, which contained key excerpts of the conversations secretly recorded in front of One Police Plaza, was entitled "Actions of Police Administrative Aide Carolyn Napoletano and Police Candidate Eric Napoletano in Connection with Homicide of Gladys Matos."

Ciccotelli characterized Carolyn as "overly possessive" and mother and son as "extremely vindictive." He said their "notably close relationship" included "characteristics not usually attendant to a mother and son."

In summing up the damning evidence, Ciccotelli made what appeared to be an extremely compelling case against both Napoletanos, but went on to declare that everyone at NYPD, as well as at the Bronx DA's office, had concluded there was insufficient evidence to justify arrests. "While there are strong suspicions by the family, Mr. Sanchez, and Detective Fazzini that Eric Napoletano either murdered Gladys Matos or arranged to have it done, repeated and thorough canvasses have failed to disclose a witness or any other concrete evidence to support their suspicions," Ciccotelli wrote. "Also, while Mr. Sanchez's statements appear to be damaging, five tape-recorded conversations with the

suspect and/or his mother failed to yield a result which
would disclose sufficient information to warrant an arrest."

Still, the deputy chief offered some persuasive observations:

CONCLUSIONS

•••**A.**   It could be argued that Michael Sanchez's actions
were self-serving—brought about by fear of being
charged as an accomplice in this crime; and while this
may be true, one only has to listen to the tape-recorded
conversations to know that his complicity is limited to
talk about what one would do if he wanted to commit
such a crime. Therefore, it is credible that his motive for
coming forward and assisting in this investigation is
simply that he feels he knows who committed this murder
and feels that the person should be brought to justice for
his crime.

•••**B.**   Both Eric and Carolyn Napoletano have not only
failed to provide assistance in this investigation, but they
have also been deceitful regarding relevant matters.

•••**C.**   Repeated accusations made by Michael Sanchez
to Eric Napoletano (during recorded conversations) failed
to evoke even one positive response normally expected
from an innocent party, such as, "What are you talking
about? I didn't kill anyone!" or "Are you crazy? I don't
know what you're talking about!" or some other such
vehement denial. The most frequent response was either a
laugh, or a statement that the police have no evidence.

RECOMMENDATIONS

The reading of the entire case folder and listening to all of
the tape-recorded conversations, causes some serious
concern regarding the fitness of Eric Napoletano to serve
as a police officer. It also causes serious concern for the
loyalty of Carolyn Napoletano, currently serving as a
member of this Department.

Even if one hypothesizes that Eric Napoletano is completely innocent of this crime, the degree of impeding the
progress of this investigation through deceit must be considered. It is therefore recommended that the information

provided herein be evaluated and appropriate action against either, or both, be taken. It is further recommended that extreme care be exercised in the transmittal of this report to maintain confidentiality. Carolyn Napoletano has made it apparent, during recorded conversations, that she has the ability to gain information on confidential matters. Disclosure that Michael Sanchez is cooperating with this Department could prove dangerous to him, and destructive to a successful result of the homicide investigation.

As telling as the memo was, very little action was taken to address its dire warnings. Eric was excluded from the next NYPD Police Academy class because of the Matos investigation, but Carolyn kept her job. In fact, she was promoted from Communications to the extremely sensitive Organized Crime Control Bureau. Once inside that operation, she worked her way into an even more critical position, senior administrative assistant to the chief of OCCB—where, as she bragged, she had access through computers and other means to just about any confidential information she wanted.

11

As the summer of 1985 wore on, it became clear that the authorities were not going to lodge criminal charges against Eric or Carolyn in connection with the murder of Gladys Matos, a situation that confounded Wanda. Severely depressed, she blamed herself for her mother's death. Fearing for her life and that of her unborn baby, she dropped her married name and departed New York for a life undercover near her father in south Florida.

Eric, on the other hand, resumed his relations with the outside world. Regaining his confidence, he became convinced that he had outmaneuvered Fazzini and the rest of NYPD. With the help of Uncle Al, he obtained yet another job, a clerk's position at a customs brokerage house at One World Trade Center. He also found himself another Puerto Rican love, a cute seventeen-year-old named Myra Acevedo.

They met in August, less than four months after the Matos homicide. Eric had taken the subway to the Bronx that evening to meet a friend. He spotted Myra while waiting in line behind her at a phone booth; he was calling home to tell his mother he had arrived safely. When Myra completed her call, Eric struck up a conversation. He began working that charm of his, and quickly gained Myra's interest. It did not hurt that he was an auxiliary cop, just like her. Eric told Myra he was single; he neglected to mention Wanda Matos or Marilyn Coludro.

Eric's new relationship blossomed in much the same way as his relationships with Marilyn and Wanda had. He promised Myra the world in terms of material goods and showered her with tenderness and affection. Seeking to establish control, he repeatedly told her that because she did not know any better, he would have to teach her how to live life to the fullest. Eric had to work a little harder this time around, but he managed to captivate Myra with his puzzling allure. Like those before her, Myra fell in love.

At first Myra's relatives were wary. Myra's mother, Carmen, was especially anxious, finding Eric to be rude and obnoxious. But he was able to overcome those concerns. "He would come early in the morning and stay by my house all day," recalled Pablo Acevedo, Myra's father. "He seemed like a good kid, so I never said anything to him."

The couple wasted little time getting married. They exchanged vows on October 19, 1985, just two months after they met. Twenty-year-old Eric was now a bigamist.

The ceremony was conducted by the Reverend Luis Sanchez at the Christian Church John 3:16 on Westchester Avenue in the Bronx. Uncle Al Jiovine was there, but Carolyn was notable by her absence. Once again, she *knew* her son could have done better.

The marriage license contained erroneous information that would have hindered anyone searching official records in an effort to keep track of Eric. The document listed the groom's name as "Eric Ernest Napolitano, Jr.," of 88-11 Thirty-fourth Avenue in Queens, Uncle Al's address. He listed his father as "Eric E. Napolitano, Sr.," born in Italy. His mother's maiden name, Carolyn Hankinson, became "Carolina Spatalino," born in Italy instead of New Jersey. He indicated on the form that he had never been married.

Eric worked hard at the relationship. He loved Myra and she loved him. They appeared to be genuinely happy. For the most part, he kept his anger in check. They argued, but Myra was a tough cookie. She gave it right back. Whenever things got rocky, Eric talked his talk, and Myra generally forgave him.

When Eric spoke of wanting to start a family more than anything, Myra could not agree more. By Christmas she was pregnant. Eric was ecstatic. A sonogram revealed that the fetus was male. Not only was he finally going to have a family of his own, but his wife was going to give him a *son*. Uncle Al would be the boy's godfather. What more could he possibly hope for?

As Myra's pregnancy headed into the third trimester the summer of 1986, Eric surely could have hoped that police and prosecutors would continue to do nothing regarding Marilyn Coludro's disappearance. She had been missing for two years. Little did Eric know, however, that Marilyn's mother, Marta Rivera, had not stopped wondering why her daughter had not called at least once to say hello. She decided to call the local police precinct one more time.

Rivera explained her circumstances to the officer on the phone: She had assumed her daughter had run off to marry Eric in 1984, but now had come to believe that something sinister had occurred.

Even the officer could not understand what happened next. His computer research for the Coludro missing-persons report drew a blank. As best he could tell, Marilyn Coludro had never been reported missing.

Rivera was flabbergasted. How could this be? She had a copy of the report herself. Embarrassed, the officer offered to take down the pertinent data so a new missing-persons report could be entered into the NYPD computer system. As per procedure, the new report also was disseminated across the National Crime Information Center's computer network. The original report had never made it on to the NCIC system. For the first time in two years, Marilyn Coludro was on record as missing in New York. And for the first time ever, she was listed as missing across the country.

The explanations subsequently proffered by NYPD for this incompetence or corruption were, at best, disingenuous. Officials suggested that an unknown employee of the department's Communications Division back in 1984 must have accidentally failed to enter the report on the nationwide system, a key function of that office. As if good police work had uncovered a two-year-old human error, the officials also maintained that the mistake had been discovered in 1986 during a "revampment" of the department's computer system. That explanation, of course, failed to acknowledge the essential role played by Marta Rivera in the creation of an entirely new document. Without Rivera's persistence, her daughter's missing-persons report would have remained missing.

And while the mystery of the disappearing report would never be solved officially, there was an obvious suspicion— that Eric's mother had somehow managed to deep-six the file. In fact, back in 1984, Carolyn Napoletano had been assigned to the very same Communications Division, a connection that represented a nightmare of embarrassment for NYPD.

* * *

In Pennsylvania, the state police computer immediately spit out the new Coludro report as a possible match to the still-unidentified body found at the Delaware Water Gap lookout. Trooper Delmar J. Wills, part of the team that had pursued more than 200 possible matches during the prior two .years, contacted Detective Robert Langer of NYPD's Missing Persons Bureau, who confirmed that the original report had "inadvertently" not been sent to NCIC in 1984.

Wills asked Langer to find out whether Marilyn Coludro had been wearing braces at the time of her disappearance, whether she had pierced ears, and whether she had a circular scar on her right knee. In fact, Marilyn had worn braces, but they had been removed. She also had five or six pierce marks through her ears.

That information encouraged Wills to keep digging. He called Rivera at her job and verified that only the wires of Marilyn's braces had been removed; the brackets had been left in place on her lower front teeth. The Pennsylvania victim had brackets in her mouth; that detail was a match. Rivera also stated that Marilyn had a small mole above her left upper lip, on the corner of her mouth; the Pennsylvania victim had a similarly placed mole.

The following morning, August 1, 1986, Troopers Wills and Dennis Mullen drove to New York City. With the assistance of Detective Langer, they met with Marilyn's relatives and showed them a photograph of the Delaware Water Gap victim. Several of the family members identified the corpse as Marilyn. But her mother was not so easily swayed. Marta Rivera did not want to believe. This was not how she wanted her uncertainty to end.

Wills and Mullen headed to Marilyn's orthodontist in midtown Manhattan. The dental chart from the Pennsylvania victim was compared with Marilyn's records; the charts matched.

Still unwilling to accept the news, Marta Rivera made an appointment to drive out to the Pennsylvania State Police barracks in Stockertown. There, Mullen politely showed her the clothing found on the victim: a size 34B bra and Jou Jou brand blue jeans with zippers at the bottom of each leg. Marta Rivera could no longer deny the tragedy; those were Marilyn's clothes.

The confirmation was little consolation, but at least

Rivera no longer had to endure the misery of not knowing. Marshaling her fortitude, she commenced the gruesome but necessary task of relocating her daughter's anonymous grave to an appropriate family interment.

Troopers Wills and Mullen now had a homicide case they could work on and an obvious suspect to pursue. Unfortunately, the trail was two years old.

They realized they needed to learn as much as possible about Eric Napoletano, but because of NYPD red tape, another two weeks passed before they obtained appointments in New York. The two investigators met with Missing Persons personnel, the sergeant who had worked on Eric's NYPD employment application, and Detective Fazzini, who briefed them on the Matos homicide. It was a function Fazzini would perform many times in the coming years: telling investigators from other jurisdictions what he knew about Eric Napoletano, his homicide suspect who got away. As difficult as it was for Fazzini to relive his investigation, he always was willing to cooperate. Since he couldn't lock Eric and Carolyn up, his only hope was that someone else would.

The detective arranged for the investigators to interview Wanda Matos's uncle, Jesus Flores, at the Forty-third Precinct. Flores recalled his niece saying that before Eric married her, he had lived in a basement with a young Puerto Rican girl. Flores said Eric had kept the girl away from her mother.

Flores then hooked up Wills on the phone with Wanda from her hideout in Florida. She explained that she was still afraid of Eric, that he had beaten her and threatened to kill her. She said Eric once had told her that just before they started dating, he had lived with a Puerto Rican girl about thirteen or fourteen years old in Marcelino Cotto's basement. She said she had subsequently been told by others that Eric had kept the girl against her will, and had even raped her. She added that the girl's name was Marilyn.

Through Fazzini's intervention, Cotto appeared at the Forty-third Precinct for an interview. He identified a photo of the Pennsylvania victim as Marilyn Coludro, then admitted she had lived in his basement with Eric for about two weeks before she disappeared. Cotto also acknowledged that Marilyn had told him Eric beat her.

Denying any involvement or knowledge of the murder,

Cotto said Eric and Marilyn had slept in his basement and borrowed his blankets. The troopers then produced the multicolored bedspread that had been wrapped around Marilyn's body.

"Whoa!" said Cotto. He admitted that the bedspread had been used by Eric and Marilyn but insisted it had not come from his house. He said it looked just like one he had seen at Al Jiovine's apartment in Queens.

In the coming weeks, with Fazzini's assistance, Wills and Mullen made several return trips to New York City. The Pennsylvania investigators met with Deputy Chief Ciccotelli, the author of the lengthy internal memo about Eric and Carolyn.

Along with Fazzini and several other NYPD detectives, they interviewed Al Jiovine. Evasive and ambiguous whenever possible, Uncle Al explained that he had met Eric when the boy was about thirteen, through a real estate broker friend. Jiovine asserted that over the years he had become very good friends with Eric's mother. She, in turn, had allowed Eric to stay over at his house on nights and weekends. But Jiovine minimized the closeness of the relationship, as if he and Eric had spent little time together.

When asked about his sexual orientation, Al lied, contending that he was not gay. Wills, for one, did not buy it, especially given the presence of a young Latino male in Jiovine's apartment.

Al also tried to downplay his knowledge of Marilyn Coludro, saying he had met her only once, when she appeared at his door crying. Great protector that he was, Al claimed he had taken Marilyn to a police station where he met with her mother, Marta Rivera, and Carolyn Napoletano. That would have been the night Eric was arrested for violating the order of protection, but Al Jiovine did not offer those details.

Wills asked about the note he had written ordering Eric to get Marilyn out of his apartment. Trapped, Al was forced to admit that he had known Marilyn, and that Eric had kept her in his apartment. But he continued to give up as little information as possible.

Fazzini proceeded to grill him about the Matos killing. Al acknowledged that he knew Eric's wife, Wanda, and also was aware that her mother had been killed. But, he insisted, he certainly had not killed her. And, he said, he had not killed Marilyn Coludro, either.

Asked about any bedspreads he might have kept in his apartment, Al provided an elaborate explanation about two red bed covers he had sent to his mother's house in New Jersey. The Pennsylvania troopers then produced the bedspread that had been wrapped around Marilyn's body.

Al stated that "at one time, over a year ago," he had two bed covers identical to the one they were showing him. Asked repeatedly where those bedspreads were these days, Al said he could not remember.

The detectives kept at it for several hours, pounding away at Jiovine's poor memory. Finally, they asked if he would help in the Coludro and Matos murder investigations. They wanted to wire him up to get an incriminating statement from Eric. Al said he had strong reservations against getting involved because of his "love for Eric." For nearly another hour, he pondered the request, then announced he would have to sleep on it. He promised to call Wills in the morning.

As soon as he left the station house, Jiovine called Eric and told him everything that had occurred: the questions the cops had asked, the evidence they had thrown in his face, and the request that he help set a trap. Eric convinced him not to cooperate in any manner. Al then purchased an answering machine to monitor his incoming calls.

When Wills did not hear from Al the next day, he called him at his office. But Al would not even get on the phone. The trooper left messages throughout the day, directing him to call back. But Al was silent. His tactic worked, too: The troopers returned to Pennsylvania without an answer.

The following day, Detective Langer of the Missing Persons Bureau reached Jiovine at his job. Al revealed that he had told Eric everything, and therefore would not be cooperating with the police. Langer then called Eric, but he, too, refused to discuss the matter.

Langer contacted Carolyn Napoletano at One Police Plaza, and determined that she had taken emergency leave that day and the day before. Such behavior was typical for Eric's mother. Whenever troubling questions were being asked about one of the women in Eric's life, she absented herself from her job. Sometimes she took sick leave, other times emergency leave, and still other times, vacation time. With the police from Pennsylvania trying to find him and his acquaintances being questioned about two homicides now, Eric also felt the pressure. Once again his life was disrupted by a fire of undetermined origin.

With Myra eight months' pregnant, an extensive blaze broke out in their apartment. The damage was so severe they had to move out. Pablo's sister made her apartment available for as long as necessary. But one evening Eric came home from work and informed Myra that they had to leave immediately.

"What's going on? What's wrong?" asked Pablo's sister.

Eric refused to say. He and Myra drove over to one of Pablo's brothers'; they would be safe there. Shortly after they arrived, Eric's mother showed up. Clearly, mother and son were scared about something.

Myra pressed for an explanation. Eric had little choice but to give up a piece of his past. He told Myra they had to move around because homicide detectives were looking for him. One of his girlfriends had turned up dead a while back. The cops wanted to talk to him because they thought he did it.

"If you're not guilty, why are you running away?" Pablo asked his son-in-law. Eric then revealed the second part of his secret: Some detective named Fazzini was also trying to blame him for the shooting of another woman. Eric provided few details. He gave the impression he did not even know the second victim. He certainly never mentioned that she had been his mother-in-law, which would have meant revealing his marriage to Wanda.

Carolyn said she had another concern about police interest in her son. She was worried about the money he had in the bank. She wanted him to withdraw the funds and deposit them somewhere else, in her name or Uncle Al's.

Pablo was dumbfounded. "If you are innocent, there's no reason to transfer the money. Anyway, if you have any money and you're nervous about it, you should leave it with my daughter. She's pregnant with your son."

Eric swore that he had nothing to do with either homicide. He contended that the police were harassing him. They had to pin the crimes on someone, so they were trying to stick it to him. Pablo wanted to believe in Eric, so he did not ask any more questions. He gave his son-in-law the benefit of the doubt, a decision he would deeply regret in the years to come.

* * *

For a fleeting moment in the wake of the Pennsylvania-Coludro investigation, it appeared that the Bronx DA's office might be prodded into taking action regarding the murder of Gladys Matos. But once again the case was mishandled.

Bronx prosecutors did convene a grand jury to hear evidence against Eric and Carolyn. Wanda Matos and her brother were even flown up from Miami to testify. But the typical culmination of a grand jury proceeding, the voting of an indictment, never occurred. Instead, the grand jury was abruptly shut down without ever hearing from Wanda or her brother.

Years later, homicide detectives investigating Eric Napoletano in several states recalled being told that the grand jury had been "postponed" to allow prosecutors and other personnel from the Bronx DA's office to work on an extremely sensitive high-profile case involving the shooting of six police officers. But that was much too simplistic an explanation for what had really transpired.

The tangled case of Larry Davis represented a major embarrassment for NYPD and the Bronx DA's office. On November 19, 1986, a large police contingent stormed a ground-floor apartment on Fulton Avenue where Davis, a drug-dealing murder suspect, was holed up. A wild shootout ensued, with the well-armed Davis wounding six officers and forcing the entire arrest team to retreat. Incredibly, Davis somehow also managed to escape, remaining at large for seventeen days, prompting one of the biggest manhunts in NYPD history.

During the subsequent two years, media attention and public pressure escalated. In March 1987, Davis was acquitted in the murders of four suspected drug dealers. In a separate seven-month trial that ended November 20, 1988, Davis was acquitted of attempted murder and aggravated assault on the wounded police officers. Noted defense attorneys William M. Kunstler and Lynne F. Stewart claimed that Davis had shot the officers in self-defense. They successfully argued that Davis believed the cops were part of an assassination team sent to silence his knowledge of corruption and drug trafficking within Bronx police precincts.

Before the Davis case faded from public view, it also became a flashpoint for racial discord in New York. Six of the seven officers who invaded the Davis hideout were white, the other Latino; the jury was composed of ten blacks and two Latinos. The jurors had believed black Larry Davis and not the white cops.

Political reality dictated that the Davis case would have required a zealous effort on the part of NYPD and the Bronx DA's office. Virtually no one would quarrel with an extraordinary pursuit of justice on behalf of dedicated police officers who put their lives on the line every day. But why had the Davis case paralyzed the entire district attorney's office, allowing the Matos case to slip through the cracks somehow? It was impossible to believe that the Matos case was not made because of insufficient evidence. Criminal cases are put together every day with considerably less evidence. In real life, there is almost never a "smoking gun."

The circumstances prompted obvious questions: Had the decision not to pursue the matter been based, at least in part, on the fact that the obvious suspects were linked to NYPD? Worse yet, as far-fetched as it might seem to some, did Carolyn Napoletano have something incriminating on someone important? Had she really known as many people in high places as she claimed? Did the tapes she recorded of personal phone conversations with NYPD colleagues contain anything incriminating?

Years later, a bitter Detective Fazzini repeatedly suggested that perjury had been committed by the DA's office in abruptly shutting down the Matos grand jury. He contended that the jurors were told their session had to be "postponed" because the key witness from Florida—meaning Wanda Matos—had not been located. According to Fazzini, however, at the precise moment the grand jurors were being fed that statement, Wanda Matos was sitting in the Bronx County Courthouse waiting to testify.

The repeated misuse of the word *postponement* was another lie. In fact, the Matos case was never again presented to a grand jury. Wanda Matos and her brother were never flown back to New York to testify.

Instead, as late as 1995, ten years after Gladys Matos's murder, the Bronx DA's office persisted with its policy of neglect. Whenever asked, officials explained that they could not talk about the Matos matter because it was "an active, pending investigation."

The Coludro homicide investigation gradually made its way into the same dead-heap pile. Troopers Wills and

Mullen kept at their task whenever they got a chance, even flying down to Florida with Fazzini—who never abandoned his pursuit of Eric and Carolyn—to interview Wanda Matos and her brother regarding what they had heard about Marilyn. Most of the time, though, they were grabbing at ghosts. Their superiors in Pennsylvania felt there was insufficient evidence to convict. With each passing month, the likelihood of a clear-cut break became more remote. Again, no one was willing to stick his neck out without a "smoking gun."

In a last-ditch effort, Wills and Mullen made a final trip to Manhattan in the hopes of confronting Eric. They were, of course, unaware that he had married again, or that his bride, Myra Acevedo, had given birth to Eric "Napolitano" Junior on September 30, 1986, at Holy Name Hospital in Teaneck, New Jersey, or that he had been moving his family from hiding place to hiding place.

The troopers buzzed Carolyn Napoletano's apartment on East Eighty-third Street, but no one responded. Later that day, they located her at One Police Plaza and asked about her son's whereabouts. She gave up nothing, stating rather officially that she would not answer any questions during work hours.

The search for Eric proved fruitless. He abruptly quit his job in the World Trade Center and was no longer seen around his mother's apartment. In fact, he was nowhere to be found.

Frustrated, the troopers returned to Pennsylvania. They had run out of options and ideas. Their investigation was essentially over.

For once, though, Eric remained in the dark. Frightened about the latest police efforts to question him, he escaped with Myra and their newborn son, Eric Junior, to the Acevedo family home in tiny Moca, Puerto Rico.

He figured the commonwealth's back hills would offer him safe haven. There was no way the Stateside cops would bother him there. As usual, Eric had law enforcement figured right.

- 12 -

IN HER WORDS

Fazzini harassed me from day one. He was like shit that you couldn't scrape off your shoe. Somehow, whatever happened to Eric, he was there. We always prayed when a cop got shot it would be him.

We first met Fazzini when Gladys's brother called and said Eric broke his windshield. He threatened us, so we decided to go to the precinct. Don't you know when I got upstairs, he was the jerk sitting there. I didn't like him right away. We thought he was a real asshole, arrogant. We said, "We were threatened." He said he couldn't do anything. You know how the police are; they don't do anything until you're dead. When you go to the police, you don't expect to be treated like he treated us. But they all are like that.

Then when Gladys was killed, we came home that night— because we were always together—and Eric said there were messages on the machine. We were tired and I said, "Eric, let's not even play them." But Eric played them, and it was Fazzini.

We remembered his name. So we figured it was some bullshit with the uncle. So I called him back and he told me he had some bad news. Eric was on the extension; I have two phones. He just told us that she was killed. He didn't give us any details. We said we'd be right up.

I couldn't cry; I was just in shock. He said he wouldn't keep us long. But we had to tear ourselves out of there, because they wanted to talk and talk and talk.

They had Eric in the room first, and they kept him separated from me. They heard what he had to say. Then I went in. They said, "Well, Eric told us this" and "Eric told us that." Then he'd tell Eric, "Your mother said this. Your

*mother said that." They were just trying to confuse us. I
know how they are.*

Fazzini started with the eyewitness shit about the windshield. But whoever said there were eyewitnesses to this
car, it was a lie. That car was in the police pound for two
months, two and a half months, before she was murdered.
All he had to do was check the police report.

I told him to speak to the owner of the car, that I was not
the owner. Al owned the car. It didn't matter that Eric had
it. And, you tell me how this car, without an engine, is out
being driven around by someone stalking her? That's what
prompted me to go to the police commissioner's office and
to Internal Affairs about Fazzini.

I had his shield number, his tax number, I had everything
down. See, that's very easy to get in the department. I wanted to
make sure they knew who he was. There were several reports of
charges on him, but all not guilty. You know, putting his hands
on people. I saw the write-up on one.

Fazzini hated me. He also did not like Eric—and Eric is a
likable person. He raced downtown to Applicant Investigation to pull Eric's file and tell them that he was wanted for a
murder, this and that. Oh, yeah, we heard it all. We heard
from people who were there when Fazzini went there. Eric
went through everything and passed to become a cop. He
was going to get called. Then a person came up to us and
said, "Good news and bad news. Good news is that the
class is going in now. The bad news is that there's a
problem." We were told, "Look up towards the precinct in
the Bronx." It was Fazzini.

He would do anything to discredit me or humiliate me or
embarrass me. He really would. I never knew the Coludro report
did not make NCIC. I find that hard to believe. I think Fazzini had
something to do with that.

My job had nothing to do with the NCIC; I couldn't have
done it if I wanted to. That could be proved with the computer that I had, with the job that I had. My computer on my
desk was strictly call box, the police emergency boxes. It
was impossible because those computers were not around
me. There was one of them in the chief's office, but there
was none of them when I worked in Communications.

Fazzini also hated me for the letters I wrote. When you
send a letter concerning a detective to all the chiefs, the
police commissioner, and the Civilian Complaint Review

*Board, he can't go around and collect them all. I hand-
delivered them. He hated that.*

*You see, cops do not like it when you think you're a little
smarter than them, or if you know things. They like you to
be stupid and they like to intimidate. We are not like that.
That is why they do not like us.*

If I had a picture of Fazzini, I'd use it for target practice.

13

Myra was overjoyed at the opportunity to rejoin her family in Puerto Rico. They could lend a hand with the baby. Eric decided he could learn to like the slower pace and casual lifestyle, the charm of Old San Juan, the warm waters off Aguadilla, and the waterfalls at San Sebastian. Sporting a goatee and mustache, he at first traveled back and forth between his new home and New York City. He needed to make money—odd jobs and driving a taxi—as well as consult with his mother and Uncle Al. When he settled in full-time in early 1987, everyone got along, but between the Acevedo and Napoletano families there were too many children running around. Myra and Eric, his facial hair grown to a bushy, full beard, began looking for a house of their own.

Although Eric was outwardly more relaxed, he remained a time bomb primed to explode. His true nature was revealed during his mother's first visit. It started with a day at the beach. Virtually every time a car pulled into the parking lot, Carolyn and Eric looked to see who was getting out. They got especially antsy whenever a police car passed through the area.

Another afternoon, in the backyard of the Acevedo homestead, he picked up a chicken and announced that the animal would be that evening's dinner. For no apparent reason, he began breathing rapidly and heavily. As his mother watched intently, he held the chicken tightly by the neck and explained that it was very easy to kill. "You just grab the head and you wring the neck—until the head drops," he said, repeatedly yanking the chicken up and down with his hand. "Then you chop it off." Just then the chicken took a peck at Eric's finger. He slapped the animal on the side of its head and screamed, "You sonofabitch!"

Eric was especially cruel to his mother, cursing and calling her "asshole," "stupid," "big mouth," and "anal."

One afternoon he directed the baby to "Smile for 'Anal Carol.' Smile for your grandma." When Carolyn scolded him, Eric went into a trance, angrily staring ahead. He then began mimicking her in a loud, high-pitched, whining voice that sounded as if he were scratching chalk into a blackboard. "It's raaaaining out. I don't like the raaaain. I don't like it here. There's too many peeeeople."

Sex was often the underlying theme of Eric's banter with his mother. On one occasion he asked one of Myra's brothers if he wanted to play billiards, then asked Carolyn if she wanted to play with the pool stick. While playing with his video camera, Eric zoomed in on Eric Junior's diaper-covered behind. "Kiss that, Carolyn. You can have this little treat," he announced. During another recording session, Eric told Myra to move her hands away from Eric Junior. He then focused the camera on his son's exposed penis and said to no one in particular, "Get it hard."

In late February 1987, Eric and Myra purchased a home twenty minutes from Carmen and Pablo. The property was fenced in, dotted with mango, avocado, orange, and palm trees, oregano and tomato plants, and plantanos trees bearing tropical bananas. The house had several bedrooms, a large living room, and a modern bathroom with shower. Eric and Myra bought about $4,000 worth of new appliances and furniture. He promised to add another bedroom and a *marquesina* as soon as possible. He also planned to build a new kitchen off the back of the house, and turn the old one into a dining room.

Eric cleared away several piles of debris from the backyard. With the help of Pablo and other relatives, he laid a concrete driveway. He put screens on the windows to keep out the insects. Inside, there were new cabinets in the kitchen and two VCRs. Eric arranged his Hardy Boys collection on a prominent bookshelf.

Although the Napoletano home had not been broken into, Eric felt the need to take "maximum security measures." He installed bars on the front door and all the windows, and a back door of solid steel. He erected a wall of fencing and gates around the property. He had an ominous new name for his home: The Napoletano Prison. "Once you come in, you do not come out," he explained. "It keeps the good people inside, and the unwanted people outside."

He appeared to enjoy his middle-class existence. He spent a great deal of time with Myra and Eric Junior, including frequent trips to the playground. He took to calling his wife "big baby" and their son "little baby." On the surface he looked like the head of a happy family. But more and more he sought to exert control over Myra. He continued to preach to her that she did not know right from wrong, that only he could show her the way. He said he had a theory about Myra and women in general: "Jesus made Earth in six days. On the seventh day, he rested. And on the eighth day, he made woman. Then nobody ever rested."

Eric had never met a mother-in-law he did not hate. He began trying to isolate Myra from her mother, even making fun of Carmen Acevedo's churchgoing. But there were certain things that Myra would never joke about. Her religious beliefs, and her family's, were off limits. She told Eric that she would not tolerate his sacrilegious behavior.

Because Myra's immediate family was intact, Eric did not confine his in-law friction to her mother. Soon an irrevocable schism would develop between him and his father-in-law. Eric realized he could not subsist on welfare benefits or keep running back to New York every time his funds ran out. Pablo said Eric could work in his candy factory. If things went well, he could become a partner. Eric accepted but quickly became disenchanted. As far as Pablo could tell, Eric could not handle hard work. He frequently complained that his pay was lousy. "He was very rebellious. All he wanted was money, money, money," Pablo recalled.

The financial problems and Eric's fighting with Pablo led to arguments between Eric and Myra, some of them quite tumultuous. On one occasion Carmen and Pablo drove over to the Napoletano homestead in the hopes of calming things down. Eric did not take too well to the interference, though, and locked all of the gates. Eric wanted them off his property. Pablo threatened to call the police; *they* would make him unlock the gates. Eric warned Pablo not to make a mistake he would regret. Unsettled by the comment, the Acevedos retreated to their own home. Eric's relations with his in-laws would never be the same, especially with Carmen. She was convinced, more than ever, that Eric was "a pig."

The next morning, Eric showed up at the Acevedo home. Leaving Myra crying in the car, he stormed in, threw the keys to his house on the table, announced that he was taking his family back to New York, stormed out, and drove away.

Pablo figured that Eric would resurface at Uncle Al Jiovine's in Queens. But when he called there to make sure Myra was all right, Jiovine indignantly denied having any knowledge of her whereabouts. Within days, Eric, Myra, and the baby would return to Puerto Rico.

Unemployed, Eric fell more into debt. He told Pablo he was behind in his car payments and said he was going to drive the car off a cliff if he could not resolve his financial problems. About a week later, that's exactly what happened.

Eric asked Pablo to send one of his sons to retrieve several items he had left in the car. Although it appeared that there was nothing physically wrong with Eric, he also wanted someone to drive him to the hospital so he could establish an injury claim.

Pablo refused to assist in the scheme. "You already told me you were going to drive the car down an embankment. I'm not going to get my kids involved in that."

Eric was incensed. Pablo could see the anger in Eric's bright-red face. Eric wanted to fight. He told Pablo not to visit his house anymore, that he was going to desert the Acevedo family.

"If that's what you want, that's fine with me," Pablo replied. "But I am not getting my children involved."

Eric felt he had no choice but to return to New York, even if the cops were still interested in him. He did not care that Myra was pregnant again and desperately wanted to remain near her family. He told one of Myra's brothers he wanted to "get into the Mafia."

Eric and Myra moved back into Uncle Al's one-bedroom apartment. With Jiovine's help, he got a job as a truck driver in Kearny, New Jersey. That October, again with Al's assistance, Myra and Eric rented the top half of a two-family house at 72 East Fourth Street in Clifton, New Jersey. On the application Eric claimed he had resided for the previous five years at Uncle Al's mother's house, and provided an incorrect Social Security number.

Eric immediately became known in the neighborhood as a nasty individual, arguing over a shared driveway and berating the landlord about living conditions and minor repairs. He fought constantly with Myra, smacking her across the face in front of others. "He would turn up the stereo so you couldn't hear her screaming," said Donna Graceffo, a neighbor.

On December 13, 1988, Myra gave birth at Elmhurst Hospital in Queens. The child was named Angelo. As had been done with Eric Junior's birth certificate, the surname was given as "Napolitano." This time around, Eric claimed he was born in Florida and listed his date of birth as March 3, 1963, instead of May 2, 1965.

Within a month of Angelo's birth, Eric was issued a class-one trucker's license and obtained another new job, as a tractor-trailer driver out of Secaucus, New Jersey. Extremely proud of his higher-paying job, Eric harangued Myra about the difference between his new pay and what he had been paid "slaving away" making candy for Pablo.

More money did not make for happier times, though. The arrival of the second child put more strain on the marriage. With increasing frequency Eric called his wife "a Puerto Rican whore" and "a worthless lowlife." He ordered her not to associate with the neighbors because they were too nosy.

Discipline of Eric Junior, clearly his father's favorite, became another flashpoint. Myra tried to keep the toddler under control, but Eric let him hit people and throw temper tantrums. Whenever Myra corrected the boy, Eric disagreed. As soon as Eric Junior began talking, he learned to swear at his mother. He also hit his baby brother and hurled big metal toys at Mommy.

On other occasions, he ran around the apartment wielding a large kitchen knife. When Myra objected, the youngster explained, "Daddy said for me to stab you" or "Daddy said I could play with knives." Myra also did not want her son playing with toy guns, but Eric equipped him with an arsenal. The child often aimed directly into people's faces while announcing, "I'm gonna kill you." In the neighborhood the youngster was known as "the little monster."

Eric was very protective of his oldest son. When Eric Junior threw his fried-chicken dinner on the floor one evening, Myra smacked his hand and told him, "God made that food!" Her husband rose from his chair, went over to the stove, and grabbed the frying pan filled with hot oil. "If you ever do that again, I'll throw this whole thing on you," Eric screamed at Myra. As an additional warning, he flicked a spoonful of the grease in her face.

Myra was stuck in the apartment, unhappy, displaying many of the sometimes contradictory characteristics of a battered woman: low self-esteem, guilt, dependence, constant fear, but a willingness to do just about anything to keep the family intact.

In early 1989, Myra expressed her unhappiness in a letter to her parents. Her mother flew up for a visit, but by the time she arrived, Eric had calmed down considerably. Myra went out of her way to put on a happy face. But as hard as she labored to make a positive presentation, Eric undermined her efforts.

In the midst of an afternoon walk with Angelo in the stroller, Eric announced to his mother-in-law, "As you can see, this is a very good neighborhood here. There's no niggers here. And we have no Spanish people either in the neighborhood. This neighborhood is all white people. Peace and quiet. You don't have to worry about no nigger breaking into your house or robbing you."

Eric assured Carmen that the lack of old dilapidated cars on the street proved that his neighborhood was racially pure. "You can tell there's no other Spanish people because if there were Puerto Ricans living here—no offense there—but you'd see cars with a red fender and a green hood and a yellow door, and we don't see any of that here."

Carmen returned to Puerto Rico assured that while things were not great, Myra was surviving. She figured that like all marriages, Myra's had hit a bump in the road. She assumed everything would be fine.

Less than two weeks later, on February 10, 1989, a fire of suspicious origin broke out in the ground-floor apartment below the Napoletano residence. At first investigators thought the blaze had been accidental, but questioned that finding after they discovered there had not been any water in the heating unit. Examining the area immediately surrounding the heater, they discovered "several cans that had their tops cut off and contained assorted burnt papers." Carolyn Napoletano later contended that police and fire officials tried to blame Eric for the blaze. It was a curious denial since no one ever made that suggestion.

Myra and her children were taken to nearby Saint Joseph's Hospital, where they were treated for smoke inhalation. When the hospital released them, Uncle Al's brother-in-law,

Larry Knoepfler, objected. He insisted that Angelo be taken
to Hackensack Hospital for additional treatment. The infant
ended up spending five days there, Myra at his side. A
neighbor would later suggest that the extra hospitalization
was part of an insurance scheme. Eric later claimed that
Angelo developed speech problems because of his injuries.

In fact, the day after the blaze Eric returned to the scene
with Uncle Al and Larry Knoepfler to remove belongings
and inquire about insurance coverage. An attorney contacted the rental agent on Eric's behalf. In an effort to avoid
a lawsuit, the realtor relocated the Napoletanos to an upstairs apartment in a four-family house at 25 East Sixth
Street in Clifton, a few blocks away. Eric ordered an unlisted phone in the name "J. Napoli." It was from this residence that Myra would disappear.

The state of the Napoletano marriage did not improve
with the change in scenery. While Carolyn always whined
that her son deserved better women in his life, Eric barely
provided. It was hard to figure where the money was going
from his supposedly well-paying trucker's job. Desperate
for basic services, Myra collected welfare in Queens, using
Uncle Al's address. Being on public assistance enabled her
to take the boys to Elmhurst Hospital for medical care. On
occasion, Uncle Al baby-sat one boy while Myra took the
other to the doctor.

Forever searching for employment linked to law enforcement, Eric applied for a job with the New York City Department of Transportation. If he could not become a cop, he
might as well become a New York City "Brownie," charged
with checking parking meters and no-parking zones and
directing rush-hour traffic. Nicknamed for the color of their
uniforms at the time, Brownies did not carry guns; pens and
summons books were their weapons. Cop wannabes became
Brownies just like they sometimes became police auxiliaries. Eric was going to become a double wannabe.

On his application, he acknowledged previous applications to NYPD, the New York State Police, and the Transit
Authority, but denied ever having been barred or disqualified from a city, state, or federal job. He claimed he lived at
354 East Eighty-third Street in Manhattan, his mother's
address. He made no mention of a wife or Clifton, New
Jersey. For the time he and Myra spent in Puerto Rico, he
scribbled, *Lived at home. My mother supported me.*

Eric was in contact with his mother more than ever. They were on the phone at all hours. If Eric was over in New Jersey during Uncle Al's workday, he called Jiovine's office on his company's toll-free 800 number. Al would then patch the call through to Carolyn at her apartment or at One Police Plaza. For Eric and Carolyn, the free calls became part of their lifestyle.

As Eric waited to hear about the Brownie job, he also applied to become a guard in the New York City prison system. One way or another, he was determined to get one of those union-protected jobs.

With the arrival of 1990, Myra felt more isolated than ever, while Eric's verbal abuse became insufferable. He continually ridiculed her ethnic background and had even taken to making fun of her accent. They rarely went out socially. If they did go out for dinner, it was for seafood at Red Lobster, a steak special at Sizzler, or hot dogs and ice cream on Route 17, near Giants Stadium. Almost always, Carolyn joined them. "For Myra's birthday, Eric and I treated her, and for my birthday, they treated me. We were always going. We always got the coupons, you know, five dollars off. We always had doggie bags coming home," Carolyn recalled.

Eric froze out Myra's family, just as he had done with Marilyn and Wanda. Eric now got angry when Myra called her mother and father. She almost never saw her relatives in the Bronx. Myra was heartbroken. Contact with her family was essential. They made her feel good about herself.

While Myra placed her faith in God, Eric deceived her more and more. On April 30, 1990, he was hired as a traffic enforcement agent. He never wore his Brownie uniform to work, though, but changed in and out of street clothes in the training academy bathroom or inside his car. As far as the City of New York knew, Eric was single without children. As far as Myra knew, her husband was still driving a truck.

Eric viewed his new job as fertile turf for an affair. When the instructors seated the class alphabetically, Eric fixed on a short black woman named Jennifer Meade. She was twenty-seven, single, and the mother of an eleven-year-old girl. After class that Monday, Eric offered her a ride to her second job at a collection agency in Manhattan. As they talked, she noticed a tattoo on Eric's left arm. He told her that "Myra" was his ex-girlfriend. He had lived with her for five years but had not seen her for the past two.

As usual, Eric moved fast. On Wednesday he presented her with six long-stemmed roses. That Friday he slept with her at a motel on Pennsylvania Avenue in Brooklyn. Eric's allure was at work again.

With the escalation of the relationship with Jennifer, he could not continue to lie about his personal life. He told Jennifer that in fact he did have children, two boys. He said they had always lived with their mother, Myra, in the Bronx, but he got to see them frequently.

Eric proudly showed off photos of his two sons. He emphatically explained that he cared more about them than anything in the world; he never wanted to lose them.

With typical obsessiveness Eric now centered his life around Jennifer and his sons. He brought Eric Junior along as he took Jennifer out to lunch on the weekend. He called her later and they spoke for an hour. Still later, he called her to tell her he was going to take his boys to Central Park to play. He took to calling Myra "what's-her-name."

Like the women before her, Jennifer liked the attention Eric showered on her. He was always polite, courteous, and treated her like a queen. The only time they ever argued was when she called him Ricky. Eric hated the moniker. "It's just some dumb name that my mother adopted for me," he told her.

Every morning before work, Eric met Jennifer in a park near the academy in Brooklyn. Every afternoon he drove her home or to her other job. They spent most evenings together, but their dates generally consisted of Eric driving her aimlessly around New York City, upstate New York, and New Jersey. All the while Eric talked about their future together. He wanted to move in with her.

Eric also wanted sex and more sex. He and Jennifer frequented cheap motels in Brooklyn, the Bronx, or New Jersey. At other times their drive-around dates climaxed in the front seat of his Toyota, usually parked near the East River waterfront, within view of the Manhattan Bridge.

More than ever Myra turned to religion. She attended services twice a week at Missionary La Roca, a storefront church in Passaic, New Jersey, usually transported by the church bus. On occasion Eric came to drive her home. But hc always stayed in his car, beeping his horn incessantly until she came out.

Eric viewed Myra's devotion to religion as competition. She now spent her evenings reading the Bible instead of having sex. He told her he could not understand why she would pray to a God, and expressly prohibited her from kneeling and praying at home. To Eric there was no God. "God never gave me anything," he said. He told Myra that he was her God. "I've given you everything."

Myra felt so alone and helpless. More often than not, Eric was nowhere to be found. Still conducting his New York life in secrecy, he told Myra his tractor-trailer job required him to make lengthy cross-country trips. On nights when he did come home, he often arrived just before dawn, claiming he had worked overtime. Myra began to suspect he was seeing someone else.

One night Eric came home with his car bashed. The vandals had also scratched a message into the paint job. *Eric, we know you're here. Fuck you. We're gonna get you.* Myra wondered who was responsible, but Eric refused to talk about it. Was someone trying to avenge the death of Marilyn Coludro or Gladys Matos? Or had Eric stepped over the line with someone else?

Pablo and Carmen were supportive of their daughter, calling more often and sending letters and holiday cards. Myra's siblings wrote more often, too. She thanked God for giving her such wonderful parents and told them she could never thank them enough. She asked forgiveness for all the times she had failed to obey.

As Eric escalated his abuse, Myra revealed his latest transgressions in a letter to her parents. She documented his name-calling and noted that he was now neglecting the children as well. He had cut her off from her religion, too, ordering the local pastor to cease all contact. She said the boys were behaving very poorly. Neither wanted to be with their father anymore. Eric Junior specifically did not want to kiss his father, prompting Eric to strike his son angrily. Myra said she now spent much of each depressing day crying. She could not go on living like this.

At a minimum, Myra decided she had to move from New Jersey. She needed to be closer to her half sister Miriam, her cousins, and aunts. After a series of long discussions Eric agreed to consider moving to the Bronx, or at least said he would. He made it clear, however, that he did not want to live in a building with any blacks. When Eric Junior began to misbehave, he warned the youngster, "If you don't behave, I'm gonna take you to a black family's house."

Myra, Eric, and the boys spent the weekend of June 2, 1990, apartment hunting in the Bronx, sleeping over with Myra's cousin, Martha Morales. Upset with Eric Junior's behavior during a visit to one of Myra's aunts, Eric grabbed the child by the arm and lifted him off the floor. With his free hand he smacked the boy across the face.

"Don't hit him like that!" Myra screamed.

Eric responded by violently kicking the child in the back.

As the argument escalated, Eric began calling Myra's father names, including Puerto Rican slurs. Myra begged Eric to stop. But the yelling got uglier. "You're not enough woman for a man!" Eric shouted. "Your body is ugly! You're not pretty!"

Myra dissolved into tears. At her first opportunity alone she called her parents. She told her mother of Eric's latest abuse. She told her father she was thinking of leaving.

Pablo tried to calm her. "From time to time things like this happen," he advised. "You're going to have to try to save your marriage. Try to work at it, okay?"

Myra tried, but Eric's tone grew more nasty. He took to telling her he no longer loved her.

On June 16, the Saturday before the final tragedy, Eric drove Myra out to Uncle Al's apartment, where he rang the doorbell and shrieked at his "father" figure: "Here! You take her!" But Jiovine refused, so Eric, Myra, and the kids returned to New Jersey.

"I'm not going to take this anymore," Myra said firmly. "I'm going to move back to Puerto Rico."

"Go ahead," Eric yelled back. "Move out. I don't care."

But of course, he did care. He cared a great deal. Myra's moving out would represent the ultimate rejection.

14

By the next morning, Myra had cooled down. Good soul that she was, she decided to take her papa's advice: Forgive and forget, turn the other cheek. It was Father's Day, and she resolved to make it a special occasion. She wanted dinner to be a beautiful celebration for Eric. After all, he had never even met his father.

Instead, Eric used the occasion to inform Myra about his mistress. The marriage was entering its fatal phase.

In fact, Eric said with his smirk, he had been seeing the woman for five weeks; Eric Junior had already met her. On top of that, Eric said, "She's black." He knew that would get Myra's goat.

The news sent her over the edge. It was bad enough that Eric was cheating, but he had to shove it in her face. She called her father. "Eric has a lover! I am *not* going to forgive him!" Myra said she was moving back to Puerto Rico.

This time Pablo did not try to change her mind. He told her to collect her thoughts and decide if she wanted him to fly up to help her pack. Pablo assured her that he and Carmen would always be there. If she did not have enough money, they would chip in the difference. "Whenever you're ready, we're ready," he assured her.

As afternoon turned to night, Eric and Myra argued nonstop. He claimed that his mistress satisfied him sexually while she did not. In between the quarreling, Eric called his mother for advice.

Badly wounded, Myra assured Eric that she knew other men. She was pretty. She could get herself someone else. She dialed the phone number of a man she had met recently. But when he answered, he told Myra he was in bed and could not come out to meet her.

Eric picked up the phone and called Jennifer Meade at her

home in Brooklyn. "Tell her not to leave," he instructed, putting Myra on the line.

Jennifer had no idea what was going on. Eric has assured her that this Myra was a former girlfriend, long out of the picture. "Do this for me. Please," Eric pleaded. She agreed, figuring it was no big deal. But as soon as Myra began talking, it was clear that she still played a significant role in Eric's life.

"Are you seeing Eric?" she demanded.

Yes, Jennifer admitted, puzzled by the angry tone.

"Have you met baby Eric? Were you talking to him?"

"Yes," Jennifer replied, confused. But before she could ask any questions, Eric grabbed the receiver and hung up.

Eric again called his mother, spoke with her for several minutes, then resumed arguing with Myra. All evening long, the phone lines raged. Myra called her relatives, Eric his.

Just before midnight, Myra called her half sister Miriam in the Bronx. She told her about Jennifer and how Eric had called the mistress right there in front of her. Eric snatched the receiver to tell Miriam of his undying love for Jennifer. He said he was going to live with her.

Myra sobbed loudly as Eric contended that she never had any time for him. Miriam tried to calm Myra, but she was hysterical. She kept repeating, "I can't believe he's playing me dirty. I can't believe it."

It was early Monday now. As soon as Myra hung up, Eric woke Uncle Al. Because he usually got up about 4:00 A.M. for work, Jiovine was not happy. This was tit-for-tat time. Since Eric had talked to Miriam, Myra joined in this conversation on an extension phone. Husband and wife traded insults, accusing each other of adultery. Al grew concerned that Eric might be beating Myra. He also was concerned about getting back to sleep. These arguments were old hat to him. At 12:21 A.M., he announced that he had to go.

Husband and wife continued to argue. As usual, Eric left for work by five o'clock. His mother called in sick at NYPD.

Myra picked up the phone and started waking relatives, beginning with a one-hour call to her half sister Janet in Pennsylvania. By 8:30, she had also talked with her cousin Martha Morales in the Bronx, an aunt in the Bronx, an uncle in Puerto Rico, and her mother in Puerto Rico. There was no way she could continue to live with Eric. He had been unfaithful.

Eric, meanwhile, called the New York City Department of Transportation's Employee Assistance Program to request counseling. He explained that he was having problems with a girlfriend who was the mother of his two children, but was hopeful of a reconciliation. He wondered if there was any counseling service he could take advantage of during work hours. Daniel Oscar Turcotte, an intern from Columbia University's School of Social Work, arranged for Eric and Myra to visit him that Friday.

Later that day, Eric told Jennifer he could not drive her to her other job. He said his ex-girlfriend was mad at him and threatening to take the children to Puerto Rico. Eric said he had to convince Myra to stay. He could not let her take his kids.

Jennifer asked Eric to explain his weird call from the night before. Why had he put this Myra on the phone? Eric explained that he had discovered Myra had a boyfriend. He had found the guy's phone number, so he had called her to make Myra jealous.

Among a flurry of calls Monday evening between the Napoletano apartment, Uncle Al's in Queens, and Carolyn's in Manhattan, Myra spoke again with her half sister Miriam. When Eric overheard Myra talking about leaving, he stormed out of the apartment, only to return in a few minutes with a rope in hand. "I'm going to choke myself in the bathroom if you don't forgive me," he screamed. Myra was in no mood for Eric's sick games. She told him that she was not going to forgive him.

Instructing Eric Junior to follow him, Eric announced to Myra and Miriam that he wanted his son to watch, saying, "Come on, baby Eric. Let's go in. Come see Daddy hang himself."

Myra told the child to stay put.

Back and forth they argued until Eric calmed down and put the rope away.

On Tuesday, Myra again spoke with her mother, adamant in her resolve to leave. She was going to call a moving company to get an estimate. Meanwhile, Eric again told Jennifer he could not see her; he was still trying to convince Myra not to leave with the kids. The last thing he wanted was for his sons to be raised without their father.

Wednesday, the twentieth, was the culminating, pressure-packed day. For the third day in a row, Carolyn was absent from work. Instead, she spent a great deal of time on the phone advising her daughter-in-law.

Because of a visit by Nelson Mandela to the city that day, Eric's training class was dismissed early. He again explained to Jennifer that he had to rush home to talk Myra into staying.

At about the same time, Myra phoned Al Jiovine on his toll-free number at work. She asked him to patch through a call to Maggie Rivera, the young girlfriend of Uncle Al's new roommate, a young Latino named Greg Velez. Myra and Maggie discussed the possibility of living together in an apartment. Jiovine attempted to dissuade Myra from leaving Eric for at least another week. He assured her he was working on obtaining a federal rent-subsidized Section Eight apartment for her.

An emotional wreck, Myra was confused. Perhaps she did not need to move to Puerto Rico. The public-assistance housing would allow her to escape from Eric without burdening her parents.

Nereida Flick, Myra's cousin who lived close by, called that afternoon to invite the kids over for a swim. Myra declined, explaining that a moving-company agent was coming to give her an estimate. She said that things had gotten so bad, she was now sleeping with the kids in the other bedroom.

Events continued to move toward their climax as Esteban Fernandez from Monti Movers in Brooklyn arrived about four-thirty. He was let into the building by first-floor resident Theresa Maltese, and her husband, Anthony. Mrs. Maltese had a complaint of her own to lodge with the Napoletanos—water was dripping through her ceiling from one of the Napoletanos boys' free-for-all bathing sessions—so she led Fernandez up the stairs to Apartment 3.

She knocked repeatedly on the Napoletano apartment door, but no one answered. Rock music was blasting inside. Fernandez turned around to leave. The downstairs neighbor was not ready to give up, though. She knocked harder, with the open palm of her hand. From inside the apartment, a male voice screamed, "I can't wait to move the fuck out of here!" Finally, Myra appeared at the door, looking distraught. She let Fernandez in, then slammed the door shut.

The apartment was in disarray. Clothing was piled on the beds in heaps. The kids were soaking wet. One of them ran around the apartment naked while the other attempted to dress himself. Eric, the father, was bare-chested, clad in a pair of jeans. Fernandez sensed considerable tension. Myra and Eric yelled at each other. Fernandez asked that the music be turned down.

The moving man surveyed what Myra wanted him to take into account: one washing machine, a console TV and two smaller ones, a battery-powered toy car large enough to hold two preschoolers, a two-piece living room set, a four-piece bedroom set, two bunk beds, four stereo speakers, and ten boxes of loose goods.

Myra made it clear that only she and the children were moving. Eric watched in silence as his wife and some stranger discussed the physical dissolution of the marriage. That was his life Myra was talking about packing up and shipping off to Puerto Rico, too.

Fernandez explained that he would provide cardboard boxes after Myra gave him a deposit. He estimated the total cost of the move at $1,336. Myra told him she would call the following day; she and her husband were going to discuss the situation some more.

About an hour after Fernandez departed—and presumably after Myra and Eric discussed her plans again—she spoke with her father. As they discussed plane tickets and other arrangements, Myra abruptly changed her mind. She informed her father that she was going to stay up north and get an apartment of her own. She said she would still not forgive Eric but would let him help her. She said Eric had now told her that he was going to move out of their apartment that Saturday. Myra apologized to her father for having bothered him. "I've worked everything out."

But Pablo was not convinced. He knew something was not right. He heard talking in the background. His daughter sounded very frightened. The confidence and spunk were missing from her voice.

"Wait! You told me that you wanted to come home. Now all of a sudden you change your mind?" There was a tinge of anger in Pablo's voice. "What's wrong with you? What's going on?"

As Myra sought to explain, the voice in the background became more clear; it was definitely Eric. Pablo asked Myra if she was nervous. Yes, she said, she was.

Just like that, the line went dead.

Pablo was really angry now. He called back and told Myra to put Eric on the phone. Eric refused. Pablo got more assertive. "I am not going to leave you there all alone in New Jersey." He said that if she was going to insist on remaining up north, she should work at reconciling with Eric. Otherwise, if something happened to her and the boys, no one would know it.

No way, Myra said, she was not going to forgive Eric. He had stepped over the line. "I'm in a lot of pain. I'm very hurt," she said. "I never thought he would do something like that."

Pablo again asked to speak with Eric, who could now be heard clearly in the background calling him nasty names. Myra pleaded with her father not to argue. It did not matter, though; Eric still would not get on the line. Instead, he said he was going out to buy candy for the boys.

Giving Myra no choice, Pablo insisted that she come to Puerto Rico. "Your mother and I will take care of you and the boys. We love you very much." Always respectful, Myra promised to reconsider her options. "I want to think about it. I love you and Mommy very much," she said. They would talk again tomorrow.

One of her younger sisters, Lizzette, then got on the line. As they chatted, Myra regained her confidence. She was already changing her mind; she would come to Puerto Rico, and take all of her furniture with her. There was no way she was going to let Eric sleep on that bed with his lover. Myra decided she would fly to San Juan with the boys that Friday. "If Eric really loves me, he will come down. Then we will work things out."

As the siblings spoke, Eric attempted to wrest the receiver from Myra's grasp. Clearly, he did not like the way things were developing. Myra asked that Pablo get on the line one more time. "I love you very much," she said. "Tell Mommy that I love her very much."

"We love you, too," Pablo said. He heard a clicking sound, as if someone was trying to disconnect by pushing down on the buttons in the phone cradle. Worried as could be, Pablo said good-bye.

He would never speak with his daughter again.

Eric grabbed the kids and headed over to Manhattan to pick up his mother. Later that evening, Theresa Maltese and hcr husband encountered Eric, Carolyn, and the two boys in the building lobby. The two women exchanged small talk on their way to the street.

Inside the building, Tony Maltese and Eric also chatted. Eric wanted to know if Maltese had heard him and Myra arguing the night before. Maltese said he had not. Eric explained that he and Myra had bccn fighting over the fact that he had a girlfriend and she had a boyfriend. Eric added that he and Myra had resumed the argument since the moving man left. He contended that in the midst of their feuding, Myra had stuffed some clothing into a sack, put the sack on her back, and walked out of the apartment. Eric said he had no idea where she had gone off to, then excused himself, saying he had to go upstairs to use the bathroom.

Tony Maltese exited the building, where he retrieved his wife from her conversation with Carolyn. A few minutes later, Eric exited the building, looking angry and agitated. Mrs. Maltese and her husband drove off as Eric opened the door to his car.

Myra Napoletano was gone, once again sending Eric back into the protective arms of his mother.

- 15 -

IN HER WORDS

A lot of things led to Myra wanting to go to Puerto Rico. First of all, Myra got married too young. Eric was like her first boyfriend and when he used to go see her, before they were married, or bring her to my house, the cousins, the sisters, the brothers had to come. Pablo wasn't letting anybody alone with her. The father didn't trust anybody.

Also, it was partly because she felt she was cheated out of—what do you call it?—dating time. She wanted to go out with other guys. There was a guy who the police talked to, but I don't know what happened to him. She had called him at his home, Abdallah. And he had called her. I guess she wanted out.

At the same time Eric was friendly with one of the traffic agents. I'm sure you have seen her, the black one. He brought her outside my house. I was in the car with her, like if he brought her home or they would take the kids. But she was never in my house.

Myra was like a daughter to me. The first time I saw Myra, she was like a little doll. I just wanted to grab her and hug her, she was so cute.

Eric and Myra loved each other, but they were jealous. And, I guess they were afraid. Eric and Myra did not have to get married, you know. They had a nice wedding. Al went, and Al's sister, Marilyn, and her husband, Larry, went. I did not go. I just didn't want to go. You know, it was too much for me already with all this happening. I was very upset about Marilyn Coludro.

And I was upset that Eric never would have met Myra if I had went out with him that night. We wouldn't have gone to the Bronx. But I had to wash my hair. Myra was using the

*phone booth and he wanted to call me, to tell me that he had
arrived safely. He was in the wrong place at the wrong time.*

*Myra and I hit it off right from the beginning. She already
knew about Marilyn. Eric told her. He didn't keep anything
from her. He told her that Marilyn had been a girlfriend
who disappeared and was found dead. I remember, she
hugged me and she said, "I understand how you feel. I
would feel the same way." I didn't like anybody Spanish. I
thought that all Spanish people have problems, like Wanda,
her broken family. Marilyn, her father was a junkie and you
heard the stories about how he used to come there and try to
get Marta and Marilyn. He used to come with a baseball bat
and hide in the stairwell. Marilyn used to tell me that, too.*

*Myra was nice. She would give. Somebody wanted to
borrow her wedding gown. She was going to give it, but
Eric said, "No, you're not." So she asked me. And I said,
"Myra, you can't be so giving. Don't lend everything. You
struggled to get that. You, and Eric, and your father and
mother bought that. Let them get it on their own. Just say
it's packed away in storage at your mother-in-law's." See,
in some things Myra was stupid, like with the wedding
gown. She didn't know how to say no; she said yes. I don't
lend anything to anybody. I won't even give you a nickel.*

PART 3

The Chase

We're good at spotting cops.

—Carolyn Napoletano

- 16 -

Nick Donato was convinced that he was dealing with a sociopathic serial killer and an equally conniving and conspiratorial mother. The challenge that lay before the young detective was a daunting one. It was now up to him to shut down this killing machine that had outfoxed all of NYPD and the New York City criminal justice system. He knew that if Eric was not stopped, he would surely fall in love again, turn abusive, be rejected, and kill.

Donato made solving the case the focal point of his life, in and out of the office. While scores of other law-enforcement personnel across the country would work on the Napoletano investigation as it continued to develop, Donato's pursuit of Eric and his mother would be unrelenting.

Upon hearing what Detective Fazzini had to say regarding the Coludro and Matos homicides, Donato recognized that Myra's decision to leave Eric mirrored the acts of rejection that had led to the earlier homicides. Control, domination, and acceptance meant everything to Eric. If Eric had allowed Myra to move to Puerto Rico, that would have meant he was no longer in control. Eric could not have that; he needed always to be in control. And his ultimate control device was murder.

Taking stock of the situation, Donato was astonished by the details of the unsuccessful New York investigations: the lost Coludro missing-persons report, the aborted Matos grand jury, Carolyn's dubious alibis for her Ricky, her unchecked obstructionism, and the Napoletanos' repeated misuse of their knowledge of law-enforcement procedures to thwart investigations and avoid punishment. The more Donato learned about Carolyn's unchallenged employment at NYPD and labor union protection, the more frustrated, angry, and professionally insulted he and his suburban partners became.

At the same time, Donato realized that he had to stay focused on the task in front of him instead of looking back at what had not happened. As he expanded his investigation, Donato surmised that Fazzini was right about Myra: He wasn't looking for a missing person; he was looking for a corpse. He hated to admit it, but he needed to track down her dental records to prepare for a postmortem identification.

Just eight hours after he first spoke with Fazzini the afternoon of July 9, 1990, the corpse in question was discovered 140 miles away, in the state of Delaware. By that point Myra had been missing for nineteen days. She would continue to be officially listed as missing for another two-and-a-half weeks until her body was identified.

A severe thunderstorm had knocked out power that evening in portions of sparsely populated Bear Township, a stretch of farmland located less than twenty minutes southwest of the Delaware Memorial Bridge, the state's main link to New Jersey. With the electricity off in their house, Richard and LaVernon Milson of 101 Labrador Lane took a walk along their dead-end road to check on a nearby transformer and traffic light. The Milsons lived in one of only two houses on Labrador Lane. There were no streetlights; a NO OUTLET sign marked its entrance.

As the Milsons walked back toward their house, they noticed a patted-down area among the tall grass running along the edge of Lum's Pond State Park. Richard Milson figured a deer had bedded down in the underbrush. He walked deeper into the field to investigate, but there were no resting animals in sight. Instead, Milson discovered what appeared to be a human skull sticking out of the ground.

Several bones were scattered about. The cadaver had been partially dug up and picked apart by animals. The exposed portion of the body was badly decomposed.

As he approached, Milson noticed some hair attached to the skull. He just looked, though, keeping his distance once he realized what he had uncovered.

Milson headed home to call 911. Within an hour, the crime scene was teeming with law-enforcement personnel from New Castle County. The case was assigned to Detective Allen E. Ruth, a fifteen-year veteran. The area was secured to await a daylight exhumation.

Ruth returned to the scene before seven to relieve the

night crew. During the next few hours a steady progression of important law-enforcement officials visited the site from the county police, the Delaware State Police, the Delaware Attorney General's Office, and the Maryland State Police.

Corporal Kenneth Conrad of New Castle County's Evidence Detection Unit began canvassing the area. He spotted a vertebra from the neck in a grassy area just inches off the roadway.

When Dr. Ali Z. Hameli, the state's chief medical examiner, and one of his deputies, Dr. Richard T. Callery, arrived, Ruth and others began carefully digging around the body so that it could be extracted without additional damage. At its deepest point, the corpse was twenty-three inches beneath the surface. The victim's legs were tucked in and the shoulders had been twisted down, as if the body had been squeezed into the narrow hole.

The extraction process was an arduous one, consuming several hours. Corporal Conrad sifted the dirt as it was removed from the grave site. Dr. Callery later compared the exhumation to an archaeological dig.

The victim was a white female with dark hair. The corpse had no identification or jewelry. The body was clothed only in a pair of yellow drawstring baggy shorts with the word FREESTYLE stenciled down the left front leg.

At the ME's office, Dr. Callery, a forensic pathologist, took X rays of the victim's teeth and compared them with records of two women missing from the county, but neither set matched.

Prior to the commencement of an autopsy the following afternoon, Ruth directed Corporal Conrad to conduct a laser examination of the victim's body for foreign hairs and fibers. The laser detected minuscule red fibers on the victim's shorts. A second laser test of the victim's scalp uncovered a fiber in her head hair. Other body hairs also were collected.

A veteran of hundreds of autopsies, Dr. Callery displayed a splendid expertise in postmortem analysis. He said the victim was in her early twenties, had given birth, weighed about 105 pounds, and was approximately five foot two inches tall—"plus or minus one and three-quarter inches." His estimates would turn out to be correct.

Otherwise, Dr. Callery was hampered severely by the advanced state of decomposition, caused by the body's exposure to the air and summer's heat. The right hand was gone. He also detected extensive internal "insect activity." The excessive degree of postmortem decay precluded his making more than a wide-ranging guess at an approximate date of death; the victim could have been dead for up to several months.

The pathologist did not fare any better when trying to determine a cause of death. He found no evidence of "penetrating, perforating, or deforming injuries" to the parts of the body available to him, but the animals had ravaged the victim's neck. The hyoid bone and the thyroid cartilage were missing, as was a cervical vertebra.

Dr. Callery simply could not solve the forensic mystery. He was forced to conclude his autopsy report with a finding that the manner of death was "homicide," but the cause of death was "anatomically undetermined." If the victim had been strangled, Dr. Callery did not have the bones to prove it.

It was obvious the victim had been murdered elsewhere and dumped on Labrador Lane. Ruth contacted the State Bureau of Investigation to obtain a list of all missing persons throughout Delaware. He then contacted each local police agency investigating a missing person who could possibly be a match. After ruling out all of the cases, he drafted a Teletype for distribution July 11, 1990, to the law-enforcement community along the Eastern Seaboard. By the following afternoon, Detectives Ruth and Donato would be on the phone comparing notes. But as events unfolded, it appeared that Carolyn Napoletano had read the Teletype first.

Lieutenant John Burke was sitting in the Detective Bureau at 10:30 A.M. when a secretary told him he had a call from Eric Napoletano's mother. Burke was understandably caught off guard. Although he had given Carolyn a business card during the Fourth of July encounter in the hallway outside Uncle Al's apartment, he had never expected her to take up the offer once the battle lines were drawn.

Looking around the office, Burke spotted an open line connected to the police department's recording system, so he had the secretary transfer the call there.

"Good morning. Lieutenant Burke."

"Good morning, this is Carolyn Napoletano," she said,

calling from One Police Plaza. From that point on, Burke could hardly get a word in edgewise.

Carolyn said she had a complaint. She had called collect the day before and the officer who answered had refused to accept the charges. She said she did not understand. "You had told Eric he could call collect, so I figured that applied to me also."

"Uh, okay," Burke replied.

It was apparent that Burke had no idea what she was talking about. "They didn't even tell you, right?" she asked.

"No," Burke replied politely.

Clearly, Carolyn was on a fishing expedition. Over the course of the next hour, she would ask a lot of questions that sounded odd considering that Myra's disappearance was still just a missing-persons case—for example, how many detectives had been assigned, what hours they worked, who was supervising them, whom they had spoken to. If she had read Detective Ruth's Teletype about the Labrador Lane corpse, she did not let on.

Carolyn claimed she was calling because Myra's sister, Miriam Colon, had supposedly been annoying Eric's landlord to ask for Myra's clothing. Carolyn contended that Miriam's actions proved she knew where Myra was hiding out. "I thought that you would like to know that."

Instead of the conversation ending, though, Carolyn commenced her inquisition. She emphasized that she knew police procedure and peppered Burke with questions. She also interspersed her queries with nasty personal comments about Donato and about Myra's neighbors and relatives.

From the sound of it, Donato was in danger of replacing Fazzini as the chief target of Carolyn's anti–law-enforcement attacks. She accused him of harassing Jeanette Konuklu, one of Myra's neighbors, "bothering her with the same questions and leaving her crying." She went on to call Konuklu "a BS artist," and said that Myra's downstairs neighbor, Theresa Maltese, the last known nonfamily member to see Myra, was "full of crap."

She went on to characterize sweet, soft-spoken Miriam Colon as arrogant. "I told Eric, 'You know, we said Myra's probably in Puerto Rico, but now I really think she's with the sister.' I really think she is, when you try to analyze it. If this was your sister, would you be calling about her clothing?"

Of course, Miriam had not inquired about obtaining

Myra's clothing; she had been trying to find out if any of Myra's clothing was missing.

Carolyn also complained that Miriam never called her or Eric anymore. But that was just more silliness; the entire Acevedo family had cut themselves off from both Napoletanos. There was no pretense about it, but Carolyn made it sound as if she was oblivious to the family's suspicions about Eric.

Instead, she said she was troubled about the way the Acevedos were behaving. Meandering again, Carolyn explained, "I'm upset. I was home yesterday. I'm very upset over this. I still have my virus kind of like hanging around. I'm not eating. Eric's not really eating—the kids are eating. We're not eating. We're not sleeping right. We're very upset. We just keep rehashing and we just feel that she's with Miriam, if she's not in Puerto Rico— She could be in Puerto Rico, and Miriam wants her clothes because Miriam goes back and forth down there or— We can't figure out why they don't call us."

Carolyn was talking a mile a minute. She sought to explain why she and Eric had waited several days to visit the Clifton Police Department after Myra's disappearance. She said that Eric and she had figured Myra went to her sister's and would come back. "As far as we were concerned, she left, she was really leaving on the twenty-ninth, that's when Eric made the flight for."

Carolyn's story left a messy trail, though. She had previously claimed the airline reservations were for the Friday immediately following Myra's disappearance, meaning the twenty-second. And, of course, even when they did show up at headquarters, Eric and Carolyn had not reported Myra missing; they had come to complain about the police.

Burke asked specifically whether reservations had also been made for the two children. Carolyn got huffy and said she had already provided that information. When Burke pressed for more details on Myra's reservations, Carolyn suggested that Myra "probably went under a different name." Burke found that interesting; he asked her what name she thought Myra would have used.

"Who knows?" Carolyn replied. "I mean, you can use any name when you go on an airline."

When Burke pointed out that Eric still had not consented to talk with Donato in person, she had a story ready for that, too. First of all, she and Eric had talked with Detectives Cooke, Snack, and Ogden. Second, the lawyer told Eric not to talk. "We also heard that you people are telling everybody, 'Why does Eric need a lawyer if he has nothing to hide?' The thing is this. Eric got a custody lawyer and he wanted to make sure that her father couldn't come and snatch the kids." She said the custody lawyer had told Eric to hire a criminal attorney. "So, now you know that for a fact!" Carolyn had an answer for everything.

But in the midst of her blabbering, she made a mistake. While explaining that she had not given Miriam her home number "because I don't want all these people speaking Spanish calling and bothering me all hours of the night," Carolyn claimed that Myra's address book and wallet were also missing. The remark about the missing wallet would prove extremely incriminating as the investigation unfolded.

Burke tried to stop the rambling, but his was an impossible mission. Carolyn now claimed that after Theresa Maltese had left for her dinner the night of Myra's disappearance, Myra had come outside, down by the Toyota, to reiterate her disinterest in joining the rest of the family for dinner.

In the middle of her stories, Carolyn stopped cold; she got another call. "Can you hold on? Eric's on the phone." Now she was tying up two phone lines at One Police Plaza.

After several minutes, she was back full of steam, with a message supposedly from neighbor Jeanette Konuklu. "Eric just told me something that I had told him Jeanette told me. But Jeanette told me she didn't tell you, because she just thought of it. So I'll tell you. Jeanette was going to help Myra dye her hair blond." Carolyn hoped that Konuklu would not be mad that she had told the story, but what the hell; "I don't see why, if it helps you."

Carolyn droned on about Myra's hair. "Who knows? She could have done it that night." Then to knock her own idea, she added that she and Eric had not found any dye materials during their search for Myra's wallet. "We spent almost an hour there, like looking around, like looking for her wallet."

Burke had deliberately let her go out of control. But he decided to take a shot at a question of substance. When Carolyn again started talking about how Myra had not wanted to join the family at the Red Lobster, Burke asked if that was where they had ended up eating.

"No," she replied. "We didn't go. We never went to eat.

We never went to eat. We just came back to my house and then he called her, and he kept calling her, and calling her. The first time he thought, Well, she's washing her hair, she's taking a shower, maybe she's resting, maybe she went by Jeanette. You know, you don't know. *And then when it got like late, Eric said he should just stay by me with the kids because, 'Give her a break,' and then, and then, she was, she was gone.*"

Now she was making no sense. What had happened to their previous story that they found the Clifton apartment empty at 3:00 A.M., then drove back to Manhattan? Why would Eric and Carolyn have driven back to Manhattan without dinner? Both their favorite Red Lobster franchises were in New Jersey, each less than a half hour from Clifton. And why would Eric have left his wife at home in New Jersey, only to drive to Manhattan so he could spend the night calling her?

Burke just listened, though, and Carolyn moved on, to character assassination of Myra. "My personal opinion is that she really wanted to go out with guys, and she had told me that when she went to Puerto Rico, her mother would watch the kids, and she would go out with guys, and I said, 'You can't do that, Myra, because you are married.' She says, 'Well, they won't know.' And I said, 'But you can't do that to guys. You have to tell them that you're married. You can't lead people on.' "

There was a point to all this. Carolyn proceeded to contrast Myra's supposed misbehaving with Eric's performance as a father. "I'm sure that they know Mommy's not there and they're clinging to him because he's Daddy. He's always got them with him. He does their laundry and he takes them out. He doesn't want anything to happen to them, and he's terrified that her family will try to snatch them. She's got a lot of relatives, like half of the Bronx is related. You would never find them. They'd shift them from one house to the other. You'd never find them again. So he's really being very cautious with them. He says they're all he has until Myra comes back—if she comes back."

As a final insult, Carolyn relayed word that Eric had told his sister-in-law, Miriam Colon, that Myra had abandoned the boys. "Miriam was screeching. I said to her, 'Miriam, it means the same thing—*abandoned*—whether she left them in the house or if she told him to take them.' "

Carolyn paused long enough for her vicious comment to hang in the air. She then announced that she had to get off the phone. Her boss at OCCB, Organized Crime, was giving her a dirty look. She had to return to work.

− 17 −

With tensions rising, the distraught Acevedo family and the cavalier Napoletano inner circle presented a dramatic contrast. Even while helping in the search for Myra's dental records, her father, Pablo, and other relatives hoped against hope that she was still alive. On the other side, while Carolyn ran interference with the Clifton police, Eric resumed his pursuit of Jennifer Meade.

Pablo had decided to stay with relatives in the Bronx until the mystery surrounding Myra's disappearance was solved. His brothers would mind the candy factory.

Donato kept the Acevedos updated as much as possible, but there was only so much he could tell them. Pablo wanted to publicize Eric's links to the Coludro and Matos murders in the local English- and Spanish-language news media, but Donato and his supervisors felt the investigation should be kept low profile to prevent the Napoletanos from finding out anything more about police activities. As always, Pablo agreed to cooperate, but his frustration was so intense he found himself unable to sit by and wait for the police. An emotional wreck, he began conducting crude surveillance on Eric.

One night he hid in front of Carolyn's apartment building from three o'clock until 8:00 A.M., when he saw Eric and the boys get into the Toyota. Whenever possible, he followed by car, hoping Eric would lead him to Myra. But reconnaissance was not Pablo's forte; Eric usually shook him in Midtown traffic or while heading across the Fifty-ninth Street Bridge into Queens.

With each passing day, Eric felt more comfortable with the idea that the Clifton police had nothing on him, and that they were going to fade away, just as their New York City counterparts had. Back with Jennifer on a full-time basis, he would often pick her up after work, take her on a long, aimless drive, then pull into a motel for a couple hours of sex. On occasion, he escorted her around New York City, pointing out Mafioso John Gotti's neighborhood, favorite bar, and social club.

Eric's relationship with Jennifer was not destined to be a smooth one, however, especially after Donato and Burke inquired about her at the Brownie academy.

One of Jennifer's supervisors told her the police had been around asking questions about Eric and his wife. The mention of Eric's "wife" really threw Jennifer. When he and his sons picked her up at the end of her shift, she told him about the questioning. "They wanted to know about me and you—and they wanted to know what happened to your wife!"

Eric no doubt realized he would have to give up part of the truth or lose all credibility. He drove to a quiet spot near the South Street Seaport, where he confessed that Myra really was his wife. But, he insisted, he had not lived with her for the past two years, and he had not been involved in her disappearance.

Eric warned Jennifer that the police were probably going to contact her directly. "Tell them, 'Go fuck yourselves. Don't talk to me. Talk to my lawyer.' " He warned that given the chance, the police would tell her he had three other wives, wives in Florida, and that years ago, two people whom he knew had turned up dead. But, Eric emphasized, none of those crimes involved him. The police were just trying to blame him, that's all.

Jennifer was more concerned about Mrs. Eric Napoletano. She did not go out with married men, regardless of how fractured their home lives were. She told Eric they were finished.

But Eric would not give up. Instead, he kept sweet-talking, until Jennifer partly gave in. She informed him adamantly that she was not making any kind of commitment, but would spend one more night with him.

Eric dropped the kids off at his mother's apartment. Carolyn being Carolyn, Jennifer had to wait in the car. The lovers then headed across Central Park and down the West Side for the Lincoln Tunnel, bound for a cheap motel in New Jersey.

Eric asked Jennifer if she thought he had anything to do with Myra being missing. She nodded. "I think you did something to make her disappear."

Eric laughed. "I didn't do nothing to her."

Jennifer told him that if he had done something to Myra, she had no doubt he would do something bad to her, too.

Again, Eric laughed. Somehow working that crazy charm of his, he put Jennifer at ease, and took her to bed for another long session of sex.

The next day, while shopping with her mother, Jennifer discussed Eric's interest in John Gotti. Her mother firmly warned her that this new boyfriend sounded like trouble. When Eric picked her up that afternoon, Jennifer again proclaimed that she would not be going out with him anymore because he was married.

Frantic, Eric worked hard to win her over. Crying, he said they were good for each other. He pleaded, "Please, don't leave me!" Again, Jennifer relented, but again only partway. She said they could still see each other for sex; they just would not live together.

Eric accepted the compromise, then turned his attention to finding somewhere to pawn off his boys for several hours. Getting away without the kids was becoming quite a task. The friend of Uncle Al's who usually baby-sat during the day was unavailable. More and more Carolyn was balking at being asked to take them. Not exactly the grand-motherly type to begin with, Eric Junior and Angelo were beginning to get to her. One recent night when she was in the backseat of the Toyota with them, she had yelled up to her son and Jennifer, "Errrr-ick! They're touching me! Do something! Tell them to stop!"

Left no alternative, Eric decided to bring the boys with him. They picked up Jennifer, then set off for another long drive. As the boys fell asleep, Eric worked his way back to the make-out park in Brooklyn. He moved Angelo's car seat from the passenger's side in the back to the driver's side. He spread Eric Junior across the right side of the rear seat.

Eric removed his pants and undershorts, then pushed the front passenger seat back into the reclining position. With his children sleeping inches away, he took off his shirt, then removed Jennifer's blouse. He lifted up her skirt and slid down her panties. Eric was in love again.

Contrary to Eric's expectations, Donato wasn't about to fade away. In fact, he expanded his investigation. There was so much to do, so many angles to explore.

The neighborhood near the Napoletano apartment in Clifton was recanvassed. The pastor of Myra's storefront church arranged for her physical description to be broadcast over a local Spanish-language radio station and relayed to the media in Puerto Rico. A check of the airlines serving San Juan uncovered a "Myra Acevedo" who had flown there during the key time period. But after considerable effort, Donato's colleague, Detective Richard Onorevole, determined that the woman listed as "Myra Acevedo and Infant" had gone on her honeymoon with a man named Carlos Infante.

A new round of interviews was conducted. Miriam Colon told the police she had heard Eric tell Myra he would "make her disappear if she left him." Neighbor Jeanette Konuklu said she had seen bruises on Myra's body and heard Eric taunt her on more than one occasion, calling her "a fucking Puerto Rican" while threatening to kill her if she ever took off with the kids.

The breadth of Donato's investigation was widened to include other law-enforcement agencies. Along with Senior Investigator Peter T. Talarico, Jr., from the Passaic County Prosecutor's Office, Donato and Burke met for three hours with the Pennsylvania troopers who worked on the Coludro case. Talarico had previously served as a police detective in Paterson, the rough-and-tumble county seat. Prosecutors from his office would handle the case if Eric was ever arrested on New Jersey murder charges.

Donato also contacted FBI Special Agent Thomas A. Cottone, Jr., to inquire about the agency's serial-killer–profile program. Cottone was attached to a satellite office in West Paterson, twenty minutes from the Napoletano apartment in Clifton. In the coming months the veteran agent would play a major role in the Napoletano investigation.

At Cottone's direction, FBI Special Agent Ivan A. Lopez checked the Napoletano and Acevedo homes in Moca, Puerto Rico, for any signs of Myra. While there, Lopez interviewed Myra's mother. Carmen Acevedo said Eric had tried repeatedly to cut off Myra from her family and had "threatened to kill her and the children on numerous occasions."

Characterizing Eric's behavior as "very weird and scared whenever he saw police officers," Carmen related that she had never liked her son-in-law because of his "bad manners and unstable personality." She said Myra had told her Eric threatened suicide, or feigned trying it, on at least two occasions—once by preparing to ingest a large quantity of pills, the other time by tying a belt around his neck. She said Myra would have left Eric years earlier except "in a strange way, she really loved him."

Carmen then let loose a bombshell: Shortly before Eric and Myra married, Eric had been driving them along Claremont Parkway in the Bronx, when his Mitsubishi hit a black man crossing the street. Carmen said she was concerned the man had been gravely injured and pleaded with Eric to stop. But Eric kept going, assuring her and Myra that even though the impact had cracked his windshield, he had not hit the man that hard.

When Carmen's comments were relayed to Donato, he added the incident to his ever-growing list of things to track down.

Just as Eric had feared, Donato and Burke interviewed Jennifer Meade. They wanted to ascertain if she knew anything material, but more important, they needed to warn her about the danger she was courting if her romance with Eric continued to develop.

In fact, Jennifer had an important story to tell: On the very morning after Myra's disappearance, she had found the usually energetic Eric asleep in his Toyota near the training academy. After she woke him, Eric had announced he had "two pieces of good news," one, Myra was gone; two, he had the kids "and she ain't gonna get them back."

Donato wanted Jennifer to know that Eric had lied to her about his living arrangements with his wife. Jennifer did not appear to be that surprised. She acknowledged that Eric had originally lied to her about being married.

To prove to Jennifer that her life was in danger, the two detectives told her about the Coludro and Matos investigations. "Whenever he gets rejected, that's when you are in jeopardy," Burke warned. Donato observed that she was traveling a path that had triggered Eric's violence in the past: She had discussed breaking up with Eric, and she had been given advice by her mother to stay away from him.

As the interview ended, Jennifer promised to take the

warning to heart. Within days, however, she would be back
in bed with Eric, a decision that would inevitably lead her to
tell him about her visit with the detectives.

That news made Eric very edgy. He demanded to know
what the cops had asked and how she had replied. He was
most bothered by her recollection regarding the number of
times they had had sex with the kids in the car.

"It was only one time!" Eric insisted, observing that he
did not want the car sex to be used against him by his father-
in-law in any custody fight.

"Okay, Eric," she said, trying to calm him down. "It was
one time, then."

Taking the offensive to protect his flank, Eric made Jennifer
promise she would never talk to the police again. He assured
her he had already told investigators everything he knew.

Her skepticism growing, Jennifer asked Eric if Myra had
been living in New Jersey *with him*. But he was resolute in
his denial, mimicking the excuses he had given years earlier
in the Coludro and Matos slayings. He said the cops were
manufacturing stories to make him look bad; they were out
to get him. "It's because Myra is missing. They don't have a
body, but they have to have a case. They have to have somebody to pin it on."

He insisted that he lived in New York with his mother. To
convince her, he went to his wallet and pulled out an identification card for an auto club. The card bore his name and
his mother's address, as if that proved where he actually
lived.

Counterattacking, Eric called Clifton headquarters the following day. Steering clear of Donato, he angrily informed
Lieutenant Burke that Jennifer had told him about her interview. Therefore, she would no longer speak with anyone
from the Clifton police. Eric said he was most upset that
Donato had told Jennifer about Marilyn Coludro, Wanda
Matos, and Gladys Matos. He accused the investigators of
talking behind his back. Burke explained that since he was
not helping to find Myra, the police had to talk to whomever
else they thought might be helpful.

"I *can't* talk to you!" Eric shouted back, reciting the
advice he had received from his attorney.

As Donato's understanding of the Napoletano inner circle
became more clear, the detective found himself learning

more about the earlier homicides. He kept running into the same people and the same troubling patterns of behavior.

"It's been his attitude about all three of them, that you're out to get him," said Marilyn Knoepfler, Uncle Al's half sister. She recalled how obsessed Eric had been with winning back Marilyn Coludro. She said Al told her several years later that the girl had been found dead in Pennsylvania, and that police had questioned him about a rope possibly used in the killing. "Al made it seem like he was more of a suspect than Eric."

Donato asked Knoepfler what she thought had become of Myra. "Eric," she replied without hesitation. Did she think Al knew any of the details? She said Al probably knew, but would keep the information to himself. "I think he would go that far for Eric."

And how far would her husband, Larry, go for Eric? "See, we talked on the way here. Larry said, 'Don't say too much.' We almost argued about it." With that, she acknowledged that Eric and her husband were quite close. "He seemed to like Larry. He looked up to Larry. Larry always had an answer for him." In fact, Eric had worked with Larry years earlier, a connection that would later figure in the developing police investigation.

More and more, Larry Knoepfler caught Donato's attention. He presented himself as forthcoming, cooperative, and suspicious of Eric, but he was less than frank while answering key questions. Donato concluded that the man knew much more than he was saying, certainly about the Marilyn Coludro homicide.

Larry described Eric as "a snot nose, arrogant, and hotheaded." He said Eric and Al argued frequently, and that Eric had joined the Marines "just to get away. He said the world hated him. He was real cocky." He said Eric enjoyed being a member of the NYPD auxiliary force because "he liked to crack heads. He would go out looking for trouble."

The anecdotal information was moderately useful, but Donato was more interested in Larry and his relationship with Eric and Al. His motor-vehicle record was a mile long, he was a nonstop insurance claim, and he had quite a checkered work record.

Over the years, as a butcher, Larry had worked at a slaughterhouse in Bucks County, Pennsylvania, and a butcher shop in Elizabeth, New Jersey. Eric had done some work for him. After working as a wholesale butcher selling to restaurants, Larry said he was "out of work for a while" after an auto accident in 1978. Of another job, he said, "I was a manager, but there was some stealing and talk of thirty thousand dollars being short." He said he was "out of work for a while" after an auto accident in the fall of 1982. Larry said Al's boss eventually got him a job importing toys, working out of his house. He said he also "worked for Tops Market in Buffalo, but was accused of selling bad meat." Then he had traveled the Northeast selling hams for Ricco's Meat Packing, and worked at Marathon House of Weenies in Rutherford, New Jersey.

In about 1985, Larry said, he began working in export packing with his cousin. He said they had a warehouse in Jersey City and had packed ninety tons of materials for Georgia-Pacific. Although Marilyn Knoepfler had mentioned that her husband had worked at a Georgia-Pacific facility in Belvidere, New Jersey, on the banks of the Delaware River, Larry avoided mentioning that specific location.

Donato was bothered about the secrecy regarding the obvious potential link to Marilyn Coludro's murder. But when he asked Larry point-blank about the job, he got defensive: "That was in 1985," Larry said, now quite positive about the year, meaning after the Coludro homicide.

In fact, the Georgia-Pacific plant was not simply in the general geographical area of where Marilyn's body had been discovered. With back roads taken into account, the proximity was startling, difficult to accept as a coincidence. Exiting to the right from the Georgia-Pacific driveway, the road led immediately to a small, narrow bridge across the Delaware River into Pennsylvania. If one took the right turn several miles down the road, traveled through farmland for several minutes, and made a right turn onto Route 611, the overlook where Marilyn Coludro's body had been dumped beckoned just ahead on the right. The trip could be completed in less than fifteen minutes.

The killer and any confederates had most likely exited Route 80 on the New Jersey side, then used the rural roads to cross the Delaware and get to the dump site. But Larry Knoepfler—or his wife, for that matter—never mentioned any of that.

* * *

In between everything else, Donato still needed to track down Myra's dental records. On the afternoon of July 12, 1990, just hours after Burke's phone conversation with Carolyn Napoletano, Donato received a call from Jim Leidy of NYPD's Missing Persons Bureau. Leidy had come across a Teletype from New Castle County, Delaware, about a homicide victim whose physical attributes matched Myra's. Donato located the computer transmission in the Clifton files, read it, and grabbed the phone.

Reaching Detective Ruth in Delaware, Donato explained his missing-persons investigation. He described Myra while Ruth described his decomposed "Jane Doe." The physical descriptions were uncannily alike, but one critical factor did not fit: the relatively brief passage of time since Myra's disappearance. Although Dr. Callery had been unable to provide a good estimate of when the Labrador Lane victim had been killed, it seemed unlikely that so much decomposition had occurred in less than a month.

Ruth cautioned Donato against getting hemmed in by the estimate. The body had been exposed to the elements. There had been some very hot, sunny days. Maybe the corpse had decomposed faster than expected. Ruth said they had to compare Myra's dental X rays with those from the Labrador Lane corpse.

Donato agreed, then explained that he unfortunately had not yet located Myra's records. He had been trying, but the task had proved to be difficult because of Myra's transient use of subsidized health care for herself and her children. Even though the Delaware corpse did not look to be a promising possibility, Donato told Ruth he would get back to him as soon as possible.

The task of finding the dental records became more imperative with the discovery of a second possible match— a corpse found by several youngsters along Interstate Route 80 in western Pennsylvania, about four hours from the Delaware Water Gap.

With Miriam Colon to guide them, Donato and Burke stopped at several dental clinics in the Bronx, without success. Myra's brother-in-law from Pennsylvania, Sammy Mendez, volunteered to check out several other possibilities. He hit pay dirt the next day, July 25, 1990.

Armed with a subpoena, Donato and Burke obtained Myra's charts at the North Concourse Dental Group on bustling Grand Concourse in the Bronx. Myra had been treated at the facility on December 5, 1989, just six months before she disappeared.

The following morning, Burke contacted the Pennsylvania State Police, but the charts did not match. He then called Detective Ruth in Delaware. Despite the original questions regarding the extent of decomposition, the records appeared to match. But Burke and Ruth could only make cursory comparisons. The situation called for expert analysis.

Burke called Donato at home. They had both planned finally to begin family vacations the following day. Instead, they made plans to drive to Delaware.

County Investigator Pete Talarico met the detectives shortly before seven. Arriving in New Castle County, they were escorted by Ruth and one of his colleagues, Detective Al Senior, to the Labrador Lane grave site, then to a meeting with the Delaware forensic pathology team: Dr. Hameli, the chief medical examiner; Dr. Callery, who had performed the autopsy; and Dr. Martin W. Scanlon, a consulting dentist.

Dr. Hameli, who had been a U.S. Justice Department consultant for the 1986 investigation to identify Dr. Josef Mengele's body in Brazil, said that Myra's dental X rays were a perfect match with the X rays of the Labrador Lane victim. The fillings on four teeth were identical; both X rays showed an open bite; X rays of the roots of Teeth 14 and 15 could be superimposed identically. The Delaware cadaver was Myra Acevedo Napoletano.

Myra's body had been dumped close to the New Jersey border, a two-and-a-half-hour drive from Clifton, a distance that mirrored the discovery six years earlier of Marilyn Coludro's body a two-and-a-half-hour ride from Manhattan. And just as there was a link between the Napoletano inner circle and the Pennsylvania dump site, there was an important connection to Myra's burial site in remote Bear, Delaware. Two years before her murder—on July 15, 1988—Eric, Uncle Al, and Carolyn had traveled together to the Wrangle Hill Auto Auction on Route 72 in the very same rural community of Bear. There, just minutes from Myra's eventual burial site, Al Jiovine had purchased a diesel-powered Cutlass Ciera.

The auction sale would remain unknown to Donato, Ruth, and other investigators because Al Jiovine had purchased the car from a resident of Lancaster, Pennsylvania. The auction handled the deal but never owned the car on Delaware motor-vehicle records.

Once again, Eric had known exactly where he was going.

Donato had mixed emotions. He was sad to learn that Myra was dead, but relieved that the mystery of her disappearance had been solved. He certainly was not shocked that Myra had been murdered. But on a personal level, he still hurt. And telling the Acevedos would be especially difficult. The detective had grown close to Myra's relatives.

Summoned to Clifton headquarters, Pablo, Miriam, and cousin Martha Morales had come to hear the worst. Still, learning about the murder of a loved one is never easy, regardless of mental preparation. The family members took the news hard. It was a heartbreaking scene.

Officials from the Delaware Attorney General's Office and Ruth's supervisors made it clear they were prepared to assert jurisdiction unless it could be proved that the murder had occurred in New Jersey. Technically, Donato's missing-persons case was now Detective Ruth's homicide investigation. But with the blessing of Clifton Police Chief Frank J. LoGioco, Donato was allowed to continue his full-time pursuit of the Napoletanos. There was no telling where jurisdiction would ultimately end up.

Donato and Ruth essentially became partners, assisted by colleagues from both departments.

Wanting more from Jennifer Meade, Donato and Ruth drove out to her home in Brooklyn that Saturday morning, July 28, 1990. For the time being, Ruth did not tell Jennifer where he was from. Donato simply introduced him as "Detective Ruth." As they exited the Holland Tunnel and headed through the New Jersey Meadowlands toward Clifton, Ruth asked the woman if any of the scenery looked familiar. At first she was not sure, but as they reached the Howard Johnson at the Clifton border, Jennifer announced, "Now I know where I am! We came here for the newspaper. He came to see what you all are saying about him."

Jennifer related how Eric had been driving out to the HoJo to purchase two major northern New Jersey newspapers routinely for the past several weeks, beginning within a day or so of Myra's unidentified body being found in Delaware. But, she continued, the trip out the night before had been more frantic than usual.

They had dropped the kids off at Carolyn's so they could drive to City Island for a seafood dinner. But when Eric returned to the car, he was in an uproar about some story that Uncle Al's mother had supposedly read in the morning paper about him. He asked Jennifer if she minded a change in the itinerary, and they headed to Route 3 in Clifton first. As always, there was no such story in the newspaper, but after speaking with his mother, Eric acted as if he knew there were major developments unfolding in Myra's case, and that an outbreak of publicity was inevitable.

Arriving at Clifton headquarters, Ruth asked Jennifer what it would take to convince her that Eric had been involved with Myra's disappearance.

"If you told me she was dead," she replied.

Ruth took a deep breath and leaned forward. "Guess what? Myra's dead."

The detective explained that he was from the state of Delaware and was investigating Myra's murder because her body had been found in his jurisdiction.

Jennifer gave the impression she was convinced of Eric's guilt, and wanted to be helpful. But she was unable to keep many of the important details in sequence, and had several key dates wrong.

Still, the interview with Jennifer was quite helpful. She told of Eric's threat to move back to Puerto Rico because the police were "following me around, tapping my phones, and talking bad about me to my captains and lieutenants on the job."

She also wrote a two-page memo for the detectives that she titled "Reasons I Feel Eric Did Something to Myra." Among her observations: The first time Eric told her about Myra being gone, "he was real positive she wasn't coming back"; he almost always called Myra "what's-her-name"; he said he was not looking for Myra; and whenever she told Eric she thought he was responsible for Myra's disappearance, he laughed and said he hadn't done anything to harm her. She said Eric also told her that he hoped Myra was all right wherever she was because he would "really be hurt if the police ever found her body somewhere dead."

Finally, Jennifer got the message. She was done with Eric. She would be safe from him, however. Unlike the women before her, she had never allowed him to become too emotionally attached. Besides, Eric had already set his sights elsewhere.

All that Saturday, Eric and Carolyn were incommunicado, failing to return a message Donato had left on Carolyn's answering machine. As the afternoon faded, Ruth called the Manhattan apartment, but also got the machine. A short time later, though, Carolyn called back.

Ruth identified himself as a detective from New Castle County, Delaware, and informed her that he had important information to pass on to her son.

Carolyn defiantly declined to put Eric on the phone. She also rejected Ruth's request that Eric personally come to Clifton police headquarters for an interview. It sounded as if Eric and Carolyn did not want to be told what they already knew.

Later that day, a strategy session was convened at Clifton headquarters with numerous law-enforcement and criminal justice officials from New Jersey and Delaware. At Donato's invitation, Detective Fazzini came over from the Bronx.

Assisted by their respective prosecutors—Assistant Attorney General Kathy Jennings from Delaware and Senior Assistant Prosecutor William J. Purdy, Jr., representing Passaic County, the court jurisdiction for Clifton—Ruth and Donato drafted search-warrant applications for the Napoletano apartment and Eric's Toyota. Purdy set out to find a judge to sign the paperwork.

It was nearly eight o'clock when Purdy, who would ultimately play a pivotal role in court proceedings, finally led everyone to the vacated Napoletano apartment. Corporal Ronald M. Webb of the New Castle County Evidence Detection Unit began a meticulous search for forensic evidence. He noticed suspicious stains in the master bedroom floorboards, extracted two samples, and also took a swab of a stain on the master bedroom closet door. Detecting staples in the floor around the perimeter of the master bedroom, Webb guessed that a carpet had previously been attached to the flooring. He extracted hair and fibers from the staples, and took a sample of a stain on the floor in the second bedroom.

Outdoors, on the north side of the apartment building, Webb found two bags of trash, including a shoe, a pillow and pillowcases, a white cloth, a piece of red rug, a purple piece of clothing, a black piece of clothing, and two wall calendars.

Theresa Maltese, the nosy downstairs neighbor, showed up to inform Donato that Al Jiovine and Carolyn Napoletano had been at the apartment that afternoon cleaning it out. Once again, the timing of the Napoletano inner circle was uncanny.

The Delaware team was determined to crack the case wide open by breaking Uncle Al Jiovine. While Carolyn and Eric stayed silent, Al returned a call from Donato and agreed to come in for an interview. Although Donato had previously spoken with Jiovine, this session would be the first in a series of long, agonizing tape-recorded interrogations by Ruth and Donato.

If Al knew Myra's body had been identified in Delaware, he was not letting on. Regardless, deception was his byword. He repeatedly lied and misled, or claimed not to hear the questions because of his hearing problems. If he felt trapped on one point, he dug himself a hole in another direction. Like Eric and Carolyn, he thought he was smart enough to outfox the lowly detectives.

After preliminary questions and misleading replies concerning how Al had met Eric, Ruth turned to the Coludro case. During a prior interview with Donato and Burke, Al had claimed not even to remember Marilyn's name, admitting only that he had met her once, while she was sitting in a car parked outside of his apartment building.

Al's memory was better for this interview, but he continued to insist that Eric had never had a girlfriend stay in the Queens apartment. After being pressed repeatedly on the issue, he conceded that one girlfriend had stayed at his place, but only for a single night.

Who was that? "Marilyn," he replied, suddenly remembering her name, or forgetting that he was not supposed to know it.

Pressed further, he also was able to remember that Marilyn was deceased. Did he know how she had died? "She was cut up." Recalling more with each question, he now remembered that the detectives who had questioned him in 1986 had shown him crime-scene photos of Marilyn's face.

It had been preposterous of him to claim so little knowledge about Marilyn Coludro. And when the detectives changed the subject to Wanda Matos, Al played just as dumb.

"I heard Eric had problems with another girlfriend at one time?" Ruth asked. Al's face was blank, so Donato stepped in. "Wanda!" He was angry because during the previous interview, Al had conceded only that "there may have been a Wanda" who lived with Eric for a month or two near the Bronx Zoo.

"Wanda? Yeah, he's married to her," Al replied. His tone was in the vein of "Oh, *that* Wanda."

Ruth wondered if Al was aware that something had happened to one of Wanda's relatives. Al said Wanda's mother "got killed, or she died, or something." Hadn't she been murdered? "That's what Eric and his mother told me," Al responded.

With dripping sarcasm Ruth asked Al how many people he knew who had been murdered, outside of the people Eric had brought into his life. Al replied that there was no one else. "So the odds of two people in Eric's little circle having gotten murdered, that could be by chance, right? A coincidence?"

Ruth was about to hit Al with the number three murder in Eric's little circle. "What if Myra was to be murdered? What would you start thinking then?"

"My God!" said Al.

Ruth raised his voice a bit. "Listen to me. I am not from New York City—"

"I'm very, I, I, I, I, I wouldn't know how to, how to answer that," said Al.

"Listen to me. I am not from New York City. I am not from New Jersey." ·

"Okay," said Al. "You said you're from an outside agency."

Ruth had Al take a guess. "Probably the Pennsylvania police department," Al replied rather curiously.

"No," said Detective Ruth. "I'm from the state of Delaware. Why do you think I would be up here?"

Uncle Al said he had no idea. Ruth was enjoying the cat-and-mouse game. "Why would I be here? All the way from Delaware?"

"I guess maybe to find out about, about My—about Myra and what-do-you-call-it, the other girl, Marilyn."

Ruth explained that he had no interest in the Coludro or Matos cases; he only cared about Myra. Backing off, he asked Al if he had ever been to Delaware. Al let out a weird "wheeesh," but did not answer the question directly. Instead, he said he had no friends there and could not remember ever doing business there. He also said he could not recall if he had ever taken Eric to Delaware.

Ruth decided to end the suspense, if there really was any. "Listen to me," he said, pausing for effect. "She's dead!"

"You're— She's—"

"I'm investigating a homicide!" Ruth said.

"She's not dead!" Al insisted. "I can't believe this." He presented himself as being frazzled, hand on forehead, stuttering, bald head lowered, no eye contact.

But quick as a fox, he somehow managed to collect himself enough to inquire, "What'd she die of?"

"She got murdered," Ruth replied. "Now it's three people in his circle. And you're right in his circle."

"How am I in his circle? How?" Al asked, indignant.

Ruth was well prepared for that one. He reached for a pile of toll records for the phone Eric had installed at the Clifton apartment in the name J. Napoli. The records, obtained several days earlier through a court order, showed a fourteen-minute call made to Al's apartment in Queens from the Clifton apartment at 2:44 A.M. on June 21, just hours after Myra was last seen. Given the length of the call, and the hour of its placement, the investigators surmised that if they learned the contents of that conversation, they might unlock the mystery of Myra's murder. In fact, though, the call would turn out to be one of the most troubling pieces of evidence in the case.

For the next half hour, and during the many hours of grilling to come, Al would repeatedly claim he could not remember the middle-of-the-night call. He did remember Eric calling at some point looking for a baby-sitter, and he recalled that his mother, Rose Dugan, had been unable to help because she was going in for eye surgery that day. But he insisted he could not specifically attach specific conversations to particular calls.

Ruth accused Al of "recall by convenience." But Al

insisted he was being honest. "I'm trying to remember and I can't."

Over and over, that was Al's answer: "I wish I could remember. I'd be more than happy to tell you. I don't. I don't. I don't recall. I really don't. I can't believe she's dead."

"She's not just dead," Ruth shouted at him. "She's been murdered. This girl has been murdered by someone in a cruel and vicious way."

Conveniently, there were some crime-scene photos on the table. "That's Myra," said Ruth.

"Where?" asked Al, unable to discern her decomposed shell.

"Right there," said Ruth, pointing to what remained of the corpse.

"Wow!" said Al.

Ruth pounded away at the link between Eric and the three murdered women: "How many people in one person's life can get murdered without people starting to believe that something's wrong with the one person who keeps bringing his folks into the circle? . . . He brings one girl into the circle and she gets murdered. Dumped in Pennsylvania. He brings another girl into the circle. You know that her mother gets murdered in New York. Another girl gets brought into the circle by him—and I'm not even saying he's doing them—I'm just saying he's the one who brings these folks into the circle, and now she's murdered down in Delaware."

Al said he was still blank on the phone call. "I'm being very honest with you; I don't remember."

Donato jumped in to inquire about Eric's fascination with law enforcement. Al recounted how Eric had become a "toy cop," passed all the examinations for NYPD, and had recently taken a job as a Brownie, "for security, for Myra, for him, for the kids." He said Eric wanted all the benefits of civil service—health insurance, pension, "the whole nine yards."

Donato agreed that Eric's reasons for obtaining the Brownie job sounded noble, taking care of his family that way. "So why is he listed as single, living at his mother's address, with his mother as the beneficiary for his insurance? And with no health insurance covering Myra or either child? And no mention of being married? And no mention of having two dependent children? Do you know why? Any idea why he would do that?"

"No," said Al. He tried to explain that he knew Eric had Blue Cross and Blue Shield coverage for the boys, but Donato did not want to hear it. Attacking as a tag team now, Ruth accused Al of being disinterested in the news that Myra was dead.

Al protested, but to no avail. "I mean, I, I, I, I can't believe that this girl, I, I don't know. It's just, she, she was too nice, I mean I, I can't explain myself. When, you know, something that's been so sweet and so nice and you can't, you can't visualize things like this, you can't."

Donato shifted the questioning to Myra's disappearance. In Al's latest version, Eric never had any intention of trying to get Myra to join the rest of the family for dinner that night. He said Eric and the boys had gone to New York to visit Carolyn so Myra could have some time to herself after a domestic disagreement.

But that version made no sense. If they weren't planning on taking Myra out to dinner, why would they have come back to Clifton at eight? They would have just stayed in New York.

Taking a new tack, the detectives switched their focus to Al's personal life. He was living these days with an eighteen-year-old Latino named Greg Velez. The young man would later say he had met Al at Tricks, a gay bar in Manhattan, and that Al had paid him $50 for regular fellatio sessions until he moved into the Queens apartment. Al had told relatives Greg was the younger brother of his girlfriend, a woman named Theresa from Virginia Beach. However, when Al's sister, Marilyn Knoepfler, asked Greg about the woman, he told her he did not even know anyone by that name.

Donato asked Al if he was involved in a personal relationship with Velez. "No. None whatsoever," he said.

"Any homosexuality between you and Greg?"

"None whatsoever," he lied.

Asked how they had met, Al lied again, claiming they had met at the Golden Cue pool hall on Queens Boulevard.

Al did not like the direction the interview was taking, and said he had to leave. But the detectives kept him talking. Purposely switching gears again, Donato inquired about Carolyn's relationship with Myra. "She loved Marilyn—I mean, Myra," said Al. "Very much so."

What did Carolyn think of Latinos? Al sought to defuse the issue, explaining that Eric's mother was "an Archie Bunker sort of person. She's got name-calling for everybody, you know."

And how did Eric feel about Latinos? Al said Eric loved them.

As the interview began to wind down, Ruth wondered if Al had any idea who could have killed Myra, or at least where they should look for clues. Al said he had nothing to offer.

Donato suggested that there was one name that kept popping up in the middle of all the homicide investigations. "Eric. I guess. That's, that's what you're saying," said Al.

"We're asking," said Donato. "You know Eric the best."

Both detectives said they had asked Eric to come to Clifton out of respect; they wanted to tell him about Myra in person, not over the phone to his mother. "We don't want to question him. All we want to do is inform him that his wife is dead," said Donato.

"I can't talk to the man," said Al. "I, I, I, I, I told him, I said, 'Well, why don't you go down there?' He said, 'I don't have to go down there.' So that's the way I leave it. I don't want to get into an argument, because if I get in an argument with him, I just lose my temper. And I, I, I just take off. I'll yell at him and scream at him. I'll call him names."

Al made it sound as if all the pressure was being put on him. He resented having to take the heat for Eric. Why didn't they force Eric to come down to headquarters? "I don't understand this justice system," Al said. "I don't think it's fair. And that's the way I feel."

"Okay. Good," said Ruth contemptuously. "I'm glad you feel that way."

The interview had run a tortuous course. Ruth left the room in disgust, but Al stayed in his chair. Donato reached for a binder of crime-scene photos and selected a particularly gruesome one of Myra's body. "Here! Live with that."

Al gasped, but still made no move to reveal his secrets.

"You can leave now. We're done," said Donato in contempt.

Al got up and departed. As soon as he could, he called Carolyn's apartment to tell her and Eric everything he had discussed with Ruth and Donato, including the official news that Myra's body had been identified down in Delaware.

Duplicitous as ever, a sobbing Carolyn would call Myra's half sister, Miriam, ten hours later—claiming she had just learned of Myra's death. She would quickly reveal the real purpose of her call, though, as she peppered Miriam with questions about the police investigation. But Miriam was not about to play the Napoletano game anymore. She curtly informed Carolyn she had nothing to say, then hung up.

Four days after Myra's body was identified, the news hit front pages in northern New Jersey. The first story, in *The North Jersey Herald & News*, included details about Pennsylvania's investigation of Marilyn Coludro's murder. Marilyn's mother, Marta Rivera, provided emotional quotes from the perspective of a victim's family, a role she would fill for the media countless times as the drama unfolded. She provided details of Eric's abuse from her daughter's diaries, and told how Marilyn had been two months' pregnant at the time of her murder.

That evening the two major Spanish-language television stations in the New York region, Univision-owned Channel 41 and Telemundo-owned Channel 47, presented comprehensive reports. The following morning, *The Record*, another major New Jersey newspaper, published an enterprising story linking Eric to the Matos murder, too. Marta Rivera again was quoted, revealing that Marilyn had been hospitalized for schizophrenia and had clung to Eric. "They tell me they don't have enough evidence. How much more evidence do they need? I only want to see justice done. I want him nailed."

The newspaper had learned of the Matos murder from Marta Rivera. "New York City police said they were not able to confirm the report Tuesday, nor provide any details," the story said.

The next series of developments in the investigation would draw more attention to NYPD, through a combination of Carolyn's employment and her obsession with the Mafia—a dangerous intermingling that would raise the possibility that she had been passing along confidential information from the Organized Crime Control Bureau to John Gotti's associates.

The events began to unfold as Donato and Burke headed off for vacations with their families. Burke would resume his administrative duties upon his return. Ruth returned home briefly to consult with his superiors, then returned to New York City, with colleague Sergeant James Hedrick and Delaware Deputy Attorney General Ferris Wharton. At the Manhattan DA's office, they met with prosecutors and Detective Fazzini. Together, they prepared search warrants for Carolyn's residence and the Toyota. The warrant issued in New Jersey for the car was not operative in New York.

In a supporting affidavit, Fazzini stated that as the detective assigned to the Gladys Matos homicide he felt there was probable cause to believe that Eric had killed his mother-in-law. He summarized his investigation, unveiling several incriminating facts for the public record, among them Eric's warning to Wanda that "she could end up like his former girlfriend, Marilyn." This comment was especially incriminating because Eric would have made the remark in early 1985, more than a year before the corpse in Pennsylvania was identified as Marilyn Coludro.

Detective Ruth implied several times in his accompanying affidavit that he believed Myra was already dead by the time Eric, his mother, and the two boys departed the Clifton apartment for dinner the evening of Myra's disappearance. He pointed out that Miriam Colon had said she tried unsuccessfully to reach Myra on the phone at the Clifton apartment that evening. He also noted that a round-trip drive between Clifton, New Jersey, and Bear, Delaware, took approximately four hours, the length of time being significant because records for Eric's home phone showed the absence of any calls between 6:49 P.M. on June 20 and 2:44 A.M. the next morning, a span of eight hours. There had been plenty of time between calls to pack up the body, drive to Delaware, bury the corpse, and return in time to call Uncle Al for a baby-sitter.

The search-warrant paperwork was completed the afternoon of August 1, 1990, and promptly signed by a judge in Manhattan. At 7:25 P.M., the search was executed by NYPD. Later, everyone returned with Fazzini to the Forty-third Precinct, where any evidence pertinent to the Delaware matter—such as the title to the Toyota and a spare set of keys—was turned over to Hedrick and Ruth.

The most startling discovery, however, pertained to Carolyn's job at NYPD. While Fazzini's post-raid invoice would simply list the recovery of "one manila envelope," he, in fact, had found portions of a personnel file belonging to an undercover cop assigned to Carolyn's Organized Crime office.

In the ensuing weeks, the seized documents would alternately be described as important or insignificant. In the version that swept through the New Jersey law-enforcement community, the data found in Carolyn's possession contained the true identity and other sensitive, personal information about a cop then working undercover, possibly on an important Mafia investigation. Discovery of the document in Carolyn's possession prompted allegations that she had been selling the true identities of cops who had infiltrated organized-crime families. Over time, the story grew even larger: The Napoletanos were agents of the Mafia, and when Eric learned he had no chance of becoming a New York City cop, he had shifted career goals toward becoming a mob hit man. Of course, mother's and son's obsessions with the Mafia did not help dispel that line of thinking: Carolyn's attendance at Gotti's criminal trial, Eric's attendance at Gotti's block parties, and Eric's braggadocio about supposedly knowing made members of the mob. At a minimum, the Napoletanos were Mafia groupies.

Carolyn tried to downplay the importance of the seized material, contending that it was simply a "Ten Card," an index card containing personnel data on individual NYPD employees. At one point she claimed, "All I did was make a photostat so that I would know what went in ink, what got typed, what you erase out, and what you change. It was really just part of my notes." At another point she offered, "Our desks don't lock and I brought all my notes home. It was just part of my notes." At still another point she said she had selected the single, specific Ten Card at random to use as a guide for working on other Ten Cards.

When her explanations were met with skepticism, she tried another approach. "It was a planted copy. Not planted like you're thinking. It was in with all my notes and Fazzini took it out of the notes and said he found it in another room. That was not so. I call it planted."

While claiming innocent motives, Carolyn still could not help but brag about her unfettered access to sensitive material: "I was told when I came there, 'If you hear something on John Gotti, you don't ask any questions. Whatever you see, whatever you hear, you do not discuss.' That was my job. I have seen a hell of a lot, and I have heard a lot."

She explained that she dealt with an undercover's "name," fake license-plate number, driver's license, change of address, change of phone number, and photos with and without beards. "It was my job in the chief's office to work with confidential information on cops," she boasted. "I dealt with personnel records, with cops' folders. I can go into my folder; I've gone in it. I handled all that information. This was everybody in Organized Crime, all the undercovers."

In the end, Carolyn was unable to justify her behavior other than to contend that she was so dedicated to her job that she had taken work home with her. Worse, she again blamed everything on Fazzini. "I know a lot about cops now to know that when they have nothing, they will make a big thing out of nothing. That's what they do," she said. "I laughed when I heard they said I was selling information to the Gottis. Anything that the police or FBI say about me selling inside information to the mob is just utterly ridiculous."

Absurdly, Carolyn thought her explanations were credible. She just could not understand why anyone would be upset that the senior police administrative aide to the chief of the New York City Police Department's Organized Crime Control Bureau had removed confidential files from One Police Plaza and brought them home—that home being the official residence of her son, the serial-killer suspect.

The hunt for Eric's burgundy Toyota Corolla had been far reaching but unsuccessful on both sides of the Hudson River. On the heels of the raid on Carolyn's apartment, a major effort was organized to find the vehicle the following evening, August 2, 1990.

Eric was working a one-to-nine shift directing traffic at 125th Street and Second Avenue in Harlem. After dismissal, he would head back to the Brownie office at Eleventh Avenue and Fiftieth Street. If he was still driving over to the HoJo in New Jersey to buy newspapers, he would lead the surveillance team to the Toyota.

With Donato still on vacation, Detective Joe Genchi and plainclothes Tactical Squad Officer Mike Vinciguerra were designated as the point men for the night's operation. The two headed for the Lincoln Tunnel in an undercover vehicle disguised as a New York Yellow Cab. In Manhattan, Genchi headed uptown, along the West Side, toward the Brownie office.

Vinciguerra would follow Eric on foot once he left the Brownie office, curiously running into an NYPD team working an undercover drug operation in the same area. Shortly before nine, Vinciguerra noticed a chunky, unusual-looking woman standing on the sidewalk in front of the Traffic Enforcement office. She was dressed in loose black clothing, with long, red hair practically covering her face. At first Vinciguerra thought she was "a bag lady" or "a witch," with her frizzy hair and macabre attire. Then Genchi noticed she had two small children standing with her.

"That's the mother!" he said. "And that's his kids!"

At about that time, Brownies started rolling into the area in groups of two or three. Dressed in their uniforms, they all looked alike. All of a sudden, the woman with the red hair started talking to a tall young male in street clothes. It was Eric. He had changed already.

For a few minutes, mother and son stood there talking, as if deciding what to do. All the while they kept glancing around, visually sweeping the area for any signs of police surveillance.

They began walking south, then stopped abruptly. Detecting no one following them, they began walking north.

Vinciguerra exited the car to follow on foot. But first he wanted to remove his gun. If he was going to follow closely, he did not want the bulge of a weapon to give him away. He began walking uptown, on the east side of Eleventh. Eric, Carolyn, and the boys paralleled his steps on the west side of the busy two-way street. Block after block, Eric and his mother stopped to check whether anyone was on their tail.

Finally, the Napoletanos made a quick left, into the entrance of a parking lot, near a group of homeless people. As Vinciguerra watched from across the street, the Toyota exited onto Eleventh, with Eric behind the wheel and Carolyn riding shotgun. The car headed south, toward the tunnel.

Genchi pulled up in the "cab," Vinciguerra got in, and they began careful pursuit along with the other nearby units in the stakeout. Despite the fact that it was nearly ten, the tunnel's intake traffic was still bumper to bumper, making surveillance a snap.

The twenty-minute drive past Giants Stadium and toward Clifton was uneventful. But suddenly, just over the Passaic River Bridge on Route 3, Eric hit the brakes.

Vinciguerra radioed to the first backup car, with Tactical

Squad members Al Franco and Michael L. McLaughlin, while Genchi pulled over toward the upcoming exit, Main Avenue, as if he were going to leave the highway.

Once the Toyota passed out of sight, over a high point in the roadway, Genchi got back on the highway proper and gave chase. By this point the Toyota had passed across the Nutley border into Clifton. The HoJo loomed ahead, the perfect place to seize the car.

But when Franco and McLaughlin sped over the rise, they did not see the Toyota. Franco radioed to the others while he and McLaughlin passed the HoJo lot and the next exit, Bloomfield Avenue. The Toyota was nowhere on the highway.

Genchi was just a few seconds from the Bloomfield Avenue exit, so he yanked the car over to the ramp. There, at the bottom, was the Toyota, stopped in traffic. Eric was headed left, under the overpass, so he could get back on the highway toward Manhattan.

Genchi pulled in behind Eric while Tactical Squad Officer Ralph Pennella, in a second unit, pulled in front. Eric was boxed in.

"Let's go, get out!" Vinciguerra shouted at Eric as the officers converged. "Get out of the car."

Eric was cocky, laughing. He was wearing an NYPD baseball cap, which increased tensions since everyone had heard about the undercover cop's file being found at Carolyn's the night before, listing his home address and the locations of his kids' schools.

"What are you doing?" Eric protested. "You're harassing me! Look, Mommy, see what I mean? They'll never leave me alone."

"Get out of the car!" Vinciguerra commanded. "Shut the car off!" He grabbed Eric's arms as he tried to reach underneath the dashboard. Vinciguerra was concerned Eric might have a gun. "Get out of the car. Put your hands on the trunk."

Eric wanted to know if he was being arrested. "No, we just want the car," he was told.

Eric Junior and Angelo were crying. Carolyn and Eric were shouting and screaming, which only seemed to upset the youngsters more. Finally, Carolyn took them across the street.

Vinciguerra again ordered Eric to lean against the trunk,

but Eric was a smart-ass. He knew what would irritate the police. Every time the officer went to frisk Eric's ankles, he turned as if preparing to make a run for it.

"Turn around!" Vinciguerra commanded.

"Oh, what the fuck is this!" Eric whined. He was really trying to push the wrong buttons. "Look, Ma. They're gonna beat me up."

"Stay there!" said Vinciguerra, at last beginning to frisk his way up Eric's leg toward the knee.

"Hey! Don't be touching my dick, man," Eric complained.

"You'd really enjoy that, wouldn't you?" Vinciguerra snapped back in anger. "I heard you like things like that."

Eric began shouting across the road to his mother. "Carol, he's grabbing my dick! He's grabbing my dick!"

"Leave him alone! Leave him alone!" Carolyn shouted. "Don't hit him."

After much ado, Vinciguerra completed the pat-down; Eric was not carrying a weapon. The officer turned to Pete Talarico, the prosecutor's investigator, who had arrived from a backup stakeout at Carolyn's apartment. "This fucker said I touched his dick. I had my hand down by his knee."

"You might have," laughed Talarico, armed with knowledge garnered from having watched a homemade porno flick of Eric and Myra seized at the Clifton apartment. "He's got some root."

It soon became clear what Eric had been fiddling with under the dashboard just before he got out of the car; he had connected the car alarm, and now it kept going on. Eric and Carolyn laughed heartily as the cops tried in vain to disconnect the device.

"You ain't gonna find nothing in this car!" Eric said. "You ain't gonna find shit!" The trunk did look immaculately clean.

Waiting for the vehicle to be removed from the scene, Eric and Carolyn kept up their tirade, especially Carolyn. "The kids are cold. It's late. They gotta get to bed. I'm gonna write somebody about this!"

"Fine. Write the governor if you want," one of the cops answered back.

"Where's that fuck Donato?" Eric asked. "That fuck won't leave me alone. I knew Donato wouldn't give up." Eric appeared disappointed at being unable to confront his new perceived tormentor, so he screamed across the street at his mother: "I told you! It's that fuck Donato, 'The Little Shit.' I told you, Ma, they're just gonna harass me. They got no reason. What's with this little town? You're making a big fucking deal over nothing. A little asshole town like this, fucking with me? You think you got something big here? It's nothing."

Eric had it backward. The Clifton police did not have 2,000 other murders to solve like their counterparts in New York City. A case like Myra Napoletano's *was* top priority.

Across the street, Carolyn continued to rant and rave, complaining the most when she was prevented from removing the kids' toys and Angelo's diapers from the car. This was a court-authorized search; she wasn't going to be allowed to remove anything. Besides, after all the guff she and Eric had given the Clifton cops, none of them was about to cut them any slack.

"Stop harassing my boy!" said Carolyn in her screechy voice.

"My kids are tired," added Eric. The moaning was unrelenting, as if creating chaos was their intention. The more Carolyn and Eric railed, the more Angelo and Eric Junior cried.

"Well then, go," one of the cops told them. "We're taking the car. You can leave."

Without skipping a beat, Carolyn demanded a ride. She said it was the least the cops could do for inconveniencing them.

"Get a taxi!" said Talarico.

As a courtesy, Officer McLaughlin was instructed to drive the family to the public phones in front of the Styertowne Shopping Center, just a short walk away. But Eric would not use those phones. Paranoid that the cops had somehow directed him to a bugged line, he marched his group to a pay phone outside a gasoline station across the street.

A short while later, everyone returned to the shopping center, where Eric paced back and forth until 11:20, when a taxi arrived. But the fare was too expensive for Carolyn's taste, so the driver left. Mother and son were livid. How dare the cops treat them this way?

Putting their heads together, they devised a two-pronged strategy. They needed a ride back to Manhattan; they also needed to address their growing public-relations problem.

They placed a call to Don Corbett, a reporter who had left his *Herald & News* business card under Carolyn's door earlier in the week.

The Napoletanos agreed to give Corbett an exclusive interview to express outrage over the way the police had left them stranded. They figured correctly that in return Corbett would give them a ride back into Manhattan. But first Thomas Franklin, a *Herald & News* photographer, arrived—at 12:30 A.M.—to snap poignant poses of Eric and Carolyn holding the groggy children, Eric still proudly wearing his NYPD cap.

For the interview, Carolyn complained that her home had been raided the night before. Of course, she made no mention of the fact that confidential NYPD documents had been confiscated.

For his part, Eric denied involvement in any of the three murders, and charged that the police were trying to frame him. "They only want to prove my guilt and not my innocence," he protested. "You can bet my word they're not going to find anything—because I didn't do anything. Why—if I did all these bad things—why am I not in jail?"

Everyone in law enforcement agreed: It was a damn good question.

– 19 –

The gathering of additional physical evidence and statements would continue through the latter half of 1990, but nothing approaching a smoking gun would ever be found. One key link was discovered, though, when Donato returned from his vacation. He drove over to the Napoletano apartment in Clifton for another look with Ruth and Detective Al Senior, also from Delaware. Outside, they noticed a large folded cardboard box lying adjacent to the trash cans. Inside the box, which bore labeling from a Toyota parts warehouse and the name Napoletano, they found a rolled-up sock and several hairs. The investigators seized the box and its contents.

Meanwhile, members of the Delaware evidence detection team seized considerable forensic evidence from the Toyota. Its dirt-laden mud flaps were removed for analysis. Numerous stains were noticed, so the trunk lining was sprayed with Luminol, a chemical reagent that can be useful in the detection of dried blood. The visible stains did not react, but several positive reactions were obtained in locations where stains were not readily discernible: on two areas of the trunk floor liner, on the right sidewall liner, and on the tire jack. In addition, positive reactions were obtained from the left rear seatback and on a child's white sock found on the rear seat. The carpet in the trunk area was then vacuumed, yielding numerous hairs and red fibers.

The materials removed from the car, as well as the cardboard box and its contents, were forwarded to the FBI lab, which was already analyzing evidence seized at the Labrador Lane grave site.

Having given it some thought, Theresa Maltese, Myra's downstairs neighbor, now recalled that Carolyn Napoletano had gone out of her way to engage her in chitchat outside the apartment building the night of Myra's disappearance. This observation raised the possibility that Carolyn had deliberately tried to keep Maltese occupied while Eric kept himself busy inside with more violent activities. In fact, Maltese now said, when Eric finally did exit the building, "He looked like he had murder in his eyes. He looked like a crazy man."

For the first time Maltese also provided troublesome details about a conversation she'd had with Carolyn at the Clifton apartment the evening after Myra's disappearance. She said Carolyn had told her that she and Eric had left Myra curbside the night before, waiting "for her boyfriend, with two big tote bags" on her shoulders.

Jeanette Konuklu, Myra's friend from next door, said she had new information to offer, too. She said she had seen burn marks on Myra's arms that looked like a cigarette had been pressed into the flesh. On other occasions Myra had displayed bruises on her legs, shoulders, and spine. Her jaw was injured so severely one time that she could not close her mouth properly for several days.

Konuklu said Eric often publicly exhibited sexually gross behavior, grabbing Myra's breasts and putting his hands down her pants in front of his children and mother at a Chinese restaurant. Whenever Myra objected, Eric told her she was nothing but "a dumb Puerto Rican." On one occasion, she said, Eric had considered connecting his car battery to Myra's body to give her a charge. She recalled another occasion when Eric wanted sex so badly, he told Myra to give it to him right then and there. Konuklu said Eric invited her to stay and watch. "He was doing it before I walked out the door," she said, also recalling that Eric Junior and Angelo had run by while the sex was in progress.

Finally, Konuklu also recalled how Eric loved to watch violent porno movies of "men killing women, and making love to them before and after." He would laugh heartily as the women were tied up and tortured, screaming in pain. She said Myra was nauseated by the films, but her objections only turned Eric on more.

On another front, Donato spoke with Al's mother, Rose Dugan, who told him Carolyn had called her several times to warn her that she was talking to the police too much. She said Carolyn had instructed her to keep quiet: "Listen to me. I've been to college!"

After interviewing Myra's mother for key details, Fazzini succeeded in tracking down a 1985 police report that matched her recollection of the night Eric hit a pedestrian and fled the scene. It turned out that construction worker Wendell R. Owens of Queens Village had died after sustaining massive abrasions, fractures, broken ribs, and hemorrhages. Eric had been responsible for another senseless killing.

Unfortunately, nothing could be done because it appeared that New York authorities had screwed up that investigation, too. The Emergency Medical Services central dispatch was never notified the night of the accident, nor was a police unit requested to respond to conduct an investigation—normal procedure when a vehicular accident results in a fatality. NYPD was not informed of Owen's demise even after the autopsy report stated under cause of death: "Pending further study. Circumstances are undetermined and pending police investigation."

Concerned about the safety of Eric Junior and Angelo, Donato began calling numerous officials in the New York City social-services bureaucracy to inform them of his investigation. He figured any kind of pressure he could put on Eric might move his investigation forward. He also prodded welfare investigators into questioning Al Jiovine regarding welfare checks issued to clients using his Queens address. When asked about Myra's whereabouts by the welfare officials, Al slipped and said she had been "murdered in Clifton." At first, Donato thought the New York social-services people might actually remove Eric Junior and Angelo from their father's care. But as time wore on, it became clear that no one on that side of the Hudson was going to move an inch unless Eric was arrested.

Still seeking better inside information, the detectives set out for another round of interviews with Marilyn Knoepfler, Uncle Al Jiovine's half sister, and her husband, Larry.

Regarding the night of Myra's disappearance, Marilyn said Al had originally told her that Myra had taken the trip into Manhattan with Eric and the boys the night she disappeared. In this version, Myra disappeared when she left Carolyn's apartment to visit her sister in the Bronx. Also, Marilyn said she realized that the story about Myra's suitcases being missing was a lie when Al relayed word that Myra's luggage and clothing had been found. Asked about her husband's employment in western New Jersey, across the river from where Marilyn Coludro's body had been found, Marilyn conceded that Larry had failed to give her details about being questioned by the Pennsylvania State Police regarding the Coludro murder. "Larry tends to be very secretive," she said.

Detective Senior from Delaware interviewed Larry Knoepfler, who again professed a lack of knowledge regarding any crimes Eric may have committed, but who now recalled a great deal regarding Eric's love of weaponry, the Mafia, and violence. Larry told of an occasion when he took Eric to a shooting range to test his nine-millimeter Colt Commander and .44-Magnum Smith & Wesson. He figured the practice session had taken place between 1984 and 1986, the same time frame as the Gladys Matos murder. According to Larry, Eric felt it was essential for him to carry a gun or knife to "protect himself from spics and niggers." He said that over the years Eric had expressed interest in joining the Mafia and had felt that being a Brownie and an auxiliary were the next best things to becoming a cop. He said Eric always carried handcuffs, frequently flashed his NYPD auxiliary badge, and liked to roam Central Park in uniform even when off duty. "He told me he wanted to be a police officer because he wanted to break heads," Knoepfler said.

The Knoepfler interviews led Donato and Ruth back to Al Jiovine. They went at him for three hours this time. He criticized some of Eric's behavior, but continued to insist that there was no way he could have murdered anyone. At times, however, Al sounded as if he wanted his "son" to get caught, only not with his help. He said "foul-mouthed" Eric had warned him not to talk with police, but to hire a lawyer. "He told me, 'You're an asshole. You shouldn't go down there.' He keeps telling me that I shouldn't be talking to you people. His mother is the same way." Al said he did not understand the criminal justice system. "Why do they allow people to be quiet?"

The detectives remained interested in the 2:44 A.M. phone call, but they failed to get Al to admit that Myra was already dead by the time of the call and that Eric had called to ask for a baby-sitter. Al remembered being asked about baby-sitting, but said he could not remember the day of the call, or the sequence of events.

Ruth said he imagined that the first person a murderer called "would have to be someone awfully close. . . . He just got done killing his wife, and he called Al Jiovine! After he just finished killing his wife, murdering his wife, and driving her body, in the car you provided for him, to Delaware!" As always, Al insisted that he was drawing a blank.

"This vehicle was used in a homicide. Do you understand?" Ruth pressed. "The name on the title is Albert Jiovine." Ruth warned Al that the car was undergoing extensive testing in the hopes of proving that Myra's body had been transported in the trunk. "Should I look at you because it's your car?"

"No! Never!" Al replied. "You should know better than that."

Ruth tried another approach. Perhaps Eric had called crying at 2:44 to confess that he had killed Myra because he could not accept her plans to leave.

Al gave up nothing. "I'm telling you the real truth. I don't remember the time, that time. I don't remember anybody calling. I don't. There's no reason in the world that I'd hide anything from you, or the police department."

But Ruth kept at him. "Two-forty-four in the morning, on the morning that Myra was killed. Eric calls you. After he drives down to Delaware, in your car, and dumps his wife, covers her up with dirt, drives back to where he lives, and the first person he calls out of the chute is you!"

"I don't recall the call," Al persisted. "I don't remember, and that's the truth."

The investigation was at a crossroads. The game plan of breaking Al Jiovine was not working. The lab work would take months. No eyewitnesses had come forward. Donato felt the investigation was in danger of falling into the same morass as the Coludro and Matos probes—a situation that warranted the convening of a coordinated law-enforcement strategy session.

As Donato readied the obligatory coffee and doughnuts at Clifton police headquarters that Monday, August 6, 1990, he was summoned from the second-floor conference room to take a call from a secretary at the Bronx DA's office. The woman said she was calling on behalf of Assistant District Attorney William Flack, the man who had convened the grand jury in the Gladys Matos case back in 1985, only to send Wanda and her brother back to Florida without ever testifying. The caller said Flack had developed a bad back. He would not be attending. No, she continued, no one would be coming in his place.

A few minutes later, Captain Ronald Naimoli of the NYPD Organized Crime Control Bureau, Carolyn Napoletano's office, called on his car phone to advise Donato that he was on his way and needed directions. Donato was a bit surprised. The organized-crime official was not on the list of expected attendees. Of course, he was welcome to attend.

By late morning, representatives from four states were on hand: New Jersey, Delaware, Pennsylvania, and New York. "The meeting was a feeling-out process, not an inquisition," Donato later recalled. The earlier homicide investigations were discussed, but not in an accusatory tone. "We didn't really worry about what did or didn't happen with the other two cases. It was strictly, 'What are we going to do about this one?' We didn't want any more people dying."

Fazzini was on hand to play audiotapes of several of the secretly recorded conversations between Eric, Carolyn, and Mike Sanchez, the friend whose advice Eric had sought before the Matos shooting. The New York detective also provided his impressions of Carolyn, advising the others how she would likely behave in different situations. It was clear that Fazzini was still bitter about the Napoletanos, and would do anything he could to help bag the mother-son combo.

Naimoli, from Organized Crime, listened intently as the others discussed his employee and her son. Before he departed, he too offered whatever help he could provide.

The following day, August 7—six days after the confidential undercover file was seized—Carolyn Napoletano was suspended from the Organized Crime Control Bureau. She was at work when a team from Internal Affairs informed her she was being relieved of her duties without pay. "They came in front of everybody, five or six of them, in suits. The lieutenant, the sergeant. Even the captain I worked with. I was very close to him. I had worked with these guys. I kept *their* folders," Carolyn later recalled. "I called my union in front of them and they told me not to say another thing. They told me to go home."

Stunned, Carolyn swore she had done nothing wrong; she had just taken some work home with her.

Because of union rules, her suspension would last for less

than a month. Firing her would have required a lengthy
hearing process and an airing of the dirty details. No one
wanted that; the department had a tradition of covering up or
downplaying misconduct. There was another logical reason
for NYPD's kid-gloves treatment: the possibility that Carolyn
did possess incriminating or embarrassing information about
people she had worked with over the years.

Incredibly, when Carolyn returned to work, she continued
to be assigned to the Organized Crime Control Bureau,
albeit to its Investigative Support Division instead of the
chief's office. "They put me downstairs, where they have
the wiretaps and the tapes. I worked right with the narcotics
people. My cop friend told me that they were told to keep
everything away from me, though. I did absolutely nothing
there. I read books all day. I typed a few letters. I learned
about the Civilian Complaint Review Board."

She contended that the ending of her suspension benefited all parties. "I had to go to the chief's office in front of
everybody and sit with the lieutenant who I hated." She said
the officials told her that although the department had found
her guilty of violating important policy, if she and the union
would not appeal, the matter would quietly be put to rest.

"That was it. It was resolved. It was forgotten. It didn't
exist. It didn't happen," said Carolyn. "In other words, 'Bury
it under the rug.' Just like that, it ended. They told me I was
reinstated. You don't ask questions. You just go back."

In its public comments about the incident, NYPD was quite
guarded, confirming only that detectives had recovered "a
confidential document listing personnel information about a
cop." Officials later alternately characterized the undercover
officer as "an investigator assigned to the Organized Crime
office" or as on assignment with the relatively insignificant
Auto Theft Squad, not on a sensitive Mafia case.

Cocky as ever, Carolyn continued to conduct her private
business on taxpayers' time, making calls and writing letters
of complaint about Fazzini. She claimed the detective had
stolen her NYPD auxiliary badge during the raid on her
apartment. "I told Internal Affairs that the man can't stand
me because I'm always making complaints about him and
writing letters about him. I told them that he took my shield
and he took my ID card. And he did! I know he did. I *know*
he did!"

Committed as ever to blaming others for her problems,

Carolyn also decided she was not going to take any more
guff from "those bozos in Clifton." She typed out a two-
page missive to the Honorable James J. Florio at the State
House in Trenton, New Jersey—as if the governor of the
nation's most densely populated state was going to drop
what he was doing to address her concerns regarding the
evening Eric's Toyota was seized.

"Eric was frisked by four police officers. Isn't one search
sufficient? Was this a training session?" she demanded.
"The police, who are sworn to protect and serve, would not
allow the little children to have their few toys. Nor would
they allow us to take diapers from the trunk of the vehicle.
This was a cruel act, would you not agree, Governor? How
do you justify this? Then to top it off, they abandoned us
with two small children."

Seven weeks later, Carolyn received a form letter in
reply. The governor's office directed her to work things out
with local police, the mayor, and the county prosecutor's
office.

In the aftermath of the police-strategy session, the detectives took a 180-degree turn in their theory about why Eric
had called Al Jiovine at 2:44 A.M. the night of Myra's disappearance. Instead of believing that Eric had killed Myra at
8:00 P.M., driven to Delaware to bury the body, and returned
home to call Al for a baby-sitter, Ruth and Donato adopted
the theory that Eric and Myra had both been on the phone
arguing at 2:44 A.M., and that Al's roommate, Greg Velez,
and his fifteen-year-old girlfriend, Magdalena "Maggie"
Rivera, had been in Jiovine's apartment playing Nintendo
and heard Myra's voice through the amplifier Al had
attached to his phone because of his hearing problem.

The detectives changed their approach because Maggie
Rivera remembered two phone calls involving Myra that
took place on the same day: From her mother's house, she
had chatted with Myra in the afternoon about their possibly
getting an apartment together, and she heard Myra's voice
on the phone during a late-night conversation Al had with
Eric and Myra in which the couple traded accusations of
adultery.

Reviewing the "Napoli" phone records, Donato found a
call from the Napoletano Clifton apartment to Maggie's
mother at 2:23 P.M. on June 20, 1990, just hours before

Myra's disappearance. The record of that call led him and Ruth to conclude that the late-night call Maggie was referring to had to have been the 2:44 A.M. call early the morning of the twenty-first. That meant Myra could not have been dead and buried in Delaware at that hour, and Eric would not have been calling for a baby-sitter. More important, the new scenario destroyed Eric's alibi. If Myra was on the phone in the middle of the night with Eric, he could not continue to claim he had last seen her at 8:00 P.M., standing curbside with her tote bags waiting for a boyfriend.

However, other facts cast doubt on Maggie's recollection of events. First of all, Maggie subsequently contradicted herself on key points. Second, Eric and Myra had engaged in a similar argumentative phone call with Uncle Al three nights earlier, the evening of Father's Day, after Eric found a piece of paper containing the phone number of a man Myra had met. Third, Greg Velez said he never heard Al mention Myra's name and never heard Al talking to anyone other than Eric during the 2:44 A.M. call. Finally, there had been no phone activity at the Napoletano apartment from 6:49 P.M. the Wednesday of Myra's disappearance until the 2:44 A.M. call.

If Myra was not already dead when Eric left to pick up his mother in Manhattan, or when he returned about eight, where had she been for those seven or eight hours? If still alive, why had she not used the phone? The woman had been on the phone nonstop to relatives since learning about her husband's mistress that Sunday. Presumably she would have called someone after Eric left with his mother and the boys. With Eric and Carolyn gone, Myra would have been free to discuss her situation without interference.

Regardless of what really happened the night Myra disappeared, the investigation was redirected on a course that boxed everyone in to the following scenario: Eric and Myra argued on the phone during the 2:44 A.M. call; when Eric called Al three hours later, he asked Al to see if his mother would baby-sit; therefore, Myra was killed between 2:44 and 6:00 A.M. Henceforth, anything contrary to the new theory was deemphasized in the investigation; anything consistent with it was accentuated.

Believing that they had made a breakthrough, Ruth and Donato took another crack at Al Jiovine. They decided

to hammer him about his homosexuality in the hope he
would give ground on the 2:44 call. They came at him
armed with compelling new information provided by Greg
Velez, news that Al had previously admitted a sexual relationship with Eric.

When Greg admitted his sexual dealings with Al, Detective Ruth had asked if Al had been intimate with Eric. Greg
answered in the affirmative, prompting the detective to
inquire further, "And how do you know him and Eric had
the same relationship?"

"Because Al told me," Greg replied matter-of-factly. He
went on to say that he believed Al and Eric still had something going. "They had to have something going, because of
Eric. When I wasn't around, Eric was around. Sometimes Al
would tell me, 'Greg, don't come by today because Eric's
staying over.' "

Confronted with the details, Al acknowledged what he
could no longer deny, that he was homosexual. He slumped
in his chair, his head bowed, unable to look at Donato and
Ruth. He said his ways were different, his homosexuality
"hard for others to understand." Smiling at the detectives,
he added in a soft voice, "It's my way of showing love for
other people."

In response to a specific question, he admitted to homosexual relations with Greg Velez, a vulnerable street kid
who lost his parents to a car crash when he was an infant.
Donato and Ruth then went down a list of other names they
had heard during the course of their investigation. To each
name Al nodded yes. And with each affirmative reply, he
sank deeper into the chair.

"What about Eric?" asked Donato.

Al nodded in the affirmative. Ruth and Donato looked at
each other. That had been easy. But the silence was suddenly broken as Al lifted his head, sat straight in the chair,
chest out, and declared, "No! No! No! Not Eric! You don't
do that with Eric!"

Donato pointed out that Greg Velez had already told them
about the sex with Eric. But Al was firm in his retraction. It
was a line he had not wanted to cross. If he admitted to
having had sex with Eric, that meant he could not deny
being a pedophile, because Eric surely would have been
underage for at least some of the sex.

During the next three-and-a-half hours, Donato and Ruth

grilled Al about the events of the night Myra disappeared, especially the 2:44 A.M. call. But Al was a different man in the wake of his admission about having had sex with Eric. He was sullen and angry. The spirit of cooperation, even if feigned, was gone. He was back to "I don't remember" and "I don't recall."

On and on they parried. Finally, the detectives told Al to leave; if he did not wish to cooperate, he would have to suffer the consequences.

Al protested. He sat there defiantly, with his arms crossed. "I'm not leaving until you tell me that you believe me." He insisted that he just could not remember the call. Maybe it was a different day. Maybe something was mixed up here.

"Yo, Al, there's the door. Good-bye, Al," said Donato, brusquely showing him the exit.

- 20 -

IN HER WORDS

Al used to have this kid Mitch, and Mitch got killed. Eric seemed to come along and was like a replacement, okay? It was for, ah, a boy, a companion, like. Eric resembled Mitch in a way.

I told you how Eric met Al through the kid he met in Central Park, Wally. The kid got talking to Eric, saying that he lived with this man, Bob. Eric and Wally got to be friendly. Eric brought him home for me to meet him. At a later date, I met Bob. And through Bob, I met Al.

Bob lived in the Seventies, off Third Avenue. I don't know how the kid was living with him. I don't remember, or I don't know. But he lived with him. No, he was not his son. Oh no, it was not a pedophile relationship. Bob liked girls. He was gorgeous. I could have went for him. Yeah, he was gorgeous. I don't know how he could associate with Al, because you know what Al looks like. And here's this guy over six foot, really good looking, nice personality and everything.

So I met Bob, then eventually Al and some other guy. I don't remember who he was. He got in the picture, and they were taking the kids someplace.

Eric resembled Mitch in a way. Then Al wanted to take care of someone, as a Big Brother, so he used me for a reference. He gave them my name, that he used to do things with my son. They called me at home for an interview, over the phone: "Did I know him well enough to trust him with my son?" I said, "Well, he has been living with him X amount of years. He was like a father figure."

They had given Al a child but there was something to do with the mother and the grandmother. Al told me the whole story, but you know, when Al talks, he always twists things around. I'm sure the mother and the grandmother kind of knew what Al was. They knew he was a pedophile. All I know is that he was never allowed to see the child again. Big Brother wouldn't let him see anybody. He was very hurt about this.

I never met anybody like Al. We used to go to Coney Island almost every Friday, to Nathan's for hot dogs. Al would always treat us. And then he treated us to cotton candy. We even went once or twice with Myra. Eric went on the rides and I kept little Eric. I couldn't go on a ride. I'd have a heart attack if I went on a ride.

We also went up to West Point, the three of us—Eric, Al, and myself.

Some days you would like him. We always talked. Al and I always talked. We talked all the time. And then he used to say that I would get into one of my snits, I'd start arguing with him and he just couldn't stand it. He'd say, "Okay, Carol. You win, you win." I could still hear him.

We were like family to him, but Al used to start trouble with us. According to Al, we didn't get along. He always had something to say about me. Negative. Nasty. He was always telling Eric these things that I said, and I didn't say them. Al wanted Eric for himself. He told Eric that if I wasn't such a snot with my mouth he would have paid all my bills. Al didn't like it when I spoke up to him. But whatever you're dishing out, I don't have to take it. I can disagree with you; it's my opinion.

I never wanted to be seen with him. In case anybody saw me, they would wonder who he was to me, because he's so ugly. One time we were going to Yankee Stadium with Marilyn and Larry Knoepfler. Eric was gonna go, too. It wound up that only I went with Al. I died. I just felt uncomfortable with him because he was so ugly and he's obnoxious.

Eric used to tease and say that Al and I should get married. I used to get mad at Eric when he started that teasing.

You know, Al had something going at the airport, he used to get envelopes. I never got any. The only thing he ever gave me, for my birthday one year, was a hundred and twenty-five dollars and I bought a cop jacket, I still have it. I went to headquarters and I got it for a hundred and a quarter. It's what the cops wear on patrol, with the patch on the side.

*No, on my birthdays I never really got anything. The iron
I have, though, he did give me that.*

*I don't think Al sexually abused Eric. I used to ask Eric
and he told me, "No." My doctor at that time used to ask
me. She said it just wasn't normal. I said to Eric, "You can
tell me. Nobody is going to hurt you if you tell me." But he
always said "No."*

*He still says "No." I know I heard stories about Al and
Eric, but I do not believe them. I just don't believe it. Because
I always told Eric, "If he is bothering you or touching you,
you tell me and you will never have to see him again. He
can't hurt you or find you." But he didn't. Al may have tried,
and Eric didn't tell me. But there was never anything.*

*I think Al is a very lonely person. I think he always has to
try to prove himself to people. Because he couldn't get
along with girls, I guess he just liked boys.*

The first two homicides continued to haunt Donato. Figuring that any evidence with the potential of putting Eric behind bars was worth going after, he considered developments in the Coludro and Matos cases to be just as important as those in the Myra Napoletano investigation.

Donato contacted Eric's first wife, Wanda Matos, still hiding out in Florida. Despite her opinion that she was to blame for her mother's death, no new evidence turned up. "I regret everything that I have done—of being disobedient to my mother," she said. "My father's and my mother's families feel like I had something to do with my mother's murder. They think I am responsible for her death. I feel bad because if I would have listened to my mother, this wouldn't have happened."

Wanda displayed more grief while recounting her nonappearance before the Bronx grand jury. "The detectives from New York had me in a hotel room. Then I went to the precinct," she said. After interviews there, she was supposed to testify, but was never given the chance. "I never got to court. The detectives from New York, they postponed it for another time. Then I came back home."

Wanda said she had wanted to stay so far away from Eric that she never bothered to divorce him. Now twenty-three, she revealed she had given birth to a girl on September 13, 1985, Tatiana Napoletano. Yes, she said, Eric was the father.

Next, Donato pursued an important lead in the Marilyn Coludro homicide, the search of a car possibly used to transport the girl's body to Pennsylvania six years earlier.

Doris DeWilde, one of Al Jiovine's half sisters, told Donato she felt there was something suspicious about a four-door 1978 Pontiac that was parked dormant in the garage at their mother's house, the Dugan residence in

Dumont, New Jersey. She said the car had formerly belonged to Al, and that over the years Eric had used it. She also recalled an occasion years ago when Eric or Al had ripped out the trunk's carpeting.

Donato called Trooper Mullen at the Pennsylvania State Police and told him of DeWilde's comments. The Pennsylvania authorities were interested, and spent the next several days in long-distance discussions with their New Jersey counterparts. Curiously, in the midst of the phone conferences, Larry Knoepfler, Uncle Al's confidant, called to let Donato know that Al planned to sever all ties with Eric. The timing of Larry's call only heightened interest in the gold-colored Catalina.

With a signed search warrant in hand, a team of detectives headed for the Dugan home the afternoon of August 28, 1990. But the Dugan driveway was empty. Half of the search party checked the neighborhood while the other half knocked on the Dugans' door. Inside, Al's mother, Rose, said Larry Knoepfler had taken the car "somewhere in town to be fixed" that very morning.

Another of Al's half sisters, Patricia Dugan, explained that when Al had given the car to the family years ago, he told them Eric had spilled oil in the trunk and removed the rug. Contradicting her sister, Doris, Patricia Dugan denied that the car had been sitting in the garage unused; she said she drove it regularly. Despite the fact that she knew Donato had been asking questions about the car for several days, she insisted there was nothing sinister about it suddenly being taken in for servicing.

The car was located at a nearby Midas Muffler & Brake Shop, and brought back to the Dugan residence. The investigators then began searching the garage, where Mullen found some thick white cord tied to a child's red wagon. When the cord, which looked like the rope used to wrap Marilyn Coludro's body, was shown to Marilyn Knoepfler, she observed that it could have been used in her husband's butcher business years ago. Also shown the strand, Larry Knoepfler agreed that it looked like butcher's cord, then insisted, "But it's not."

When the car was processed at the New Jersey State Police Lab, technicians seized a multicolored comforter and a piece of trunk carpeting that reacted positively to a

Luminol test, indicating the possible presence of blood. The car's interior and trunk also were vacuumed.

In fact, the trunk carpeting did not contain blood, and no useful fibers were detected. The lead did not pan out after all.

Left little choice, Donato and Ruth once again turned their attention to the owner of the Catalina, Uncle Al Jiovine. When he appeared at Clifton police headquarters by invitation, Jiovine was driven to the county prosecutor's office in downtown Paterson. Maybe a change of scenery would help his memory.

This was to be a group interview: Ruth, Donato, Lieutenant Burke, Detective John Downs from Delaware, and Captain Frank Failla and Bill Purdy from the prosecutor's office. Everyone had grown extremely tired of Al's lack of cooperation. The tone of this session was downright nasty, yet again, no ground was gained. Al insisted he could not recall the key 2:44 A.M. call.

Purdy told Al he had no doubt that Myra had been on the phone at 2:44 A.M., and that she was killed shortly after the call. He warned that when Eric was eventually tried for murder, Al would either be called as a witness or be sitting next to his "serial-killer son" as a codefendant for covering up. The prosecutor offered immunity but told him he had to tell everything he knew.

Al held his ground. He said he received so many different phone calls that the conversation in question could have occurred "at three o'clock in the morning, eleven o'clock at night, or one o'clock in the morning."

But, Purdy countered, there were no calls listed on the phone bill for those other times. And there weren't—for that particular night.

The interview deteriorated into a shouting match. Purdy ended it by declaring, "I can't wait to see you on the fucking witness stand!"

With the local officials getting nowhere, it was time for the investigation to take another turn. The FBI officially opened a kidnapping case file with Myra as the victim.

The FBI had been in on the Myra Napoletano case almost from the beginning, when Delaware officials sent their forensic evidence to the FBI lab for analysis. Donato had met several times with Special Agents Thomas A. Cottone,

Jr., and Drusilla L. Wells in New Jersey. Cottone, a short, tenacious man who joined the FBI in 1972, was named lead agent on the Napoletano investigation.

On September 5, 1990, Cottone convened a meeting of detectives and prosecutors from the four states along with seven FBI agents, and Gregg O. McCrary, a serial-killer specialist from the FBI's National Center for the Analysis of Violent Crime at the FBI Academy in Quantico, Virginia.

To Nick Donato, the meeting crystalized where the investigation had been and where it needed to go. "Things were starting to bog down, all of the things we had hoped for in August. Now come September, we started to realize we may be sucking wind here. Al Jiovine wasn't coming clean with us. We pretty much knew he wasn't going to come across. We couldn't talk to Eric, and anything Carolyn would come across with was basically misguided and had nothing to do with the investigation."

Several ideas were tossed around at the FBI meeting. Someone suggested wiretaps, but because of manpower demands, that was considered an option of last resort. Surveillance of Eric was discussed, but the FBI's resources in New York were being pushed with intelligence demands because of tensions in Iraq.

McCrary, the FBI profiling expert and a twenty-two-year veteran of the federal agency, impressed everyone as he went down a list of typical serial-killer characteristics. It sounded as if Eric qualified for virtually every category.

With McCrary's expertise, the group immersed itself in the psychology of the Napoletano inner circle. It was reassuring for the local investigators to hear McCrary confirm their suspicions that Eric had selected minorities to fall in love with because his upbringing made him paranoid and insecure. "We understood that—look at who he was raised by, Carolyn and Al," said Donato. "But we needed to hear from the people who do this every day that we were on the right track."

McCrary explained that someone like Eric needed to feel self-assured, protected, and able to exercise control over his life and those around him. He selected young minorities, perhaps on the rebellious side, who were looking for a better way of life. The women, in turn, looked up to Eric as their savior. By selecting minorities, Eric convinced himself he was in a position of superiority. It gave him confidence.

A teenage Eric Napoletano displays one of his favorite weapons.

Dressed in his New York City Police Department auxiliary uniform, Eric leans against a precinct patrol car.

Carolyn Napoletano holds her grandson Angelo, while Eric sits with Eric Jr. at a Clifton, New Jersey, shopping center after police seized Eric's Toyota. (Thomas Franklin, *North Jersey Herald & News*)

Eric's third wife, Sandra, poses with Eric Jr. (left) and Angelo at their New Mexico home.

Myra Acevedo Napoletano with her son Angelo

Myra with Eric during a happy moment in Puerto Rico.

Angelo (left) and Eric Jr. with their grandfather Pablo Acevedo, Myra's father. (Laura Seitz, *North Jersey Herald & News*.)

Marilyn Coludro, Eric's first known victim, in a photo distributed to the local news media in 1984 by the New York City Police Department Missing Persons Bureau. (*New York Daily News*/NYPD)

Marta Rivera, Marilyn Coludro's mother, holds a photo of her murdered daughter. (Collette Fournier, *The Record*, Hackensack, New Jersey.)

Police aerial photo of Labrador Lane in Bear, Delaware. Myra Napoletano's body was found July 9, 1990, less than ten yards from the edge of the dead-end road.

The body of Gladys Matos, shot six times on April 29, 1985, on a Bronx street corner. (NYPD)

FBI surveillance photos taken outside Eric's apartment in Albuquerque, New Mexico, the morning of his arrest, March 27, 1991.

FBI SWAT team enters Napoletano's apartment.

Eric is escorted to a telephone booth, where he makes a wiretapped call to Albert Jiovine and Carolyn.

Eric heads to the phone booth again, moments after assuring FBI Special Agent Sarah Burcham that her colleagues would never find any evidence against him.

The key investigators, from left to right: Clifton Police Dept. Lt. John Burke; FBI Special Agent Thomas A. Cottone, Jr.; Clifton Police Dept. Det. Nick Donato; and Senior Investigator Peter T. Talarico, Jr., of the Passaic County Prosecutor's Office.

Corporal Allen E. Ruth of the new Castle County Police Dept., the lead detective in the Delaware investigation of Eric Napoletano. (New Castle County Dept. of Public Safety.)

Senior prosecutor William J. Purdy, Jr. (left) with his assistant, Walter R. Dewey, Jr. Purdy lodged murder charges against Eric after authorities in Delaware, New York, and Pennsylvania declined to take action.

Eric with First Assistant Deputy Public Defender Louis Acevedo at his arraignment. (Laura Seitz, New Jersey Court Pool.)

Jennifer Meade, Eric's lover at the time of Myra's murder, tells the jury Eric was "real positive" his wife would not be coming back. (Danielle P. Richards, New Jersey Court pool.)

Eric laughs during his sentencing as a sobbing Carmen Acevedo, Myra's mother, bemoans the lack of remorse shown by her daughter's killer. At left is Ernest M. Caposela. (Ed Hill, New Jersey Court Pool.)

Det. Nick Donato and Eric Napoletano exit U.S. District Court in Newark on April 11, 1991. (Jim Annes, *North Jersey Herald & News*.)

Carolyn Napoletano—charged with conspiracy and tampering with evidence—refused to stand for this mug shot at Clifton police headquarters. (Clifton Police Dept.)

Codefendant Albert "Uncle Al" Jiovine tries to hide behind his copy of court documents. (Amanda Brown, *North Jersey Herald & News*.)

Eric's penchant for minorities might also have been a subconscious attempt to get back at his mother, who was so demonstratively prejudiced. While hating minorities, Eric was always around them; he fell in love with them, then bad-mouthed and abused them. "He felt good enough to kill and walk away from it with no guilt," said Donato. "This was a guy who wasn't 'guilty.' He had no conscience about killing someone he felt had wronged him."

Throughout all of the legwork and strategy sessions, Donato did his best to keep track of the Napoletanos. He learned that Eric had called in sick to his Brownie post on Friday, August 24, 1990, and had resigned the following Monday in order to report to a new night job repairing subway tracks. Donato immediately briefed Transit Authority officials on Eric's background.

Carolyn Napoletano was on the move, too. A check with NYPD officials by FBI agent Cottone revealed that she was still an employee, but after seven years at One Police Plaza, she had been transferred from the Organized Crime Control Bureau, reassigned to the First Precinct, just outside the Holland Tunnel. She would be broadly disliked by uniformed and civilian employees, angry that instead of getting rid of her the brass had dumped her in their precinct. Carolyn would later brag that she still had unfettered access to confidential documents.

With each month, concern for the well-being of Eric Junior and Angelo grew. After all, Eric's history demonstrated that he hurt people close to him. If he ran out of women, would he turn his violence on his sons?

Pablo Acevedo decided he could no longer sit on the sidelines while his grandsons' lives were in jeopardy. He hired a civil attorney to file for visitation rights as a prelude to requesting custody.

Donato continued to brief the New York City social-services system to the situation, but without criminal charges against Eric, Pablo's civil action represented the only hope.

On the first court date, November 5, 1990, Eric, Carolyn, and the boys failed to appear. On November 13, the Napoletanos were again absent. Eric's attorney said she had tried repeatedly to contact him. Stiffed on her fee, she asked to be relieved. The family court judge agreed, then issued a default judgment against Eric. Pablo and Carmen were granted unsupervised visitation for a minimum of three hours per week.

Abruptly, though, Eric had disappeared. Unbeknownst to everyone except his mother and Uncle Al, Eric had moved to the Southwest.

The last, and decisive, phase of the investigation was about to take place.

- 22 -

No matter where Eric fled, he could not escape his demons. He was now practicing his brand of rough love in New Mexico, the Land of Enchantment. On the afternoon of December 4, 1990, he was driving a battered station wagon five miles east of downtown Albuquerque when he stopped for a red light. As he waited for the traffic signal to change, he abruptly turned around and began punching Eric Junior in the backseat, over and over. The four-year-old boy cried as he sought to protect himself. Eric continued to whack away nonstop, though, and the boy fell to the car floor. Watching in horror from the car directly behind, motorist Cindy Luetters wrote down the station wagon's license plate. This was middle America, where people still cared. Luetters called the New Mexico Department of Human Services.

The car would subsequently be traced to the stepfather of Eric's newest lover, Sandra Christine Walsh Martini. Sandra had met Eric in 1989 at a party in New York. She next saw him riding a bus the following summer, shortly after Myra's disappearance. They talked, a date was arranged, and a relationship developed. As Jennifer Meade faded, Sandra had taken center stage. Following the usual pattern, Eric had fallen in love.

He had told Sandra that Myra was alive but had run off. He said he did not know where she was, but suspected she was with her parents. Sympathetic, Sandra had agreed to help Eric care for his two boys.

When Eric learned of Pablo Acevedo's visitation petition, he quickly agreed with Sandra's suggestion that they move away from New York. Eric didn't want to leave, since he knew he would never make the same money elsewhere. But he had no choice; there was no way he was going to let Pablo get those kids. They decided to drive out to Albuquerque, where Sandra's mother and stepfather lived.

On Tuesday, November 6, 1990, the day after the original court date for Pablo's petition, Eric rented a fourteen-foot truck, using a Chase Visa card issued in his name, but on Al Jiovine's account. Al reacted with an angry farewell note, telling Eric to use Carolyn's line of credit, not his. *I do not want you to call me,* he wrote. *You are a sneak without telling me. I do not want to know you. Good-bye.*

Several days later, Eric, Sandra, and his boys arrived in New Mexico. Eric applied for welfare, spelling his last name with an "i." He was granted food-stamp benefits of $277 per month. They stayed with Sandra's mother, Claire O'Connor, for a few days, then got their own apartment. They moved again within a month, though, because of a dispute between Eric and another tenant. Displaying wild behavior, Eric Junior worked his way through a succession of baby-sitters. Sandra's mother refused to care for the child because he kept hitting her.

Using Sandra's family's address, Eric received a New Mexico learner's permit. He again misspelled his last name, and claimed he had never been issued a driver's license in another state. Eric did, however, use his correct Social Security number.

Eric was full of ideas again. Maybe he would become a cop, or start a junkyard, or open a discount beer and soda store. He visited an army recruiter. He and Sandra talked about getting married. They even got the kids a pet dog.

Motorist Cindy Luetters's distress call about the child being beaten in the car was referred to social worker Marion Schroeder, who called the Albuquerque Police Department. The owner of the 1982 Dodge station wagon, Daniel O'Connor, lived just a few blocks from where the attack had taken place.

Schroeder opened a case file. After ascertaining that there were no children with the last name of O'Connor registered in the local school, she drove to O'Connor's home. He showed her his van, but it bore a different license plate. O'Connor was evasive when asked if he had any other vehicles. After some discussion, O'Connor told Schroeder he would tell her about his car, but only if she promised not to tell anyone he had provided the information.

O'Connor then revealed that his stepdaughter, Sandra, was living with a man named Eric and his two children. He said he had lent them his station wagon. O'Connor swore that he did not know Eric's last name. Persuaded to cooperate, he found a piece of paper with their address on it.

Schroeder headed over to 13220 Mountain Road, N.E., Apartment C, a four-family house, where she encountered a tall, thin man who identified himself as Eric Napoletano. When asked to explain his relationship with Daniel O'Connor, Eric said he was "just a friend, not a relative."

Eric was defensive. He denied knowing anyone named Sandra. Asked about any children, Eric said he had two boys with him, but denied being in the car with them at the time and place Schroeder cited. He also denied having hit either of them. Schroeder asked about the boys' mother. Eric said her name was Myra Acevedo, but claimed he did not know her whereabouts.

As they talked, Schroeder learned from Eric that he had applied for welfare. He explained that he was being evasive because he feared she was checking up on his application. Once Schroeder convinced him that she was not a welfare investigator, Eric became more forthcoming, but not more truthful. He said he and Sandra were engaged, that she visited his apartment frequently, but did not live there. He said he and his sons had moved to New Mexico about a month ago.

Eric expressed frustration over being unable to find work paying more than four dollars per hour, especially since the people over at welfare would not provide him with day care.

As the conversation continued, Eric recanted several of his earlier denials. He admitted he had been out with his boys in the car and had hit Eric Junior "one or two times" after the boy took off his seat belt to stand up. "It's my right to hit my children," Eric insisted. He asserted that he did not abuse them or leave any marks.

The official was not swayed. She outlined New Mexico's child-abuse law and observed that there were nonviolent ways to discipline, such as time-out periods.

Schroeder said she wanted to talk with the children. Eric Junior went first, distracted and reluctant to answer questions. The most Schroeder could get out of him was that his father hit him with a belt whenever he was bad. Just then his father entered the bedroom and frantically began removing the boy's clothes. He said he wanted to prove that his son did not have any bruises.

Screaming, Eric Junior resisted. But Eric showed no

regard for his feelings. Schroeder asked Eric to stop, or at least slow down so his son would not be so frightened. But Eric refused. He stripped the boy nude, frightening him to no end.

Eric brought Angelo into the bedroom, and proceeded to strip him, too. Two-year-old Angelo obeyed, though, and offered no resistance.

True, there were no visible marks or bruises on either child, but that was not entirely the point. Schroeder explained that she was concerned about Eric's parenting skills. She raised the possibility that the boys could be placed in Protective Services Day Care. Eric sounded very interested in the free program. Anything to get the kids off his back.

Eric and the boys spent Christmas in Albuquerque. Two weeks later, he married Sandra in El Paso, Texas. Court records indicate that the officiating judge waived the seventy-two-hour waiting period due to "hardship." For once Eric spelled his last name correctly. Sandra kept the news from her parents.

The newlyweds moved into an apartment without a phone. Still unemployed, Eric was full of complaints. He took to calling his new mother-in-law "bitch," "the witch," "scumbag," "scuzzy," and "fucking asshole." He also started calling Eric Junior "Spic" and little Angelo "Boo-Boo" because he frequently hurt himself.

Three months of special day care was approved for the boys. Psychological counseling was approved for Eric Junior, and Schroeder referred Eric to Parents Anonymous. But as always, he did not need counseling; he just needed the day care.

Within days of obtaining the supervision, Eric claimed that Eric Junior's clinical psychologist, Dr. Harold E. Paine, had recommended that his son be around older children. But when Schroeder contacted the doctor, he said Eric Junior was already in a class with children his age and older. Also, the staff at the Chelwood Kiddie Kollege day-care center had not reported any problems with the boy's behavior. The time away from home was doing him good.

On the other hand, Dr. Paine, he was concerned about the father. Characterizing Eric's parenting skills as "very low," and his overall behavior as "arbitrary and coercive," the doctor said he was going to offer Eric counseling on the issue of parenting rather than recommending a program for the child.

Confronted about the problems with his nurturing and disciplining skills, Eric finally agreed to join Parents Anonymous. But, he said, he had complaints that needed to be addressed. He had not received his welfare check for February, probably because of his change of address, so he had no money for rent or utilities.

Schroeder referred him to the Salvation Army and reemphasized the need for him to join the parents' organization. Eric reacted with a new excuse: He had no money for gas to get there.

This was a losing battle for Marion Schroeder. She told Eric she was going to keep checking on him. She said it was imperative that he join the parents' group.

But Eric blew her off. He was not about to stand up at some therapy session and give his life story, even a fake version.

Back in New York, Christmas had come and gone sadly for Pablo and Carmen Acevedo. They had visitation rights but no children to visit. Eric had not even been served with the court order. Worse, seven months had passed since Myra's murder, and her body had still not been released for a proper Christian burial. Donato learned from a Transit Authority detective that Eric had not been at his new job since mid-November. Also, the Acevedos' civil attorney relayed word that she had been told Eric and his sons had left the metropolitan area with an unknown woman. The hunt was on.

Donato turned again to FBI Special Agent Tom Cottone, arming him with pertinent information, such as Social Security numbers, birthdates, and credit-card account numbers for all members of the Napoletano inner circle. Hopefully, modern computer technology would detect a Napoletano presence.

The strategy worked. On January 22, 1991, Cottone called Donato with news that an "Eric Napolitano" had obtained a driver's permit in New Mexico using the same date of birth and Social Security number as Myra Napoletano's husband. The licensing data had been tracked down by FBI agents in New Mexico after Cottone traced the

U-Haul rental charged to Uncle Al's credit card, and determined that the truck had been returned in Albuquerque.

A New Mexico FBI team, led by Special Agent Julian M. Gonzales, quickly compiled a dossier on Eric's new life: The woman he was living with used the names Sandra Walsh and Sandra Martini, and had at least two daughters, Nina, seventeen, and Amanda, twelve; the utilities in Eric's apartment were registered under his name but with an incorrect date of birth and Social Security number; Sandra's stepfather, Daniel O'Connor, operated an appliance-repair service out of his home; Eric told welfare officials he was single and said the boys' mother—"Myra Acevedo"— resided at 354 East Eighty-third Street, in New York City, Carolyn's address.

FBI agents in New York additionally learned that Sandra had been living on and off as "a street person," suffering from "chronic drug- and alcohol-abuse problems" that led to her losing custody of her children. Twelve years older than Eric, Sandra was not an exact fit for his victim profile, but she still qualified as a likely target for murder.

The presence of a new woman in Eric's life was cause for considerable concern. Cottone decided to host another joint law-enforcement meeting. The agent was fast becoming as involved in the case as Donato, successfully pushing federal prosecutors and his bosses to make the matter a high priority. The meeting, attended by many old faces and several new ones, marked a crucial turning point in the Napoletano investigation. The usual representatives were present from Clifton, Passaic County, Delaware, and Pennsylvania. Fazzini was on hand again. Prosecutor John D. Ryan, chief of the Bronx DA's Major Offenses Bureau, attended in place of Prosecutor Flack. Robert C. Stewart and Glenn J. Moramarco represented the U.S. Justice Department's Strike Force out of Newark.

Robert B. Fram from the FBI lab in Washington explained that his research had detected a match between the red fibers found on Myra's shorts and the ones recovered from the Toyota trunk liner. In the coming months, Fram would link similar fibers in samples Donato had collected from under radiators and door sills at the Clifton apartment, as well as from vacuum debris removed under the spare tire in the Toyota, and from the Toyota parts carton. The fibers were turning up all over the place. But their potential evi-

dentiary value remained in question because their origin
was still unknown.

Agents Cottone and Drusilla Wells briefed everyone on
the situation in New Mexico. Since police pressure had sub-
sided in the weeks leading up to Eric's departure, it appeared he had run to avoid the Acevedos' family court
petition. As a result, Eric's actions increased concern about
the safety of Angelo and Eric Junior.

As the FBI meeting wore on, it became clear that the
Delaware prosecutors had lost their gusto. Detective Ruth
had already told Donato he was going to fade from the
scene. There was no solid physical evidence, no murder
weapon, and Al Jiovine had not been broken. There were
other homicides coming in, and it was time to move on.
Also, he was transferring to the K-9 Unit.

New York and Pennsylvania were still waiting, too,
finding cover behind their claims of insufficient evidence.

Tom Cottone, though, was eager to keep pushing, even if
the FBI's theory for entering the case—that Myra had been
kidnapped across state lines for the purpose of murder—
would be difficult to ultimately sustain in court. Cottone felt
strongly about the federal jurisdiction. At a minimum, he
believed it was strong enough to obtain subpoenas and a
wiretap order.

That left the real onus on Prosecutor Bill Purdy from Passaic County, an experienced attorney who had handled about
seventy trials. His father had spent years working in the
criminal justice system, first as a sheriff's deputy, then as an
investigator in the same county prosecutor's office. The
younger Purdy could still remember his father telling him at
the dinner table, "The courthouse is the whorehouse."

After graduating Seton Hall Law School in 1984, Bill
Purdy had spent one year as a judicial clerk, then served
briefly as an assistant prosecutor on juvenile cases in
Hudson County, New Jersey. When he learned of an opportunity to join the Passaic County Prosecutor's Office, he
grabbed it.

Nearly forty, Purdy was a low-key, likable bachelor.
Sandy-haired, wearing glasses, athletic and bearded, Purdy
was treasurer of a community theater. During his college
years, he played folk guitar in bars. A righteous man, he was
personally affronted by Carolyn Napoletano's involvement

in law enforcement, viewing her role in the murder conspiracy as a disgrace to every honest cop.

"Somebody has got to do something," Purdy said, taking the floor at the FBI meeting. "Let's all go with our best case. Even if we lose, at least we tried." But the suits wearing the dusty unsolved cases in New York and Pennsylvania sat in silence.

"We're all convinced he's killed three people. Letting him run around Albuquerque is useless," Purdy agreed. "We can't just say, 'Well, there's nothing we can do about it.' "

His words were met with more silence. He sensed where his appeal was headed—nowhere. "If no one else is willing, I'll go first."

Purdy made his commitment without concern for glory or career advancement. He cared about doing the right thing. Someone had to get Eric off the street.

Despite the expense, the possibility of wiretaps now received top priority. Led by Assistant U.S. Attorney Stewart, a tenacious veteran prosecutor, the feds moved swiftly. As a preliminary step, a grand jury subpoena was issued for phone records of Sandra's stepfather's home and business, and all calls made from "any telephone facility in New Mexico" to Carolyn's home phone or to the 800 number at Uncle Al's employer in Manhattan. In the wake of all the questions about the 2:44 A.M. call, Al had removed the phone from his apartment.

The records review was a huge success. Eric and Al had not stayed angry at each other for long. There were several dozen calls from Daniel O'Connor's business to the 800 number in Jiovine's office. More important, there were scores of crosscountry calls to Al's office from nearly a dozen different phone booths in the northeast section of Albuquerque.

The records could not show whether Al had been transferring any of the calls to Carolyn. But a conversation Agent Cottone had with Detective Fazzini quickly cleared up that uncertainty.

Fazzini reported that Eric's mother had lost the "senior" in her job title, and was back to being a "police administrative aide" after being found guilty of improper personal use of NYPD phones.

As usual, Carolyn saw a conspiracy behind her employ-

ment troubles, and she tagged Fazzini as the ringleader. She
said she was transferred out of the Organized Crime Control
Bureau because "nobody wants to have somebody who is a
problem. And they didn't want to be the ones to demote me."

In fact, she had been turned in by a civilian co-worker.
The colleague had observed her removing the phone from
her desk, taking it to a secluded area of the station house,
and spending long periods of time in whispered conversation. When the co-worker asked Carolyn who she was
always talking to, she claimed that her "uncle" at the phone
company was patching calls through to her son, Eric. "They
were cruel to me at the First, very cruel," Carolyn later
asserted. "I was working with hateful people. They didn't
want a supervisor in there. They were black and Puerto
Ricans. They were bitches."

The information from Fazzini clinched the decision on
where to place the wiretap. Eric was using the toll-free line
to Jiovine's office for all of his calls back home.

Working night and day, Prosecutor Stewart, Cottone, and
Dru Wells compiled an impressive twenty-three-page affidavit to accompany the wiretap application. The three homicides and the related investigations were summarized. The
affidavit also alleged that Eric's mother and Uncle Al were
"accessories after the fact" to the Coludro murder, and
"accessories before the fact with respect to the Myra
Acevedo kidnapping-murder." It was additionally alleged
that Eric, Carolyn, and Jiovine had "conspired to tamper
with potential witnesses," that Sandra's life was in "serious
danger," and that there was "reason for concern about the
safety of Eric's two young children."

In asking for the wiretap, Cottone and Wells laid out a
plan of attack: After establishing telephone surveillance, a
search warrant would be executed for physical evidence.
Given Eric's "volatile nature," they believed he would not
be able to face a renewed investigation alone, and would
therefore contact the two people who had always supported
him through "the various episodes of girlfriend- and wife-
beating and the three homicides—namely, his mother and
'Uncle Al.' " The agents also observed that Eric's "pathological relationship" with Carolyn and Al had withstood the
pressures of at least three murders. "Thus, it is highly
probable that he will turn to them once again, and that they
will form a united front to save him."

In this respect, Carolyn's prior conduct was highlighted. Describing her as "the driving force behind the obstruction efforts to date," the agents noted Carolyn's assignment in the NYPD Communications Division at the time the Coludro missing-persons report failed to make the national computer system, her "ironclad alibi" for Eric in the Matos shooting and the night Myra disappeared, her driving off with Eric to buy a gun, her coaching of Mike Sanchez in the Matos investigation, and the fact that "a personnel file for an undercover New York City police officer" had been recovered during the raid on her apartment. "The unauthorized possession of this file was a serious breach of Departmental regulations," the agents observed.

The affidavit covered another important aspect of the case: Gregg McCrary's research on serial killers—by definition, anyone responsible for three or more homicides in separate incidents—and his story of the three murders linked to Eric. McCrary and his colleagues concluded that Eric demonstrated virtually every characteristic typically found in a sexually sadistic serial killer. The only characteristic they were unaware of was cruelty to animals.

McCrary observed that there was a certain predictability in a sexually sadistic serial killer's criminal behavior. He noted that Eric had demonstrated a preference for victims whose affections and trust he first gained, such as a wife or girlfriend. Such victims were typically lured by offers of care, kindness, and security. With the victim emotionally committed, the murderer would change his behavior dramatically and embark on a course of violent domination and humiliation.

"Her life then becomes a nightmare, but she feels powerless to extricate herself from the situation," McCrary wrote. "If she gives any indication of leaving, the offender perceives this as a critical and intolerable threat to his ability to control. It is this prospect of losing control over the victim which generates the uncontrollably explosive rage within the offender."

To McCrary, it was not a question of whether Eric would kill again. "It is only a question of time until his next victim does something, or refuses to do something, which he perceives as a threat to his control over her. When that happens, he will react as he has always reacted. . . . The documented case histories demonstrate conclusively that offenders like Eric Napoletano cannot stop killing of their own volition. They stop only when they are stopped by external forces."

None of Eric's latest actions in New Mexico would have made Agent McCrary change his findings. He and Sandra obtained a binder for $20,000 worth of renter's insurance. Along with Uncle Al and Carolyn, he immediately began working on an insurance scam. While visiting with a State Farm agent, a quote was prepared for a $50,000 universal life-insurance policy on Sandra.

On March 5, 1991, Marion Schroeder, Eric's social worker, received an anonymous referral alleging that a little boy had been sexually abused in a van by a man with a cyst on his forehead. The source of the allegation stated that he had walked up to the windows of the van, looked in, witnessed the abuse, and noticed the cyst. The only other information provided was the van's license plate and the fact that it had been parked in a lot adjacent to a convenience store in Albuquerque.

Schroeder determined that the van was registered to the Chelwood Kiddie Kollege, the day-care center attended by Eric Junior and Angelo. The facility was located next to a 7-Eleven, and had a parking lot alongside its main building.

Surveying the scene, Schroeder observed that the parking area was not secluded. If anyone had observed the type of conduct alleged by the tipster, they surely would have seen the huge CHELWOOD KIDDIE KOLLEGE building sign and the CHELWOOD KIDDIE KOLLEGE markings on both sides of the van. So why had the caller reported only the license plate?

Inside the facility, Schroeder determined that the center's only male employee, George Baca, had a large cyst on his forehead. She concluded that someone was maliciously trying to point a finger at the man. As they discussed the situation with Mary Aigner, the center's director, Baca tried to recall if any parents had recently expressed dissatisfaction with the services.

Baca and Aigner both immediately thought of the young father of two boys who had been involved in a dispute just the day before. The parent had attempted to leave the younger of his two sons for the day, but staffers suspected he had a case of pink eye. When the workers refused to accept the boy, the father became irate. He yelled and screamed, and when Baca also failed to satisfy him, the man fled in a rage.

Schroeder interrupted to inquire if they were talking about the Napoletano children, whom she had referred to the facility. Baca and Aigner said they were. Aigner said that lately the boys had been arriving unkempt and unfed, or eating candy bars at seven o'clock in the morning. Eric Junior also had developed a very aggressive behavior pattern, often provoking physical fights.

Baca said the boy's father had been encouraging the improper conduct, instructing him, "If somebody hits you, hit them back." As if to provide a rationale for his position, Eric told Baca that the boys' mother had been "murdered back East."

Schroeder was shocked. Eric had never mentioned that fact to her. He'd claimed he had no idea where Myra was.

The next day, Eric called Schroeder to complain about the quality of care at Chelwood Kiddie Kollege. He said he still did not have a job or phone, and was planning to move to California at the end of March because welfare benefits were much better there than in "stingy New Mexico." He complained that he had paid taxes for years. It was time for him to get something back. He whined that there were plenty of people collecting benefits who did not deserve them. "It's my turn," he declared.

- 23 -

The federal phone tap was approved on March 7, 1991. Agent Dru Wells would later say that the court order marked the first time the FBI had used a wiretap in a serial-killer case. Because of technical difficulties, actual monitoring did not begin for another week. But the bug paid off quickly, confirming a close ongoing relationship between Eric, his mother, and Al Jiovine. Many times Eric and Uncle Al spoke alone. Other times Eric dialed the 800 number, then had Al patch the call to the First Precinct, where Carolyn answered, "Roll call."

Just as the FBI had predicted, on still other occasions, the three of them talked together on a conference hookup, sometimes using code words such as "Timberland" to refer to Delaware, "South Jersey" to refer to New Mexico, and "S" for Sandra. Eric invited Jiovine to fly out for a visit. He could spell his last name with a "G" in case the cops were tracking him.

When Eric and Al talked alone, Al acerbically criticized Carolyn and Sandra, the current women in Eric's life, while Eric exhibited extreme hostility for his new mother-in-law. "She's a bitch," he announced one day to Uncle Al.

"Sounds like your mother," Al replied.

"Yeah, kind of," Eric agreed.

"Nobody could be that bad, though," said Al.

"Welllll, I don't know—"

"She's as bad as your mother?" asked Al.

"Close to it. I'll put it that way," said Eric.

"Can you imagine having two of them in the house?"

"Yeah, right," said Eric.

In one call with his mother, Eric inquired about the status of the investigation into Myra's murder. "I was talking to Al, and I told him, 'They still have the car and they still have her. They're probably still investigating.' But they

can't be getting any new information. So it's probably kind
of shelved."

During another intercepted discussion about the investigation, Eric asked, "Hey! There's nothing new going on
with those assholes over there?"

"Nope," Al replied.

"Because I was thinking if they still got the car, and
supposedly the body, that they must still be investigating.
But what I honestly think is the case has gotta be shelved
because they're not getting anything—nothing new is coming in."

Eric sounded confident, with one reservation: "The only
thing is, unless they have my mother's phone bugged—and
your phone bugged. I doubt they could have your work
phone bugged. It's impossible. But what are they gonna
attempt to gain from it?"

"I don't know," Al interjected.

"I don't think a judge would give those assholes a court
order to bug your work phone," Eric said. "I really don't
think they would. You know what I mean? From bugging
your phone, even though you talk to me, you're talking
eight, nine months ago. Am I gonna be talking about it on
the phone?"

Eric said he wanted to speak with his mother, so Al
patched the call through to the precinct. Carolyn said she
was going to take a couple of days off to study for a civil
service exam and see a doctor for stronger painkillers. She
complained that her arm was killing her after a busy Saturday night doing laundry. "I washed the socks first. They
were fine. And I put in the five, ya know, those real heavy
bath towels I got? I put them in and then I put in the other
towels. And when the wash was finished, all the water
didn't soak out, and I had to wring them out, and I hurt my
arm." She also complained that the dryer had stolen two of
her quarters.

At times, it seemed as if paranoia about phone taps was
all they could think about. Carolyn lamented to Al, "It's
a shame. I can't even talk to you." Eric said he had read
a book that detailed the FBI's electronic surveillance of
John Gotti. Carolyn said she had changed her phone
receiver at home in case the police had planted a bug inside.
She doubted the precinct phones could be tapped because so

many people used them. She also doubted Al's 800 line could be bugged because it was a business. But Eric warned her not to rule out that possibility, suggesting to Al that he twist off his mouthpiece to check after they hung up.

Despite their misgivings, though, the Napoletano inner circle did not limit telephonic communications. They kept talking and talking—for the investigators.

When Eric wondered if he should purchase Larry Knoepfler's vintage Lincoln for his new wife, Sandra, Al remarked, "And then something is going to disappear!"

Eric asked Al what he meant by the comment.

"Then that's going to disappear, too," Al said.

"The car?" Eric asked, obviously feeling the need to differentiate between the vehicle and its future operator.

When Al replied in the affirmative, Eric chuckled, then added coyly, "Well, you never know what's going to happen."

Throughout the next week, it became clear to the monitoring agents that Eric, Carolyn, and Al were conspiring to defraud State Farm Insurance by filing a false personal-property claim under Eric's new renter's policy. Eric said he had taken several rolls of film showing his valuables, and hoped that operating manuals and warranty cards were sufficient proof of ownership for "stolen" electronic equipment.

While discussing an about-to-disappear video camera, Al inquired, "What happens if you buy something from someone who is no longer living?"

"Oh, I got you," Eric replied. "Good! Aha. You're right." Deciphering the coded talk, the monitoring agents discerned that Eric and his confederates were going to involve Myra posthumously in the scheme. "As a matter of fact, she gave it to me as a present," Eric added.

On another occasion, Eric and Al agreed they needed to make sure the "gifts" from Myra had been manufactured before her death. Al wondered how insurance companies handled the lack of a receipt for a gift given by someone "no longer in service." For emphasis, he repeated the key phrase: "Okay? 'No longer in service.' "

As Al, Carolyn, and Eric developed the insurance scheme, Al revealed one afternoon that his car had been stolen from his garage. Eric did not believe him. "No, really!" Al insisted. "Truthfully, this time, truthfully." Eric was stunned.

The irony of it all. But then his paranoia set in. He recalled that the cops had taken a ring of keys during the raid at his mother's apartment. He was sure a spare set to Al's Olds had been taken. "They might have given them to some junkie or crackhead. You don't know. I'm just saying," said Eric.

Even new crimes were uncovered by the intercept. Conversations between Al and his now-former roommate Greg Velez, being monitored to check for obstruction of justice, revealed that Jiovine had agreed to underwrite a retail drug-trafficking partnership. Greg would sell the drugs primarily in West New York, New Jersey, where he had moved with Maggie Rivera. Al urged Greg to be careful during conversations on the 800 line, though, because "they can bug my phone for, you know, Delaware."

The stakes were raised considerably and Eric's demeanor changed radically after a process server delivered a family court show-cause order under his mother's apartment door on Friday, March 22. Myra's parents wanted Eric to appear in court on April 1 to explain why he should not be arrested for disobeying the visitation order.

Talking surly, Eric now made it sound as if the goods involved in the property insurance scheme would not necessarily be "stolen." Perhaps they would disintegrate in a massive fire. Perhaps Sandra would fall asleep smoking just before the blaze began. It sounded as if Eric was preparing to kill again, with a plan to make money in the process.

Fearing that Pablo might locate him and take the kids, Eric purchased a nine-millimeter Ruger. He began strutting around Albuquerque with the weapon sticking out of his pants. He had considered buying an AK-47 or an Uzi, both assault weapons, but told his mother and Al he had decided to keep things low-key.

Eric consulted a lawyer, only to be told he needed to retain one in New York since that was where the Acevedos had filed their petition. Eric told Al to instruct Carolyn to find an attorney who charged by the hour, someone who could file a couple of documents to get Pablo and Carmen off his back. "Tell her she's gotta get me a fuckin' lawyer that'll charge one hundred dollars an hour. She has to! I can't fork out twenty-five hundred dollars."

* * *

Concern continued to grow in law-enforcement circles about Eric's mental stability. Cottone decided the FBI had to make a move; lives were at stake.

A new affidavit was prepared to support applications for search warrants on Eric's apartment, car, and person. Similar paperwork was prepared for Carolyn and Al's apartments. The affidavit summarized the eavesdropped conversations and asserted there was probable cause to believe Eric had murdered Marilyn Coludro, Gladys Matos, and Myra Acevedo Napoletano. The documents also alleged that Eric, Al, and Carolyn had conspired to commit insurance fraud.

On the afternoon of March 26, 1991, a U.S. magistrate in Albuquerque approved the search warrants regarding Eric. Specific notice was made of the FBI's particular interest in red fibers that could be connected to Myra's death. Search warrants also were approved in New York for Al's and Carolyn's residences. Arrest warrants and criminal complaints for all three were prepared by Cottone, then signed by a federal magistrate in Newark. A separate complaint named Al and Greg on drug-conspiracy charges.

Conversations intercepted throughout that day further confirmed the urgent need to arrest Eric. The main topic of discussion was the fast approaching court date in New York on the Acevedos' visitation show-cause order. But venom, deception, and threats of violence overtook the legal debate.

Carolyn assured Eric that she had been busy interviewing civil attorneys. She related how she had told one of them of her instructions that her son never get involved with a Puerto Rican girl again. "I said, 'It's their families.' " After making her standard vile comments about Marilyn Coludro's mother, she questioned the lineage of Wanda's brother, then added, "And now it's Myra's fucked-up family."

Eric and his mother were on a roll. They agreed that if they put their heads together, they could muck up the court system and effectively shut Pablo down. "We could delay him a whole bunch of times," said Eric. "Or we could also put in a stay on the judge's order for visitation, or file an appeal."

Carolyn said she was concerned that Eric could be arrested for violation of the visitation order. Eric said he had already spoken with local authorities. "I called the cops. And I also talked to lawyers. They *could* arrest me out here. The cop said it depends if they put it on the NCIC computer."

Carolyn said one of the attorneys advised her to tell anyone who asked that she did not know where her son was living. But, Carolyn continued, she was concerned about saying that, in the event the police "put two and two together" about the calls to Al's 800 line. "Now, then, I *am* lying, because I have said I do not know where you are." But with Carolyn, there was an explanation handy. "In a way, though, I'm *not* lying, because you're calling me through someone."

"That's it!" said Eric in agreement. "That's it, exactly."

Eric begged his mother to convince one of the lawyers to give him a discounted hourly rate. "If I only pay out two hundred, I've still got that thousand dollars if I gotta vacate very quickly. . . . If I robbed a bank, or if I rubbed them out to get them to leave me alone, I wouldn't mind running. But why should I run and be a fugitive?" He said if he had to, he could obtain phony documents and establish a new identity. "I fear for my life and for my children's safety. I did not flee; I relocated." Carolyn chimed in that she was going to go out and buy a black wig for disguise.

In her search for the perfect lawyer for her son, Carolyn said she was next going to see "a firm of three Jews," but she said she feared they really needed "a sharp lawyer" like Gotti attorney Bruce Cutler. She said she told one attorney "how Fazzini prevented you from coming into the department," and how he had supposedly failed to check out their alibi in the Matos shooting. She said the lawyer told her that given all the circumstances, he could see why Eric had fled.

Eric again protested. "Wait! Wait! Wait! Listen, you gotta remember this. I did not flee. I relocated."

Suddenly, there was a commotion at the precinct. The people behind Carolyn were talking too loud. The pressure was getting to her. "I can't hear too well because of all this goddamn noise. I am going crazy in this place! I cannot stand it!"

Eric was talking over his mother now, practicing his explanation for why he left town. "You can say that it was impossible, that it was impossible for me to—"

"Somebody just told me that they're looking for me upstairs," Carolyn interjected.

"Listen! Will you let me finish the fucking sentence!" said Eric. "Say that it was impossible for me to function in New York as a single parent and work and everything. That's why I moved."

"I know that," said Carolyn, assuring Eric that she believed his explanation, even if no one else did.

The background noise at the precinct picked up again. Poor Carolyn couldn't conduct her personal business over the din. "Listen to me! Lis-ten to me! Don't make me scream," she commanded, raising her voice. "I am going crazy here! I cannot stand these people! I'm going crazy with the noise! I cannot tolerate it!"

"All right," said Eric.

"My body cannot take all of this!"

"Okay, okay," Eric assured her. "Oh-kay!"

Carolyn said she had to go. The bosses were looking for her. It sounded as though someone upstairs wanted her actually to do some work.

"All right! Let me go!" Carolyn pleaded.

One more time, Eric begged his mother to convince one of the lawyers to charge by the hour. "Because these kids, *there's gonna be bodies lying around* if anybody comes and tries to take them!"

"I have to go!" said his mother.

"And you'd better get that thing off your hip!" instructed Al.

Back in New Jersey, Agent Tom Cottone's concerns were heightened by the hour. Eric filled in the remaining piece of his serial-killer profile when he brought "the little ani-mule"—his nickname for his sons' dog—to the phone booth.

"What are you doing? Dragging him on the ground again?" Al asked upon hearing a disturbing noise in the background. "He's only a baby, Eric. Don't start hurting him."

Eric assured Al he was not harming the pet even though it

was biting his shoelaces. As the two men talked about finding a cheap lawyer, however, Eric interrupted, "Hey! Hey! Fuckin' pig!"

"Don't curse," Al pleaded.

The dog could be heard yelping as Eric kicked away.

"Oh, you motherfucker," said Al in anguish.

"Sonofabitch!" said Eric.

"You motherfucker! I heard you hit him," said Al.

"He ran under a fuckin' car almost, out in the fuckin' street."

"That's your fault," said Al. "He doesn't know any better. He's a dog. Not a human being, like you."

Later that day, Eric called family court in Manhattan to ask if he could be arrested out of state for noncompliance with a visitation order. An official explained that family court judges had jurisdiction only in New York, but the FBI could step in if a criminal warrant had been issued. Claiming he and his sons were now residing in California, Eric said his ex-wife's parents wanted him arrested on the grounds that he had fled New York to avoid the court order. Displaying an incriminating knowledge of where Myra had died, he then added, *My wife was killed in Jersey.*

The most troubling comments of the day were uttered while Eric lamented to Carolyn and Al about the expensive legal fees he faced for his battle with Pablo. "I know a cheaper way. I was cleaning my gun last night. I took it apart. You know, I can buy a whole new barrel for twenty-five dollars, just the barrel. The whole gun is four hundred. I can buy just the barrel, you know, for ballistics tests."

"You won't let that gun go off by mistake," Carolyn advised.

"Oh, no. No. No," Eric assured her. "If Pablo comes up the steps and I'm going down the steps, and I trip and it accidentally"—Carolyn started laughing—"discharges."

Carolyn laughed louder.

"Come on! Listen to me," Eric insisted.

"Listen, you might accidentally shoot—"

The FBI monitoring agents could not make out all of the words. Eric and his mother were stepping on each other's lines.

"Anyway," said Eric, "what's to say—"

Now Al joined in. "And the, and the— Hey! Hey! Hey! And the barrel falls out."

"Yeah, right!" Eric agreed. " 'A semiautomatic pistol malfunctioned and shot the victim ten times yesterday,' " Eric mimicked as the others laughed loudly.

"Listen, you might accidentally shoot yourself," said Carolyn.

"Yeah, well that's a problem," said Eric ominously.

There was silence on the line for several seconds. "Do you feel calmer now?" mother asked her son soothingly.

"Yeah. I am," Eric replied.

But Al was far from relaxed. He still did not like Eric walking around town with a gun strapped to his hip. Eric explained that when he went to his sons' psychiatrist's office he got strange looks from the office staff.

"You *are* psycho!" Al yelled as Eric laughed.

"She keeps looking from my eyes down to my gun. Shit, you know, it's funny because I'm in a nut-doctor's office."

For once Carolyn grew restless with the small talk. "Listen, if I can't get a word in, I'm gonna hang up. I told you. People are nosy. I don't need anybody hearing anything."

"He's acting childish," Al insisted. "He's acting like an asshole."

Carolyn asked if other people displayed their weapons. Al interjected, "No," but Eric insisted that they did, and told a story of an Albuquerque man who had foiled a bank robbery by shooting the bandit six times. "Now he's a hero!"

"Eric, I don't think it's funny," said Al.

Suddenly, mother and son began arguing about whether any of the New York lawyers should be told he had remarried. Eric was adamant that his wedding be kept secret, even though he had earlier told his mother to pass along the information. "You're gonna fuck me up if you mention that," Eric screamed. "Because they'll come down here and swarm all over. You don't understand. Believe me."

Carolyn insisted that she could not lie to the attorneys. "Fuck! No!" Eric was angry, loud, abusive.

"Eric, you're sick, Eric," said Al.

"I'm gonna hang up," said Carolyn. "I'm not even gonna go to the lawyer. I'm sick and tired of you yelling and treating me like shit." Eric quieted down, so she continued. "One day you tell me one thing, the next day you tell me something else."

Cottone had heard enough. Things were really getting

shaky if Carolyn thought Eric was becoming unstable. Eric could break at any moment. Threats of "bodies lying around" could not be taken lightly. Neither could talk of Sandra "falling asleep" with a lighted cigarette. Or banter about guns going off "accidentally." Sandra and the boys had to be rescued immediately.

The FBI was going to take Eric down.

PART 4

The Collar

Little Eric was fine until Eric told him Mommy went to Heaven. From that night on, his eyes were very sad.

—Carolyn Napoletano

- 24 -

The word went out that the feds were arresting Eric Napoletano. The overall operation would be run by Agent Cottone
out of the FBI's command center in Lower Manhattan,
where investigators and prosecutors from New Jersey, New
York, Delaware, and Pennsylvania rendezvoused with
scores of federal agents and Justice Department attorneys
for last-minute planning. The operation in New Mexico
would be commanded by Agent Gonzales. He and Cottone
would remain in touch by cellular phone. Eric's arrest warrant and the search warrants for Carolyn and Uncle Al
would not be executed immediately to give Eric the opportunity to make an incriminating call to his mentors over the
tapped 800 line.

Out in Albuquerque that Wednesday, March 27, 1991, the
FBI established observation posts in two apartments, one
across the parking lot from Eric's second-floor apartment,
the other within view of his favorite phone booth two blocks
away. Shortly after 6:00 A.M., New Mexico time, Eric departed his residence. He paused for a second, then stepped
back inside. Two minutes later, he exited wearing his Ruger
in a holster strapped to his right side. He headed west,
toward the phones.

As soon as Eric was out of sight, a five-member Special
Weapons and Tactics (SWAT) team led by Special Agent
H. Douglas Beldon stormed the apartment. The current Mrs.
Eric Napoletano answered the door. She and his boys were
sent to the back bedroom along with the family dog. The
agents hid to await Eric's return.

In what had become a daily ritual, Eric chatted briefly
with Al Jiovine at his Manhattan office, then headed back to
his apartment to use the bathroom. Climbing the stairs, he
entered the apartment, then turned to close the door.

"FBI! FBI! Freeze!"

Eric spun around to face the voices. There were three machine guns and something that looked like a grenade launcher staring him in the face. Everyone was dressed in bulletproof vests and jackets adorned with "FBI" in bright yellow letters.

"Freeze! Put your hands up!"

Eric hesitated for a moment, then complied with the request.

Special Agent Roger E. Babcock removed the gun. It was unloaded, but Eric was carrying a clip containing fifteen rounds.

Eric was handcuffed, placed on a chair in his kitchen, and advised that search warrants were being executed on his person, car, and apartment. The two boys were placed in protective custody, and removed for transportation to a safe house, the All Faiths Receiving Home. Gonzales, a thirteen-year veteran of the FBI, relayed word back to New York that Angelo and Eric Junior had been rescued. There was universal relief.

Gonzales informed Eric that he was not under arrest. He was free to leave and do whatever he wanted. In fact, he could even make phone calls if he wanted. However, if he wished to stay, he would have to remain handcuffed.

At first Eric decided to watch, but within the hour he grew impatient and asked if he could go to a nearby phone booth. Beldon and SWAT team colleague Carlo M. Stella gladly placed Eric in a Bureau car and drove him there. Since Eric said he wanted to return to the apartment, the cuffs were left on. At the phone booth, Stella removed one of the cuffs and attached it to the structure. He and Beldon then backed away to afford Eric the appearance of privacy.

Eric picked up the receiver and dialed toll-free to Uncle Al. The monitoring agents back in New York would get every word.

"Yeah, Al. Listen! You gotta listen to me! It's very important," Eric said rapidly. "The FBI just came to my house when I walked back in. They came and they had machine guns pointed at me and everything. They took the kids away. And they said the kids are gonna stay in the custody of the State because of—what did they say? That I'm a 'danger to the children.' And Al, they're searching my house. They got my gun. I don't know if they're gonna confiscate it. They said I could probably get it back later. But

they took the kids! I gotta give you the name of the FBI
agent in charge. You gotta call my mother. She's gotta get
the lawyer. I gotta get them kids back. She's gotta go to
court right now. They said I probably can't get 'em back
until I go to court in New York. They got me handcuffed
to the fuckin' phone booth over here, Al!" Speaking with a
nervous stutter, he provided Al with Agent Gonzales's
name, office address, and number to pass along to Carolyn.
She would know what to do.

Al asked about Sandra. Eric explained that the agents had
taken her to her rehab clinic. "She's not under arrest. And
right now they say I'm not under arrest."

"Under arrest for what?" Al wondered.

"I don't know—for the murders. They got— They
want— They— They're here looking for evidence for the
murders and kidnapping. And this and that. But they said
they haven't made the decision if they're going to let me go
yet. At this point I'm not under arrest. But they're not gonna
find no evidence, you know."

Eric said he needed to speak with his mother, so Al dialed
the First Precinct. "Gotta get a hold of her. This has gotta be
straightened out," Eric said, sounding extremely concerned.
"I gotta get them kids. *I can't have anyone asking them
shit!*"

"Roll call, Napoletano."

"Yeah, Carol. Listen, it's me."

"He's in trouble!" Al interjected.

Eric explained again that his apartment had just been
raided. "I gotta give you the FBI agent's name. You gotta
call the lawyer and straighten this shit out."

Calmly, Carolyn assured her son that she would handle
the situation. "How did they get to you?"

"They said they were given it by the FBI in Newark
yesterday, and they know nothing about it. So the FBI in
Newark had to say I'm a danger to the kids."

Again, she assured him she would reach the attorney.

Eric was frantic. "She's gotta go to court and get that shit
kicked out so I can get my kids back. Carol! Just get everything straightened out."

Talking in code, Al expressed concern about the manuals
and warranty cards he had sent Eric for the insurance scam.
"Yeah, they got 'em. They got everything," Eric replied.

"They can't keep that stuff!" Al protested.

Carolyn interjected that none of that mattered. They had more important things to deal with: the call to the lawyer. "Let me go. Let me call her now, all right?"

"Love you!" Eric told his mother.

Back at his apartment, Eric became bored sitting in his kitchen. The agents suggested he go get some breakfast. Eric got up to leave. This time he said he was not coming back, so the handcuffs were removed.

Marching right back to the phone booth, Eric called Al, who connected him to Carolyn. She was now using a phone on the street outside the precinct. "These guys are going through everything. They went through the meat in the freezer," Eric said. "They're walking around with cellular phones. I mean, just like you see in the movies." He said they had even offered him doughnuts.

Eric began reading portions of the search warrant to his mother. "It says they want any letters written in 1990 between Al Jiovine, Carolyn Napoletano, and myself. So, anything I have in there in 1990 that relates to that. They're looking for any evidence into, it says, the beatings of Wanda Matos."

"There's nothing," said Carolyn confidently.

"Right," Eric agreed. "And the murder of Gladys."

"There's nothing."

"The kidnapping and murder of Myra."

"There's nothing," mother again assured son.

"And the murder of Marilyn, because they're saying in here that her body was found somewhere in the Delaware Water Gap, or something like that; it's federal property."

"Okay," said Carolyn, taking control. "I have not sent you any letters. I have only sent you newspaper clippings. And if they ask you why, you say, 'My mother keeps me up to date.' "

"They're going through everything," said Eric. "Boxes of fuckin' cereal. Every fuckin' thing. These guys aren't leaving an inch unturned. They looked under the table. They're fuckin' checking out little Eric's fuckin' Jeep. These guys are fuckin' good." He said it was crucial to get the kids back. They *had* to be kept from talking.

"I know. I know," said Carolyn. "Does Sandy know anything?"

"No," he said. "They're probably interrogating her, because they haven't brought her back yet."

Eric said he only heard snippets of the conversation in the bedroom. "They kept telling her something and she kept saying, 'Oh, no. He wouldn't do that. I know him.' " Eric said he did hear Sandra tell the agents that they were married. "You know, you can't teach these women to shut their mouths."

"Ummmm," said Carolyn.

The conversation drifted back to the visitation issue. "I gotta get my kids back," Eric told her. "You just get that case kicked out of court today!" Carolyn said she would call the FBI in Albuquerque to see if the secretary would connect her with "those dicks." Carolyn was shouting in the phone now, and Al complained that the echo was "mind-boggling." She apologized. "I'm sorry. I'm talking loud. Okay, Ricky?"

Eric became more aggressive in his demands. "What about getting the kids back? What are you gonna do? I wanna know what evidence these guys—"

Al interrupted: "Jesus Christ! This is getting impossible." Angrily, he ended the call.

Carolyn was aflutter. She sensed that the situation was considerably worse than it first appeared. Why would the FBI have taken the kids? Her Ricky sounded uncharacteristically unnerved on the phone. He was almost crying.

She told her precinct boss she was ill and going home. She asked if she could get a ride in a patrol car, but was informed that none was available. Someone suggested she take a taxi. The temperature inside the First Precinct suddenly got very chilly.

Carolyn left the station house, but before going home, she headed for Eric's lawyer's office.

Eric paced around the apartment parking lot. He struck up a conversation with Special Agent Sarah Burcham, who had driven the Napoletano boys to the safe house. Eric explained that Eric Junior had been under a psychiatrist's care since Myra's death. He contended that any separation from him would be detrimental because of the boy's emotional problems. Eric said his son feared he was going to leave him, and as a result, followed him around constantly and would not let him out of his sight.

Eric assured Burcham that the agents would not find any incriminating evidence; even if he had committed a crime, he wouldn't keep any evidence with him. He lashed out at Myra's father, Pablo Acevedo, and NYPD. He said Pablo was trying everything possible to steal Eric Junior and Angelo. He also contended that Pablo was a violent man who beat his kids with whips and would no doubt abuse Eric Junior and Angelo if he gained custody.

"I fear for my life," Eric said, contending that Pablo might go so far as to kill him to gain custody. That was why he had gone to the local Wal-Mart department store to buy the Ruger.

When Eric entered a neighbor's apartment, Burcham asked him to return to the parking lot. Eric obliged, then asked, "What were you afraid of, that I was gonna go in there and get a gun?"

"Well, the thought crossed my mind," the agent replied.

Eric turned to head for the phone booth again. Al told him Agent Gonzales was still supposedly in a meeting, and that the custody attorneys were still not in their office. Eric said he could not understand how the kids could have been taken based on the warrant. "They're searching for weapons and bloodstains, this and that related to the murder of Wanda's mother, the kidnapping and murder of Myra, the beatings of Wanda, all this other kind of shit."

"Ooooh, boy," said Al.

"So I'm telling them, 'Look, my weapon was purchased five days ago, and that's not anything.' "

Eric hung up and returned to his apartment to check on the search and Sandra's whereabouts. It was time for the FBI to turn up the heat. One of the agents told Eric that Greg Velez was being held in New York City and was speaking to the FBI.

Sandra had returned from the clinic, so Eric grabbed her and headed back to the phones. He wanted to debrief her along the way on what the agents had asked her.

"I've gotta get the kids back. That's what I'm worried about," he told Sandra. With each remark, it was clearer that he feared they might say something incriminating.

When Al got on the line, Eric was quite stern. "Listen. The FBI told me something! I want to know, what did you tell Greg? They said that they're holding this guy Greg and he's speaking to the FBI right now. They say that you have told him everything."

"I told him nothing," Al protested.

Eric did not sound convinced. "You've told him nothing? Well, what possibly could you have—"

Al got nervous and started stuttering. "He just, ah, all he said was that he, he, he had suspicions that you, that, that you, were somehow involved somehow. I said, 'You're wrong, you're entirely wrong.' That's his, that's his assumption. Not mine."

"Well, they're trying to swarm in on me and get some evidence."

"I don't know what they're talking about," Al assured him. "You know, ah, Greg has his feelings. You know he doesn't, he, he doesn't know which way to go. That's what he said."

Eric asked if his mother had gotten home yet. He kept repeating how she had to make the lawyers get his children back.

"This pisses me off because I paid four hundred and fifty dollars for my nine-millimeter, and now they got it." Eric was off on a tangent about the weapon, but Al was concerned about his lover and partner in the drug business. "But what's Greg got to do with it?"

"Because they got Greg and they say that you've told Greg everything, and that Greg is telling them everything. I don't know what that means."

"I don't know what it means either," Al insisted.

"I'm asking you!" Eric shot back. Again, Al asserted that he had no idea what Greg could be talking about. Anyway, Al contended, even if Greg had said something, it was hearsay.

"I know," Eric agreed. "Probably, yeah. If you, if, if, if I allegedly had said something to you, or somebody else. And then somebody had said it to him, it's hearsay—but it could be enough, yyyyou, yyyyou know what I'm saying?"

The more Eric thought about it, the more worried he became. "Well, answer me this, have you said anything incriminating? Yes or no?"

"Who?"

"Have *you* said anything incriminating?"

"No!" Al replied.

"That's all I wanted to know."

* * *

Eric headed back to the apartment parking lot, where someone from the FBI conveniently let slip another piece of information for his benefit. Crestfallen, Eric grabbed Sandra and rushed back to the phone. "Okay, Al!" said Eric sternly. "What I heard is, supposedly, that these guys have your whole phone bugged at work, and that's how they knew I had a gun. Supposedly that made them a little nervous. Supposedly they know this stuff about the Mafia and all this other shit that we've talked about on the phone."

"Oh, come on," said Al.

"I know. I said the same thing," Eric said. "It's good fantasies for these guys, practice for them."

Eric returned to his key obsession, his kids. Al said Carolyn was at the lawyer's office now. He would put the call through.

Eric identified himself, but attorney Angela Scarlato told him Carolyn had just left. At that very moment, Carolyn dialed Al's office from a pay phone on the street outside.

Al was as busy as an overseas operator. He complained that his boss was on the other line fuming. "His 800 is getting tied up too much." Apparently the customers were unable to get through. "P-p-p-please. I can't stay on the line," Al stammered.

"Wait!" Carolyn pleaded. "What did she tell Eric?"

The question went over Al's head; he was focused on his irate boss. He told her the man had also been contacted.

"What do you mean? The FBI called your boss?"

"That's right. Because the 800 has been bugged."

"The 800's what?"

"It has been, uh, tapped," said Al. "Tapped. They tapped the 800."

"So they've been listening all along," Carolyn said bleakly.

"Oh yeah. They knew about the weapon."

"And also they got, uh, Greg apprehended." Al said he really, really had to go. His boss was livid.

When Carolyn walked into the lobby of her apartment building on Eighty-third, she was met by a wall of law-enforcement personnel.

"Hello, Carolyn," announced a familiar voice. It was Fazzini. He would not have missed this for the world.

"Oh, no," she replied. "You couldn't make enough of a mess the last time, now you have to come again. I have nothing."

The FBI agents produced the federal search warrant. Carolyn looked over the paperwork and nodded. "Follow me," she said, cognizant that she had no choice.

After being read her Miranda rights, she smugly sat down at the kitchen table to paint her fingernails.

Eric and Sandra spent the next hour walking the Albuquerque streets, then returned to the apartment parking lot and jumped into the station wagon. With Eric behind the wheel and the FBI in loose surveillance, they departed for Sandra's mother's house.

When they arrived, Eric dialed Jiovine to tell him Carolyn had left word with Sandra's relatives that a contingent of FBI agents were at her apartment—"with Fazzini." Oh how Eric hated to say that name.

Eric said the agents had told him Greg was saying that "he heard Myra's voice on the phone—"

"Whhhhat?" said Al.

"At three o'clock. Remember that phone call, the time I called you from my house in Jersey?"

"Yeah," said Al.

"Greg's made a statement saying that he heard Myra's voice on the phone at three o'clock in the morning."

"So what?" Al asked.

"I'm saying, 'So what?' too, but—"

"I don't understand this!" said Al.

"This is what they're saying, that this is what Greg said," explained Eric. "But that's bullshit. You *know* that's bullshit!"

"He heard *Myra's* voice on the phone?"

"Right. But that's bullshit!" Eric shouted. "Because I, *I* called you. You know? This *is* bullshit. You know what I mean?"

"There's some kind of misunderstanding there," said Al.

The dialogue suggested two opposing scenarios: Myra could not have been on the phone because she was already dead; or Myra had been on the phone, but to support Eric's alibi, they wanted anyone listening to think otherwise.

Al acted as if he were in a fog. "I don't understand what's going on. I mean, why are they at your mother's house? There's nothing to do with the children."

That was the point, Eric said. "It doesn't have to do with the children. It has to do with me, and the alleged crimes they allege that I committed!"

"Whew! Oh, boy," said Al.

"This is what it has to do with. What I'm saying is being that you are named in the warrant—"

"Huh?"

"You are named in the warrant! It has your name in it!" Eric began to read from the paperwork, how the FBI was looking for weapons, videotapes, and photographs depicting him "engaged in sadistic activity," red fibers, and any correspondence related to any of the murders, to tampering with witnesses, tampering with evidence, or to a conspiracy.

"What's that got to do with me, though?" Al asked. Eric suggested that agents were probably on their way to his apartment in Queens at that very moment; maybe he should call a lawyer.

"Well, there's nothing I can do about it," Al said philosophically. With that, he got off the phone. Instead of seeking legal advice, though, he signaled Greg on the beeper he had bought him for their drug business.

When Greg called back from an outdoor phone booth, Al chose his words carefully. "Easy, easy, easy, easy, easy. I wanna tell you something. Say nothing," Al instructed. "Are you okay?"

Greg assured him that he was fine. "What happened?"

"I got something to tell you, you won't believe." Al asked Greg if he had been contacted by the FBI. Greg said he had not. Al let out a big sigh. "They are now breaking down my door."

"Whaddaya mean, 'Breaking down your door'?"

Al quickly reviewed the morning's developments. "They're claiming they got you, and that you made a statement that I told you that Eric did it."

"Getthefuckouttahere!"

"No! This is what they're telling Eric: You made a sworn statement that Myra did call at two forty-four or three forty-four that one morning. That you remember exactly the time, and that she called. That it wasn't Eric who called."

"Getthefuckouttahere!" Greg repeated.

Talking in code, Al also warned Greg to hide the drugs from their business. "You know," said Al.

Greg reacted angrily. "Dammit. Shut up, Al."

Al tried to comfort his friend. "You know, Greg, you're my main concern. You know, *you're like a son to me.*"

Eric drove back to his apartment building. As he exited the car, which was adorned with a bumper sticker reading HAVE YOU SLAPPED YOUR BITCH TODAY? he was surrounded by Agent Beldon's SWAT team.

Mama's Boy was arrested without incident. Beldon informed Eric of the warrant issued in New Jersey for kidnapping and interstate transportation for the purpose of murder.

Still linked to Cottone in New York via cellular phone, Agent Gonzales relayed word of Eric's arrest. Carolyn would be taken into custody at the completion of the search of her apartment. A separate team headed over to Jiovine's office.

When Gonzales received confirmation of the New York arrests, he passed that news on to Eric. While being fingerprinted, Eric inquired about the charges against his mother and Al.

"Aiding and abetting," Gonzales explained.

"Like if I whacked someone and another person threw the gun away?"

"Yeah, something like that," the agent replied.

Asked to provide details about his life, Eric, now clad in a T-shirt bearing a Puerto Rico logo, gave up little. The agents noted on official records that Eric had three tattoos, a parrot on the right arm with the name *Myra*, an eagle and snake on the left tricep, and a heart and rose on the right upper back, with the name *Sandra*. He answered truthfully about who his mother was; as for his father, Eric replied, "Unknown."

Eric looked as if he was deep in thought, so Gonzales asked him what he was thinking. "You guys are very professional, but as far as the case goes, it's a bunch of BS. If it took you guys ten months to solve this case, then you don't have much."

At Eric's Albuquerque apartment, Special Agent Fram, the forensic expert, seized several items containing red fibers. The FBI still hoped to be able to find something to match up with the fibers found on Myra's shorts and in the Toyota trunk. Several manuals and photos showing Eric wearing a gold watch and Myra using video equipment were taken as evidence of the insurance fraud, along with a sheet from Eric's notebook listing $9,255 worth of tools, cameras, TVs, jewels, coats, silver, VCRs, sewing machines, and video equipment that was going to be "stolen" or "burned." Two notes from Uncle Al added another $2,002 for an amplifier, tuner, and compact-disc player.

Several porno films were among the eighty-eight video-tapes seized, including "Black Vixens in Heat," "Hot Sex in Bangkok," and "Taboo: American Style," a movie about incest. Many of the movies had themes of violence, torture, and sadomasochism. In addition, there were copies of gory horror films, cop movies, and TV crime programs. The agents also seized four hats, "two police baseball type caps and two police type hats with visors," all bearing the NYPD insignia.

At Al's apartment, agents removed a pair of handcuffs from a birdcage, a knife from a bedroom closet, a canister of tear gas from a living room cabinet, and a machete. Piles of papers, photo albums, loose pictures, Eric's Marine Corps mementos, and personal letters to Eric also were seized.

At Carolyn's, the agents would find the jackpot. In a strongbox they discovered a copy of Myra's New York City birth certificate, a Puerto Rican driver's license issued to Myra Acevedo Olavarria; Myra's NYPD auxiliary police identification card; and two Social Security cards, one issued to Myra Acevedo Olavarria, the other to Myra Acevedo. Discovery of these cards was extremely significant: Carolyn had claimed Myra left with her wallet. Why would Myra have failed to take such important documents with her? How had they ended up at Carolyn's?

A large assortment of TV news stories about John Gotti, three color photos of Eric brandishing a handgun, a pair of handcuffs from a bedroom dresser, court papers pertaining to Pablo's visitation petition, and virtually every episode of *Miami Vice* on videotape were also seized, along with microcassette tapes of personal phone conversations Carolyn had recorded with men who were obviously employed by NYPD. A list of home phone numbers for ranking members of the department was also confiscated.

The agents also discovered unused airline tickets for a flight on November 10, 1990, to San Juan. Eric must have considered fleeing to his home in Moca before heading out to New Mexico.

And, in Carolyn's purse, the agents found her NYPD identification card and a "Far Side" cartoon. The cartoon depicted a farmer holding an ax in front of a flock of chickens while pondering, "Okay, who's it gonna be? Whoooooooooo's it gonna be?" On Carolyn's copy, the names *Dickhead, Pablo, Miriam, Ruth, Spic & Spook,* and *Slut* had been assigned to the individual chickens. "Dickhead" meant Detective Fazzini; Pablo and Miriam meant Myra's relatives; Ruth meant the detective from Delaware; "Spic & Spook" meant two Internal Affairs detectives whom Carolyn had lobbied unsuccessfully to lodge charges against Fazzini; and "Slut" meant Marilyn Coludro's mother, Marta. Over the course of the next several months, Carolyn would reveal nasty nicknames for other adversaries: Purdy would become "Dirty Bird" and "Dirty Birdy," while Donato and Cottone would become "Those Two Little Shits" because of their height.

Carolyn had assumed the search team would find nothing and leave. Informed that she was being arrested in connection with the kidnapping and murder of her daughter-in-law, she lost her detached indifference. As handcuffs were produced, she protested vigorously. "Where am I going to run to? I have two bad arms. I can't walk out of here like this. I've lived here a long time."

The agents told her no one would see her; they would bring an FBI car right up to the front of the building. Breathing deeply, Carolyn stood up, her knees wobbled, then she fell to the floor.

"Call an ambulance. We'll take her to Bellevue," Agent John M. Winslow suggested, referring to the Midtown hospital with a well-known psychiatric unit. Someone else shouted, "No, we'll take her to the hospital on Rikers Island," the unpleasant linchpin of the city jail system.

Carolyn went from apparent unconsciousness to bright-eyed alert. She said she did not need medical attention. She was ready to proceed downtown.

When she arrived at the FBI office, she reverted to her role of abused, harassed victim. Agent Wells held her up by the arm. "Ooooh, ooooh," Carolyn said in pain, feigned or real.

"She'll keep this up all night!" Fazzini warned.

The agents escorted Carolyn down the hall, enabling Fazzini, Donato, and Ruth to deliver long, hard looks in her direction. This was payback time.

To be on the safe side, the feds had Carolyn examined by a nurse. Because of the delay caused by her collapse, it was too late to bring her before a magistrate. She was going to have to spend the night at the Metropolitan Correctional Center, across the street from One Police Plaza. None of the law-enforcement personnel shed a tear over that development.

Carolyn found some consolation with her plight, though: One of her fellow inmates that evening was her idol, John Gotti.

Downtown at the First Precinct, Carolyn was quietly suspended. Her court-appointed attorney successfully argued for low bail in U.S. District Court on the grounds that she had never been arrested before and worked for the New York City Police Department.

Released, Carolyn had nothing to say; she was no stoolie. Uncle Al took a different approach, however. One night behind bars coupled with a conversation with his lawyers worked wonders. He said he was ready to talk about *all three murders*—and to put Carolyn at the center of the cover-up conspiracy.

Late that afternoon, Al and one of his attorneys, Edward W. Cillick, sat down at a conference table at the U.S. Attorney's Office in Newark. Federal prosecutor Glenn J. Moramarco was joined by Assistant District Attorney John D. Ryan and detectives Fazzini and James McGovern from the Bronx, two prosecutors and Detective Ruth from Delaware, Passaic County Prosecutor Bill Purdy and Detective Donato from Clifton. Under a proffer agreement, none of Al's statements could be used against him in any subsequent criminal proceeding. But any information derived from the interview could be used as leads to develop new evidence, which could be used against him. Also, all bets were off if it was determined that he had lied.

Al was committed to providing as little information as possible. He would give up Eric and Carolyn, but not himself.

Representing New York, John Ryan went first, directing Al to begin with the Coludro murder. Al said Eric had called him at work late one afternoon in 1984, very frightened: "He said, 'Al, something happened very bad. Please get to a phone.' "

Al said he left work immediately and called Eric from a pay phone. "He told me he just killed Marilyn at my house.

I hurried home on the subway. The house was dark. He was upset and shaking. He pointed at the bathtub and there was Marilyn." Al said all he could see was the top part of her body. "I looked at her for a second or two, I turned around. My stomach just went all different directions. He pointed to me and said, 'You don't say nothing to nobody. Do you understand?' "

Al contended that shortly after he glanced over at Marilyn's head sticking out of the tub, Carolyn arrived at the scene. Eric said he needed help in cleaning up and disposing of the body. "I said I couldn't help. I wouldn't. I had to leave the apartment. I had to. I just couldn't handle it. My legs were weak. My stomach was upset and I felt like throwing up. I fear that man more than anybody—more than anybody else here would ever realize."

Al said that while Carolyn and Eric went to get his car, he left. "I went to downtown Manhattan and walked around for hours in a daze. I didn't even know who I was." He claimed his walk had lasted for seven or eight hours. When he returned, he continued, Marilyn's body was gone, but Eric was still cleaning up.

Al said he asked Eric what he and Carolyn had done with the body. "He said he took it someplace in Pennsylvania. And he threatened me again."

And how did he know that Carolyn had gone for the ride? "I know he was with her because he told me he was with her. They went and got my car."

Al was supposed to be coming clean about everything he knew. But it became apparent he was still not going to tell the full story about the time Marilyn Coludro had spent in his apartment with Eric. "He brought her over my house for one day and he was traveling around to all various different places with her in disguise and all like that. He just brought her over one night for, I think, a couple hours. He had a bad incident with her. He was playing games with her. I told him not to."

Ryan tried to get Al to admit that Eric was living with him at the time. "Oh, boy! I don't know. I think he was. I'm not sure. Either my apartment or his mother. He was back and forth."

Well, did Eric periodically stay overnight with Marilyn? "I don't remember her sleeping over. I really don't," Al insisted.

It was obvious Al was not going to budge on any issue involving himself. So Ryan moved on, asking Al to recount Eric's description of what he had done to Marilyn. "He said something about cutting her throat. That's what he told us," meaning himself and Carolyn. Al said Eric also told him he had used a knife from the apartment, but had never shown him which one. Al explained that he had not asked too many questions. "I was too nervous and too scared."

Ryan then asked the really tough question: Had Eric explained why he killed Marilyn? "It was something about protecting me and his mother. Something about protecting us from being in danger by her and her family." What did that mean? "I have no idea. It's been such a long time. He said something about, 'I don't want you to get in trouble with her family or my mother to get in trouble, and that's why I did it.'"

Al's version was sketchy. Ryan tried to circle back for more details. Had he seen any blood? No, Al said. Not even in the bathroom? "I didn't go over there. I was too scared." Had he at least noticed a wound around Marilyn's neck? "I didn't notice anything. I just noticed that she was protruding out of the tub." And what part of her body? Just the head, he said, just the head.

Al was very uncomfortable, even with the gentle questioning. The subject matter was getting to him, or at least he was making it appear that way. Prosecutor Moramarco suggested a recess. When they resumed, the questioning shifted to the Gladys Matos shooting.

Al recalled that after Wanda left, Eric tried relentlessly to find her. He said Eric had wanted to get back at her somehow, so when he could not find her, he decided to kill his mother-in-law. "I tried to persuade him not to, but you don't talk to that man that way."

Al said he drove Eric somewhere near 110th Street in Harlem to buy a gun. Eric instructed him where to park, got out, and walked around the corner. Al said Eric returned several minutes later, but empty-handed. According to Al, he then drove Eric to Carolyn's apartment and went home. "The next thing I remember, he killed her. He told me that his mother was with him up in the Bronx. He took my car and I didn't know it, and he went up there with his mother. He told me what he did. He shot her."

Asked how he had learned of the murder, Al said Eric and

Carolyn called him at work together, on two extensions. "He told me he just shot Gladys. His mother was on the phone, too, and she told me the same thing, that she was sitting in the car. He told me he emptied everything out of the gun, five or six rounds. He told me he shot her in the head area."

Al's story of this murder was consistent with the facts known to police.

Ryan wondered if Eric had mentioned what he did with the murder weapon. "He told me he threw it away someplace near the airport, but he wasn't going to tell me where." According to Al, Carolyn then took over the phone conversation. "She said they were going to make an alibi that they were sleeping at the time it happened, or they were downtown in a restaurant."

The prosecutor asked if Carolyn had discussed Eric's intentions with him. "No. I don't believe so. I'm trying to remember. I don't believe she did." But had Carolyn admitted being with Eric for the shooting? "When it took place she was sitting in the car," he replied.

And she and Eric had both told him of their plan to give the police a phony alibi? "Exactly. That same day," Al said. "They told me they were up already in the precinct where it happened for an hour or so."

Ryan was finished. It was clear he was not going to get any more. There was one more homicide to cover, so he handed off to Detective Ruth for questioning about Myra's murder.

After quickly getting the pleasantries out of the way, Ruth bore in on the 2:44 A.M. call. "Did you have an early morning phone call involving her?" As usual, Al said he did not remember.

"A two-forty-four-in-the-morning phone call?"

"I don't remember. And that's the truth."

And so it went, first Ruth, then Donato, again going after Al regarding the call, assuring him that Greg and Maggie now remembered it vividly. But Ruth misrepresented what Greg and Maggie had stated about the supposed phone call. He even tried a subtle threat: "When I asked you about the two forty-four phone call, you realize that there's been a federal investigation going on?"

It did not matter to Al. He still could not recall the all-important call, threat of a prison term and all. "I don't remember. I wish I did," he said emphatically.

Al was considerably more enlightening, though, about other aspects of Myra's murder, those that did not involve him directly. He said Eric and Carolyn had both told him about the killing "the next day, or the day after that." And what had they told him? "That they took care of Myra." Ruth wondered how Al was sure that when Eric and Carolyn said they "took care of Myra," they meant she had been murdered. "He told me he killed her," Al replied.

Changing his story a bit, he then stated that he had actually spoken first about Myra's death with Carolyn alone. "The mother called me at nighttime. I don't remember the exact words. It was like saying, 'Well, we got rid of Myra.' She didn't tell me anything about the death, how she was killed. The best I can recall, she said, that Eric 'took care of Myra.' " He said Carolyn never used words like *killed* or *murdered* on the phone. " 'Took care of her.' She's very careful what she says on the phone." He said she never told him if she had participated in the killing or the disposal of the body.

Al said Eric called him the following day at work and repeated the confession. Eric did not tell him how, when, or where he had killed Myra, just that he had. He said Eric had also neglected to tell him how he had transported the body to Delaware. "The only thing I can think of is the Toyota. I'm just assuming." Al was not asked directly if he had accompanied Eric on the burial trip, but Ruth asked if he had ever been to Delaware with Eric. "Not that I know of, no," said Al, trying to leave himself breathing room.

Seeking to explain why Eric had killed Myra, Al said, "Eric was very unhappy with the situation. They were arguing and always bickering about whatever the situation was. She was concerned about the children. She wanted the children to be with her."

Al's attorney interrupted to observe that it was now 7:05. He had told everyone at the start of the interview that he had to attend a meeting at seven. He said he had to go, but suggested they could "possibly continue at a later date."

Al was free to leave, released on $20,000 personal recognizance bond. The authorities knew he had not come clean about everything, and parts of his story sounded self-serving. But he had given up Eric on three murders—and

Carolyn, too. As potential suspects, mother and son had played NYPD and the Bronx DA's office for suckers. In the Matos case, and the Coludro case to a lesser degree, Eric and Carolyn *had* been smarter, or at least more persistent and vigilant, than the cops and prosecutors they had dealt with. For seven years, they had won.

- 26 -

IN HER WORDS

Had I not passed out, had I just gone to court, I would never have went to MCC for the night. So I was there, and John Gotti was there. They had the nurses there. They took my blood pressure. They gave me bananas. They gave me orange juice. I didn't cry. I was like in a state of shock.

Detective Ruth was there. He is a jerk! He is a jerk! He came in and said, "We got the three of you now. You're going where the sun don't shine." I just looked right through him. Everybody came up and said something to me really nasty, nasty, just like him. I totally ignored them.

Other ones asked me if I would like to make a statement. I said, "No way, not the way you people twist things around. I am not talking to anybody." They kept after me, and kept after me, saying, "Well, Al's in there and Al said this and Al said that." And then they said, "You are going to jail." I said, "I'm not talking to anybody." And I didn't.

That's an awful experience going into prison. You got to take your clothes off in front of them people. I died! I died! I died!

But they were very nice to me. I couldn't climb up on the upper bed so they asked the girl to come down. They were all black girls. They were all in there for drugs.

They asked me what I was there for.

I said, "They said that I helped my son kill his wife."

And they said, "No! You're such a nice person."

They went and scrounged up cookies and milk for me. I was so nervous. I kept going to the bathroom. The guards made me tea. The doctors gave me a physical and they gave me my medicine.

The next day, when I went to court, they let me out on my

own recognizance. I got a federal lawyer in Manhattan. He was nice. He said it was all bullshit. Everybody thought it was bullshit.

27

The social-services system in Albuquerque had to determine where to place the Napoletano children. At the same time, the FBI had to establish whether Eric's boys knew anything about their mother's murder.

Marion Schroeder, the social worker assigned to Eric's abuse investigation, had heard about his arrest on the morning news. Immediately recognizing the name Napoletano, the social worker called All Faiths Receiving Home and confirmed that the children were there. The FBI had left instructions that the boys should be released to the Acevedos. But the maternal grandparents had to be investigated before the children could be given to them. New Mexico authorities had received allegations, presumably from the Napoletano inner circle, that Pablo was abusive and therefore not an ideal caretaker.

Schroeder contacted Agent Gonzales, who informed her that the FBI did not object to the state of New Mexico's involvement. He said the agencies needed to work together; there was official concern that Eric Junior might have witnessed his mother's murder.

The social worker also reached Agent Cottone in New Jersey. He specifically warned her that he did not want Carolyn Napoletano anywhere near the children. Nick Donato, who happened to be in Cottone's office preparing to fly to New Mexico to testify for law enforcement at Eric's federal removal hearing, told Schroeder he knew the Acevedo family quite well and could vouch for their stability and sincerity.

At Donato's suggestion, Schroeder called Myra's half sister, Miriam Colon, who assured her that Pablo and Carmen were loving, dedicated, and deeply religious; they would make terrific substitute parents. Miriam expressed a desire to visit with the boys as soon as possible.

Schroeder decided that the children could be released to the Acevedo family pending a final determination. Because of the boys' ages, and Eric Junior's increased acting out, she recommended that two adults come to pick them up. It was decided that Pablo and Miriam would make the trip. Working through the All Faiths auxiliary, TWA workers donated employee travel coupons.

The Acevedos formally filed for permanent custody in New York, and New Mexico officials decided to do whatever they could to help. While the attorneys hashed out the technicalities, Pablo and Miriam would fly to Albuquerque to testify at a temporary custody hearing. Any interviews with the boys would await their arrival.

The feds knew they had to proceed carefully with the children. For background, Agent Norman M. Scott spoke with Schroeder. The social worker said she had never been able to prove that either child had been the victim of physical abuse. She said she believed Eric Junior might eventually talk about any physical, sexual, or mental abuse inflicted by his father, but it would take weeks, and possibly months, under the direction of a psychiatrist to extract such information. She felt that extensive therapy was in order before the older boy was even asked if he had seen anything significant the night his mother was murdered.

At All Faiths, Eric Junior asked how his father was doing. He was told that Daddy was in jail, and that he and Angelo would be staying at the safe house while their father worked out his problems. Eric Junior replied, "My daddy didn't shoot anybody."

There were two other important issues the FBI in New Mexico had to pursue: interview Sandra Napoletano to determine if she possessed any useful information, and investigate a claim by a federal prisoner that Eric had made incriminating jailhouse statements.

Agent Gonzales found Eric's third known wife to be a steadfast defender of his innocence and integrity. But she did admit that on the day he was arrested, Eric had warned her to be careful about what she said to the FBI, and to remember what the agents had asked her. Curiously, Sandra said she remembered reading a document about Myra's body being found in Delaware. She was not sure, but believed it was "an office communication from the police department." For

some reason, she remembered the date mentioned in the
document, July 19, 1990, eight days prior to the Delaware
corpse actually being identified. If Sandra's recollection was
correct, it meant she had read one of Detective Ruth's Tele-
types soliciting information about the Labrador Lane corpse,
once again suggesting that Carolyn Napoletano had been
well informed all along and had kept Eric posted.

To investigate the jailhouse snitch's claims against Eric,
Agent Gonzales headed out to Sandoval County Detention
Center, where Eric had been held until his federal removal
hearing. Fred Fottler, incarcerated on federal drug charges,
said he was not looking for anything in return for his story
and was even willing to take a lie-detector test. He said he
had met Eric when they were being transported from the
Santa Fe County Detention Center to the U.S. Marshal's
Office in Albuquerque. "I saw you on the news," Fottler
remembered telling Eric. "The news was marking you for a
serial killer."

Eric, who claimed he was an ex-cop, had asked how the
TV stations were playing the story. "Am I a star now?" he'd
wondered.

Fottler said he'd replied that the news had been quite
negative, and told Eric it appeared that the case against him
was quite solid. He said Eric had laughed and bragged,
"They ain't got shit on me. The first murder, I killed my
girlfriend. They came and questioned me. I told them, 'Are
you going to arrest me? If not, get the hell out of here!'
They came to question me about my mother-in-law, and I
told them the same thing. They ain't got shit on me. They
can't prove it or they would have arrested me earlier." If
Fottler was telling the truth, Eric had admitted flat-out to
Marilyn Coludro's murder.

On April 8, 1991, twelve days after Eric's arrest, Pablo
Acevedo and his stepdaughter, Miriam Colon, arrived in
Albuquerque. The next day, they were reunited with the
boys. Four-year-old Eric immediately ran into his grandfather's arms to give him a big hug. Pablo began crying.
Then Angelo, two years and four months, ran over and
climbed into Pablo's lap, cuddling. Both boys appeared to
be very comfortable with Pablo and Aunt Miriam. It was
apparent to the social-services staff that the boys had an
especially strong attachment and love for their grandfather.

Pablo and Miriam were allowed to take the boys to a McDonald's for dinner. Schroeder picked them up an hour later and brought everyone back to All Faiths. As Pablo and Miriam prepared to depart, the children became distraught. Angelo had to be physically pulled away from his grandfather's arms, screaming and crying uncontrollably. By the time Pablo and Miriam reached the parking lot, they too were sobbing. They vowed to see that things were made right. They had to, for Myra.

As Schroeder drove the adults to their motel, Miriam revealed that Eric Junior had made a terrifying accusation when she took him to the bathroom at McDonald's: He said he was angry at his father "because he put a rope around Mommy's neck."

Miriam asked why Daddy had done that. "Because they were fighting." She asked if anyone else had been in the room. He said Angelo had been with him. Miriam told Schroeder she froze at that point, then changed the subject.

The next morning, Schroeder told Agent Gonzales and Detective Donato about Eric Junior's disclosure. The boys were due in court that morning for the custody hearing, and Gonzales asked Schroeder to interview Eric Junior afterward.

The court session went well; the State of New Mexico decided it was in the boys' best interest to be placed with the Acevedos immediately. The State would retain legal custody and act in a protective capacity until the State of New York decided on the petition filed there for permanent custody. The judge said the Acevedos could take the boys with them. They would catch a flight to New York that afternoon.

But first Eric Junior and his aunt were taken to the FBI office for an interview. The youngster balked, stating, "I want to talk about something else." But as Schroeder inquired gently, he gradually opened up.

The boy related how he had woken up and heard loud sounds during "the night Mommy went to God." When he climbed down from the top bunk bed to look out of his room, Daddy was screaming and Mommy was crying. Then, he continued, he saw his mother sprawled out on the floor, "sleeping," with his father standing over her.

Young Eric described a rope he said his father kept in the apartment "for people when they don't make food or clean their room." He said that his father put one end of the rope around his mother's neck and placed the other end over the top of a door and tied it to the doorknob.

Schroeder asked Eric Junior how his father had been behaving during this sequence. "He was screaming," he replied.

"Was anybody crying?" The boy said yes, Mommy. "He did it, but he didn't want to do it. He put the rope around the doorknob."

Schroeder produced three anatomically correct dolls, one for Daddy, one for Mommy, and one for little Eric. "If it's hard for you to tell us, maybe you could show us." She proposed that they play-act about the night of Mommy's murder. She established a scene where it was late at night, and Eric Junior heard Daddy making noises.

The youngster jumped right in. Daddy had been "yelling at Mommy." He then skipped right past the murder. "We went for a drive in the car—me, Angelo, Daddy, and one of my friends." This would have been the ride to Delaware.

As Schroeder prodded, Eric Junior said the friend was a man. She asked if she could guess his name. The boy agreed to the game.

"Was it Bob?" No, said Eric Junior.

"Was it Jim?" Again, the answer was no.

Agent Gonzales handed her a piece of paper with a name written on it. "Was it Al?"

"Yes," the boy replied emphatically. "How did you know?"

In response to more prodding, Eric Junior said that the ride had been a lengthy one, it had been dark out, and he eventually fell asleep. He and his brother were in the front seat, Al in the back, and when he awoke he was back home.

"And where was Mommy?" Schroeder asked.

"Up with God."

Schroeder circled back in the hopes of drawing out some details about the murder itself. "What did they do when they got mad at each other?"

"They fought," the boy said.

"Did you ever see anyone with a rope around their neck?"

"Yes," said Eric Junior. "My mommy."

"Was it that night?" Yes, he replied.

The boy was getting increasingly uncomfortable. Schroeder asked him what he had seen when he looked out of his room. "I saw my dad."

She tried for more. "What did you see?"

"I thought we were done talking about it," he replied.

Schroeder was running out of chances. "Maybe if you tell me what you saw, we can be done."

"My dad took the rope. He put the rope on the door."

"Where else did he put the rope?" Eric Junior did not answer.

"On her neck?" Again, he did not answer.

"On your mother's neck?" Yes, the youngster replied.

Schroeder could not continue to ask leading questions or her efforts would do more harm than good. The interview was terminated. Eric Junior looked emotionally drained.

Aunt Miriam and the boy were transported back to All Faiths. As soon as they arrived, Eric Junior became a bundle of energy again. He hustled everybody together so they could leave for the airport. Schroeder took them to the motel, where the adults packed.

"Why aren't you coming with us?" Eric Junior asked.

"I live here. I have a family here," Schroeder explained. For a second he seemed confused. But then he looked up and smiled. "Okay." Satisfied, he joined the other family members.

A short time later, they were off to New York to be reunited with Carmen, who was flying up from Puerto Rico, and the rest of the family.

Marion Schroeder closed out her case file, but not before adding an ominous recommendation that Eric Junior receive "trained psychotherapy as soon as possible to enable him to address the emotional needs created by losing his mother, being removed from his father, any trauma from placement in substitute care, and most especially, issues arising from his witnessing events the night of his mother's death." The system had an obligation to keep Eric Junior from following in his father's footsteps.

28

Eric Junior's eyewitness account of his mother's murder altered the homicide investigation considerably more than the divergent theories about the 2:44 A.M. phone call. If Myra had been killed inside the Clifton apartment, the federal kidnapping charges were doomed; she could not have been transported alive across state lines. Less than twenty-four hours after the youngster made his claim, his father was brought into U.S. District Court in Newark, where the kidnap complaint was dismissed. There was a silver lining in all this, however: The boy's statement meant that Bill Purdy could now assert jurisdiction under New Jersey law for murder in the first degree.

Eric was taken aback by the developments. He had come to court intending to complain about the way he was being treated in federal custody. Instead, Donato, Cottone, and Talarico arrested him on the new charges and transported him to Clifton for processing.

The next day at the arraignment, Purdy revealed that Eric Junior had given an incriminating statement against his father to officials in New Mexico. State Superior Court Judge Sidney H. Reiss set bail at $2 million.

Eric's new attorney, First Assistant Deputy Public Defender Louis Acevedo—no relation to the victim's family—argued that such high bail was tantamount to none at all. Acevedo, who had once served as a trial commissioner for police-corruption cases at NYPD, said reasonable bail would allow Eric to get a job and support his children.

Judge Reiss was not impressed. "He is a danger to society. There's a lot more here than smoke." Despondent, Eric was put on twenty-four-hour suicide watch.

With the federal charge against Eric no longer operative, it was inevitable that the charges against Carolyn and Jiovine would also have to be dropped. As an alternative,

Donato signed a local complaint charging Carolyn with hindering Eric's apprehension and prosecution.

The noose around Uncle Al tightened in a different way. Because he had failed to remember the 2:44 A.M. call during his sworn plea-bargain talk, he was charged by the feds with making false statements. Greg Velez said he was now certain he had heard Myra's "muffled" voice on the phone during the 2:44 A.M. call on the night she disappeared. He also now said he had heard Al ask Myra if Eric was hitting her, but Greg had not heard her reply. Greg also said Al claimed he had "killed a man" in a gay love-triangle dispute. Perhaps coincidentally, the federal drug charges filed against Greg and Al the day of the kidnapping and obstruction arrests were suddenly dropped.

Al's attorney, Edward W. Cillick, contended that his client had simply forgotten the phone call during the first statement because he was nervous and tired. Of course, that was an incredible claim, given the number of times Al had been asked about the call.

Facing five years in federal prison, Al was allowed to remain free on a $30,000 personal recognizance bond.

Because Carolyn's federal public defender, Thomas Roth, had been alerted to the developments, she had not been present in federal court for the announcement. This left Donato and Cottone very disappointed. They were already angered at the fact that Carolyn had violated the terms of her $20,000 federal personal recognizance bond by contacting a potential witness, Larry Knoepfler—Uncle Al's brother-in-law. They would not have minded arresting her on the State charges.

Instead, Carolyn was allowed to surrender for processing at Clifton police headquarters, in the company of an assigned local public defender, Russell G. Bickert. After the Clifton municipal judge, Harry Fengya, set bail at $25,000, Carolyn was escorted to the processing area for fingerprinting and mug shots.

"Give me your finger," said Detective Joseph Tuzzolino, grabbing Carolyn's right hand. Her fingers were adorned with long, reddish-orange decorative nails. Turning away to prepare to make a print, Tuzzolino felt a strong tug, then a release. Turning back, he felt the fake nail separating from Carolyn's body.

"Whoa!" Tuzzolino said as he skeptically watched the defendant drift to the floor. A veteran of thousands of fingerprint jobs, Tuzzolino later recalled, "Most people, when they faint or have a heart attack, go down like a tree being cut. But she floated down nice and easy."

Donato had watched as Carolyn's knees unlocked slowly. She had not hit her head on the floor, and her arms had not folded under her. He removed her eyeglasses and ascertained that her breathing was not hampered. Carolyn's act was a carbon copy of her behavior the day the FBI had arrested her.

"Relax," Donato advised Tuzzolino. "This isn't the first time she's done this. She'll be all right."

As a precaution, an ambulance was called, but Carolyn stated that she did not want to be taken to the hospital. Shortly thereafter, she was transported to the county jail to join her son.

Carolyn benefited greatly from the change in prosecution strategy. Instead of facing life, or at least a lengthy federal prison term, she now faced only eighteen months for a fourth-degree crime. Carolyn would have been charged with a more serious third-degree offense, but under New Jersey law, hindering-apprehension and hindering-prosecution charges were reduced to fourth-degree offenses whenever the defendant was a parent helping an offspring. Also, a fourth-degree conviction carried with it a presumption against incarceration, a presumption difficult to overcome when the defendant has an otherwise clean record.

Still, from Purdy's perspective, the lesser charges were better than nothing. He figured that at a minimum, even a fourth-degree conviction would cost Carolyn her New York City Police Department job. He was a realist; he could only do what he could do. If Carolyn had played such significant roles in the other murders—helping clean up Uncle Al's bloody bathtub and removing Marilyn Coludro's body; and helping buy the gun, then accompanying Eric to the Gladys Matos shooting—it was up to New York to charge her.

The next morning, April 18, 1991, Carolyn was brought before Judge Reiss wearing a blue business suit, high-heeled pumps, and shackles. The bail hearing provided Purdy with an opportunity to detail his fifty-year-old defendant's links to NYPD and the three homicides to a degree he would probably not be allowed to under the stricter rules of evidence at a criminal trial.

Purdy maintained that the reduction of the crime to fourth-degree was an unfortunate technicality. "The offense that Carolyn Napoletano was attempting to hinder the prosecution of was, in this case, a murder committed by her son." He summarized the key evidence: her visit to Clifton headquarters with Eric to complain that the police were harassing them, her being the primary source for several explanations as to where Myra had gone off to, and her volunteering to police repeatedly that she and Eric had returned to the Clifton apartment at 3:00 A.M. to find Myra gone while, in fact, Myra had been heard on the phone at that hour.

The prosecutor claimed there were ongoing investigations into the other murders. He said the history of those probes "tells us that Carolyn Napoletano has been involved since 1984, having an active knowledge of these investigations and an active knowledge of these homicides, and has at all times attempted to provide alibis for a suspected murderer."

"Did you say nineteen eighty-four?" the judge asked.

Purdy nodded in agreement, then explained that Carolyn had provided an alibi for her son in the Matos shooting. "There have been no charges filed, but this is a very active investigation. I have spoken to the district attorney's office in New York and it is ongoing. Charges are expected to be filed in the near future."

The prosecutor argued that intercepted conversations between mother, son, and Uncle Al about Eric's possible quick departure from New Mexico showed "a blatant disrespect" for the judicial process and law enforcement. "There was discussion—open discussion—regarding possible violence. By this, I mean the shooting of a potential witness in this case."

"All three are involved?" Judge Reiss inquired.

Purdy replied in the affirmative. "It's all too casual, their approach to avoiding the judicial process. It seems to be the most economical means to get rid of the witness."

Continuing to escalate his argument, Purdy pointed out that Carolyn was employed by the New York City Police Department.

"*Had* been employed?" Judge Reiss asked.

"*Has* been employed," Purdy replied. Discreetly avoiding an in-depth discussion of the NYPD-Napoletano link, he

said that New York police authorities had been contacted in
the wake of Myra's homicide, and that a search warrant was
subsequently executed on Carolyn's apartment. "Based on
some information that was found there, she was transferred
from her job as secretary for the chief of a division. Civil
service being what it was, Mrs. Napoletano continued her
job with the police department. I don't think that should
benefit her at this bail hearing. I think that what we know
about Mrs. Napoletano and her involvement in covering up
crimes, in scheming, in protecting a murderer—"

"Well, let me just interrupt you to ask this question," said
Judge Reiss. "Do you think that her knowledge of the criminal justice system was used in furtherance of the scheme
that they were setting up?"

Purdy said it was obvious that Carolyn had "knowledge
of the criminal justice system and was able to make contacts. There is certainly reason to suspect she took an active
part in causing reports not to be filed. She also, with the
purpose of hindering an investigation, has caused complaints to be filed, Internal Affairs complaints, against
detectives who were involved in the investigation of her
son. And that was openly discussed on the telephone conversations. Her involvement with the police department is
an insult to law enforcement!"

Bickert, Carolyn's public defender, rose to argue for the
same bail conditions set in federal court—$20,000, with
actual cash not required unless she jumped. The defense
attorney suggested that if Purdy wanted to talk about more
serious allegations, he ought to charge his client with more
serious crimes. Then they could argue about higher and
stricter bail.

Judge Reiss said he would not even consider less strin-
gent bail conditions. "What the prosecutor has presented to
me concerns me substantially because of her knowledge of
this system and her use of such knowledge in fostering
interference with the process. I don't consider this to be a
run-of-the-mill mother trying to protect her son when she's
using the system against itself, having the knowledge that
she does." He set bail at $20,000 surety, meaning that Caro-
lyn would have to put up the entire amount, or pay a fee to a
bail bondsman, if she found one willing to get involved with
her. "I thought what I was dealing with was a mother trying
to protect her son. That's one thing. But someone who is in

the system, and is using the system against the system, for
whatever purpose, that's an entirely different thing."

Carolyn was taken back to the county jail. Within a week
Bickert had convinced a three-judge appeals panel to reduce
her bond to $2,500, drawing even more attention to the rela-
tive insignificance of the charges. Within a week of the New
Jersey arrest, she was freed.

She ultimately also got her job back. After being suspended for nearly two months, she was reinstated on the
payroll when union lawyers successfully argued that under
civil service rules, she could not be suspended for more than
thirty days without a hearing. Carolyn promptly vowed to
fight for her back pay.

As if moving her around solved the problem, Carolyn was
again transferred, this time to the Midtown North Precinct.

While the legal drama unfolded, Pablo Acevedo, Miriam
Colon, and the boys departed Albuquerque for New York's
LaGuardia Airport, where they were greeted by the children's seventy-eight-year-old great-grandmother, Evange-
lista Acevedo, four great-uncles, three great-aunts, and three
uncles. The authorities in New Mexico had been very
friendly and generous, moving Pablo to tears. But he realized that his final battles were yet to be waged.

He wanted to move the boys to Puerto Rico as soon as
possible, but he had to obtain custody in New York family
court. In the meantime, he and the boys moved in with
Miriam Colon.

Eric Junior continued to act out. One day he locked his
grandmother, Carmen, in the bathroom. When she later
asked him to explain his behavior, the boy said he had
simply done what his father used to do to his mother.

Now in the constant company of family members, Eric
Junior's memory grew more vivid. Pablo put the youngster
on the phone one day to tell Donato he had a secret about Al
Jiovine having been in the car when he went on "the long
drive."

Donato discussed the situation with Purdy, who agreed
that Eric Junior should be interviewed again as soon as possible. Several days later, the boy was brought to the Passaic
County prosecutor's office, to a special toy-filled room,
where Donato conducted a videotaped interview for nearly
two hours.

Eric Junior reiterated the basic scenario he had described during his New Mexico interview, with several additions. He said that when he saw his father with a rope in his hand, hurting his screaming mother, "I kicked my dad away. I kicked him." Presumably talking about the burial ride to Delaware, he said that he and Angelo had sat in the front seat with their father, while Uncle Al had sat in the back.

Parts of the expanded story were improbable or inconsistent with known facts. He said his mother was wearing a skirt when she was killed, but the body had been found with shorts. Also, the seating arrangements only made sense if another adult was in the backseat with Al, but the boy made no such mention. Also, the boy now described the ride as "a short trip."

It was difficult to ascertain whether Eric Junior had witnessed his mother's murder. At a minimum, though, it appeared he had watched many nights of terrifying domestic violence.

After the interview was completed, Pablo and Myra's sister, Miriam, asked Donato if Eric Junior had mentioned anything about Uncle Al feeding him peanuts during the Delaware trip or that Myra's tongue had been hanging out of her mouth while the rope was around her neck. Such inquiries crystalized the downside of using the boy as a trial witness. Any defense attorney would surely wonder why the youngster had made wild accusations to his relatives but was unwilling to repeat them to authorities.

Three weeks later, Donato received another call from Miriam Colon regarding Eric Junior's recollections. She said he now contended that Daddy had made him help dig the hole for Mommy's grave with a shovel. In relaying the story to Donato, Miriam said the boy told her his father had put on gloves, then forced him and Angelo to wear gloves also. In this version, Angelo sat in the backseat with Uncle Al, Eric Junior knew his mother's body was in the trunk, the digging had definitely taken place at night, and Daddy had thrown the gloves away "in the grass."

Miriam also revealed that Eric Junior's emotional problems had deepened. "He's afraid of the night when he goes to sleep. He can't stand the night. He always has problems. We have to tell him stories so he can fall asleep." She said Eric Junior had taken to cursing his father, saying things like, "He's an asshole. He don't know no good."

Donato asked Miriam if she or any other family member had ever mentioned anything about Myra being buried. She insisted that no one had discussed such details in front of him.

"How in the hell would this kid know—"

"That's the reason! He saw everything! Donato, believe me!"

The detective assured Miriam he did believe her.

"He saw everything," she continued. "That's the reason he can't stay still. He hurts his little brother. I feel so sorry for him. He scratched his face and everything. We tell him, 'Don't do that,' but sometimes he can't be calmed down. He's always got to be hitting."

Donato and Purdy suggested counseling, but Pablo was determined to handle such matters himself. He assured everyone that things would be fine once he got the boys back to Puerto Rico. He would raise them properly. No one could doubt his sincerity, but Pablo faced a mammoth task.

Meanwhile, Eric decided to fight for his children from behind bars. "They're still his kids. Just because someone is accused of something doesn't mean he's going to give up his rights to his children," said Stephen Posner, one of his civil attorneys in New York. In one hearing, Posner assured the court that Eric had a "meritorious defense" and claimed it was likely the charges would be dismissed. He also accused the Acevedos of feeding the children unproven accusations about their father.

In the wake of frantic collect calls from Eric, Sandra left New Mexico, and upon her arrival in New York, she announced that she wanted to join the custody suit. Pablo was livid, calling Sandra an "unfit mother" who was simply doing Carolyn Napoletano's bidding to delay the process. He pointed out that Sandra had never even tried to visit the boys after Eric's arrest.

The custody lawyers battled it out for the next several weeks, but ultimately there was nothing to contest. On July 11, 1991, Family Court Judge Leah Marks awarded the Acevedos permanent custody of their grandsons. Authorities in Delaware finally released Myra's body. At long last Carmen and Pablo headed home to Moca to give their daughter a proper Christian burial.

- 29 -

IN HER WORDS

I do not believe this with little Eric. I just can't believe it. I don't know where he would have gotten it from. I just know that he was very sad. I think that when you say to a little kid, "Did this one do this? Did this one do that?" the kid is going to say yes and not really know what he is saying. And I think that when Donato got down on the floor playing with blocks, I think he was putting words in his mouth.

If it was said, they had to say it to him so that he repeated it. But I don't believe it. He was a little kid then, he was like going on four.

You have to remember one thing, from the time that Myra disappeared those kids were with me. They were with me constantly. I would take them to where they went to the baby-sitter's and I would pick them up, then go get Eric.

If I thought for a moment that Eric did it, I would be afraid of him. I would never want to be around him. But I know him really good.

Eric doesn't have a mean bone in his body. He doesn't get into fights with people or anything. He never fought with anybody. He's never come home bruised or bloody. I don't care what anybody says.

I know that Al told stories that Eric broke my arm, because I've had two broken arms. I was with Al and Eric when I broke my arm the first time. But Al lied and said that Eric pushed me. They didn't know that I fell until I screamed because they were both walking in front of me. We had walked down the steps; it was like a sheet of ice. How they didn't fall, I don't know.

I would never have broken my arm if I didn't leave the house. I was already in bed but Eric had a moped, registered at Al's mother's house. He was out riding on it and I don't remember why he had to come home, but Al said he couldn't get him to come home. I said, "Well, I'll go out with you." Al came by to get me and we went out there and we went in the police station. Al did all the talking, he and Eric were friendly with the mayor's son out there. But they didn't know where Eric was. All of a sudden they spotted him. It was like a movie. Eric came in and they impounded the bike. They said that I had to pay for storage. I remember I said, "I ain't paying for nothing." Al paid, and as we were walking down the steps—Al was in front and Eric was in the back—I walked right where they walked, and I fell down. All my weight went on my shoulder and I just yelled "Aawww." Al said, "Oh, it's nothing." He said, "Come on, get up. I've got to go to work tomorrow."

Then Eric went inside to tell them that I had fallen. So the cop came out—and they are assholes out there in Jersey. I mean, even though I was born there. You know some things you remember to your dying day? The cop says, "What hospital would you like to go to? We have a number of hospitals." Like I could pick a hospital! So Eric and I went in the police car. Eric, I remember he was hugging me and telling me he'll help me and he'll do anything for me. I knew it was broken.

I'll never forget it. We laughed over it later. That was a lawsuit. I sued the borough of Dumont. I got money for that.

The second time, I was in the department about six months, and I broke my arm in the house. Eric didn't do it, but Al said he did. I had a shag rug and I slipped on it and I went into the doorknob—no, that was my eye, I'm sorry. That was my eye. I fell in the bathroom. I am accident prone. I can't tell you how many accidents I've had. I have had stitches in my head. I've had a broken toe. But I got the broken toe so little Angelo wouldn't get hurt. Eric had taken the kids down in the elevator and then he came back because he had forgotten something. When I opened the door he just came in, but the elevator was still there and the kids were still in the hall. You know how kids are, so I went running and as I did, I had newspapers in a plastic bag like you get in the supermarket, it caught on my toe and I dragged big stacks of like two weeks of the Times *and the*

Sunday papers, everything, all out in the hall with me, and I broke my toe. Just so I could save Angelo.

The second time with the arm, Eric wasn't home. I had to walk over to the hospital in my nightclothes. I worked midnights then, and I was getting up going to work when I slipped with the slipper. You know on the marble sill going into the bathroom? And I fell down between the toilet and all my weight went on my arm and I broke it. When it rains, sometimes I have to put my sling on because it is really bad.

I've been sick a lot. In the past ten years, I have been really sick. But I don't resort to drugs. I mean, I'm a prescription junkie, if you want to call it that, because I have so much wrong with me. I have arthritis in my fingers. The medicine is also for my arms. They never healed right. The medicine is half painkiller, half anti-inflammatory. I also take an extra pill that is a combination of vitamins. And I get a B-twelve shot every week.

I'm anemic. During the week, it takes everything I have to get up and get to work. I know that I can always be taken to the hospital, or I can always leave. They'll take me home in a patrol car. When I come home, I fall asleep watching the news. I am so tired during the week. I do not like people sitting with me on the bus. I have to sit in the front. I get claustrophobia and I always feel sick because I cannot stand that stopping and starting, and those bumpy roads when it goes off the highway.

I'm a mess.

- 30 -

Purdy's New Jersey grand jury returned an eighteen-count indictment against Eric, Carolyn, and Al on June 6, 1991. In addition to the charge of murder against Eric, he and his mother were accused of conspiracy, hindering apprehension by lying to the police, hindering prosecution, theft of Myra's wallet and identification cards, tampering with evidence, and tampering with witnesses—Carolyn for warning Uncle Al's mother she was talking too much to the police, and Eric for his advice to Jennifer Meade not to cooperate. Al was charged only with two counts of conspiracy in the continued hope that he would cooperate fully.

Under federal speedy trial provisions, Jiovine's trial on the obstruction charge was set for July 8 in Trenton, New Jersey. On the eve of the trial, with Maggie and Greg prepared to testify about the 2:44 A.M. phone call, Al blinked. In an unusual move, he agreed to plead guilty without obtaining any concessions from prosecutors. Perhaps he was relieved to avoid bigger legal problems, such as charges of murder or accessory before the fact on one or both of the first two homicides.

Assistant U.S. Attorney Moramarco insisted there be no deal on sentencing. He was going to seek the maximum five years without parole. He did promise that if Al cooperated with the Bronx investigation, and any others that might develop, his good deeds would be made known to the court. The more Al cooperated, the better chance he would have at a reduced sentence.

Moramarco realized that he needed to secure the longest possible sentence as an incentive for Al to cooperate—along with the pending State conspiracy charges. "It is our hope and expectation that there will be other indictments," the prosecutor said.

In court to enter his plea before U.S. District Judge Garrett E. Brown, Jr., Al admitted that he had withheld material information from federal agents, that he in fact did remember the 2:44 A.M. call. But in admitting his guilt, Al was not required to provide an in-depth accounting of how he now remembered the crucial specifics of the phone call.

Al played the wounded bird when he appeared before Judge Brown again, on October 28, 1991, for sentencing. His lawyer explained that Al had a "love-fear relationship" with Eric—possibly even a physical one—that had prevented him from betraying Eric, even with the grant of immunity. The attorney characterized Al as a good citizen, active in charity work, and the sole support for his elderly mother, Rose Dugan.

Prosecutor Moramarco opposed the defense request for a reduced prison term, pointing out that if the defendant had spoken up sooner, two women would still be alive. Moramarco made it clear he thought Al was still lying about his knowledge of all three murders. He said Al had been asked on numerous occasions to reveal what he knew and had either declined or provided "bits of information" authorities already knew.

Judge Brown sentenced Al to the maximum five-year term. He observed that given the circumstances, the federal sentencing guidelines called for an even stiffer prison term, but he was prevented from dispensing one because of the statutory limitation for the specific crime charged.

Always the manipulator, Al wanted a couple of days to get his affairs in order. But Judge Brown ordered that he be taken away. Al appeared to be in shock. He was finally going to have to answer for his years of silence.

Since Al Jiovine's credibility and eventual cooperation were both tenuous, further investigation was still needed. More than ever, Detective Donato and Agent Cottone were now partners—a fine display of FBI and local law-enforcement cooperation. The more useful evidence they could uncover, the less Bill Purdy would have to stake his trial presentation on Al Jiovine. For a great deal of the time, however, Cottone and Donato found themselves chasing people who were potentially harmful to the State's case.

The two investigators turned once again to Marilyn and Larry Knoepfler. Jiovine's half sister alleged that Al was involved in a kickback scheme with a trucking company in Seattle. Matter-of-factly, she said envelopes of cash were being sent in Al's name to their mother's house via DHL, about $1,000 once a month.

Larry Knoepfler presented himself as being uncharacteristically helpful this time around. He now offered that Eric had accompanied him years earlier on several deliveries for a meat-distribution business he ran out of his parents' home. He also volunteered that he had told Eric of his experiences working in a slaughterhouse and had shown him how to cut sides of beef, how to tie double knots around pigs' hind legs, how to hang them upside down, and how to drain the blood from the jugular veins. This description easily matched the way the coroner in Pennsylvania had said the blood had been drained from Marilyn Coludro's body. Larry seemed intent on making Cottone and Donato aware that he was not the only one with knowledge of the butcher's business.

Larry said he also now remembered the specific reason Eric had asked in 1985 to be introduced to Mafia figures: Eric had decided to become a mob hit man. Larry additionally claimed that he once found a torture-bondage magazine under the seat in Eric's car and recalled Eric claiming that he often picked up hookers when he drove a taxi during his trips back to New York from Puerto Rico.

Al's brother-in-law also described a lock-blade knife Eric used to carry in a sheath on his side and a "Rambo-style" serrated survival knife he kept in his car trunk. He recalled that when Eric had been an auxiliary cop, he had secreted a small handgun on his ankle and kept a knife and a club with him. Clearly seeking to separate himself from any possible connection to the Coludro homicide, Larry also now specifically remembered having given Eric some cord from his garage that looked like the type used to tie up Coludro's body.

With this new information, Donato and Cottone could not help but think that Larry was being more forthcoming in order to divert any possible interest in his background. The investigators became even more convinced that Larry knew much more than he was saying. His credibility as a potential witness was too suspect.

Another potential trial witness who would surely never be called was Theresa Maltese's husband, Tony. He had a significant story to tell, but it conflicted with the operative theory on the 2:44 A.M. call, and he had a criminal record for a sex crime involving a child.

Donato had always wondered what Theresa's husband had witnessed in the Clifton apartment hallway the night Myra disappeared. But he had proved to be impossible to track down in the months after Myra's body was identified.

In fact, Theresa had lied repeatedly about her husband's whereabouts, variously claiming he was not at home at the moment or visiting relatives in Florida but unreachable by phone. Then, without going into detail, neighbor Jeanette Konuklu informed Donato that she was no longer allowing Theresa to baby-sit for her.

Donato ultimately determined that Tony Maltese—bald, five-foot-nine, and 210 pounds—was an inmate at Mid-State Prison in Wrightstown, New Jersey, serving a plea-bargained four-year sentence for sexual assault and endangering the welfare of a child. He had entered the prison system on July 20, 1990, just one month after Myra's murder.

More intriguing than Maltese's background was the story he told Donato about Myra's final hours: While his wife had been outside talking to Carolyn that evening, he had engaged Eric in conversation in the building lobby. According to Maltese, Eric asked if he had heard him arguing with Myra the night before. The man told Eric he had heard loud words exchanged. Eric said that he and Myra had been fighting about his having a girlfriend and her having a boyfriend. Eric then explained that he and Myra had resumed arguing that afternoon, after the moving man left, until she tossed some clothes into a backpack and walked out, leaving him and the two children in the apartment. Eric said he had no idea where Myra had gone off to, then excused himself to go upstairs to use the bathroom.

Maltese's story was, of course, quite tantalizing. But like Eric Junior's, it complicated the case. His version of events suggested that Myra was already dead by 8:00 P.M., or that Eric was on his way upstairs to finish the job. By necessity, Maltese would have to be kept on the sidelines to keep the new 2:44 A.M. scenario intact and to avoid the possibility of a tough cross-examination about his criminal record.

Another potential witness, Bob, the businessman who had introduced Eric to Uncle Al, was located by the FBI in Charlotte, North Carolina, residing with his "foster child,

Wally," now a grown man. Interviewed by Special Agent James R. Fitzgerald of New York, Bob provided a version of how and when the various parties had met that differed considerably from the one related by Al Jiovine. Bob asserted that Wally and Eric had been friends with Jiovine's young roommate, Mitch, before Eric met Al, and that Eric knew Mitch so well he had attended his funeral following the young man's accident on the Queensboro Bridge. Bob the businessman made no mention of any trips to the zoo with the two boys or links to the Catholic Charities organization, as claimed by Carolyn and Jiovine.

He went on to explain that he had sent Jiovine a condolence card regarding Mitch, Al called to thank him, then he met Al for the first time several days later, when Jiovine visited his apartment on East Seventy-eighth Street in Manhattan. He said Eric happened to be there with Wally, so he introduced Eric to Jiovine.

As provocative as those relationships were, Bob revealed an even more fascinating liaison: During the course of young Wally's friendship with Eric, he—Bob—had the occasion to date Eric's mother, Carolyn. Bob said the relationship had consisted of "approximately six to eight dates."

Bob insisted he had not known that Eric had moved in with Jiovine until Carolyn told him. He said his relationship with Carolyn lasted only a short time. "He described her as becoming overly obsessive with him and their relationship. She was a bother to him," Fitzgerald wrote. "He also stated that Carolyn told him she was seeing a psychologist to help her with various mental disorders. She did not confide in him what these mental problems were." Bob claimed that after breaking up with Carolyn back in 1981 he had not seen or heard from her, Eric, or Al again.

The last of the rogues' gallery of troublesome potential witnesses—a conniving, high-profile jailmate of Eric's named Arthur Seale—came forward to contact Cottone and Donato.

Eric considered himself a leader in the Passaic County Jail, a dubious honor that made his mother proud. He also considered himself a good judge of character, but he should have been more careful than to befriend Seale, the admitted kidnapper and killer of Exxon executive Sidney Reso. Eric took to Seale as soon as he arrived at the county facility, where he was being housed as a federal prisoner. Eric was impressed with Seale. He had been interviewed by Barbara Walters; news stories of his case had been circulated worldwide.

Seale quickly sensed an opportunity. Through his attorney he sent word to the prosecutor's office that he possessed incriminating information on Eric Napoletano.

Tom Cottone, who happened to be one of the FBI's case agents on the Reso investigation, and Donato, who had recently begun working out of Cottone's office on loan to the FBI Violent Crimes/Fugitive Task Force, headed over to the county jail for an interview. Seale told the investigators that Eric viewed himself as president of the cellblock and considered Seale vice president. He quoted Eric as having told him, "Okay, so I did it. But they don't have any real evidence, like hair, blood, or fibers." Seale then started to go on about his and Eric's opinions of other inmates in the unit. Cottone and Donato wanted to know what other specific information he possessed that implicated Eric in any of the murders. Seale said he had already told them everything he knew. Cottone and Donato got up to leave. They had been there less than thirty minutes. He had nothing useful to offer.

In contrast to the relative speed of Al's federal case, the legal combatants in the New Jersey prosecution settled into a deliberate pattern of pretrial posturing.

The case was assigned to Superior Court Judge Vincent E. Hull, Jr., for whom Purdy had clerked years earlier. One of the most respected and skilled jurists in the state, Hull presented a dignified profile: formal, gray-haired, former prosecutor and state deputy attorney general. Years ago he had been involved in the prosecution of one of the most controversial cases in New Jersey history, the murder trial of former boxing champion Rubin "Hurricane" Carter.

There was talk of the Napoletano trial beginning in early to mid-1992, but that seemed unrealistic given the myriad pretrial motions. For starters, Eric's public-defender team of Louis Acevedo and Susan McCoy wanted the news media banned from pretrial hearings. They reasoned that much of the evidence introduced at pretrial proceedings would be unduly prejudicial, such as the FBI's classification of Eric as a sexually sadistic serial killer preying on Latina women, testimony about the other two murders, Eric's homosexual relationship with Al, his secret move to New Mexico, his

mental instability, his propensity for violence, and any char-
acterizations of him as a bigamist, adulterer, wife beater,
and sexual deviate.

Acevedo cited a great many newspaper and TV reports on
the case, but was especially perturbed about statements
made by Lucy Crespo, a Christian Radio Vision host who
had talked with Myra in the weeks before she died. Crespo
had told Donato that two months before Myra's death, she
told her that Eric had locked her in a room for three days
and would not let her see her children. In an interview with
Channel 41, Crespo contended that Eric harbored intense
hatred for his mother, to the point where he would have
liked to inflict on her the violence he had imposed on Marilyn Coludro, Gladys Matos, and Myra Napoletano.

"Ms. Crespo provides a diagnosis of Mr. Napoletano even
though she holds no doctorate or medical degree," Acevedo
chided.

To drive home his point that a barrage of negative publicity could make it impossible to select an impartial jury,
Acevedo told Judge Hull he had overheard five Spanish-
speaking inmates at the county jail debating the "appropriate disposition" for Eric because his victims were all
Latina women. Without skipping a beat, Judge Hull
retorted, "Well, I don't think they're going to be sitting on
the jury."

The judge denied the motion to close the courtroom,
saying that adequate alternatives existed: A larger than
usual pool of potential jurors would be summoned; exhaus-
tive voir dire would be conducted relative to potential
jurors' knowledge of the case; pretrial hearings would be
conducted that summer, with the trial starting in the fall to
afford a media cooling-off period; and the most crucial
hearings would be conducted after the jury was selected and
before the start of testimony.

Understandably, the defense team was concerned about
the possibility that the jury would hear testimony regarding
Eric's relationships with Marilyn Coludro and Wanda
Matos, and the subsequent homicides of Coludro and
Wanda's mother. Purdy argued that such testimony was
admissible under New Jersey Court Rule 55, which stated
that evidence showing a person had committed a crime was
inadmissible merely to prove his disposition to commit

another crime, but was permitted to prove some other fact at issue, "including motive, intent, plan, knowledge, identity, or absence of mistake or accident."

Purdy contended that evidence of the prior crimes established Eric's "continuous state of mind" to "demean, abuse, and murder these women." He told the court he was prepared to demonstrate that Eric had wooed Marilyn, Wanda, and Myra "through promises of undying love and commitment," and that these Latina women were particularly susceptible to his overtures "due to their social, economic, and intellectual status."

"The State contends that the defendant has not only an affinity for young Hispanic women, but a perverse desire to control and dominate them. When the women asserted independence, or otherwise made efforts to terminate the relationships, Napoletano was compelled to maintain his dominance by committing murder," Purdy wrote. "In each case, the defendant ended the deteriorating relationship by murder. In Wanda's case, her mother refused to divulge her whereabouts, so the defendant struck out at the mother as a substitute. The pattern is further evident from the fact that the defendant, after ending one relationship, was seemingly compelled to become involved in a similar relationship to feed his need for domination."

According to Purdy, several key points of similarity in all of the homicides implicated Eric in Myra's murder: the type of woman, the nature of his relationships, the pattern of abuse, the termination of the relationship by murder, the disposal of two of the bodies under basically identical circumstances in isolated, rural areas located in outside jurisdictions, "and the accessory role of his mother in avoiding detection."

In a second Rule 55 dispute, Purdy contended that evidence of threats, arguments, and violence between Eric and Myra also was admissible. Such evidence included derogatory ethnic epithets, observations by witnesses of bruises and burns on Myra's body, overheard arguments and fights about their impending split, and Eric's vow to kill Myra if she ever took the kids and left.

As to be expected, defense attorney Acevedo opposed admission of any mention of the first two murders. "Neither one of these defendants have ever been as much as charged with any crime or offense related to those homicides. Those homicides are seven and eight years old, and no charges have been filed against anyone. It is amazing how the State of New Jersey can prove something that the State of New York has been unable to prove."

Another legal maneuver involved a technical request by Purdy to use the statements of one co-conspirator against another under court rules allowing exceptions to the hearsay rule. The evidence in question concerned statements the defendants had made to police as well as conversations intercepted by the FBI wiretap. Citing a long line of supporting court rulings, Purdy argued that Carolyn and Al had made statements to the police "with the purpose to thwart the investigation," for example, volunteering false information about Myra's possible whereabouts or failing to recall a particular phone call. Purdy contended that each of the defendants was liable for the actions and statements of their codefendants "when they occur in furtherance of the conspiracy."

Purdy argued that the relationship between the defendants was further established by evidence of the two prior homicides. "The evidence will demonstrate that Albert Jiovine and Carolyn Napoletano have knowledge of the homicides and they assisted Eric in efforts to prevent law enforcement from obtaining evidence and information. The relationship between the three defendants, the homicides, and the coverups, are all corroborative of the existence of a conspiracy." If no one in New York was going to use all of that evidence, Purdy was certainly going to try.

Acevedo opposed the prosecutor's strategy on the grounds that the evidence was inadmissible hearsay. Further, he argued, allowing such evidence would "create substantial danger of undue prejudice," or confuse and mislead the jury. He made the additional argument that if Uncle Al did not testify, his statement quoting Eric's supposed confession that he "took care of Myra" could not be used at trial because it would violate Eric's Sixth Amendment right of confrontation and cross-examination.

Acevedo ridiculed Uncle Al's inability to remember the "infamous two forty-four A.M. telephone call" for so long. He also questioned the State's claim that the call helped prove the existence of a conspiracy. "It is truly an amazing feat how anyone could conclude that a person's failure to recall a particular event is 'substantial enough to engender a strong belief in the existence of a conspiracy.' " The defense attorney pointed out that Uncle Al told police that Eric had confirmed making the call, but Al still could not recall it. He suggested that if Eric and Al had conspired to create a cover-up, Al would have simply echoed the story Eric had told to the police.

Judge Hull ultimately rejected most of the defense requests. He said the state had met the necessary burden to sustain an indictment. He scheduled pretrial suppression hearings to begin July 7, 1992, during which he would rule on the conspiracy issues and the admissibility of numerous statements and wiretapped conversations. The judge said he would decide Rule 55 issues—most important, any testimony about the first two murders—immediately before the commencement of trial testimony.

Carolyn waived her right to be present at the suppression hearings. She claimed she had run out of vacation time; attending would "impose an undue financial hardship." Uncle Al—temporarily transferred from the federal prison at Bradford, Pennsylvania—attended every day wearing the same red golf shirt and a worried frown.

Eric looked taut and considerably thinner. Apparently, his stay at the county jail had not been a pleasant one; he claimed the deputies had beaten him. He attended clad in a gray sweatsuit the first day, then wore a blue jacket, dark pants, and white shirt. His attorneys had obtained the new outfit from the local Salvation Army office.

During court, Eric often whispered to his attorneys, scribbled on a notepad, and rolled his eyes when Purdy was speaking. During one session he repeatedly referred to the prosecutor as "that asshole."

Seeking to prove the existence of a conspiracy—a necessary legal technicality—Purdy pointed out how Al had claimed he was staying away from the Napoletanos, yet phone records showed fifty-nine calls from his Queens apartment to Carolyn's during the six weeks after Myra's disappearance and thirty-two calls from Carolyn's to his apartment in a corresponding time period.

On the third day of hearings, Judge Hull ruled there was sufficient evidence to show that Eric, Carolyn, and Al had indeed been part of a conspiracy. He okayed use of the wiretap tapes as evidence, subject to limitations because of his co-conspirator concerns. The judge said he was swayed by two key elements: For Al, it was the 2:44 A.M. phone call; for Carolyn, her possession of Myra's Social Security cards, Puerto Rico driver's license, and New York City auxiliary police ID card.

In ruling against Purdy on the co-conspirator issue, Judge Hull said that significant portions of the wiretap tapes along with several other pieces of evidence would be admissible only against the defendant the evidence applied to. For example, the "Far Side" cartoon altered to include nasty names for Fazzini and the others could conceivably be admissible against Carolyn, but not against Eric. Since mother, son, and Uncle Al were slated for a joint trial, such evidence would have to be excluded.

Judge Hull ordered excised from the tapes all references to drug dealing by Al, the insurance scam, Eric's walking around Albuquerque with a gun on his hip, weapons, the dispute between Pablo and Eric, Eric's comments about Jews being cheap and "Jew lawyers," Eric and Carolyn's claims that Fazzini had prevented him from joining NYPD, any talk of the "coffee shop" alibi because it referred to the Matos shooting, and—pending an overall decision on Rule 55 material—any references to "other crimes evidence," most notably the first two murders.

On the final day of hearings, July 14, 1992, Judge Hull ruled that witnesses would be allowed to testify about Myra's fears during the waning days of her life. He specifically approved such testimony from Pablo and Carmen Acevedo, and neighbor Jeanette Konuklu. And in a major boost to the prosecution, the latest Greg Velez–Maggie Rivera version of the 2:44 A.M. call, in which Al asked Myra if Eric was hitting her, would also be allowed.

The suppression hearings had been very uncomfortable for Al since he had to sit next to Eric in court each day. He had never even looked at his "son," much less spoken to him. He did not relish the prospect of having to sit at the same table throughout a lengthy trial. Also, he was sure he would prefer conditions at the federal prison in Pennsylvania to spending time in one of New Jersey's maximum-security facilities. He was willing to talk in exchange for a deal that would fold any state-prison time into his federal sentence. Purdy decided it was worth getting Al more solidly on board.

On July 23, 1992, Al sat down with Donato and Investigator Pete Talarico from the prosecutor's office to tell yet another version of events. He said he now specifically remembered that when Carolyn first called him with news of Myra's murder, she had told him in code, "Al, he did it again, to M." During the next two hours, Al leveled accusation after accusation. He said Carolyn had called him again the Friday after Myra's disappearance to tell him Eric was on his way over to Queens, and would beep his horn for him to come outside. Al said they met on the corner of Eighty-eighth Street and Thirty-fourth Avenue, next to the park near his apartment building. "It was dark in that area," Al recalled. "He whispered to me, 'Are you wired?' Then he said, 'Al, I had to kill her because she was taking the kids to Puerto Rico. I took her to Delaware.' At that point, the whispering stopped and I told him, 'You must be sick.' When I was turning around, he called me a 'fucking asshole.' Then I turned around and walked away."

Al said that when he and Eric were together the next afternoon at the Clifton apartment, Eric told him "he cleaned the car up so they would never find any evidence."

Al also now remembered that Eric called Myra names such as "spic" and "bitch," kicked Eric Junior when the boy grabbed someone else's toys without permission, and referred to police investigators as "dickheads" and "assholes." He also now recalled how Carolyn told him "Eric punched her in the eye, whereas she had to go to Doctors Hospital, down at the corner of Eighty-eighth Street, near her home in Manhattan. I also recall an incident outside the Dumont Police Department, where Eric and Carolyn had an argument, and Eric pushed her against a van. She either dislocated her shoulder or broke a bone. I believe the Dumont police took her to Holy Name Hospital in Teaneck." In telling that last story, Al neglected to mention that Carolyn later sued the municipality with his help, based on a different version of events.

Al now recalled the 2:44 A.M. phone call better, too. Eric had been angry because Myra wanted to go to Puerto Rico. Eric had wanted her to get subsidized housing in New York. Eric had told him, 'Here's the fucking bitch, you talk to her.' And Myra had gotten on the phone crying that Eric was having sex with Jennifer Meade, then coming home for sex with her. "I asked her if Eric was hurting her or hitting

her, and there was no response. She was crying and I heard
Eric yelling in the background, 'Fuck her. She's not going
anywhere.' "

As tidy as Al's story appeared on the surface, his credibility still strained belief. He claimed Carolyn's "he did it
again to M" call had been her first to him in sixteen months
because she owed him $800. Given the relationship later ex-
posed on the FBI wiretaps, it was hard to believe that Carolyn
had called him so casually after such an extended separation
to announce that her son had committed another murder.

As always, dealing with Al was no simple matter. Still, he
did represent the least of the evils.

The next day, Al appeared before Judge Hull to admit that
he had conspired with Eric and Carolyn to cover up Myra's
murder. He admitted that when he told police she might have
flown to Puerto Rico or gone to live with relatives in New
York, he already knew she was dead. He also knew that Eric
had killed her and that her body had been buried in Delaware.

Al also confessed that Carolyn and Eric had told him to
lie to the police, and that when he reported back after telling
the police a phony story, they praised him, saying, "That's
good. That's the way it should be."

In return for pleading guilty to one count of conspiracy to
hinder Eric's apprehension and agreeing to testify against
Eric and Carolyn in a manner consistent with his latest statement, the second conspiracy count was dismissed. The State
agreed to limit Al's exposure to a five-year prison term,
promising to make it concurrent with his federal sentence. If
he succeeded in getting his federal term reduced for cooperation, the New Jersey sentence would be reduced, too.

Outside of court, James A. Kilpatrick, one of Al's attorneys, explained to Diane Haines of *The North Jersey Herald
& News*, "This has been a weight on his mind for the last
two years. He feels good about what he did today." Defense
attorney Susan McCoy reacted quite differently: "His credibility is really questionable. We're not really concerned
about it."

Al had a concern, though, for his safety. As a result, he
was kept in isolation, away from Eric, until he could be
transferred to the jail in adjacent Bergen County.

With Al finally on the side of the good guys, the focus
turned to Eric and Carolyn, and the upcoming trial. The

wiretaps, as well as the defendants' statements to police, were powerful evidence, a colorful glimpse of their everyday life intermingled with criminal talk of schemes and cover-ups.

Everyone on the government side had been looking forward to having Eric and his mother sitting there side by side as the tapes were played. But Judge Hull's ruling on the co-conspirator issue left Purdy with a tough decision. He needed to present as strong a case as possible against Eric. He could not afford to let important evidence go unused for cosmetic gain. He had no choice but to file a motion seeking separate trials.

On September 4, 1992, ten days before the scheduled start of jury selection, Judge Hull granted Purdy's request—unopposed by the defense. The judge said he wanted to make sure he protected Carolyn's constitutional rights while allowing the State to present as complete a case as possible against Eric. Understandably, Eric's case would go first.

That should have been the end of the courtroom foreplay; the attorneys should have retreated to their offices for a week of final preparations. But a percolating legal and personal dispute between defense attorney Acevedo and Prosecutor Purdy was about to explode. Before it was over, the trial would be delayed another seven months, Acevedo would be under criminal investigation, and Eric would be assigned a new attorney.

PART 5

The Trial

They say I never shut up.
That's why I can't take the stand.

—Carolyn Napoletano

- 31 -

A criminal trial is supposed to be a "search for the truth," but Lady Justice often has one eye closed. The evidence in *State of New Jersey* v. *Eric Napoletano* would be presented in the spring of 1993 as the "facts of the case," but Prosecutor Bill Purdy's procession of witnesses would really only support his "theory of the case." As with most murders, there would actually be three versions of events: the government's version, the defendant's version, and the way things really happened. This trial would turn more on what the jurors did not hear rather than on what they did.

Sensing that Judge Hull was not going to allow any testimony about the murders of Marilyn Coludro and Gladys Matos, or the fatal hit-and-run on Wendell Owens, Purdy formally withdrew his motion for pretrial hearings on those issues. Because no testimony would be produced about prior acts of violence, the jury would not hear from survivor Wanda Matos. Similarly, the jury would not hear from Gregg O. McCrary, the FBI's serial-killer expert from Quantico, and would not be told about Eric's violent parenting skills.

While Eric Junior's story of watching his father kill his mother had formed the basis for New Jersey assuming jurisdiction, the youngster also would be kept off the stand. In making that decision, Purdy had to consider the boy's age, his ability to remember details, the traumatic effect testifying could have on him, and the fact that his version discredited star witness-to-be Uncle Al Jiovine, who continued to insist that he had not taken the ride to Delaware.

Finally, the jurors would not hear any oral argument or crossexamination from defense attorneys Louis Acevedo and Susan McCoy. "Acevedo versus Purdy" had promised to be quite a show. The tension had been building for months. Acevedo had assured anyone who asked that he was "going to kick Purdy's ass." But the confrontation was not to be. The defense lawyer was taken off the case—the climax to a lengthy and bitter dispute over the "search for the truth" as it applied to the 2:44 A.M. phone call.

Trying to assess the extent of damage that testimony on the call could cause, Acevedo and Public Defender's Investigator Frank Scott interviewed Maggie Rivera and Greg Velez. In stunning tape-recorded conversations, the teens both recanted their incriminating statements about Myra having been on the phone at 2:44 A.M. the night of her disappearance. Greg claimed he had told the truth the first time he talked to police when he said he remembered the call and was sure that Myra had not been on the phone. Maggie said the late-night call she had recounted for police had occurred "on a different night." Both teens said they had claimed Myra was on the phone because of threats that Greg would be arrested on the federal drug charges.

When investigators Pete Talarico and Harold C. Pegg, Jr., from the prosecutor's office reinterviewed Maggie, she promptly recanted her recantation. However, the defense was not told of this development for the next four months, until two weeks before the scheduled start of trial.

At that point, Purdy filed a motion seeking Acevedo's disqualification on his perception that the defense attorney would be "a necessary witness" at trial regarding his role in the recantations. The prosecutor maintained that Acevedo's disqualification would ward off a successful appeal on the grounds that Acevedo might have foregone certain tactics for fear he would be personally incriminated. It was important, Purdy agreed, that Acevedo not be allowed to get up at the end of trial and pronounce, "I was there. I know what happened." Purdy's boss, Passaic County Prosecutor Ronald S. Fava, revealed that his office was conducting a criminal witness-tampering investigation against Acevedo.

The attorney angrily charged back. He mocked the threat of criminal charges, asserting that Purdy had to know that the credibility of Greg and Maggie was marginal, at best. By Acevedo's count, Greg had recanted three times, Maggie twice. Acevedo observed, "They change their stories depending on who they are being interviewed by."

Judge Hull ruled that Acevedo could stay on, but prohibited his involvement when it came to oral argument and cross-examination regarding Greg, Maggie, and related police witnesses. Both sides appealed, and the Appellate Division of Superior Court sided with the prosecution, removing Acevedo from the case entirely. The justices observed that Acevedo's limited role might be challenged on appeal as "denial of effective counsel." The start of trial would have to be delayed indefinitely to allow for more appeals.

The legal maneuvering pushed Eric over the edge. Just before 3:00 A.M. on September 23, 1992, he tried to commit suicide by slashing his neck and both wrists with disposable razor blades. "I'll show those bastards who are fucking around with my trial date," he screamed as he exited a shower area with a blade in each hand.

He was rushed to Barnert Hospital in Paterson. An artery on Eric's left wrist was severed, requiring transfusions of blood. He was subsequently transferred to the psychiatric unit at Saint Mary's Hospital in Passaic, then transported to the Forensic Psychiatric Hospital in Trenton, part of the state prison system, where he was examined for several weeks.

On October 2, 1992, the New Jersey Supreme Court declined to consider any aspect of the recantation dispute, meaning that Acevedo remained off the case. But that did not end the dispute. Acevedo's boss, Michael J. Marucci, questioned how Sue McCoy, or anyone from the public defender's office, could continue to represent Eric. Marucci said that if Eric was convicted, the defendant could complain that McCoy had fashioned her case to protect Acevedo. Marucci filed a motion asking that his entire office be disqualified.

At a hearing on November 5, 1992, nineteen months after Eric's arrest, Judge Hull sought the defendant's opinion. "Your Honor, I feel like I'm a one-legged man in an ass-kicking contest," Eric said. "I have been in jail for a very long period of time. I would like to get a trial as soon as possible. I'm innocent. I will be acquitted at trial."

Judge Hull asked Purdy if Acevedo was still under criminal investigation. The prosecutor replied in the affirmative and added that he had no idea when the probe would conclude. With that, Judge Hull said he had no choice but to disqualify the entire public defender's office. "Even if there is not a conflict of interest, there is an appearance of a conflict of interest."

* * *

Finding Eric a new lawyer proved to be almost as complicated as getting rid of Acevedo. The defendant needed a so-
called pool attorney, private counsel assigned to a poor
defendant who, for whatever reason, cannot be represented
by the public defender's office. But there were problems
with the usual solution.

The New Jersey legislature, the county governments, and
the state Supreme Court had become embroiled in a catfight
over financing of the public defender's system. With
funding for pool attorneys temporarily in limbo, there was
no mechanism for Eric—or any defendant in his predica-
ment—to be assigned pool counsel.

The county assignment judge, Sidney H. Reiss, realized
he could not wait for the politicians before getting the
Napoletano case back on track. So he turned to Ernest M.
Caposela, a certified criminal trial attorney who over the
years had handled hundreds of criminal defenses, including
complicated murder trials and court-assigned pool cases.
His Clifton office was just a few blocks from the Napoletano apartment.

Caposela talked it over with Judge Reiss, and on November 18, 1992, he agreed to take the case. He figured he
would get compensated eventually. Besides, Ernie Caposela
thrived on the game of courts, and this was a big case. "He
gets the same defense whether I'm paid or not," he said.

Like Purdy, Ernie Caposela was a local boy. His father,
the son of Italian immigrants, had worked for years in
Paterson's "Silk City" mills. Caposela played varsity baseball and football at a Catholic high school, then graduated
from Fairleigh Dickinson University in 1975. He worked
college summers as a lifeguard at the Jersey shore, later as an
intern for the Internal Revenue Service. After receiving a
master's degree from New York University Graduate School
of Public Administration, Caposela went to work in Manhattan for a Lexington, Kentucky, consulting-clearinghouse
organization called the Council of State Governments. In
1978, he enrolled in the University of Louisville Law School
and worked part-time for the local U.S. Attorney's Office.
He liked Kentucky, but feared he would be viewed as an
ethnic outsider. Also, his parents had developed health problems and he felt he owed it to them to be nearby. So, after
graduation, he returned to New Jersey to practice law. In

1990, he married one of his father's neighbors. Eve and
Ernie's first child, Jake, was born only weeks before he took
on Eric's case.

Judge Hull set April 19, 1993, for the start of jury selection, and approved Caposela's application to hire former
Secret Service Agent Francis R. Murphy as his investigator.
Over the years, Murphy had guarded Presidents Ford, Carter, and Reagan, as well as George Bush as vice president.
He knew the local turf, too. In the late 1960s, he had been a
police officer in Paterson, the county seat.

The defense team began reviewing court transcripts,
police reports, witness statements, and FBI lab results. In
the meantime, the funding dispute was resolved; Caposela
was going to get paid.

Caposela said he viewed his entry into the case as a fresh
start for Eric, and would therefore not rule out any kind of
defense. He spent several hours with Eric at the county jail
the day he took the case, and countless more with him in
subsequent weeks, generally spending the entire day with
him on Saturdays. He now arrived at his office by 8:00 A.M.
and did not depart until after 10:00 P.M. There were still
other clients to serve. As he sank deeper into trial preparation, his wife began bringing their son to the office each
evening for a good-night kiss.

Still recovering physically and mentally from his suicide
attempt, Eric began to accept Caposela. "I've never asked
him if he did it. I don't have to do that," Caposela explained.
He said he viewed Eric as "a love-starved kid. People like
Bob the businessman and Uncle Al gave him things he never
got from the father he never knew."

Eric read the grand jury testimony, pointing out places he
thought witnesses might be vulnerable. The defendant thought
he had plausible explanations for every troublesome fact that
Prosecutor Purdy might produce. Caposela listened politely—
it was obvious that Eric was very intelligent and streetwise—
but only to a point. Eric wanted to testify, to provide explanations for the inconsistencies. But Caposela concluded there
were far too many things to explain away, and codefendant
Carolyn, for once, could not come to her son's rescue with
corroboration.

Caposela looked elsewhere for his defense, aided by large
time charts that he hung in his office law library. He and

Murphy blocked out the uncontestable: times of the known toll calls, police interviews, and Eric's work shifts. Then they mapped out different burial-ride scenarios, taking into account whether Myra would have been killed by 9:00 P.M. or after the 2:44 A.M. call. They concluded that Myra was either killed and buried on the Wednesday night before the 2:44 call—as Detective Ruth had first believed—or she was buried late the next night, Thursday, regardless of when she was actually killed.

Cataloguing the discovery material was an immense task. Reading through the thousands of pages of witness interviews, Caposela prepared two sets of notes for each potential cross-examination, one filled with positive points that helped his case, the other filled with things to watch out for. Those sheets of paper would be the blueprint for a defense consisting essentially of cross-examination of the State's case—a straightforward "prove-he-did-it" defense. Caposela and Murphy decided not to interview Uncle Al; he would be confronted at trial.

Murphy's job during testimony would consist of keeping track of exhibits and defense documents, and, perhaps more important, baby-sitting Eric. The defendant had displayed his fidgety, manic states during jailhouse conferences. The defense team did not want him behaving that way in front of the jury.

Caposela instructed Eric to look directly at Purdy during negative testimony. "If you can't look at your accuser, you have a problem." He also planned to hold Eric's arm and pat him on the back to show jurors he was not afraid. "It's all part of the theater, all part of the drama," Caposela explained.

In searching for a defense, Caposela found himself most worried about Al's testimony. "I might be able to leave a subtle inference that Al did it, but my fear is that the jury will say, 'Well, if Al did it, he had Eric help him.' So that won't necessarily do me any good."

Caposela was also concerned about "bad character evidence"—witnesses all too willing to say negative things about Eric's treatment of Myra. And, although he would argue otherwise in court, Caposela realized the State had compiled a great deal of legitimate evidence. "This is still a very strong circumstantial case. Eric wouldn't let go of the kids and she wasn't leaving without them."

Regardless of the trial's outcome, Caposela assumed that

Eric would never again be free. "Whatever the reason, they've never arrested him for those New York cases. But I know in my heart that if I get him an acquittal here, they'll charge him immediately in New York. There's no way the FBI isn't going to pressure New York to do it. The feds put too much into this case. To them, they know they have a serial killer."

The State's list of potential witnesses included more than 150 names from all across the country. Purdy decided to enlist the aid of Walter R. Dewey, Jr., an assistant prosecutor normally assigned to Judge Hull's courtroom. Purdy and Dewey had been close friends since they worked on juvenile cases together back in 1987. They played guitars together at prosecutors' conventions. Purdy had even been in Dewey's wedding party. Purdy knew he and Dewey could work together without a personality clash.

Working six or seven days a week, the two prosecutors sharpened the focus of their case. They knew they had to work carefully with many of their civilian witnesses, truly a cast of dubious characters led by Uncle Al. Purdy would never feel totally comfortable with Al as a witness. He was, after all, a pathological liar and a member of a vicious murder conspiracy. The trick would be to convince the jury that Al was telling the truth on the witness stand.

Placement of Jiovine in the order of appearance was a particularly troublesome decision. Dewey thought Al should go last, but Purdy was concerned how that would look to the jury if Al's memory changed again. Purdy decided to give himself some breathing room by saving several other witnesses for last.

During those same months of delay, Al gained more confidence, at least about his status in the criminal justice system. He began boasting that there was no way he was going to serve the entire five years. It sounded as if Al had everyone where he wanted them. To keep him under control, Federal Prosecutor Moramarco filed papers to delay consideration of Al's petition for a reduction in sentence until after Eric's trial.

As the new trial date approached, Caposela filed a flurry of motions, including a request for another hearing on the wiretap excerpts. Judge Hull ultimately agreed to excise all references to Eric's fascination with Mafioso John Gotti, Eric's plans to vacate New Mexico quickly if a New York judge issued a warrant for his arrest on the child-custody dispute, Eric's characterization of Sandra and her mother as "bitches," the FBI SWAT team members wearing bullet-proof vests and pointing machine guns at him, the fact that the FBI had taken his two sons because they regarded him as a threat, and Eric's concern about Sandra talking to law enforcement: "You can't teach these women to shut their mouths."

Judge Hull left open the possibility that he also would prohibit use of the wiretapped conversations for the morning Eric was arrested on the grounds that the defendant was "in custody" when he made his handcuffed phone calls. The judge said he would explore the legal issue at a Miranda hearing after jury selection, but before the start of testimony. That way jurors could be instructed not to watch TV or read the newspapers about the dispute.

Jury selection began as scheduled, and consumed a day and a half. Potential jurors were asked to note on a questionnaire if they had heard details of the Napoletano case. In the first panel, 25 of 81 said they had, while 19 of 38 cited familiarity in the second panel. Those knowing too much were disqualified following questioning by Judge Hull in private.

Sixteen jurors were selected, a surplus of four that would be reduced to three the next morning when the employer of one of those selected decided the man was essential to the company's work on military contracts. The deciding jurors would be drawn by lot just prior to the start of deliberations.

Judge Hull sent the jury home to await completion of the Miranda hearing. Four witnesses, all FBI agents, would testify: H. Douglas Beldon, the SWAT team leader for Eric's arrest; Sarah Burcham, who had spoken with Eric in the Albuquerque parking lot; Julian M. Gonzales, who had directed the New Mexico operation; and Thomas A. Cottone, Jr., the overall case agent back in New Jersey. The issue was straightforward: When was Eric in custody, and if he was in custody, did the actions of the FBI agents constitute "custodial interrogation"—the threshold required for the reading of one's rights?

Purdy had Beldon read from the original FBI affidavit, and as he reached the section stating, "The mother has been the driving force behind the obstruction efforts to date and she is likely to be particularly vocal in facing this latest problem," Eric glanced at Murphy, raised his eyebrows, and smiled broadly. Laughing at his mother's recounted words and actions would become one of Eric's trademarks as the trial progressed.

Beldon acknowledged that Eric had been handcuffed during the hours prior to his official arrest, but the agent insisted that if Eric had said he did not want to remain in the apartment during the search, or did not want to return to the premises after making phone calls, he would not have been cuffed. He observed that Eric certainly had not been handcuffed to the phone to coerce him into calling Uncle Al.

Agent Gonzales acknowledged that he had hoped Eric would call Jiovine's 800 number, and admitted he had specifically told Eric he was free to make phone calls. Under cross, Caposela got the agent to concede that when Eric was cuffed to the phone booth he was not free to leave. But, Gonzales contended, Eric was only "being detained" at that point. He said Eric was never "in custody" until he was "under arrest."

Judge Hull placed the dispute in perfect focus, though: "If Mr. Napoletano had decided to go to the airport in Albuquerque and take a plane, would he have been allowed to do so?"

"Your Honor, I don't know if I could answer that question," Gonzales said, forced to dodge. "I think I would have called New Jersey to find out what they wanted me to do, and I would have done whatever they wanted."

Next, Agent Cottone emphasized that the wiretap had been put in place also to monitor the safety of Sandra and the boys. He then highlighted portions of the intercepted conversations where Eric repeatedly told Uncle Al and Carolyn he was *not* under arrest.

The opposing attorneys launched into lengthy arguments. Purdy maintained that all the statements had been made voluntarily; Caposela argued that Eric's Miranda rights had been violated before and after his arrest.

In ruling, Judge Hull gave a split decision. He tackled the most serious issue first—all of Eric's remarks made to Agent Gonzales after the arrest, for example, Eric's observation that the FBI's case was weak since it took ten months to arrest him.

The judge said the evidence clearly indicated that Eric

had made the remarks after his Miranda rights had been read to him, and in reaction to comments from Gonzales. Judge Hull said case law barred the admission of comments made "wherever a person in custody is subjected to either expressed questioning or to its functional equivalent." He said none of Eric's post-arrest comments would be allowed at trial.

Judge Hull said he would allow the wiretaps of the final day to be played to the jury because while Eric had been in a "custodial setting" at the phone booth, he had not been subjected to "custodial interrogation." He ruled that law enforcement just happened to be listening in as Eric called "confederates" for "support and assistance."

The judge saved the toughest issue for last: Eric's conversations with Agent Burcham in the parking lot. He observed that Agent Cottone's strategy to provide Eric the latitude to make phone calls that morning was "in hindsight, a brilliant strategy because the first place the defendant ran was to the telephone booth." But, the judge continued, the fact remained that the handcuffs constituted custody. He said he was barring Burcham's testimony "as a matter of fundamental fairness."

The legal foreplay was over. Finally, the "search for the truth" could begin.

Judge Hull's courtroom was jammed that Thursday morning, April 22, 1993, as Bill Purdy and Ernie Caposela prepared to make their opening statements. The sheriff's deputies acted more official than usual as they took up positions behind Eric and throughout the courtroom proper. The air-conditioning system in the building had not been turned back on for the summer season yet, so the courtroom was warm and stuffy. In the coming days, the heat would become oppressive, measured at 87 degrees in one of the courtrooms late one afternoon. Print and television reporters—English and Spanish—jockeyed for the best seats. Photographers directed their still and video cameras at the defendant's table, hoping for a dramatic close-up of Eric looking mean and angry. Marta Rivera, Marilyn Coludro's mother, optimistically told reporters, "I waited nine years for this!"

Everyone looked for Eric's mother, but the search was in vain. Carolyn remained in Manhattan, a no-show for her only child's murder trial.

Attired in a gray suit with suspenders and a neatly trimmed beard, Bill Purdy appeared nervous as he stepped up to the podium. He quickly warmed to his task, though, explaining to the jurors who he was, where he worked, and his role at the trial. He warned the jurors not to look for all the answers in the first one or two witnesses, promising there would be hundreds of pieces of circumstantial evidence. "A case such as this is sometimes compared to putting together a jigsaw puzzle. Piece by piece we build that puzzle."

Seeking to explain his case in its purest form, Purdy argued that Eric had murdered his wife, then buried her body in Delaware to avoid detection. "And his mother and Uncle Al helped to cover it up." He appealed to the jurors to

conduct a thorough "search for the truth," a task he
acknowledged would be difficult because the case was
"filled with dirty little facts."

The prosecutor sought to distinguish between victim and
defendant: the kind, caring, simple wife named Myra versus
the cruel, vicious, cheating husband named Eric. And he
sought to contrast the two families at the heart of his case:
the concerned, religious Acevedo family versus the bizarre
Napoletano clan.

"You will see a lot of Myra's family here," he assured the
jury. "Her mother and father, cousins, sisters. The people
who cared about her will testify. You will see a very tight,
close family in the Acevedos, people who were concerned
about her when she was missing." Of the victim, Purdy
observed, "You will hear about a woman who was almost a
prisoner in her own home," a dedicated mother virtually cut
off from her family and social contacts. "Her life was her
children."

Turning to stare at the defendant, Purdy continued, "You
will hear about another family certainly, the Napoletanos.
I'll refer to them as Carolyn, Eric, and this Uncle Al, who is
actually not related, but he's a gentleman who had contact
with Eric Napoletano since Eric was about twelve years old.
And you will hear very strange things about their relationship. Is it a father relationship? Is it a friend relationship?
You also will hear about a strange relationship between a
son and his mother. You will hear how they talk to each
other. You will see it is unusual. To call them a family is
almost an abuse of that term when you hear about the conniving they did, the sneakiness, the deception to cover up a
murder!"

Outlining his case, Purdy offered a preview of the witnesses he planned to call, notably failing to mention Uncle
Al Jiovine. Instead, he stressed the wiretap issue heavily,
promising jurors they would get "a sense of who these
people are, and who they are to each other . . . how they can
hardly live without each other, how they seek each other for
counsel and advice and support. I defy you to say that these
are the conversations of innocent people.

"You won't hear Eric, Al or Carolyn say who did it, but
you will hear them be very careful about talking on the telephone because they think the phone is bugged. You will

hear them very relieved because they think the investigation
is shelved. . . . And those conversations will be completely
consistent with 'consciousness of guilt.' "

Sounding as if Carolyn was on trial, too, Purdy explained
why Eric and his mother thought they had the police figured
out: "Carolyn Napoletano was, and is, in a clerical position
with the New York City Police Department. She has been
for several years. I've told you that Eric Napoletano was
trained to be a traffic-enforcement officer. He's got a certain fascination with police activities as well. You will hear
about that also. They work in the New York City system.
But we hicks here in northern New Jersey work a little different, okay? They were expecting perhaps a New York
City response to this incident. They were expecting a detective to come in with the missing-persons report, do the cursory work, then say, 'Don't have a body, can't find her, next
job. Wait for the body to turn up before we do anything.'
I'm not saying there are not cops like that in New Jersey.
I'm sure there are. But you will not hear about any of them
on this case, and certainly not Detective Donato."

Caposela's opening was brief, with standard themes: The
defendant is presumed innocent, listen to the evidence, and
the real truth comes on cross-examination, not during the
worry-free direct questioning by the prosecutor.

He warned the jurors to keep open minds and not to convict his client because he was not a nice person. "Sometimes
we say things in private or we use mannerisms in private,
and certainly if we knew that the public were listening, we
might not act that way," Caposela said. "You are going to
hear Eric Napoletano speaking with some other individuals.
And yeah, he comes across sometimes as obnoxious, as
spiteful; sometimes you will hear profanity. But he is not on
trial for his bad personal characteristics; he's on trial for the
murder of Myra Acevedo Napoletano."

Standing near the four large crates of defense documents,
Caposela made it clear he had no doubt Uncle Al would testify and in fact would be the linchpin of the prosecution's
case. He wasted no time challenging Al's credibility, contending that he had been asked dozens and dozens of times
about the 2:44 call, always answering "I don't know" or "I
don't remember."

"So ask yourself, how are you going to feel about convicting Eric Napoletano of murder when Albert Jiovine takes this stand? You will see he was tricked. They appealed to his emotions. They even threatened him."

He suggested that despite "one of the most extensive investigations ever conducted," not one useful piece of forensic evidence had been linked to his client. "Nothing. That's what the evidence will show. Nothing. . . . The prosecution in this case is based on pure speculation and painting a picture of bad people. And when I say 'people,' I'm not just talking about this defendant but his mother, Carolyn Napoletano."

Seeking to establish Eric's pattern of abusive treatment of Myra as far back as possible, Purdy summoned Donna Benson, the downstairs neighbor from the first Clifton apartment, as his first witness. Benson described a stay-at-home existence for Myra, saying that Myra rarely went outside her home without her husband. When Purdy asked whether the witness had ever heard "any discussions" coming from the Napoletano apartment, Caposela objected, stating that such an open-ended question would likely elicit an "objectionable hearsay response." Judge Hull sent the jury out of the courtroom, the first of many such excursions the panel would take so potential testimony could be given a practice run under Judge Hull's tight restrictions.

Benson then stated that she heard the couple argue a lot, with Eric calling Myra "a lowlife" and always telling Myra the children were his. She said Eric's behavior had given her "a very bad feeling."

Caposela rose to object. "What this witness just said is the gravamen of my objection, that this made her feel bad and upset her in some way. This is classic 'bad character evidence' if I have ever seen it. . . . He's a 'bad person,' so they feel bad for Myra."

Judge Hull said he would allow Benson's comments about having heard the couple argue, with the understanding that she refrain from giving opinions as to how she felt or what she thought of the victim and the defendant.

With the jury back in the room, Benson grew expansive. She said she had heard Eric call Myra "whore, slut, and bitch." The witness also said Myra was diminutive in stature and kept a nicely furnished, spotless home.

* * *

Theresa Maltese, the short, stout, and nosy downstairs neighbor, took the stand next. Her soft voice resonated with nervousness. She made a wretched witness, unable to answer the most straightforward questions. When Purdy asked her what kind of clothes Myra wore, she replied, "Very nice clothes. Average clothes. Jogging pants. Nice clothes. She wore nice clothes. She was very well dressed in clothing."

Maltese said she had stayed away from Eric, associating just with Myra and the boys. She also stayed away from mentioning her husband, Tony. When asked to recall the circumstances under which she saw Myra in the hours before her disappearance, she gave a flawed version of the visit by the moving man, as if she were the only member of her family on the premises that afternoon.

She said she first went upstairs to complain about the water leaking from the kids' bath. "I knocked on the door, no one answered. Eric yelled from the background." She now claimed she had not understood what Eric said. "And then Myra came to the door." She said she told Myra there was someone ringing the doorbell for her. "It was a moving-truck man and, I guess, maybe that's— She came— He came up, and came in the house, and she slammed the door in my face. That's it."

"You let the moving man in?" Purdy specifically asked.

"I let the moving man in the apartment, and then she let him in the apartment upstairs." Her husband, Tony, was nowhere to be found in this muddled version.

Purdy still looked to grab his payoff—the pretrial observation Maltese had made about Eric to detectives: "He looked like he had murder in his eyes. He looked like a crazy man."

But when Purdy asked her to recount her observations of Eric exiting the building, she balked. "He didn't say nothing."

Purdy pushed harder. "How did he look at that point?"

"Well, he didn't look too happy. That's all I know. He didn't look happy." When Caposela objected, Judge Hull instructed her to say "what you saw about his face."

"He just looked— I mean, well, just, you know— I mean, like— He came down and he just stood at the car. He stared at me. And that was it. And he looked like he wasn't too happy."

"Go ahead, Mr. Purdy," said the judge sternly.

"Where did you go?" Purdy asked. Maltese proceeded to bring her husband into the picture. "I went in the car and I went out to dinner with my husband." Her comments left the impression that Tony had merely driven by to pick her up, and that she had gone outside to meet him curbside. Purdy skillfully kept the illusion alive. "Your husband wasn't living with you at the time, is that correct?" No, she said, he had not been living with her "for a long time."

Purdy directed Maltese to the night after Myra's disappearance, when she saw Eric and Carolyn at the Napoletano apartment. Maltese said mother and son both told her that after she left for dinner with Tony the night before, Myra had come downstairs carrying two suitcases and "was standing outside waiting for somebody." She said Eric told her Myra had a boyfriend.

Purdy wanted to refresh the witness's memory regarding the crucial information she was failing to recall. He reached for Exhibit S-40, a copy of the statement she gave police on August 3, 1990. "Just take a look at that. Do you recognize that?"

"I don't read," the embarrassed witness replied to the even more embarrassed prosecutor. "I never learned how to read."

Certainly, no one could accuse the State of having over-prepared the witness.

Because of Tony Maltese's criminal background, Caposela had wondered during trial preparation if the man would make a reasonable alternative suspect. If Carolyn and Eric had been out all night, Tony could have killed Myra when he returned from dinner with Theresa. But there was no motive, so the strategy had been abandoned before it really got started.

That did not prevent Caposela from suggesting the idea during cross-examination of Mrs. Maltese, though, in the hope that even one juror would be concerned enough to find reasonable doubt.

In response to a question seeking precise details about the moving man's visit, Maltese explained, "Well, I had my husband—my husband was with me."

"So your husband was also with you then when you went to the top of the steps?"

"Yes," the witness replied. "He was with me for a while, but I didn't mention him in the picture, like. I didn't want to mention him in the picture at all."

Caposela said he did not understand. Up to that point he had been under the impression she had been alone on the stairs.

The witness tried to get cute. "I was alone—after he came down to open the door for the guy." In this version she and Tony had gone upstairs to complain about the water dripping through the ceiling, and when her husband went downstairs to let in the moving man, she told him to go into her apartment.

"You said you didn't want to mention him or you didn't want to put him in the picture. Do you remember you said that?"

"I don't see him very much. He doesn't live with me. We're separated," she replied, without detail. "That's why I don't want him to be in the picture of this."

Caposela asked her if she remembered being interviewed by Detective Donato. She said she did. "And did he ask you about Tony Maltese, about your husband? Did he ask you where he was and tell you that he wanted to talk to him?"

"No," she replied incorrectly.

"You don't recall Detective Donato ever asking you, 'Mrs. Maltese, I would like to talk to your husband, Tony Maltese. Can you tell me where is he?' "

"No, he never—"

"Never?" Again, she replied in the negative.

Caposela kept at it until the witness conceded, "Yeah. I told him I didn't know where he was. . . . I didn't want him to be involved because it was another problem."

Where was all this headed? Certainly not to a discussion of what Eric had said in the hallway shortly after the moving man departed—that Myra had already left. Caposela abandoned his effort, with the jury not being informed of Tony's background.

Mercifully, the first day of testimony in this supposed search for the truth came to an end. Maltese's testimony had come dangerously close to perjury.

Outside in the hallway, the prosecution team looked dejected. Purdy was tense and angry. Dewey stormed away cursing. "It's like I never talked to the witness in my life," Purdy said.

Equally unimpressed, Marilyn Coludro's mother repeated the comment she had given reporters that morning, only with a different meaning: "I waited nine years for *this*?"

- 33 -

The State's presentation moved swiftly to the events of
Myra's final days, generally told from the perspective of her
family—parents, sisters, and cousins—and at an important
moment, through the eyes and ears of Esteban Fernandez,
the moving man. Purdy had two goals during this segment
of testimony: to continue contrasting the Acevedo and
Napoletano families, and to establish Eric's "consciousness
of guilt."

Fernandez vividly described the disintegrating marriage.
"She was the one who was moving to Puerto Rico and he
was apparently planning to stay," the moving man said,
detailing how he had discussed the family possessions with
Myra item by item.

The witness also neglected to make any mention of Tony
Maltese. "I went to the door and there was this old lady
from the first floor. She asked me who I was and where I
was going to. I told her I was from a moving company, that
I was there to see Myra Napoletano for an estimate. And
right away she got ahead of me, and up the stairs, and
started knocking on the door. At the time we heard very
loud music from the apartment."

"You followed her up the stairs?" Yes, he replied.

"You are at the top of the stairs with this lady from the
first floor?" Purdy asked ever so carefully.

"Yeah. She was the one who was knocking on the door."

The next witness, Myra's next-door neighbor, Jeanette
Konuklu, presented more rocky terrain. Dramatically dab-
bing her nose with a tissue, she professed that she and Myra
had been "best friends." They hung out every day, went
food shopping together. She had planned to help pay for
Myra's plane tickets to Puerto Rico.

As Konuklu began to recount a Monopoly game that had
taken place at Myra's apartment around Christmas 1989,

Caposela rose to object. Fearing more "bad character evidence," he wanted to hear the story before the jury did.

With the panel out of the courtroom, the witness said Eric had become angry over the fact that he was losing. "She was wiping us out. So he came across the table and said something about, 'You dumb fucking Puerto Rican.' . . . They had an argument. The last statement he made was, 'If you think you are ever fucking taking these kids away from me, I will fucking kill you.' "

Caposela argued that the comment about Myra's heritage was "highly inflammatory." He pointed out that the State was claiming Eric had murdered Myra because she planned to take the kids to Puerto Rico, "not because she was Puerto Rican."

The judge ruled that Konuklu could testify only about the threats she said she heard Eric make in relation to the children, not about Myra's heritage.

Purdy then warned her to listen carefully to his questions and to "only answer exactly what's asked." Judge Hull suggested that leading questions would be appropriate.

With the jury back, Konuklu explained how Eric had become upset because Myra was beating him in the Monopoly game. In response to a question, she said the arguing escalated beyond the results of the game, to the point where Eric threatened Myra.

"And could you please tell me, to the best of your knowledge, the exact words that he used when he made that one threatening statement?" Purdy asked. "I want you to use the language that you told the police before in your statement."

"You dumb fucking Puerto Rican," she blurted.

"I object, Judge!" Caposela pleaded.

Judge Hull instructed the jurors to leave the courtroom.

Caposela was at wit's end. "Judge, we just went through ten minutes of trying to make sure that that did not come out before the jury. That was, I think, the place where the leading question would have been appropriate because of the danger."

Purdy explained that he certainly had not intended for the witness to have made the ethnic comment. He said he had asked her to use the exact language because she had previously "expressed some reservation" about using the profanity "fuck" in court.

Judge Hull was visibly upset, but denied Caposela's

motion for a mistrial. He instructed Purdy to ask a narrowly focused and leading question that would elicit a comment only about Eric's threat to kill Myra if she left with the kids.

When the jurors returned, Purdy specifically asked Konuklu if she recalled what Eric had threatened to do if Myra took the children. "He said that if she were to take the f'ing kids from him, he would kill her," the witness replied, now unable to utter the "F" word.

Turning to the substance of Konuklu's testimony, Purdy elicited the fact that she knew Myra had been saving for the trip to Puerto Rico. The money, which amounted to about $400 at the time of her disappearance, was kept in a brown wallet secreted behind the lip of a bedroom hutch. The witness also maintained that she had seen Myra's Social Security card in the wallet. She said that when she sneaked into Myra's bedroom to look for the wallet, it was gone.

Cross-examining, Caposela focused on Konuklu's claim that she had seen Myra's Social Security card in the wallet, presumably one of the cards with the last names "Acevedo" and "Acevedo Olavarria" found in the strongbox in Carolyn's apartment. The defense attorney asked Konuklu what was the last name on the card she saw.

"Offhand I can't remember," she replied. "It was tilted into the light, but you could see 'Social Security.' I know what that looks like. It was in blue."

Could she see the name on the card? "No, not clearly. No."

Caposela pointed out that she had testified during pretrial hearings that she could see the name "very clearly," and had sworn the name she saw on the card read "Myra Napoletano."

"If you see someone's Social Security card in their wallet, you assume it is theirs when they tell you it is theirs," Konuklu replied defensively.

On and on they went. The witness said she "vaguely" remembered seeing Myra's name on the card. "I don't know if it had her last name now or maiden name. Like I said, it was tilted. It had a cover on it, a clear plastic cover, so when light hits, it does reflect the light." But she had been certain enough to testify about the name last July. "Yes, at that time," Konuklu answered. "What I'm trying to say is I saw 'Myra.' Being she is married, it would have her married name on it, right?" The witness was filled with assumptions, precisely the picture Caposela sought to paint. "I mean, mine does."

Caposela suggested that she was making an assumption. "Maybe at the time," she replied. "All I know is, it had 'Myra' as the first name."

Why, then, had she testified that she had been "absolutely certain" that the name on the card had been "Myra Napoletano"?

Konuklu said she did not know. "Maybe I was confused."

Caposela had made his point. He could argue that everything out of Konuklu's mouth was subject to an "assumption test." The witness was another minus for the State.

Eric's behavior in court was running hot and cold. One session, he arrived at the defense table calm and silent, sucking on cough drops; the next moment he was smiling and superkinetic. In his perked-up mode, he furiously scribbled notes for Murphy and Caposela, feeding them questions to ask. His animated note-taking got so wild one afternoon that Caposela lamented, "I'm losing control of my client."

There were occasions where Eric mumbled "Asshole" under his breath in Purdy's direction, but he generally kept his mouth in check, sitting between Caposela and Murphy, rubbing his right thumb and index finger down the bridge of his nose or along the edges of his mustache.

During one recess, Eric tried on a pair of eyeglasses, then asked his legal team if he looked more dignified. Caposela and Murphy looked at each other and smiled. Murphy told Eric to remove the lenses and sit down.

Walter Dewey would handle the next set of prosecution witnesses, all police officials. They would recount the events at the Clifton apartment and police department headquarters in the days immediately following Myra's disappearance.

In detailing the Napoletano family's visit to Clifton police headquarters, Sergeant John R. Zipf described Eric's arrogance and how neither Eric nor Carolyn had filed a missing-persons report regarding Myra's disappearance. Instead, he said, "It was like where did I have the right to send somebody to his house!"

Officer Joseph Klein informed the jury that when he asked Carolyn where Myra was, she replied, "That's for you to find out!" The line was a zinger. Purdy was an expert at using Carolyn's mouth to help sink her son.

Detective William Cooke recalled how Eric and his

mother had been evasive when he and colleague Ed Snack
interviewed them three nights after Myra's disappearance.
"She stated she didn't like to give her address out," Cooke
said. Purdy asked if Eric had said where Myra had gone.
"He said he thought she was with her sister, Miriam, in the
Bronx."

The jury heard the story Eric and Carolyn had given the
detectives about the key Wednesday night, how Myra had
had a "hard day," so Eric had taken the boys to his mother's
house, how he had tried to reach Myra on the phone, and
how after failing to reach her, he came back to the apartment at 3:00 A.M. and found her missing.

Next, Detective Paul Ogden recounted Eric's story of
having made "arrangements" with American Airlines for
Myra's flight to San Juan, and how Eric claimed when he
returned to the Clifton apartment at 3:00 A.M., Myra was
gone along with two suitcases, her pocketbook, and her
birth-control pills.

Granted permission to read directly from his report,
Ogden quoted Eric as saying he felt bad about Myra being
missing, "but his girlfriend's there to talk about this, and
that helps." He also recited from his report that Eric had told
him if Myra came back, "he still loves her, and he will take
her back."

Lieutenant John Burke took the stand to introduce the
tape recording of his disjointed conversation with Eric's
mother. The jurors were riveted as they listened to Carolyn
weave her web for fifty-three minutes. Her silly comments
and domination of the conversation on the tape prompted
chuckles from Eric and members of the courtroom audience.

Generally, Caposela treaded lightly with the police witnesses. He did not contest their versions; Eric and Carolyn
had done and said exactly what the cops claimed. He just
disagreed with the police spin on things. He sought to show
that Eric and Carolyn were secretive about where they lived
and worked because of New York City residency requirements for Eric's Brownie job. Plus, they had said only that
they "believed" or "felt" Myra could be with her sister
Miriam in the Bronx.

Cousin Martha Morales started off the parade of family witnesses. Testifying under her new married name, Rodriguez,
Martha said Myra had called very upset about 6:00 A.M. the

Monday before her disappearance. She said Myra cried as she
revealed that Eric had told her about his mistress the night
before. Martha said Myra told her she planned to take the boys
and move to Puerto Rico by the end of the week.

Martha helped Purdy paint the portrait of Myra the loving
caretaker. In the year before Myra's death, Martha said, she
had started to attend church regularly, and had begun to
wear simple-styled clothing and less makeup. "She was an
excellent mother. She kept her kids well dressed, clean at all
times. She would always carry extra clothes with her just in
case the kids would get dirty." She was emphatic in her
denial when asked if Myra ever had a boyfriend, and
explained that as far as the Acevedo family knew, Eric
drove a tractor-trailer.

Myra's sister, Miriam Colon, testified about the numerous
phone conversations she had with Myra in the days before
her disappearance, and with other relatives immediately
thereafter. The testimony documented the Acevedo family's
growing concerns that week. Miriam also managed to get in
several biting observations about the Napoletano family, for
example, how Carolyn had not attended Myra and Eric's
wedding.

Miriam recounted her call with Myra late the evening of
Father's Day, when she told her of Eric's affair. "I had to
calm her down," Miriam recalled. "She said she couldn't
believe it, that her husband was playing her dirty." She also
related how Eric had gotten on the phone to tell her that "he
met this other woman, Jennifer, and he loved her and was
going to live with her and leave my sister. And then he told
me that he felt two loves, one for Jennifer and one for my
sister. At that time I told him, 'You can't have two loves.
You can't love my sister and her at the same time. How
could that be?' And he said, 'Well, it happens.' "

Miriam said she spoke with the Napoletanos on several
occasions after Myra's disappearance. She said neither Eric
nor his mother ever accused her of hiding Myra, but he did
suggest his wife might have run off to Puerto Rico with
friends. She also testified that neither had ever mentioned
any supposed airline reservations.

Nereida Flick, Myra's cousin, told the jury how Myra had
declined her invitation to bring the kids swimming the afternoon of her disappearance because of her appointment with
the moving man, and how later that week she called, then

visited, the Clifton Police Department to file the missing-persons report on behalf of the entire Acevedo family.

Looking scared and melancholy, Myra's mother, Carmen Acevedo, took the stand assisted by an interpreter. She told of her daughter's chaperoned dates with Eric, the time Myra and Eric had spent living in Puerto Rico, just minutes from the Acevedo home, and her final conversation with Myra, when she said she intended to come to Puerto Rico with her two children.

Myra's father, Pablo, took the stand next, the trial's twentieth witness. It took great restraint, but Pablo kept his anger in check. The witness came off as a sturdy family man, dedicated to his children, stepchildren, and grandchildren.

Asked to describe Myra's demeanor during his phone call with her on June 20, 1990, several hours before her disappearance, Pablo said, "She was like she had never been. She had a nervous tone of voice." Following the pattern, Caposela objected to the characterization, but this time Judge Hull disagreed.

"I will allow the witness to testify with that description," he ruled. "The witness is the father of the decedent." Pablo appeared to relax a bit from that point. He recounted Myra's plans to come to Puerto Rico, his offer to pay the rest of her moving costs, her change of heart, with Eric's voice in the background, and finally, his recommendation that if she was going to stay up north, she mend fences with her husband.

He said he asked to speak with Eric, but that his son-in-law refused to get on the line. "I kept insisting for her to go to Puerto Rico. She was nervous. She was upset. She told me that she loved me and my wife, and we agreed that we were going to call her the next day to see if she had changed her mind." But his calls the following day went unanswered, he told the jury.

By the weekend, Pablo said, he had grown so concerned that he flew up to New York to investigate himself. He said he called the Clifton apartment "every moment" that he had free, and when he finally reached Eric at Carolyn's apartment in Manhattan, "he told me that Myra had left to go to her sister's house, or that maybe she left with a boyfriend she had."

"And you had already been in contact with all of Myra's sisters?" Purdy asked. Pablo replied that he had spoken with everyone in his family.

When Judge Hull sensed that Purdy was about to pursue a line of questioning regarding what Eric Junior had told Pablo about Myra's whereabouts, he interrupted and sent the jury out for their midmorning recess. Running through the prospective testimony, Pablo said there had been silence on the phone line when he first asked the boy, "Where's your mother?" He said that, after "five or six seconds—as if someone had stopped the conversation," the youngster replied, "We're looking for her."

Caposela expressed concern that if the jury heard about the time delay it could conclude that his client had told Eric Junior what to say.

Purdy agreed that such an inference was prejudicial. "And that's specifically the reason we want to offer it. I think there are inferences that can be drawn from this conversation. There are inferences that can be drawn from every bit of evidence. Simply because the inferences are against the defendant does not make them objectionable."

Judge Hull decided to allow Pablo to testify as to the time gap between his asking Eric Junior where his mother was and the response, but he would not be allowed to say he believed Eric had interfered with the phone call.

On cross-examination, Caposela wanted to make the point that Pablo had not considered his son-in-law dangerous if one of the options he discussed with Myra was for her to get back with Eric. When asked, however, Pablo replied, "She answered me that she would forgive him as a person, but she wasn't going to forgive him in relation to being his wife again."

Testimony from the Acevedo family had painted exactly the picture Purdy had hoped it would. By necessity, the prosecutor again headed into troublesome territory: Uncle Al's call to his mother asking her to baby-sit for Eric's children.

Al's mother, Rose Dugan, hobbled to the stand. Gray-haired and seventy-nine years old, she had hearing and memory problems worse than her son. Her testimony could have shed important light on the 2:44 A.M. phone call dispute; in one of her interviews she had said that when Al called her at about 6:00 A.M. to baby-sit he told her Eric had called him with the request at about 3:00. If Eric had asked for a sitter during the 2:44 call, Myra was probably already

dead. That would have suggested that Al had remembered
the call all along, but had not wanted to remember the topic
of discussion.

Regardless, none of those issues would even be broached
with Dugan. Instead, she testified in nonspecific detail
about her son's call the morning after Myra's disappearance. She said Al told her "Myra had to go someplace," and
needed someone to baby-sit the children. She told the jury
that she declined the request because of her previously
scheduled eye surgery that day.

Covering ground quickly, Purdy inquired about the visit
to her home by Al and Eric on the Saturday following
Myra's disappearance. She recalled that as the two men
were leaving, Eric said, "What will we do if the cops are
there?"

Purdy completed his direct examination in less than five
minutes, staying so far away from details about Al's baby-
sitting call that he had failed to establish what time Dugan
thought the call had been made, never mind if Al had mentioned to her what time Eric had called him.

"Did you elicit a time at which this telephone call came
from her son on Thursday, June twenty-first?" Judge Hull
asked Purdy.

"I believe I referred to a time of 'morning,' " the prosecutor replied. Pressed to give a better answer, Dugan said
the call from her son had occurred "about a quarter to
seven."

Caposela also was not about to pursue who said what to
whom in any great detail because he had concluded by this
point that the jury probably would not care if Myra had been
killed at 8:00 P.M. or 3:00 A.M. Instead, he sought to focus his
cross-examination on the concern Eric had voiced when he
visited her home the Saturday after Myra's disappearance.

Despite her testimony only moments earlier, the witness
claimed the defense attorney had to be referring to the prior
Saturday—an impossibility given the date of Myra's disappearance. "It wasn't the twenty-third 'cause I just had my
operation and I had a patch on my eye," she now stated. "It
must have been the week before."

Caposela wanted to make sure she was talking about June
16, 1990. "Yeah," she responded. "Because the twenty-
third, I couldn't do nothing, 'cause I had the patch on my

eye and I had to go back to the doctor. So it wasn't that weekend."

He graciously gave Dugan several opportunities to get back on track, but as the defense attorney continued to quiz her, she became more resolute. "It must have been the week before," she said. "It wasn't after my operation, I know."

Purdy tried to straighten things out on redirect, but got nowhere. Left no alternative, he finished with the witness, then promptly called her daughter, Marilyn Knoepfler, to the stand. Immediately, the prosecutor linked the two witnesses for the jury: "The lady who was just in here is your mother, is that correct?"

"My mother, yes," Knoepfler replied.

Knoepfler remembered her mother repeating Eric's comments about the cops to her, and the fact that the conversation had occurred on the Saturday after Myra's disappearance, and after her mother's eye surgery.

Jennifer Meade took the stand the afternoon of the fourth day of testimony to paint the picture of motive. "We're going to get killed," Caposela confided. "There'll be blood all over the place, and I can't lay a glove on her. She's bad on dates, but that's it."

Eric's former mistress recounted how Eric had told the Brownie training class he was single and lived at home with his mother, that he had romanced her with a bouquet of roses, and that, after Myra's disappearance, he had suggested they move in together.

The witness recalled that when she had asked Eric about the tattoo with *Myra* on his arm, he had told her the woman was an old girlfriend he had not seen in two years. Purdy asked if Eric had told her he had children with Myra. "Not at that time," she answered.

Had they gone on dates? "We mostly drove around. For about three, four hours."

Purdy turned his questions to the key week, with Jennifer recalling that Eric had called her that Sunday evening to put his supposed long-lost girlfriend on the phone.

She recalled Eric telling her later that week that he could not drive her to her second job because he had to go talk Myra out of moving to Puerto Rico. Had he ever expressed concern about Myra taking the children with her? "Yes," Jennifer said. "He was very worried about that."

She said that on the Thursday morning of Myra's disappearance, she found Eric asleep in his car instead of in the park where they had arranged to meet. After waking him, she continued, Eric told her he had "two pieces of good news about Myra: one, she was gone; and two, he had the kids." Jennifer delivered the incriminating line powerfully and succinctly.

Jennifer said she had assumed Myra had custody of the children, so Eric's comments had thrown her. "I said, 'She's coming back because those are just babies and she ain't going to be gone too long.' And he said, 'She's not coming back!' "

Purdy was on a roll now. He referred to the time when Jennifer eventually learned that Eric had been married to Myra. "Now, did you hear him use that name, 'Myra,' a lot?"

"No," Jennifer said. "He called her 'what's-her-name.' "

She was asked to explain what Eric told her after he learned she had spoken with Detective Donato. "He told me not to talk to them anymore, just to tell them, 'Talk to my lawyers.' "

Purdy wanted more. He asked her to recall Eric's specific comments. Jennifer nodded in approval. "His exact words, the best I can remember, are, 'Don't talk to them no more. Tell them to talk to your lawyer, especially if "That Little Shit," Detective Donato, talks to you, tell him to go fuck his-self.' "

Jennifer made a terrific witness. Coupled with the testimony of the police personnel and the Acevedo family, her story provided the jury with a solid reconstruction of Myra's final week, while undoing any damage inflicted by Theresa Maltese and Jeanette Konuklu. The prosecution's case was firmly back on track.

34

IN HER WORDS

All that week I was at home sick, with the flu or something, and I spoke with Myra. Either she called me or I called her, which the phone bills will show. She was undecided about going to Puerto Rico, whether to take her furniture and everything, or just go on vacation. Her father said she should just come on vacation. Because once you give up the apartment, you can't come back to it.

One time when I talked to her, she was going to let the mover in the apartment. The next time, she wasn't. During one phone call, when we were speaking, Eric came home. Then the doorbell rang downstairs. She said it was the moving man. It was at five o'clock, the news was on, I remember. Myra said she wasn't going to answer it.

But the downstairs neighbor, "Nosy," went out and opened up the door and let him up. Then Myra started cursing and calling her all these names. Myra gave the phone to Eric. So I was talking to him when I was listening to all this.

I didn't talk to her after that until she called to say that Eric was on his way with the kids. So I quick got myself ready.

When we got to the house in Clifton, Eric went up. By the time he went through the door, Theresa and her husband came home. They had left hurriedly when Myra was fighting.

Theresa was getting out of the car. I put my head out the window, because we were in the back, and I said, "Theresa." She said, "What's going on?" I said, "I know about your fight with Myra. I heard it. I was on the phone with her." See, that's what she didn't know.

Then I said, "Well maybe Myra's calmed down. Eric just

went up. She's going to come down. But I don't know if she is going to go out. Why don't you go up and apologize?" Theresa said, "No." She said she was just coming to get money.

Theresa was just about walking away from me, still talking, when Eric came down. They said hello to each other. She didn't say anything else. As Theresa moved away, Eric said, "She's not going to come; you talk to her."

Theresa got in her car. She left. Eric did come down by himself, like Theresa said. But then he went back in the house and Myra came down with him, just for a second.

It was like I didn't know her. I should have sensed something. Now you know. She wasn't herself. She wasn't happy. She wasn't laughing. She didn't want to go to dinner. We used to go to Red Lobster all the time. We were always going there. We always got the coupons, five dollars off. We liked the food and we always had doggie bags coming home.

Myra went back upstairs. Anybody who was out could have seen Myra. They were in the playground, they were all over. But you know how it is, people don't want to get involved because when you try to do good, the police are the ones who mess you up.

We left Clifton. We came back to New York. We didn't go out to dinner. I wasn't feeling well and— I mean the kids had something like in my house, you know. But, no, to go out and eat, no, no. I don't remember if we found a parking place or if Eric parked by the hydrant out in front of the house, because that was our spot.

We kept calling her—no answer. I don't know if we got out there at two, a little before, or a little after. We were there for a while. The kids were sleeping. We had to carry them up.

We were in Clifton a short time before Eric called Al. Eric wasn't sure if he should call. He was trying to get me to stay home with the kids and I had already been out of work four days. So that was when he called Al, the famous two forty-four A.M. phone call.

Eric asked Al, "Did you see Myra? Did you talk to her? Did you come by and get her? Could your mother watch the kids tomorrow?" And it was "no" to all of them. Al said his mother couldn't because she was going in for surgery.

See, they said they heard Myra yelling in the background.

I was right there and I was not saying a word. It was Eric doing all the talking. He called Al to find out if he had seen her, if she had come over there, if she had called. Then Eric told him she was missing. The only reason Maggie and Greg were there was because Al's hard of hearing. They had the answering machine turned up so loud that they could hear Eric asking for him. They had to wake him up. But they were confusing it with another call, where Al said Maggie and Greg heard them fighting.

Shortly after the phone call, we left with the kids. We didn't know what to do, so we came home. But we continued to call, to see if she came back. Eric went to work in the morning.

We didn't stay in Clifton because, number one, Eric was working here in the city. Number two, I had been home sick and I was going to go back to work that day. Number three, Myra had started to pack. The kids wouldn't have been able to sleep in their beds. She had boxes on them and stuff piled ready to go. She didn't pack like a normal person. She had kids' winter clothes, then maybe she had summer clothes in there, and maybe she had sheets and towels. It was a disaster. Everything was all over.

Eric never went back there anymore—not to sleep. The kids never slept in their beds again either until they went to New Mexico.

I know without a doubt that Eric didn't do it. I was with him. And I saw Myra and I talked to her that night. He couldn't have done it before he left because he didn't go back into the house with Myra. He was driving us away. Myra just hugged the kids good-bye and we pulled away.

When her father, Pablo, called after she was missing, I talked to him. He said, "We all have to stick together. We have to care about one another."

35

Nick Donato had waited a long time for his moment. Not allowed in the courtroom during the preceding testimony, the State's key law-enforcement witness had no idea how the case was progressing. He was itching to get started. Even Judge Hull sensed the detective's anticipation. Purdy said he hoped Donato was standing by in the hallway. "I'll be surprised if he's not," said the judge. As Purdy announced, "The State calls Detective Nicholas Donato," the rear door to the courtroom opened, and there he was. Judge Hull could not resist observing with a friendly smile and a nod, "Standing right at the door."

Throughout that afternoon and the following morning, Donato touched on the high points of his lengthy investigation. His responses were crisp and knowledgeable. When uncertain of a fact, he had no misgivings about referring to his typewritten report.

In recounting his Fourth of July encounter with Carolyn and Eric outside Uncle Al's apartment, Donato described how Eric had angrily interrupted his mother as she attempted to give her version of events. "When his mother was speaking to us, he continually would say to her, 'Carol, shut up. Carol, shut up.' They actually got into a fight, a physical fight, where they were pushing and shoving one another back and forth. He was trying to push her back into Al Jiovine's apartment and she was pushing back to stay in the hallway. He was saying, 'You don't have to talk to them. Shut up.' And she was saying, 'No, I can handle this.' "

Donato recalled that Eric told him the police should be talking to the Acevedos about Myra's whereabouts and had warned him and Burke to stay away from him. "Mr. Napoletano said, 'Don't be coming to my job, don't be talking to my friends, and don't follow me around.' Right at that point

Carolyn Napoletano chimed in and said, 'Yeah, and that goes for me, too. If you show up at my job, I'll have you escorted out.' "

"Did she tell you, at that time, where she was working?" Purdy asked. Donato said he was not certain if she had mentioned her employer's identity that day, "but I do know where she worked—the New York City Police Department."

Purdy used Donato to introduce various phone records and a summary of the most pertinent calls. Each juror was given a copy of the specialized list, Exhibit S-62. Donato reviewed the key calls, especially the 2:44 A.M. call to Uncle Al's. The detective pointed out that neither Eric nor Carolyn ever mentioned the late-night call, claiming only that they had returned to the Clifton apartment at about 3:00 A.M. to find Myra gone.

Finally, the detective testified about the search he conducted in the Napoletano apartment for reddish fibers, explaining that he had scraped samples from "all the hard-to-reach places, or the most unobvious places, especially because we were talking about a fiber." Experts would tie in this testimony later.

On cross, Caposela turned to what was going to be the cornerstone of his defense, a frontal attack on Uncle Al's credibility. In response to Caposela's questions, Donato had no choice but to confirm that Al was quite a liar: He had even lied about who used the Toyota. The defense attorney reviewed the numerous times Al had been interviewed by police. "And during the course of these interviews, one of the prime questions was about a phone call that he was purported to have received at two forty-four in the morning on Thursday, June twenty-first, is that correct?" Donato agreed.

"And in fact, he was asked by Detective Ruth, in your presence, many, many times about that, is that correct?" Again, Donato agreed.

Caposela said that rather than go through each instance, he would represent that Uncle Al had been asked about the phone call "in excess of one hundred thirty-five times." Donato said he could not agree to such a specific number, but conceded, "He was asked repeatedly, yes."

"And each and every time he was saying something like, 'I don't remember' or 'I didn't get the call,' is that right?"

"A lot of 'I don't recalls,' " said the witness. "A whole lot of 'I don't recalls.' "

Caposela wondered if Donato, as a professional investigator, had concluded that Al had "a selective memory."

"That's a consideration," Donato replied.

"Is that a fair term? In other words, when he wants to tell the truth, he does, and when he doesn't want to tell the truth, he doesn't?"

Donato had nowhere to run. "Mr. Jiovine has lied to me. Let's just say that."

Caposela delved into Donato's search for information about the color of the Toyota's trunk liner. The detective had tried to ascertain whether the car could have previously had a different-colored rug, perhaps made of the matching red fibers. The defense attorney had good reason for asking the carpet questions; he was preparing for his cross-examination of Uncle Al. In one of his final pretrial police interviews, Jiovine had said he was sure the carpet in the trunk had been burgundy.

In fact, Donato acknowledged, all 1989 Corollas came equipped with gray trunk lining. For extra emphasis, Caposela said he wanted to know specifically about the carpeting in Eric's car. "Your recollection is that it was light gray in color?"

"I believe so," Donato replied. "It certainly wasn't red. I would remember that!"

Walter Dewey stepped up to question the next witness, Daniel Oscar Turcotte, the New York City Department of Transportation summer intern who had fielded Eric's request for marital counseling with Myra less than a week before her disappearance. The witness recalled the "urgency" of Eric's original call. "He had presented a kind of crisis with his personal relationship," Turcotte said. But instead of arriving for the appointment with "the mother of his two children," Eric had appeared with "a young Afro-American woman."

"And when he appeared for his appointment, what did Mr. Napoletano say? How did he behave?" Dewey asked.

Caposela rose to object. The attorneys went to yet another off-the-record sidebar, before the judge sent the jurors out of the courtroom. This time the skirmish centered on state law regarding the confidentiality of sessions with marriage counselors.

Dewey insisted that his questions were proper because the New York City DOT had not released Turcotte's files to Eric's first attorney, Louis Acevedo, until it had received a signed waiver of confidentiality. Caposela said he was unaware of any such waiver; he certainly had never been given a copy. He further argued that the confidentiality privilege was only Eric's to waive.

Dewey argued that marital counseling was not the issue; when Eric arrived at the DOT offices, he said he needed child care.

"Are we going to hear comments that the defendant made about Myra Napoletano?" Judge Hull asked. Yes, said Dewey.

Caposela jumped back in, reading from Turcotte's report, how Eric was "very manic," "arrogant," and displeased with the agency's responses and recommendations. Dewey let on that Turcotte was prepared to go beyond the written report in his testimony.

"Well, where is the waiver signed by the defendant?" the judge demanded. Dewey said it had never been produced for his office. Louis Acevedo had prepared it, and sent it to the DOT—"whereupon, they released this information." The prosecutor argued that Turcotte was on the defense list of potential witnesses. Judge Hull said that was immaterial. He needed to see a signed waiver. And it was clear that if Eric had to sign one now, Caposela was not about to let him do so.

Judge Hull told the attorneys to take a few minutes to try to untangle the confusion in private. "And I would have appreciated knowing that this would be an issue in the case before the witness took the stand!" he admonished.

Following a recess, Caposela told the judge he was officially contesting Turcotte's testimony under New Jersey Statute 45:8B-29 pertaining to marriage-counselor privilege.

Judge Hull said he would hear the testimony in camera, then decide if it was privileged. He sent the jury home for the day and told everyone not connected to the case to leave the courtroom.

With the courtroom sealed, Turcotte resumed his story at the point where he had asked Eric what happened to his plan to reconcile with his supposed girlfriend. "He was very angry. He said, 'Fuck that bitch! Forget her! I need child care, and I need it now! And you've got to help me get it.' "

Caposela and Turcotte went back and forth over the witness's use of the word *manic* in his report. Turcotte said Eric had been gesticulating. "It seemed very difficult for him to be seated for any length of time. He would stand up— He would just do a lot of talking with his hands and so forth."

The witness said that his supervisor, a woman identified only as Anna, had noted that Eric answered her questions very quickly and directly. He said that when his boss inquired, "Are you always like this?" Eric had replied, "Yes. Not only am I like this, but my mother's like this, too."

In response to Caposela's question, Turcotte recalled that Anna had suggested Eric might be suffering from a psychiatric disorder and might "benefit from further psychiatric assistance."

Judge Hull sent Turcotte out into the hallway. Caposela argued against allowing the testimony because of the marriage-counseling privilege and, as a fallback position, because it would be unduly prejudicial.

Dewey argued there could be no privilege; Eric had told Turcotte he no longer wanted marital counseling—he wanted day care. "It had nothing to do with supposed reconciliation or hope of her return, because, quite frankly, Judge, he knows that she's never returning."

Judge Hall ruled that the conversation was not entitled to confidentiality protection. While Eric had called for marital counseling, he had shown up asking for emergency day care.

Caposela won one concession, however. Judge Hull ruled that Turcotte was not qualified as an expert witness, and therefore could not characterize Eric's behavior as "manic." He said that Turcotte could testify "as to the manner" in which Eric spoke, "without rendering an opinion as to whether or not he suffered from some type of mental problem."

The next morning, Turcotte told the rest of his story smoothly and competently to the jury. He still got in his buzzwords, characterizing Eric's mood as "angry" and "agitated," and pointing out that Eric had changed his request from needing marital counseling to demanding day care.

"He told me, 'Fuck that bitch. She came in a few nights

ago with our children and dropped them off, said she was going to the store and she hasn't been back since. And, frankly, I don't give a fuck if she ever comes back because she's unfit to take care of our children.' " Turcotte's delivery got better with each run-through.

There was little Caposela could do on cross-examination. He asked Turcotte where in his report he had recounted Eric's story about Myra's failure to return from the store.

"This is anecdotal. He said that to me. I didn't include it. This is not a verbatim report but a summary of the interview, which I would do regularly with all employees," Turcotte replied. "I tend to just put a couple of very small quotes in my report."

"So you pick and choose which material you're going to quote and which ones you're not going to quote, correct?"

"I certainly do," the witness shot back.

"I have nothing further." Caposela returned to the defense table, his efforts severely damaged by the testimony.

It was time to hear Greg Velez, now twenty-two, and Maggie Rivera, now seventeen. Greg went first; his story was more vulnerable. Short and stocky, he strolled to the stand wearing a New York Knicks T-shirt, a Raiders football jacket, Nike sneakers, and a designer-label baseball cap. One of the sheriff's deputies told him to take off the hat. The courtroom was hotter than usual, so within a few minutes Greg voluntarily abandoned his fashion statement and removed his jacket, too.

A resident of the Bronx these days, Greg explained that he and Maggie were living together with their two children. Maggie had given birth to a daughter, Ashley, just three months earlier. Jonathan, their son, was now three.

Purdy covered the touchy ground Caposela would surely grab: Greg's relationship with Al. The witness said he was a street kid who did not know where his parents were, he met Al at a gay bar, and he went home with him "to make a little extra money."

Purdy quickly moved to the crucial 2:44 A.M. call. He told Greg to refer to the giant calendars for June and July 1990 hanging on the courtroom wall if he needed help keeping the dates straight. "I can't see. I wear glasses and I don't have them," Greg said.

"If you need help remembering the dates, take a look at that calendar. If you have to, get down," Purdy said firmly. He really did have his work cut out for him with these witnesses.

Greg went on to tell his latest version of the 2:44 call for the night Myra disappeared: He had been playing Nintendo in Al's living room with Maggie when the phone rang; he answered it; Eric was on the line, so he woke up Al.

Purdy asked Greg if he had been able to hear any of the voices on the other end of the phone. "Yeah, kind of muffled," he replied.

"And could you hear Al's voice?" Yes, he said.

So what had he heard? "Well, I heard Eric. I heard Al ask Myra if Eric was—was he hitting her. And I couldn't really hear what she said on the phone."

"You heard a voice on the other end of the phone?"

Yes, Greg said. "I heard a voice."

"And it sounded like Myra's voice?" Purdy asked.

"Yeah," he contended. "Because the TV was lower. I heard—"

"Does the Nintendo create a lot of noise?"

"Yeah, but I lowered it," said Greg.

Purdy produced a copy of Greg's August 9, 1990, interview with Ruth and Donato. Had he told them he remembered hearing voices?

"Yes," Greg replied incorrectly. In fact, he had told the detectives he heard only one voice on the other end, Eric's, and had pointedly denied hearing Myra.

Under cross-examination, Caposela pounded away at that very issue, reminding Greg of all the occasions he had said he did not remember hearing Myra's voice on the 2:44 call. Had the police asked him about the call the evening of Father's Day? "I don't think so," Greg said. Hadn't he said on August 9, 1990, that he never heard Al mention Myra's name during the call? "I don't remember saying that," he now claimed.

Caposela read the key questions and answers from the transcript, where Greg said he had not even heard Myra's name mentioned and where he said it appeared that Al had spoken only with Eric. Greg said he still did not recall saying those things.

Under more questioning, he also claimed not to have known that his drug-dealing charges were dropped the very week he testified against Al in federal court.

Caposela worked his way to Greg's recantation, reading

into the record the entire transcript of his interview with lawyer Acevedo and Investigator Scott.

On redirect, Purdy had the perfect comeback, however. He played the seven-minute tape of the recantation interview, then asked how long Acevedo and Scott had been there. About an hour and a half, Greg replied. The prosecutor asked if the taping had taken place at the beginning or end of the ninety minutes. "At the end," said Greg.

"Now what were you doing for the other time?"

"We were just rehearsing it," the witness replied.

Magdalena "Maggie" Rivera's testimony followed similar lines. Purdy started with a brief bio: street kid who gave birth to her first child when she was fourteen.

Moving to the 2:44 call, Maggie said she and Greg were playing Nintendo while their son slept in a nearby crib. The phone rang, and went to the answering machine. "It's me, Eric," the voice on the line had said. Greg picked it up, then went to wake Al.

Dressed in a cartoon-character T-shirt and dungarees, Maggie told the jury she could hear both sides of the conversation because of the volume-enhancing device on Al's phone. "Al is deaf so he puts the volume up high and you can hear the people who are calling talking. . . . I wasn't trying to listen, but I—I could hear because he had it loud. I heard everything."

She said Eric began by "telling Al that Myra had a boyfriend. And Al started laughing. He said, 'Myra's got a boyfriend?' Myra got on the phone. She was like, 'No, that's a lie! I don't have no boyfriend. He's the one with the girl'—she used 'black girl'—'He's the one with the black girl.' And they were arguing back and forth. And then Al asked Myra, 'Is Eric hitting you?' and she told him, 'No,' that he wasn't hitting her. And then they just kept on arguing about the boyfriend and the girlfriend stuff and then after that they hung up."

This still sounded like the Sunday night call, except to the jurors, who did not know the whole story. In fact, it made no sense that Al would have been hearing about Myra's supposed boyfriend for the first time during the Wednesday evening call. Surely, Eric would have made the claims to Al during their phone conversation late the evening of Father's

Day, three days earlier. That was when Eric and Myra had traded charges of adultery.

It was hard to imagine Eric having waited three days to tell Al such a story. Al was one of the two people to whom Eric told everything.

On cross, Caposela read a portion of one of Maggie's prior statements, where she said she believed her afternoon chat with Myra inquiring about possible apartments and the 2:44 A.M. call had occurred on different days.

Maggie said Detective Donato had specifically pointed out the record of the 2:44 call to her. "Did Detective Donato point out any other phone calls on that sheet?" Maggie said the record of one other call had been shown to her, the Wednesday afternoon chat she had with Myra about apartments.

Had Donato pointed out any phone calls for that Sunday? Or Monday? Or Tuesday? No, the witness replied three times.

Caposela grabbed Maggie's recantation statement, and read the entire transcript to the jury, where she had insisted of the 2:44 call, "It was a different night. It wasn't that night."

But on redirect, Purdy again countered by playing the tape of Maggie's recantation interview. Her tape ran only four minutes.

"How long were these gentlemen at your house?" Purdy asked.

"They was there a pretty long time," she replied, explaining that "every time I would say something they would tape, you know, tape me, they would stop it, rewind it and make me say it another way. They would stop the tape recorder and then if it didn't sound right to them, they would rewind it to the beginning and start over again."

Purdy wondered if the defense team had questioned her about the authenticity of her signature on her earlier police statement. Yes, they had, Maggie said. But, she told the jury, she had assured Acevedo and Scott that her signature was genuine.

"They asked you no questions on the tape recorder about that, right?"

"No," she replied. "They didn't ask me that on the tape recorder."

So why had she told Acevedo and Scott that the key call involving Myra had taken place on Father's Day night?

"When they asked me the first time, I told them that it wasn't on Father's Day, that I was sure it was the twenty-first at two forty-four, you know, at two forty-four. Then he took out the warrants. He started saying 'Oh, you know, he's going to get locked up anyway, so you'd better cooperate with us.' Then they started showing me the papers and they was telling me, 'Look, you know, it's right here. You know it was Father's Day, you know it was Father's Day.' So I just said that. I didn't want them to put Greg in jail."

The search for the truth was traveling quite a tortuous route. If supposedly streetwise Greg and Maggie were to now be believed, the origins of the dispute over the 2:44 A.M. phone call could be traced to their belief that somehow a public-defender attorney and his investigator could have gotten Greg arrested.

Over the course of the next several days, Purdy and Dewey called a series of witnesses to cover the Delaware connection and take care of technical evidence—for example, a Social Security Administration official to explain that cards had been issued to Myra in the last names "Acevedo" and "Acevedo Olavarria," but not in the name Napoletano; and a Toyota-dealer representative to confirm that a bumper had been shipped to Eric in the large cardboard box seized outside the Clifton apartment.

The Delaware witnesses formed an eclectic group: Labrador Lane resident Richard Milson, who had found Myra's body; Corporals Kenneth Conrad and Ronald Webb, the police evidence-detection technicians; Detective Ruth, who detailed—complete with aerial photos of the Labrador Lane area—the comprehensive investigation he had conducted; Dr. Martin W. Scanlon, the dentist who had matched Myra's Bronx dental records with the X rays of the Labrador Lane corpse; and Dr. Richard T. Callery from the Delaware Medical Examiner's Office, to explain his exhumation and autopsy.

While questioning Conrad, Dewey spread out the Toyota parts box on the courtroom floor to prime the jury's imagination. The investigator said he had found loose hairs in the carton and shipped them off to the FBI lab for analysis.

Through Detective Ruth, Purdy introduced a forty-minute composite of Al Jiovine's three taped interviews, replete with a sampling of the 135 questions about the 2:44 A.M. call.

With the jury out of the courtroom Dr. Callery previewed fourteen color slides as part of his clinical explanation of decomposition and scattered bones. The State was not required to prove a manner of death, but juries like to know such things. Dr. Callery wanted to explain why he had been unable to determine how Myra had died.

For once the testimony got to Eric. At first he tried to avoid looking at the slides by grabbing a transcript to read. However, Dr. Callery was very descriptive and had a smooth delivery. Eric could not resist a peek, but the slides repulsed him. He was visibly shaken—first looking scared, then sad, as if about to cry. The back of his neck began to throb. He pushed his chair back, out of vision of the projection screen. He wiped his right eye and refrained from watching the rest of the presentation.

Caposela argued that there was no need for such graphic testimony since he was not contesting the adequacy of the exhumation or autopsy. He contended that there were other "noninflammatory" ways Dr. Callery could make the same points.

Judge Hull agreed. "They can do nothing but inflame this jury, or perhaps make the jury sick. The State will not be allowed to use them."

With the jury back, Dr. Callery provided a fascinating dissertation about his efforts at the crime scene and on the autopsy table. Through words alone he painted a gore-filled picture that had several jurors squirming in their seats: e.g., "the skull was skeletonized. There was no flesh on it, no eyes"; "all the soft-tissue skin was gone"; the key internal organs—the heart and lungs—had been "devoured by insects and decomposed." He said when he finished assembling the pieces, there was a space where the neck belonged. "It was like a jigsaw puzzle with parts missing," a situation that had prevented him from determining whether the victim had been strangled.

He said he also had been unable to analyze another body part uniquely susceptible to early decomposition. "The brain had been devoured by insects. It had decomposed. And the brain decomposes differently than the rest of the body. Rather than becoming soft and the consistency of a pudding, the brain becomes liquid. It's called liquefactive necrosis. All of the structures that you'd normally want to examine are lost."

Still, Dr. Callery testified, given everything he knew about the case—along with the circumstances of the burial and his autopsy—he had concluded within "a degree of medical certainty" that the state of decomposition was consistent with Myra's death having occurred on or about June 21, 1990.

Under cross-examination, Caposela questioned how Dr. Callery had been able to mark the box "homicide" on Myra's death certificate. The defense attorney wanted to make the point that the pathologist had based his determination on facts provided to him by law-enforcement authorities, not on his autopsy findings.

"No, not really," the doctor replied, explaining that he had made such determinations for decomposed corpses on other occasions. "Young women don't end up in shallow graves after dying of natural causes in rural areas of Delaware," he stated tightly.

"Is that why you marked that box?" Caposela asked.

"Absolutely," Dr. Callery replied.

As the witness sought to elaborate, Caposela cut him off to prevent further damage."You've answered the question. That's fine. Thank you."

Special Agent Robert B. Fram, of the Hair and Fiber Unit at the FBI lab in Washington, was the leadoff witness for day eight of testimony, Monday, May 3, 1993. Eric had turned twenty-eight the day before. Caposela treated him to a Crystal Pepsi.

Fram had worked on about a thousand cases during his twelve years with the FBI. His testimony for this trial had been delayed for several days while he sifted through evidence in the Branch Davidian cult case in Waco, Texas.

Fram provided the jury with a primer on the "transfer theory" by which hairs and fibers move from one person or thing to another when they make contact: "By looking for foreign hairs or fibers on an item—in other words, a hair or fiber that doesn't belong on an item—and attempting to associate it back to a source, I can show the possibility of contact between those two people or between a person and an object."

Fram said he had found fibers on Myra's Freestyle shorts that were foreign—three different types of synthetic fibers, all red. He said two were acrylic, the third was a polyester.

"They're relatively fine fibers. They're not carpet fibers. They could possibly come from an item of clothing, but probably something like a blanket or a throw rug, something like that made up of very fine fibers."

"And conversely why would you say they would not be from a carpet?" Prosecutor Dewey wondered. Fram said that carpet fibers were "much coarser, much thicker."

Fram said it was possible the three fibers had originated from the same item. "Oftentimes they're blends. They're all red, a little different, they have differences, but you can expect that." He explained that there were "a thousand different fiber types out there"—polyester, acrylic, and nylon—and about 7,000 different dyes. Fram said fibers move around a great deal, citing studies showing that only four percent of fibers planted on an item remain after thirty-six hours. Of course, he added, if an object was buried, the fibers would not transfer off.

Dewey introduced various fiber evidence that Fram had analyzed. In a vacuuming of the Toyota trunk, Fram said he found a dark brown head hair that "exhibited the same microscopic characteristics as head hairs from the victim. Either she was in the trunk, or somehow hair from her got into the trunk." On three pieces of trunk carpeting, he found "a combination of red synthetic fibers" that "exhibited the same microscopic characteristics and optical properties" as the fibers he had found on Myra's Freestyle shorts. He said his findings indicated that Myra's shorts and the pieces of trunk lining had come in contact with the same item.

Moving to the cardboard Toyota parts box, Dewey asked Fram to walk to the center of the courtroom well, where the carton lay. The prosecutor inquired first about the pair of socks found inside the box. "Yes," said Fram. "These are the socks in the box."

Fram said his examination of the hairs recovered from the socks and the inside of the Toyota box had yielded a dark brown head hair with the same characteristics as Myra's. He said he also found "all three of the fiber types, the two red acrylic fibers and the red polyester fiber."

Dewey produced Exhibit S-86, fibers and hair removed from staples on the floor in the Clifton apartment. Fram said he found a red polyester fiber and a red acrylic fiber, both consistent with having come from the same source as the other red fibers.

Fram said he also found "numerous red polyester fibers" under the Toyota's spare-tire cover that exhibited the same properties, and detected relevant polyester and acrylic fibers in scrapings Donato had taken from between, behind, and under the radiators and floorboards in four rooms at the Clifton apartment.

Fram had matching red fibers popping up all over the place—in the box, the trunk, Myra's shorts, and the Clifton apartment—impressive evidence, given the number of fibers and dye types in commercial circulation. The cardboard Toyota parts box was the clincher, though, propped up on the courtroom floor for the jurors.

The forensic testimony was some of the most powerful the jury would hear. On cross, Caposela made a valid point that Fram had failed to find any fibers from the trunk liner on the box or on Myra's shorts. But that fact failed to cloud the frightening image Fram had projected of Myra wrapped in a blanket, being put into the cardboard parts carton, carried to the curb, and placed into the Toyota trunk for the trip to Delaware.

Purdy switched the focus of his presentation to the wiretaps. He called FBI Special Agent James R. Fitzgerald from the New York office to explain the technical points of the eavesdropping operation. Fitzgerald, who had supervised the tap on Al's 800 line, said he had provided Agent Cottone with copies of the tapes every day. Cottone, in turn, had provided them to each of the law-enforcement agencies on the task force.

Fitzgerald pointed out that Uncle Al Jiovine often patched in Carolyn when Eric called. But the jury was not told that she was always on duty at NYPD's First Precinct when the connection was made.

Purdy's investigator, Pete Talarico, took the stand to verify chain of custody of the tapes provided by Agent Cottone, to confirm that he had made excerpt tapes at Purdy's direction, and to put into context several of the eavesdropped discussions, for example, references to family court papers served by Pablo Acevedo's attorney.

Over the course of that afternoon and the next morning, the jury heard 129 minutes of excerpts culled from the two weeks of FBI intercepts. Much was missing, but plenty of good stuff remained as Talarico piped the intercepts through a cheap boom box.

The jury acquired a strong sense of the three personas—Eric, Carolyn, and Uncle Al: their subterfuge, their scheming, their knowledge of police procedures, their know-it-all mindset. The three sounded so confident on the phone assuring each other that there was no evidence, but those same words sounded so circumstantially damning in the courtroom. If these three weren't in cahoots covering up Myra's murder, why were they talking the way they were talking—whispering, using code words, and bragging how the cops had nothing on them?

- 36 -

The critical moment in the "search for the truth" had arrived. It was time for the jury to meet Uncle Al: pedophile, convicted perjurer, co-conspirator, and confidant of Eric and Carolyn Napoletano.

Bill Purdy, of course, knew that the testimony could explode in his face. He had no assurances regarding Al's intentions. Al could go silent, tell a new story, go back to forgetting the 2:44 A.M. call, or cause a mistrial by blurting out something about the earlier murders.

Purdy had no choice, though. The State needed Al's testimony. The testimony from Greg and Maggie about the 2:44 A.M. call could not bear the weight. And, as part of the conspiracy, Al could provide jurors with an inside view, however filtered. The strategy would be simple: Don't ask. Don't tell.

As Al took the stand clad in a blue sports jacket and tie, Eric doodled a bird on his yellow legal pad, as in stool pigeon. He wrote the name *Sammy "The Bull" Gravano* underneath, a reference to the Mafia informant who had testified against John Gotti. The defendant fixed a steady glare at the man in the witness box, but Al would not look in his direction. Eric had claimed he was not angry at Al; he just considered him a weakling for letting the cops push him around.

Purdy began by walking Al through a sanitized version of his biography: import manager, $30,000 a year, resident of Queens, met Eric and Carolyn back in May or June of 1978.

Even cleaned up, the story got ugly fast. Purdy asked how he had met the Napoletanos. "Well, I was involved with the Catholic Charities, the Big Brothers, and I knew a gentleman that was also involved. He introduced me to Eric through his mother."

Well, whom had he met first, Eric or his mother? Al said
he had met Eric first.

"And how old was Eric at the time?"

"About thirteen," Al answered, slouching, his voice getting softer with each response.

"And did there come a point shortly after you met these
two individuals where Eric came to live with you?"

Yes, said Al, Eric had come to live with him in Queens.

"And why did this person come to live with you? Did his
mother come to live with you, also?"

"No, just Eric," he replied, answering the second question, avoiding the first.

"Well, what arrangements were made between you and
Eric's mother?"

"That he had to go to school and that he stay with me."

"And was any— Were you paid any money to take care
of him?" Purdy asked.

"Yes, I bought him, I think, clothes and whatever, whatever, the necessities, food and things like that."

Al must have misunderstood. "No," said the prosecutor.
"Did anyone pay you any money to take care of him?"

"No, not at all, no," Al replied.

Never asked, and therefore never answered, was the question of whether Al had ever extracted a sexual quid pro quo
from the young and vulnerable Eric.

Purdy asked if Eric had ever brought girls home. Al said
he had. "And you were aware of relations he had with
women before he met Myra Napoletano?" Yes, said Al.

Purdy's line of questioning was clever. It helped mini-
mize any hint of something sexual going on between Eric
and Al, and avoided any hint of jealousy on Al's part. On
the other hand, Al had to admit his homosexuality, at least
involving Greg. He had no choice since Greg had confirmed
it. Al explained that he had Greg move in with him "because
I was by myself. I was alone." He said he continued having
sexual relations with Greg despite the fact he knew Greg
had a pregnant girlfriend.

When Purdy asked Al why Eric's phone was listed under
the name "Joseph Napoli," Al started to lie. "Because he
was working in New York—" He caught himself. "He
didn't want anybody to know he was living in Jersey." Of
course, Al could not be asked if the "anybody" meant
people like Detective Fazzini from New York.

Turning to the key week, Al said he remembered patching a call between Myra and Maggie Rivera one afternoon. Seeking to make his key link, Purdy then asked Al if he remembered the 2:44 A.M. call.

Without hesitation, Al replied affirmatively: "Eric and Myra called me." He said he spoke with Eric first, then Myra.

But Al proceeded to describe a conversation very different from the one Maggie Rivera had recounted for the jury. "Eric was complaining about her intentions of going to Puerto Rico and he did not want her to go. He wanted her to take that Section Eight housing, you know. And they were screaming and hollering—I *can* hear, you know—and she was crying and—"

"You have a device on your phone that keeps the volume up, is that correct?" asked Purdy. Yes, said Al.

He said he had not heard any threats of violence on the other end of the line. "Just screaming. She was crying. She wanted to go to Puerto Rico, and he was going with Jennifer, having an affair with her, and then coming home and having an affair with Myra. She didn't want that."

Al said Eric called him later that morning at work, "around six- thirty." And what had Eric told him then?

"He told me he *went over to the apartment* and, he said, Myra was gone; and he called me, and he needed somebody to baby-sit his two sons, Eric Junior and Angelo; and he asked me if my mother could watch them."

Al's explanation was outrageous. The trial was supposed to represent—finally—Al's moment of candor. As if there weren't enough versions of the night Myra disappeared, here was Al slipping the jury a hybrid new one. If Al was telling the truth about the 2:44 call, then he was lying about the 6:30 chat.

Why would Eric have said he "went over to the apartment" if he and Myra had been there for the call at 2:44? For Al's testimony to be the truth, Eric would have had to leave the Clifton apartment sometime after the 2:44 A.M. call, and returned before 6:30 A.M. to find Myra gone. He would have had to drive over to Manhattan in that time, too, since the 6:30 call to Al was made from Carolyn's apartment. He presumably would have taken his kids on the middle-of-the-night journey, too.

"She was gone. She wasn't there," Al remembered Eric

telling him. But Purdy did not ask Al to explain any further.
The issue was not whether Eric had lied when he called Al
at 6:30; the issue was whether Al was still lying, under oath.
But neither side in the courtroom would pick up on Al's
comment, either by oversight or conscious decision.

Al was only one-quarter of the way through his testimony. His additional self-serving explanations would con-
sume seventy-two more pages of official transcript. He went
on to tell the jury: He met Eric in a park, where his "son"
told him he had killed Myra because she was going to take
the kids to Puerto Rico; Eric told him he had taken Myra's
body to Delaware; he had protected Eric because he cared
for him; he had protected Eric because he was afraid of him;
Eric told him the cops would never find any evidence in the
car because he had it cleaned; he conceded that he'd lied
"quite a few times" to Detectives Ruth and Donato; he lied
in a federal statement even though he had been given immunity; he had allowed people to believe he was Eric's uncle,
stepfather, or even father; and, almost breaking down, he
explained, "Yes, it was a very close relationship."

Purdy could not avoid Al's federal obstruction of justice
plea. "I still withheld information," Al admitted. Purdy put
Al's plea and sixty-month sentence on the record. Al noted
that he also had pleaded guilty to one of the two counts of
conspiracy to hinder apprehension cited in the New Jersey
indictment.

"And this plea requires that you testify truthfully today?"
Purdy asked. Yes, said Al.

The prosecutor asked Al if, prior to making the New
Jersey deal, he had expected early parole on the federal sentence. "No. I didn't expect any," Al claimed. But that position was not forthright, either. Federal prosecutors had been
on record for months as saying that they would seek a sentence reduction if Al cooperated in other prosecutions.
Purdy read the key elements of the New Jersey plea deal to
the jury, including the part where any sentence would be
concurrent and coterminous with the federal term. Had any
promises been made regarding any specific reduction in his
sentence? Al claimed that only a recommendation would be
made to the sentencing judge. Al was playing the game of
semantics to the hilt.

* * *

With any chance of acquittal riding on a successful attack of Al's credibility, Caposela began his cross-examination with the plea bargain, pointing out that because the state and federal sentences were concurrent, Al had saved himself five years right there. And if he succeeded in getting the feds to reduce their sentence, the plea bargain required that his New Jersey sentence be reduced by a corresponding amount. Caposela suggested to Al that he was avoiding a bundle of time behind bars. Al agreed, "For a person who is sixty-two years old, to be very honest with you, yes."

Perhaps triggered by Al's use of the word *honest*, Caposela abruptly jumped back in time, to when Al said he met Eric. The defense attorney exposed the charade used for years by Al and Carolyn to wrap the respectability of Catholic Charities around the origins of the boy-man relationship back in 1978. "Let me take you back to when you met Eric Napoletano, and you say you met him through Catholic Charities; is that correct?"

"No," he now claimed. "I said I was involved in the Catholic Charities."

"He was not, but you were involved?" asked Caposela incredulously.

Al nodded in agreement. "But his mother had intentions of joining the Catholic Charities."

"All right," the defense lawyer continued. "So it's not your testimony that you met him through Catholic Charities. But instead you met him through a mutual friend—is that correct?"

"Yes, who was involved with the Catholic Charities."

Caposela asked for the friend's name. Without any hesitation, Al provided Bob the businessman's full name.

Had the man told him how he had met Eric? "He said he met him in a park someplace."

This was pulling teeth. "He said he met him in a park?"

Yes, Al said, in Central Park.

Caposela dug deeper, inquiring whether Bob the businessman had a son.

"No," said Al. "He had a young man that was living with him."

Hadn't Eric first met the young man, Caposela asked. Yes, Al replied, explaining that he was unsure whether Bob had also been present for the initial meeting.

Caposela continued to press, asking Jiovine to explain how he had come to learn of Bob's introduction to Eric.

"He called me and told me that," Al replied.

"That he had a young man—"

"Yes," said Al.

"He had a young man who, who could come and stay with you?"

"Yes, exactly," Al replied with an air of innocence.

"And then you did eventually meet Eric Napoletano, correct?" Yes, said Al.

And who introduced them, Eric's mother or Bob the businessman? Al said that Bob had introduced them, at Bob's house.

"And you talked to Eric at that time?" Yes. "And you said to him, 'Would you like to come live with me?' Is that what you said?" Al said he was uncertain "if it was right away."

Well, Caposela wondered, had he called Eric's mother? "His mother was very evasive about anybody taking him over to their house," Al replied. "She wanted to check on me, what kind of a person I was, where I worked and all." Al's answer sounded sincere, but it failed to explain how he and Eric had somehow managed to become good buddies before he had ever met Carolyn.

Caposela dug in one additional level. He still wanted Jiovine to explain how things had gone from his meeting Eric at Bob's house to Eric's moving in with him. "Did you call Carol and say, 'I met your son'?"

The witness replied that he believed Bob the businessman had taken care of "all of that."

"*He* did all of that?" Caposela asked back.

"He did all of that for me because he knew her and I didn't."

Al's reconstruction of his life was a sham. Caposela's questions on the Al-Eric-Carolyn-Bob connection stripped away any remaining cover. And the defense attorney had barely touched the surface.

Caposela headed for another area of Al's biographical misrepresentation, his stint in the Marines. Had he ever told anyone he had been a drill instructor? "I might have said that to Eric, but I wasn't," he replied.

Hadn't he also made that claim to the police? Al said he could not recall but admitted he had been only a vehicle operator.

"You kind of embellished a little, made yourself a little more important?" Caposela suggested.

Al nodded in agreement. "Sort of put a little cream on the cake, yes, to make an impression, you know."

Caposela then picked up on Al's 135 memory lapses regarding the 2:44 call, getting the witness to admit that he also had lied to investigators about his relationship with Greg Velez. "It's not easy when you're going to the police department being questioned when—for the first time in your life. It's tough, very tough on a person," Al explained.

"Isn't it easier to tell the truth than to lie?" Caposela wondered.

"Well, maybe," Al answered weakly.

Caposela asked Al if he remembered talking with Myra the evening of Father's Day. The subject had never been mentioned in his three lengthy tape-recorded police interviews. Amazingly, Al now claimed full recall.

"Did they both talk to you on the phone? In other words, did Eric talk to you and then did Myra talk to you?" Caposela asked. Al agreed with the description. "And they were arguing, were they not, about Eric having a girlfriend, correct?"

"Yeah," said Al. "And she was having intentions—she wanted to move to Puerto Rico or get that Section Eight housing."

"And then Eric would get on the phone again?" "Ah-huh," said Al, concurring.

"And did he talk about Myra having a boyfriend?" Yes, Al conceded.

"And it was going back and forth. They were arguing with each other, right?" Again, Al agreed.

Caposela had made his point. Al would not have been surprised three days later, at 2:44 A.M., if Eric claimed Myra had a boyfriend. And his testimony served as additional evidence that Maggie's recollections before the jury also were incorrect.

Caposela pulled out the "Napoli" phone bills. "I've never seen them," Al claimed. But as Caposela showed the Sunday night call to him, Al nodded knowingly in agreement. "I was awake," he said, meaning he was not mixing it up with the 2:44 call three nights later, meaning he now remembered both calls. But his version of the Sunday conversation matched Maggie's trial version of the 2:44 A.M. call. It was a tortured, evil web.

Caposela asked Al why he had lied to police about his relationship with Greg. "Maybe I was too ashamed of myself." The defense attorney assured Al he was not trying to embarrass him about his way of life. "I'm just here to try to find out what occurred in this case. We are all here in search of the truth at this point."

"Exactly," said Al.

Well, what about the claim that he had met Greg in a pool hall? That had been a lie, right? "Yeah," said Al softly.

What about his claim to Donato that he lived at 130 Erie Street in Dumont, New Jersey? "That's my permanent residence."

"But you really spend most of your time, a great percentage, almost ninety percent of your time, in New York City?"

"In Queens, that's right, as a matter of convenience," Al explained with a straight face.

The next topic of inquiry was Al's claim that he was scared of Eric. "I *am* afraid of him."

"But you weren't so afraid of Eric that you said to yourself, 'I better not talk to the police anymore because I'm afraid of Eric,' right? You didn't do that. You still—"

"I had the other side of me that told me I had to go," Al protested. And, he added, "I knew I wouldn't say anything to the police that would be detrimental against Eric."

Caposela and Al sparred for another thirty minutes. Caposela wanted to expose Al for the lie he uttered after he had supposedly become a cooperating witness, about the color of the Toyota trunk lining. If there was one claim in all of Al's drivel that suggested he would say anything to save his hide, it was his statement that the trunk liner had been burgundy, suggesting a solution to the hunt for the reddish fibers. In fact, the Toyota people insisted that Eric's model of 1989 Corolla had come with gray carpeting, period. On top of that, some of the matching red fibers had been recovered from the gray carpeting.

"During any of these interviews, did the color of the carpet of the trunk ever come up?" Caposela asked.

"I believe so, yes," said Al.

"And your answer to that was what, that it was burgundy?"

"It was a burgundy color, right," said Al.

"Was that because you saw it? You saw a burgundy carpet in the trunk?"

"I saw a burgundy carpet in the back at the Toyota dealer. I never seen it in that car."

Al now sounded terribly rehearsed. But he was intent on continuing. "I never seen—" Caposela sought to cut him off. "They showed me a 1989 Toyota Corolla and tires, the jack—"

"Mister Jiovine, the question—"

Al was determined to get his point in. "Also, the carpet was burgundy in color," he insisted.

"So, when you went to buy the car, it's your testimony that you looked in the trunk?" Caposela asked.

"That's right."

"And there was a burgundy carpet in there?"

"That's right," Al repeated.

For sure, Caposela had scored some bull's-eyes. But would anyone on the jury care how many of these intricate details had occurred the way Al claimed? Al had come across as a hapless, bungling sap saddled with a bad memory and dirty secrets. But when it came to the single issue that really mattered—Eric's whispered confession that he murdered Myra and buried her in Delaware—Al had come across as quite authentic.

Caposela had been left a Hobson's choice. He had concluded that he could not credibly suggest Al was the sole murderer. And pressing him on issues like whether he had taken the ride to Delaware would not help Eric beat the charges. If Al admitted to his role, it would only mean he had taken the ride with Eric. Caposela's only option, then, had been to beat up on Al's credibility without really offering a suggestion as to why Al persisted in being evasive or untruthful on certain points.

Purdy had problems, too. He could not ask Al if he had taken the burial ride down the New Jersey Turnpike because under his "search for the truth" Eric drove alone, or perhaps with his mother and two boys. And Purdy could not knowingly allow perjury.

So, there would be no confrontation about the burial ride—all of which worked in Purdy's favor. He was able to present a theory of the case less than accurate on several specific details but without having to worry that the defendant might stand up and scream, "Wait a minute! That's not the way it happened!"

Al was excused and taken back to his jail cell. Figuratively, he had just gotten away with murder.

- 37 -

IN HER WORDS

I want you to understand what kind of a liar Al is. He lies about anything. We always have stories about Al. Every time Eric and I talk about it, we laugh.

Every year, my mother makes homemade fruitcake. I don't eat fruitcake unless my mother made it. She's been making it for years. She always gave Al one for Christmas. It's so rich that you can only eat one piece, a half a piece. But, oh, no, not Al. He says he ate almost all of it on the way home from Dumont. I says, "But Al, you couldn't have." He says, "I ate it all. There was traffic." I says, "Al, you couldn't have, you couldn't have!"

So a couple of months later, because you can have this stuff for a long time—I still have some in the refrigerator— we go to Al's house. He was not home from work yet. Eric says, "Go get us some cans of soda." Al is funny in covering food, so we didn't want to take anything that's not covered up, or that we're not opening. Then I started yelling. Eric comes out, "What's the matter? What's the matter?" I said, "Look! Look! Remember the fruitcake he 'ate'? There it is. There it is." It had a little label on it, "To Al, Love, Flo." I wanted to take it home, but Eric said, "No, we can't take it." Isn't that funny? That's the kind of liar Al is.

Then you got to hear the other one about— Do you know that Al gets mail on holidays? Nobody else does, Al got mail—swore up and down one holiday that he had mail in his box. Yes, he gets mail; we don't. He lies about anything.

When little Eric's birthday came, we decided to have a party for him in my house. And we decided that we would have to get something for Angelo because he's a baby and he don't know. So Al's bringing gifts from his mother and his sister. One of his sisters was going to get Angelo a

winter jacket, so I said what size to get to allow for a
sweater underneath. Do you know that Al gets like two sizes
smaller?

So we give it back to him and he says he's going to take it
back to his sister. A month goes by; it's getting cold. I ask
him. "It's coming, it's coming." I call his sister, and she
tells me that Al said that the jacket fit perfectly. Now I told
her what I told you, and I told her that Angelo does not have
a jacket now. This is how the man lies.

There are other things, but those were the three best. I
mean, really a liar. I think that knowing what he's like, if
anybody like the police threatened him, he would say anything. He would sign anything, say anything, write anything. But he can't remember the phone call. He lies so
much that I really don't think he knows what the truth is
anymore.

38

Essentially, the trial proper was completed, save for brief testimony from five more FBI agents, Eric's ex-landlord to recount that Eric told him he had "bought" Myra plane tickets, the young man Myra had called the evening of Father's Day, and three quick witnesses appearing on behalf of the defense. The jury would get the case in a couple of days.

Special Agent H. Douglas Beldon, the only FBI representative from New Mexico to survive the Miranda hearing, told the jury about his SWAT team's raid and Eric's arrest.

Subway dispatcher Ahmad Abdallah, the man whose phone number Eric had found three days before Myra disappeared, was summoned to explain his two contacts with Myra—one in person, the second on the phone—to prevent Caposela from proposing him as an alternative suspect. Dressed in a tan-colored business suit, Abdallah said he lived in Brooklyn with his wife and three kids.

He said Myra was crying uncontrollably when he met her near the federal courthouse in Lower Manhattan on a Friday about a month before her death. "I was a little hesitant at first, but I thought I might be able to help," he said. "I didn't know what was wrong. She looked very young to me. I thought she might have been sixteen or seventeen. She had a very young face." He said he asked her if everything was okay. "I tried to comfort her."

He said Myra told him that she had an appointment to inquire about subsidized Section Eight housing and afterward she accepted his offer to discuss her situation over lunch at a nearby pizza shop. Abdallah contended that Myra claimed—as she had to Section Eight officials—that she was living with an older guy, meaning Al; she had come up from Florida to escape from another guy, meaning Eric; and she needed a place to live with her sons.

"I said, 'Well, I do come across things. I know several landlords in Brooklyn. If I come across anything I'll give you a call.' " But, Abdallah told the jury, Myra would not give him her phone number. So he had given her his.

In response to Purdy's questions, the witness remembered receiving a phone call from Myra late one night while he was in bed with his wife. After being shown the phone records, he recalled that the four-minute call had occurred the evening of Father's Day. "I told her I didn't have anything for her. She seemed kind of upset."

"Mr. Abdallah, did you at all discuss dating Myra?"

"Not at all," Abdallah assured Purdy.

"Did you ever make any plans to meet her at all after this time that you met her?" No, he insisted, that was not why he had given Myra his number.

Running out of options fast, Caposela opted to conduct an aggressive cross-examination. He immediately tried to make the witness look like an unsavory opportunist. "You say that you approached her because she looked young and she was crying; is that correct?" Abdallah answered in the affirmative.

"Did you ever ask her if she goes out? I'll use the term 'Do you go out?' Do you understand what I mean by that? By that I mean, 'Do you date? Do you see people?' " The witness said he did not recall asking such a question.

Caposela refreshed Abdallah's memory with a copy of a statement he had given investigators back in 1990, where he said he had asked Myra if she went out, and she had said she did not.

Purdy rose to object. He wanted to know where Caposela was headed. Judge Hull turned to the jury box; the jurors were already on their way out.

The prosecutor explained that he had been very careful to limit the introduction of statements attributable to Myra. He warned that if Caposela was going to bring in any of Myra's comments through Abdallah's police interview, he was going to bring in the part where she told Abdallah the man she was running away from had been "pretty abusive to her."

"It's my position that they were flirting; that she was looking for someone," said Caposela.

Judge Hull was not going to allow some roundabout testimony speculating that Myra had a boyfriend, especially at this late stage. He suggested that Caposela ask his question without referring to the interview transcript. Otherwise, he might allow Purdy to develop a line of questioning about the abusive man from Florida. "In reality, she *is* talking about her husband, and I'm going to allow the prosecutor to pursue it on redirect if you continue to push this on cross-examination."

Caposela argued that the witness was trying to tell the jury that he had innocently tried to assist Myra in her plight, but that the statement he gave police "makes it sound like he was trying to arrange a date with her."

"Mr. Caposela, you do what you want. And you understand what perils may be down the line," the judge said angrily. "There are ways of cross-examining the witness. There are alternative methods. But you choose the one you wish to do."

Caposela put down Abdallah's statement on the defense table. He got Judge Hull's message, but he was still determined to make his point. With the jury back he asked, "Mr. Abdallah, on that date when you met Myra, did you flirt with her?"

Visibly upset with the unfolding events, the man tersely asked back, "Did I flirt with her? You want to elaborate on 'flirt'?"

"Well, I mean did you want to date her?"

"Absolutely not," the witness insisted.

The defense attorney turned to the phone call of Father's Day evening. Abdallah said he spoke only to Myra. "And did she ever say to you that she wanted to meet you someplace or—"

"She wanted to go somewhere or to meet, and I didn't understand what she wanted, or I didn't want to. At that point I realized—" Caposela cut him off.

"Okay. Well, she asked you, 'Can we meet?' or 'Can you come out?' "

" 'Can we talk' or something," Abdallah replied. "I don't remember exactly what it was."

Caposela realized this was going nowhere, and he retreated. "I have nothing further."

Purdy had only one question on redirect, designed to contrast Myra's call to Abdallah with Eric's call to Jennifer Meade the same evening. "Mr. Abdallah, she didn't put her husband on the phone for you to talk to, did she?" the prosecutor asked.

"No, she didn't," Abdallah replied.

Purdy walked back to his seat and sat down.

The agitated witness stormed off the stand. Abdallah hustled through the well of the courtroom, grabbed his briefcase from the floor with a sweeping motion, and stalked off toward the exit, mumbling under his breath the entire time.

The State's final four witnesses were FBI agents who had participated in the raids on Carolyn's or Uncle Al's apartments. One of them, Special Agent John Triolo, testified that he had seized Myra's birth certificate, two Social Security cards, Puerto Rico driver's license, and New York auxiliary police identification card from a strongbox at Carolyn's apartment.

Purdy was finished, save for a final attempt to get permission to play two additional snippets of eavesdropped comments to the jury: Eric's remark, "These kids, there's gonna be bodies lying around if anybody comes and tries to take them," and the Eric-Carolyn-Al discussion about how Pablo Acevedo might "accidentally" get shot if he came to New Mexico looking for his grandchildren. Purdy wanted the excerpts admitted on the grounds that they showed Eric's motive for murder, "a misguided devotion to these children," and a terrible reaction, "however inappropriate," to Myra's plan to leave with the children.

Judge Hull observed that the State had already received the benefit of testimony about Eric's threats to kill Myra if she ever left with the kids, about their arguing at 2:44 A.M., about Eric's call for a baby-sitter at 6:30, and, finally, Eric's expressed desire, as intercepted on the wiretap, to keep the FBI from talking to the two boys at all cost. "I find that what is now being offered is too remote and too prejudicial," Judge Hull stated.

After entering several more exhibits into evidence, Purdy announced, "Your Honor, that concludes the State's evidence. The State rests." Fifty-two witnesses had testified over a three-week period.

With the jurors out for lunch, Caposela made the standard motion for judgment of acquittal on the grounds of insufficient evidence. He also specifically requested the dismissal of Count 14, which charged Eric and his mother with the theft of the $400 that Myra had been saving in her now-missing wallet. Caposela argued that the jury could only decide the theft allegation on "pure speculation." He asserted that no evidence had been presented to support that the wallet had been taken as a theft.

Judge Hull agreed and dismissed the theft charge. But he left all other counts intact, including one that alleged the wallet and the ID cards had been taken to hinder Eric's apprehension.

Caposela called his first witness that afternoon, lawyer Lawrence M. Fagenson. He explained that his firm provided legal services to local members of the Communications Workers of America and had gained Eric as a client by virtue of the defendant's union job as a Brownie.

Since Eric had waived lawyer-client privilege, Fagenson testified that Eric told him his wife had left, and as a result the police had been questioning him. "I told him he should have no further communications with the police department." The attorney said he personally contacted the Clifton Police Department and left an explicit message that he represented Eric and "did not want them speaking to him relative to any of the facts and circumstances of the case, and that if they had cause to arrest Mr. Napoletano, they should contact me and I would arrange a voluntary surrender."

Caposela next summoned Assistant U.S. Attorney Glenn J. Moramarco to emphasize that the pending motion to reduce Al's federal sentence depended on his cooperation in the prosecutions of Eric and Carolyn—the point being that Al had quite an incentive to testify exactly the way the government wanted him to.

With the jury out of the room, Caposela conducted the required voir dire of Eric regarding his decision not to testify. Staying seated at the defense table, Eric replied, "Yes," "That's correct," or "I understand" to a series of questions. Eric said he was aware that he did not have to testify and that the jury could not infer anything negative from his failure to do so. He acknowledged that Caposela had advised him not to take the stand but that the decision was ultimately his alone.

"Knowing that, what is your decision? Do you want to take the witness stand and testify in your own behalf, or do you choose not to testify?" Caposela asked.

"I decline to testify," Eric replied, sounding like a Mafioso dodging a congressional subpoena thirty years ago.

As his third and final witness, Caposela called Lieutenant Diana Brown of the New York City Department of Transportation, Eric and Jennifer's Brownie training instructor. Her testimony was designed to show that Eric had not left work on Thursday, June 21, 1990, the day after Myra's disappearance, excessively early, thereby minimizing the time he would have had available to make the burial ride on that particular evening.

In testimony elicited to explain why Eric had lied about where he lived, Brown also confirmed that under New York City government regulations, one had to reside in New York to work as a Brownie.

That completed the testimony portion of the trial. Neither side had called defense lawyer Louis Acevedo and his investigator Frank Scott regarding the recantations and the 2:44 phone dispute. Through an attorney of his own, Acevedo had sent word he would decline to testify without immunity. The prosecutor's office, in turn, had declined to act on that suggestion.

The appropriate defense exhibits were entered into evidence, and the jury was sent home. Summations would begin in the morning.

The courtroom was sweltering on Thursday, May 6, 1993. The front row was filled again with TV cameras and still photographers. Many members of Myra's family were on hand, including her mother and father, Carmen and Pablo. Marilyn Coludro's mother, Marta, also was in attendance; so were Detective Donato and Investigator Talarico.

Caposela went first, and categorized his remarks into six well organized areas: "bad character evidence"; motive—whether Myra had really decided to leave with the kids for Puerto Rico; the 2:44 A.M. call; the cover-up, focusing on what the State claimed the wiretaps showed; fiber and hair analysis; and Eric's confession. The phone call and the confession to Uncle Al both obviously hinged a great deal upon Jiovine's credibility. "If you believe him, it almost makes all of the other ones irrelevant," Caposela conceded.

He appealed to the jurors not to accept the perceptions of the witnesses as fact. For example, Donna Benson said Eric dominated Myra, and would not let her out. But at the time Myra was pregnant. He contrasted Benson's testimony with Jeanette Konuklu's claim that she and Myra went out together frequently. He questioned Konuklu's credibility. "She did not like this man. She did not like the way he treated his wife. She had an agenda."

Daniel Turcotte, the DOT social worker, received similar treatment. According to Caposela, Turcotte's agenda was to make sure the jurors knew Eric had dismissed his missing wife with "Fuck that bitch!" Caposela asserted that Turcotte also did not like Eric. "And he didn't want you to like him, either."

As to the question of whether Myra had decided to go to Puerto Rico, the State's motive, Caposela pointed to Myra's failure to give the moving man the requested fifty-dollar deposit.

Caposela's view of the 2:44 phone call was straight-forward, and expected: He contended that the call with Eric and Myra arguing had actually occurred the prior Sunday evening. "It makes sense, wouldn't it? Isn't that when all of the calls about the girlfriend and boyfriend are occurring?" He also pointed out that Al had denied the police version of the conversation even after the cops threatened to charge him with being an accomplice.

"He said, 'Give me a Bible. I'll put my hand on the Bible to show you that I'm telling you the truth.' A Bible! Just like this one that he put his hand on when he came in here. . . . He was willing to put his hand on a Bible back then and lie. Now, we have to decide when he came in here and put his hand on *this* Bible whether he lied."

Caposela warned the jurors what could happen if they convicted Eric on Al's testimony. "As you walk out the door into the hallway, guess who walks up to you? Al Jiovine. And he says, 'Mister or Miss Juror, you know what? I didn't tell the truth in that courtroom when I testified. I didn't tell the truth.' Would you be shocked? Would your reaction be, 'Hey, you know what, it figures. I suspected.' If that's what your reaction is—'It figures. I suspected. He probably did'— then you have a reasonable doubt about his testimony. You have a reasonable doubt about whether that man tells the truth. And that's the testimony that you're being asked to convict somebody of murder on."

Next, Caposela addressed the cover-up issue. He said he anticipated that Purdy would dwell on the way the defendants acted, the way they said things on the wiretaps like, "They won't find anything." But, the defense attorney argued, Eric acted that way because he was afraid of Pablo Acevedo's efforts to gain custody of Eric Junior and Angelo. And he acted that way because his attorney told him not to speak with the police.

Caposela argued next that the brouhaha over Myra's missing wallet and ID cards was based on Jeanette Konuklu's erroneous claim that she had seen Myra's Social Security card in the name Napoletano. He contended that there was no merit to the State's assertion that Eric and Carolyn had taken Myra's wallet to make it look as if she had left. Why hadn't the prosecutor shown the Social Security card to Konuklu on the stand? "Why not just show her the card? 'Is this the card that you saw? We found this card in Carolyn Napoletano's strongbox. Is this the card that you saw in Myra's wallet?' Wouldn't that be the logical thing to do? Well, the prosecutor didn't do it. Know why he didn't do it? He didn't know what she was going to say. He wasn't sure that she was going to be able to identify it."

Turning to the forensic evidence, Caposela acknowledged that he was fascinated by Agent Fram's hair-and-fiber testimony and guessed that the jurors had been, too. But, he continued, "As interesting as it was, it had a lot of flaws." He reiterated that fibers and hairs get transferred in many ways, by attaching to clothing, shoes, and the body. "We take socks and throw them in the box, and the hairs are on the socks, and then the hairs wind up on the box. You know, it sounds like something from Dr. Seuss." Caposela delivered the line with a smile, but the jurors stared back solemnly.

He argued that it should have come to no one's surprise that Myra's hair was found in the trunk of the Toyota. "That was her family car." He recounted how Fram had agreed with the premise that someone could lose a hair in the trunk while removing a bag of groceries, and how fibers could be transferred when a piece of clothing retrieved from the floor of an apartment was stored in the trunk of a car. "There's a multitude of ways these things could be transferred."

Caposela moved to the most difficult piece of evidence he faced: Uncle's Al rendition of Eric's confession. It was the weakest portion of his summation. "I'm not telling you not to believe him because he's a bad man." He suggested that deep inside, Al might actually be a decent guy. "I'm not saying that a liar can't have a heart."

So what *was* he saying? Caposela never really did say. He suggested one possible explanation for Al's failure to recall the 2:44 A.M. call—he honestly had not remembered it. But that detracted from his argument that Al was a liar. In the end, what could Caposela have said? Reasonable jurors could accept that Al had forgotten the 2:44 call, or maybe the argument had occurred on another night, or maybe Myra wasn't on the phone, or maybe Eric had even told Al he just killed Myra. But why would reasonable jurors accept that Al had concocted the story of Eric confessing to murder?

And so Caposela moved on to a list of issues that were bothering him. He began with the fact that no one had heard from Myra during the eight hours before the 2:44 A.M. call. The previous call had been made at 6:49 P.M. "If she was home, why weren't there any phone calls out of the apartment?"

He wondered, If Eric had killed Myra, did he kill her in the apartment? And if so, how did he kill her? And if so, how did he get her out of the apartment? And if so, when did he get her out of the apartment? Caposela argued that if Eric had killed Myra shortly after 2:44, then the neighbors should have heard.

Caposela asked the jurors to consider each of his questions "and each and every piece of evidence in this case" a link in a chain. If they found reasonable doubt with any one of the links—whether it be Uncle Al, Greg Velez, or Special Agent Fram—they had to find Eric not guilty. "The pieces that are missing are essential parts of this puzzle," he maintained. "They are huge pieces at the center of this puzzle—and they are missing. There is no evidence in this case that will convict Eric Napoletano of murder beyond a reasonable doubt."

Caposela began walking back toward the defense table. He had kept his promise to be brief, just over an hour. "I wish you Godspeed in your deliberations. Thank you."

The defense attorney had put in many hours preparing his case. He was an honorable man, on many levels beyond his original willingness to take the case without guarantee of pay. But he had been given an impossible task. In his heart, he knew the jurors would not concern themselves with such details as where, when, and how Myra had been killed, or why she had been buried in Delaware. All that would matter to them was whether Eric had been the murderer.

Slumped in his chair, Eric observed, "Ernie, I thought you were going to do a good job, and you did. You did better than I thought. But you know what, I'm gonna get fucked."

Purdy commenced shortly after eleven o'clock. For the most part, Eric sat motionless, looking stunned, his fingers clasped in front of him, wrists resting on the tabletop.

The prosecutor observed that he would react to some of Caposela's comments as well as make points of his own. "Near the end of his summation he told you that we're here to protect a sacred right, the right of the defendant to be presumed innocent and get a fair trial. We're also here, I think you understand, because another sacred right has been violated, a life has been taken."

Using his favorite analogy for a circumstantial case—a jigsaw puzzle—Purdy argued that Caposela would have the jurors spread 1,000 pieces on a table without having any idea how to go about unraveling the mess. He suggested that solving the puzzle became much easier once everyone looked at the assembled picture on the cover of the box. Still, he added, "You have to put it together." And when this case was put together, he argued, the resultant picture would convince them that "Eric Napoletano murdered his wife."

Purdy argued that Caposela was incorrect in claiming that every piece of the puzzle had to fit. He said that was not the way it worked, that all he had to do was "prove each and every element of the offenses beyond a reasonable doubt, not each and every fact." He cautioned the jurors not to play detective. The State did not have to prove how Myra was killed. "You shouldn't waste five seconds in your deliberations on that question."

He said other details "simply are unknowable," like "exactly what happened in that apartment at 2:44 A.M., what time the defendant actually drove to Delaware. . . . Focus your attention on the facts that you do know. The questions you have to answer are, Is the defendant guilty of the charges? Did he murder his wife? Did he try to hinder his apprehension by giving the police false information? Did he engage in a conspiracy with the other defendants to try to cover this up?"

Alternately raising and lowering his voice for dramatic effect, Purdy ticked off the relevant pieces of the circumstantial puzzle: The Napoletano marriage had been deteriorating; Eric had treated Myra badly; she had planned to leave, the moving man had come to give her an estimate; she had discussed the move with her family; she had been saving money for the move; she told Eric she was going to take the kids with her; Eric was obsessed with his kids; he had threatened to kill her in the past; Eric had a mistress; and Myra did not have a boyfriend.

Purdy was inspired. "But that is not all there is in this case. There's so much more! So much more!

"He never expected them to find the body, and he never expected these people to come into court . . . to haunt him," Purdy said. "He thinks he can lie to one person, lie to another, tell a third and fourth lie to two other people, and nobody is going to put it together." Purdy reasoned that there was a two-pronged explanation for Eric's behavior: He, Carolyn, and Uncle Al all thought they were smarter than everyone else, and if the cops never found the body, they would not have a case.

Indirectly referring to the prior homicides, Purdy wondered at one point what Myra had done to deserve her fate. "Her crime was what? Loving her babies? Wanting to take them with her? Leaving this murderer, who is going out with another woman?"

As Carmen Acevedo cried softly at the mention of her daughter's name, the prosecutor turned to one of the centerpieces of his case, the wiretaps. He said the excerpts offered a rare opportunity to look inside the criminal mind. "We heard how these people relate to each other. We heard how they planned, how they conned, how they schemed with each other. . . . You heard them talking, screaming. You heard them being concerned about the phone being bugged. You heard them trying to cover up."

Purdy recited some of the wiretap excerpts. Carolyn, talking on the phone at the First Precinct, had assured Eric and Al there was no way that her work phones could be bugged. " 'There are three other people besides myself in this room making phone calls,' " he quoted her as saying. Eric had concluded that Al's Y.G.M. phone also could not be bugged: "I don't think a judge would give those assholes a court order to bug your work phone." Eric had asked, "Anything new from those assholes?" meaning the police in

New Jersey. And Eric had said he would need money, "if I gotta vacate very quickly."

There was Eric's "slip of the tongue," where he told the family court official, "My wife was killed in Jersey"; Eric's pronouncement on the day of his arrest that he could not have anyone talking to his children; Eric's concern that Greg Velez could have told the FBI "everything"; Eric's concern that even if Greg's words were hearsay, "it could be enough."

"Is this an innocent person, talking that he's afraid that hearsay could be enough?" Purdy asked.

Also, why had Eric asked Al if he had said anything incriminating? "Who could say anything incriminating except someone who knows something?"

Purdy proceeded to Carolyn's explanation of when a lie is not really a lie. He injected extra inflection for this one. Quoting Carolyn, Purdy explained, " 'I *am* lying because I have said I do not know where. But in a way, I'm *not* lying, because *you're* calling me *through someone*.' " Purdy argued that Carolyn's comments were a clear indication of the defendants' "approach to the 'truth' throughout, how they can scheme, and step around it, and sidestep it. All three of them are up to their hips in this muck, and they are all helping each other."

Directing his attention to the 2:44 call, Purdy argued that of course Myra had been on the line. If Eric had come home shortly before the call to find his wife gone, had he gone to neighbors to inquire if she was there? Had he called Myra's sister, Miriam, in the Bronx, to tell Myra to get home? Then the next day, and the day after that, had he gone to the police? Well yes, eventually, Purdy said—but only to complain about them snooping around his apartment.

The prosecutor explained Greg's initial failure to remember the 2:44 call on his being a street hustler, dependent on Uncle Al for money, food, shelter, and transportation in return for sex. "Is he going to give that up?" As for Maggie, he emphasized how she had linked the 2:44 A.M. call with a phone conversation she had with Myra about apartments twelve hours earlier.

He blamed Al's inability to come clean about the call for so long on his father-son relationship with Eric. The prosecutor said that once investigators heard the "other" Al on the wiretaps, they knew they were dealing with "two different people," and realized that Al actually did possess intimate knowledge of "the facts of this case."

"So, you have to determine in asking whether that phone call came in and whether it was significant, why Al Jiovine wouldn't talk about it?" That was a good question indeed, but also for the possibilities Purdy did not mention—that Eric had called at 2:44 to say he had killed Myra and had just returned from driving her body to Delaware, or that Eric had called at 2:44 to tell Al he had just killed Myra and needed a baby-sitter.

Purdy covered another batch of circumstantial pieces of the puzzle: Eric told Jennifer that Myra was not coming back; Eric told Daniel Turcotte that Myra had left the kids with him to go to the store and never came back; Eric was so confident she was not coming back that he demanded day care; just two days after Myra's disappearance, Eric and his mother told the landlord he was going to vacate the apartment; because of Carolyn's employment at NYPD, she and Eric knew how city cops work, and figured "no body, next case"; Eric did not file the missing-persons report; Eric confessed to Al; Al should be believed even though he got a plea bargain because he still had to do five years; such plea deals were a fact of life, a necessary evil; the "very compelling" fiber evidence suggested the three fibers came from a common blend; and ID cards that one would expect to find in Myra's missing wallet were found in Carolyn's apartment.

The prosecutor contended that Carolyn's taped conversation with Lieutenant Burke was filled with lies. He recommended that the jurors listen to the tape again, "if you can sit through it." He told them to listen "even more carefully for what she doesn't say." He said Carolyn had implied to Burke that Myra had taken her wallet because she and Eric could not find it, but had failed then to tell the lieutenant, "By the way, she didn't take her Social Security cards and her driver's license, the only forms of identification that I think she had."

As far as Purdy was concerned, Carolyn did look for Myra's wallet for more than an hour, as she had claimed. But he characterized her disclosure of the search as "another slip of the tongue. They knew that wallet was there. They knew there was money in it. What they didn't know was where it was. . . . So they had to look for it. Because if they didn't look for it, and they didn't find it, and the police came to that apartment and found the wallet, then the story about Myra leaving voluntarily and probably being at her sister Miriam's might not hold much water."

Purdy lamented law enforcement's inability to explain Myra's whereabouts for eight hours the night of her disappearance. He reiterated that a cooperative Uncle Al could have explained if Eric had taken the phone away, or tied her up in the closet, but he had not.

Out of necessity, then, Purdy was forced to address the alternative scenario: What if Myra had not been on the phone at 2:44? "What would that suggest to you in light of all of the other evidence—her plans to go to Puerto Rico, the threats to kill her? The only thing that would suggest, if Greg and Maggie were somehow wrong about that call, is that Myra was dead sooner. That's all that would suggest!"

Purdy was right, of course. But in light of the recantations and the sudden recovery of Al's memory, if Myra had not been on the phone, the alternative scenario also would have suggested perjury on the part of Al Jiovine, Maggie Rivera, and Greg Velez.

As predicted by Caposela, the prosecutor did address the site selection of Delaware for Myra's burial. "Why Delaware? Because he didn't want the body to be found. Look at this area, look at how remote this is. Why put a body here?" As Purdy displayed a blowup photo of the Labrador Lane area to remind jurors of the rural landscape, Myra's relatives—seeing the photos for the first time—broke out in tears, then sobs. Myra's cousin, Martha, whispered, "Is this where she was buried?"

Continuing, Purdy said Eric had intended for the body to stay hidden forever. "It wasn't meant to be dug up by animals. It wasn't meant to be exposed by the elements."

As to his guess for when the body would have been transported to Delaware, Purdy pointed out there would have been "more than sufficient time" during an eight-hour span between late Thursday night, when Eric left the Clifton apartment with his mother, and Friday morning, when he met Jennifer in Brooklyn.

Summing up, Purdy told the jurors their verdict would come from within. "You will know it with certainty, and you will feel it as your intelligence, common sense, and experience analyzes this evidence. And in your heart of hearts, you will say 'Yes, I believe he did it.' "

The Acevedo family was united in loud grief. "That's right. That's right," several relatives said to each other, shaking their heads up and down in agreement. "What more evidence do they want?" asked cousin Nereida Flick.

Purdy returned to his seat. He had addressed the jury for 2½ hours, with a lunch break in between. His dramatic readings from the wiretapped words of Eric, Carolyn, and Al had been the high point, better than a replay of the tapes would have been. Purdy had given it much more meaning and feeling from the heart—for Myra and her family, and for everyone in law enforcement and criminal justice who performed their jobs the way they were supposed to be performed.

That night was a tough one at the Passaic County Jail. The authorities brought in a suspect charged in a vicious sexual attack on a five-year-old girl. The inmate was put in the special segregated wing, Eric's home. The inmates attacked the suspect, and Eric later claimed he had helped in the pummeling. "Talk about a crazy motherfucker! That guy's certifiable!" said Eric. "I hate being around these career criminals." He apparently subscribed to a strange jailhouse morality: Hands off of little kids. The rules of the jungle do not prohibit killing their mothers.

The next morning, Judge Hull delivered his instructions to the jury. Twelve deciding jurors were selected from the fifteen who heard the case. The remaining three became alternates, and were escorted to an office for safekeeping by Sheriff's Deputy Archie Vogel, who had supervised the security detail for the trial.

At 10:35, on Friday, May 7, 1993, the jury got the case. They would consider twelve charges against Eric: one count of murder, three counts of conspiracy to hinder apprehension, six counts of hindering apprehension, one count of tampering with a witness, and one count of tampering with evidence.

"I hope they hang you by the neck," said Myra's cousin, Martha, as Eric shook hands with Caposela and was led to his holding cell. The defendant was still smiling, but it looked more like a nervous grimace now.

Wearing a beautiful diamond-studded brooch that spelled the name *Jesus*, Carmen Acevedo began praying. The family set up camp in the hallway. Within an hour, the jury sent out its first note: It wanted the law explained on the various charges wrapped into the murder count. Judge Hull decided he had to reread his entire instruction on murder and the lesser included offenses: passion provocation manslaughter, aggravated manslaughter, and reckless manslaughter.

The jury returned to their room at noon, were brought their lunches, and sent out a second note by midafternoon. They wanted the testimony of six witnesses reread: Theresa Maltese, Sergeant John Zipf, Detective Cooke, Detective Ogden, Detective Donato, and Jennifer Meade. They also wanted a repeat instruction given on the definition of the charge "tampering with a witness."

The jurors returned to the courtroom, where Judge Hull reread the requested legal definition. He sent them back to their room, essentially to wait for the official court reporters to locate their notes of the requested testimony. A short time later, reporter Irene M. Hayes reread Zipf's brief testimony. The judge advised the panel that the Donato readback would take "several hours," and sent them back to their room to await court reporter Sharon Palmer's arrival to perform the Cooke and Ogden readbacks.

The jurors sent word they were withdrawing their requests for readbacks of Meade and Donato. That left Theresa Maltese. It was too late in the day. Judge Hull had promised no night work. He sent the jury home for the weekend.

Always on the lookout for even a glimmer of reasonable doubt, Caposela wondered if maybe, just maybe, the jurors wanted to hear Theresa Maltese's testimony again because they were concerned that she had left her husband, Tony, "out of the picture."

The final flurry was swift on Monday, May 10, 1993. The jurors resumed deliberation after Palmer reread Theresa Maltese's testimony, but the panel stayed in the back room for only another fifty-one minutes. This time they had a verdict. Officially, five hours had been spent in the jury room, but most of that time had been spent waiting for the readbacks and eating lunch on Friday.

The court clerk went down the counts, one by one, beginning with the most important. "How do you find the defendant, Eric Napoletano, as to count one, murder?"

"We find him guilty of murder," replied forewoman Ruth Taylor.

Eric remained seated in his chair, his fingers in their now

familiar clasped position, with Caposela to his left. He showed no emotion, other than to close his eyes for just a second.

From the Acevedo family section, controlled, muffled voices cried out, "Oh, God!" and "Yyyyyes!"

The forewoman went down the list. Eric was guilty on every count. The jurors would not look at Eric. He did not glance their way either, choosing to stare straight ahead.

"What is the present bail?" Judge Hull asked.

"Two million dollars, Your Honor," Purdy replied.

"There will be no bail for this defendant pending sentence," the judge declared.

Eric turned once again to shake Caposela's hand. He was then led away past the TV cameras, still wearing his silly smile.

Outside the courtroom, as congratulations were exchanged between the families and the key players, Pablo Acevedo stood off in a corner of the corridor, tears streaming down his face. "I am at peace now," he said simply.

But his less forgiving niece, Martha, relayed a different sentiment for other members of the family: "My cousin would be alive today if New York had done something."

39

Six weeks after the verdict, on June 25, 1993, Eric was brought into court for sentencing. As usual, he shook Caposela's hand as soon as he arrived at the defense table. He let out a deep loud laugh, then broke into a broad grin. Caposela appealed to his client to calm down. The attorney would have preferred to be elsewhere, but his presence was required.

Myra's relatives gathered in a large circle around her mother, Carmen. Marta Rivera, mother of Marilyn Coludro, came over from Manhattan in the hopes of being able to address the court. Sitting across the left front row of the courtroom were Detective Al Ruth, Nick Donato, FBI agents Tom Cottone and Dru Wells, Lieutenant John Burke, and Investigator Pete Talarico. Walt Dewey joined Purdy at the prosecution table.

By contrast, Eric's coterie could not even fill the seats on a motorcycle. His mother was still nowhere to be seen. Uncle Al remained in prison. And Frank Murphy had gone on to another case. That left Caposela to handle Eric. As the day turned emotional, it became a burdensome task.

The proceeding did not hold much consequence for Eric, save a change of address from the county jail to the state prison system. Caposela had prepared him for a lengthy sentence—at least thirty years.

Judge Hull opened the proceeding by asking the defense attorney if he had any objections to the probation office's presentencing report. In fact, Caposela observed, he did take exception to references about "other pending investigations in New York City" and the FBI's characterization of Eric as a sexually sadistic serial killer. "I don't think any of that information is appropriate for the court to consider in its sentencing."

Bill Purdy said he appreciated Caposela's technical

objection and agreed that everyone had an obligation to focus only on the crimes for which the defendant was convicted. Still, the prosecutor noted, "The law requires us to sentence the whole person. And it's indeed difficult to sentence the whole person knowing what we do know about Mr. Napoletano, not only about the two prior homicide investigations, but other things that came up during the course of this trial and pretrial hearings."

Judge Hull said he was going to excise from the report all references to criminal matters other than Myra's murder. "The court has taken no testimony with respect to any other murders. In fact, there are no charges to my knowledge pending with respect to any other murders." He also ordered the deletion of the FBI's serial-killer affidavit and a letter from Marilyn Coludro's mother concerning the lack of action on her daughter's murder. He said he sympathized with the woman but observed, "This letter is not properly before this court for purposes of this sentence. It may very well be appropriate in another jurisdiction, specifically in New York, with respect to the court system there, or to law-enforcement agents in the City of New York."

Caposela rose in response to Judge Hull's request that he give his recommendations for sentencing. He explained that his client had instructed him to limit his remarks. He said Eric understood that Judge Hull had little flexibility when it came to sentencing for murder: life with parole eligibility after thirty years, or thirty years without parole.

The defense attorney contended that when the other murders were not considered, Eric's conviction did not warrant a life sentence. He acknowledged, though, that it was difficult for him to explain the difference between a life sentence and a term of thirty years without parole to someone twenty-eight years old.

Judge Hull turned to the defendant. "Mr. Napoletano, is there anything you would like to say before sentence is imposed?"

"No comment, Your Honor."

Purdy rose to speak. "Your Honor, this day is a long time coming for the family of Myra Napoletano, who lost their sister, cousin, daughter, and mother around June 20th, 1990. It's been a long time coming for law-enforcement officers who worked on this case." He asserted that circumstances required a life sentence. "What was done in this case is more than what was marginally or minimally required to commit the offense of murder. Mr. Napoletano's actions, his character, his contempt for law enforcement, his contempt for human life, his contempt for decency all go into the aggravating factors which the court must consider."

He argued that the offenses involved in the other guilty verdicts were "sufficiently distinct from the murder" to warrant separate, consecutive prison terms, with additional periods of parole ineligibility. He contended that Eric's "ability to manipulate the system" was especially reprehensible given his knowledge and contempt for law enforcement.

Eric broke out in a wide grin as Purdy spoke negatively of him. He stuck his chin out proudly and grabbed the lapels of his suit coat to puff. His smile widened as Purdy spoke of Myra's vulnerability.

The prosecutor summarized Myra's decision to break free from Eric's domination. "She had had enough of his antics. She had had enough of his philandering. She was going back to church. And he would have none of that.

"The coup de grâce," Purdy continued, "was the fact she was going to leave him and take the children and look for a life away *from—this—nut*!" Purdy had pivoted toward the defendant to snap out the final three words angrily.

Eric lost his grin—but only for a few seconds—redrawing it as Purdy referred to the defendant's adultery and other mistreatment of his wife. The prosecutor again pointed in Eric's direction and referred to "the smugness Mr. Napoletano has shown in court, and shows today."

Eric exaggerated his toothy beam.

Beginning to show his anger, Purdy argued that Eric had shown no remorse for his crime, not even during the intercepted phone conversation with his mother and Uncle Al. "Did we hear any kind words about Myra? Any sorrow that she's gone? Any sorrow that the children are without their mother? Any words such as, 'I wish I hadn't done it'? or 'I'm sorry it had to happen this way'? That's not the person who we hear on the tapes. And that needs to be addressed today."

He said Eric's callous attitude permeated every charge in the indictment, such as count two, where he had been convicted of hindering apprehension by hiding evidence, specifically by burying the victim. "This further shows not only his contempt for law enforcement but his ability to manipulate the system as well, by first going out of state, finding this isolated area, and showing a contempt for the victim by burying her in this manner."

Eric was really over the edge now, moving around in his chair, laughing, giving the impression he was enjoying Purdy's attack.

Judge Hull's face began to turn red with anger. "Mr. Napoletano, is there something to smile about during the course of this proceeding?"

"Uh, no comment," Eric replied to the judge, finally reining himself in. Sitting still again, he opted for a modified smile, carefully keeping his teeth covered while he fondled his mustache with the thumb and first two fingers of his right hand.

Purdy argued that if Eric were ever freed he would almost certainly commit another serious crime. He noted that the court was required to contrast the aggravating factors for a heavier sentence against the defense's claims of mitigating circumstances. Raising his voice, he asked that "little or no weight" be given to mitigating factors "because as I read through them and I think of Eric Napoletano, *I* have something to laugh about in court today." He said that none of the listed criteria applied, especially the one stating that the defendant had no history of prior criminal activity and had led a "law-abiding life" for a substantial period of time before the murder. "What we've heard on the wiretap of his contempt for law enforcement is almost laughable."

Eric snarled at the prosecutor.

Purdy then made a special point of mocking another possible mitigating factor, whether imprisonment "would entail excessive hardship to himself or his dependents." In fact, Purdy argued, "the opposite is true. Only his imprisonment guarantees that his children may have some hope for a normal existence."

Asking for the maximum possible sentence, Purdy turned to the spectator section. "The grief that he put the family through is substantial. The way he acted toward the family added to their grief." Purdy then explained that Myra's mother, Carmen Acevedo, was present and wished to be heard.

The petite woman, shaking and on the verge of tears, approached the well of the courtroom. Interpreter Hayley Encarnacion stood next to her to translate. Once again the contrast between the Acevedo and Napoletano families would be made crystal clear.

"I want to say a few words. I want to express what I have suffered with the death of my daughter," she said in Spanish, her voice cracking, her sorrow-filled eyes covered with tinted glasses. She explained that she was speaking in the name of all of her relatives, especially her husband, who had stayed behind in Puerto Rico to take care of the children and the family business.

"My daughter was a little child when she married him," Carmen said, staring sternly at the defendant, unwilling to utter his name. "When they got married, I gave her to him and I told him, 'Take care of her because she is a good child, a good daughter.' I never had any problems with her. He was her first boyfriend and her first husband. I never had problems with her in school. She was an intelligent child, very good and very innocent.

"When I found out that my daughter had disappeared, I suffered a lot. I couldn't believe it. I am thinking of those two children who are now orphans. When I found out that she had disappeared, I already knew that he had done something to her. I knew from the very beginning that he was the one who had killed my daughter. And I say that before God, because I am a Christian woman and I am not lying. We have suffered a lot and our family has been united."

Carmen again looked over at the smiling defendant, now reading the letters members of the Acevedo family had sent to the court asking for his execution. "To him, this means nothing," she said. "Because as I am looking at him, he keeps laughing. This is a serious thing, but to him it is as if nothing has happened."

Eric threw the letters back on the table in disgust.

"But I feel that in my heart, and my heart is very sad. And his older child, the older one has suffered very much with his mother's death. He always asks me about his mother and he always wants to go, almost every day, to the cemetery just to look at her stone.

"Despite that, he is a very intelligent child, and he knows very much about this case, and he knows what has happened to his mother," she said, finally getting into the public record her family's position regarding Eric Junior's intimate knowledge of his mother's death. "With God's help, I am going to raise him and he is going to be a productive person in society."

Accepting that Eric was not facing the death penalty, Carmen said that she was asking Judge Hull "in the name of my husband and my relatives" that Eric be given "a life sentence without any possibility of parole. I am afraid that if he gets out, he will hurt me and my children."

She paused for several seconds. The tension hung painfully. There was hardly a dry eye in the room, even among the hardened law enforcement personnel.

Judge Hull told the interpreter to explain that he could not legally impose a sentence denying any chance of parole.

Carmen bowed her head, disappointed. "In any case, if it cannot be a life sentence, and anything happens to my family, we will know that it's coming from him because we have no enemies."

She returned to her seat, where the rest of the family members were sobbing uncontrollably.

It was time for sentencing. Caposela told his client to straighten up, and Eric stiffened to attention. Judge Hull said that based on the trial record, as well as evidence the jury had not heard, he felt the aggravating factors substantially outweighed the lone mitigating one, that Eric had no prior convictions.

Judge Hull cited as aggravating factors Eric's deception, his repeated lies to police, his removal of Myra's personal property, his attempts to convince Jennifer Meade to withhold information, his burial of Myra's body out of state, his efforts to conceal his whereabouts, the wiretap discussions about insurance fraud, and his bragging about having a gun that could be used against Pablo.

"Accordingly," the judge said, he was sentencing the defendant on the murder charge to life in prison, with no parole eligibility for the first thirty years. "With respect to the second count, hindering apprehension by burying the body of Myra Napoletano in Delaware, I find an additional aggravating factor, and that is the heinous, cruel, and depraved manner in which that crime was committed to hinder his own apprehension. The court was privy to the testimony of the authorities in Delaware as to how that body was found and the condition that body was in as a result of the manner in which Myra Acevedo was buried."

As a result, Judge Hull said, he was imposing an extra,

consecutive, five-year sentence, with a requirement that an additional two and a half years be served before Eric would be eligible for parole. That meant he had to serve thirty-two and a half years before he could even ask for parole consideration. The other charges were folded in.

The judge told Eric he had forty-five days to appeal. "And if you cannot afford the services of a lawyer, you can apply for the public defender to represent you on an appeal. Do you understand that?"

"Yes. Thank you," Eric replied, now the model of decorum.

"We'll take a recess," Judge Hull said as he briskly left the bench.

Eric stood up so the sheriff's deputies could cuff him. He turned to the Acevedo family to flash his silly smirk as a final display of contempt.

PART 6

Epilogue

It was always Eric and I,
only each other to count on.

—Carolyn Napoletano

40

IN HER WORDS

We know Eric didn't do it, but say anybody kills anybody. You just dump them on the street, or you dump them in the water. Why are they going to go two states away, or something like that?

I think Al did it. I think he did Myra, I really do.

Marilyn, I don't think so. I don't have any feeling about that because I think that she just ran away. But with Myra I have the gut feeling.

With Gladys, no, I think, which I told the police, which I told Fazzini, I think that Gladys had a boyfriend.

I know that Al did away with Myra. He had no alibi for that night. Eric and I were together. I think it was because of the welfare thing. Al wrote a letter saying that she lived there with her two children, and that she lived with him. I really think because of the welfare thing that he wanted to get rid of her so she didn't have to be using his address anymore. You know what I mean?

See, I did not know about the welfare until after she was killed. What I found out later was that she was after Section Eight. Then she would have gotten away from Al, but I think that he just didn't want to be associated with her anymore.

The prosecution says that Eric had a motive and the motive was that his wife was going to take his children. That's ridiculous. He said if she wanted to go there to clear her mind, he felt safe. Because, her family wouldn't have let her run around down there. He said he would send her money, and he would come down for a long weekend or whatever, because they always have those ninety-nine-dollar fares. That's the only time I went.

They don't know where she was killed or how she was

killed. And Al seems to know so much about this. And let me say this to you: Say Eric did this, and he knows that Al has a big mouth and can't keep anything to himself, is he going to tell Al?

They have intimidated Al so much that Al will say anything. He twists things around. He's a liar. He's a pedophile. He will say and do anything.

Any seed that they plant, it will sprout with Al. The police intimidated him, like they did with Maggie and Greg. He always went because they intimidated him.

They told Al that he was going to go away, but that they would reduce his sentence if he would turn. They kept pressuring him. They were after him, and after him. Finally, he did it. I guess he figured that he would do anything to save himself, even if it meant lying and letting other people go to jail.

Al was good to Eric, but I can't see that he could turn on him and make up the lies. I told Eric a long time ago, "One day Al will be trouble, mark my words."

I personally feel that the police or the FBI tampered with that jury. I just don't alone think that they read "serial killer" in the paper. I think that they tampered with them. They didn't have anything, so this is how they did it.

I think that somebody bought somebody. I mean there is a lot of that; we know that. I said to Eric, "Everybody thought it was bullshit and look where you are. If you had Bruce Cutler, you'd be home."

How could Eric be involved? How could he, if I were with him, and I saw Myra? The next day he went to work and he was accounted for. And then he came home. So when did he take this body? And how did he take it? They didn't find anything in the car. That's why I will not plead guilty. He couldn't have done it, and he wouldn't have done it. He did love her.

I could cry now because I miss him. He would make a good lawyer. He would have made a good cop. He really would have. Pals? Yeah. He was really good.

41

Life had turned bleak for Eric Napoletano back at the county jail. He had spent all those months flexing his machismo, assuring his fellow inmates that he was going to walk because "Dirty Bird" Purdy had nothing on him. The verdict had brought him abuse and ridicule, however, and the situation worsened after sentencing. Inmates now called him names and pushed him around. He was no longer *the man,* no longer the president of his wing. He was now just an ordinary jailhouse punk.

Transferred to the state prison system, Eric attempted suicide, or his version of it, several more times. On one occasion he cut his wrists. Another time he dropped gym weights on his body. His antics were beginning to wear thin, though. For someone who had killed so efficiently, he was incapable of completing the job on himself.

Prison officials concluded that Eric was simply trying to maneuver himself into a permanent home in the softer environment of a psychiatric hospital setting, so they shipped him back to maximum security, where he played chess and promised to help his mother prepare for her trial.

The victims' families struggled to cope with their lingering pain. Wanda Matos remained underground in Florida, estranged from her relatives. Marta Rivera, Marilyn Coludro's mother, renewed her efforts to obtain justice in her daughter's case. Pablo and Carmen Acevedo returned to Puerto Rico with Angelo and Eric Junior in the hope of living normal lives. The youngsters visited their mother's grave on a regular basis. In a poignant display of thanks, the family presented plaques to the prosecutors and key investigators before leaving the New York metropolitan area.

Over time Eric Junior calmed down, but he again expanded on his story that he had seen his father kill his mother. He now specifically recounted how his father had tied one end of the rope to a doorknob, thrown the rope over the top of the door, then tied the other end to his mother's neck. He also now contended that Uncle Al Jiovine and his grandmother, Carolyn, had both taken the burial ride to Delaware.

Pablo acknowledged that the boys remained "a little hyperactive," but said he was confident he could help them overcome any remaining emotional trauma without formal therapy.

Pablo was melancholy while reflecting on how things could have been. "Eric abused the confidence our family placed in him. We gave him love and support. We made him part of the family, and he took advantage." Having learned so many more disturbing facts about his son-in-law in the years since Myra's murder, Pablo said he now believed that in a strange way, death had set his daughter free. "Myra is better off now than before. She's resting. She's gone. But we have her two children—and we love them very much."

Other key players in the Napoletano drama also concentrated on resuming their usual routines:

- Bill Purdy took on more responsibilities, handling many of the high-profile homicides in the county prosecutor's office.
- Defense attorney Ernie Caposela returned to his private practice, continuing to accept pool attorney cases occasionally. He received a letter of thanks from Robert N. Wilentz, chief justice of the New Jersey Supreme Court. "Your willingness to undertake such representation without any assurance of eventual compensation speaks well for the profession and its dedication to the system of justice."
- The criminal investigation into defense attorney Louis Acevedo's role in the Maggie Rivera–Greg Velez recantations was closed without any charges being filed. In the interim, Acevedo was promoted to head the regional public defender's office in Bergen County.
- Scandal upon scandal continued to surface in the New York City Police Department. Confidential logs of police wiretaps disappeared from the Communications Division at One Police Plaza. The Mollen Commission, established to examine police corruption throughout the

city, determined that NYPD brass had done little to ferret out bad cops, even when confronted with incontrovertible evidence. The commission concluded that NYPD was incapable of policing itself. And, of course, Carolyn Napoletano was not even a cop; she was merely a civilian employee.

- FBI Agent Tom Cottone continued to work out of the FBI satellite office in West Paterson, New Jersey. Like the others in law enforcement familiar with the Napoletano case, he was most horrified about the role played by Eric's mother, especially given her employment. "For somebody who hates law enforcement as much as she does, it is kind of bizarre for her to be working for a law-enforcement agency," he said. "I've had a lot of cases where the mother would obviously protect her son, lie to law enforcement, or just refuse to cooperate. This is the first one I have ever seen where the mother would be as intimately involved in these homicides as she is."

- Nick Donato worked on loan with the FBI Violent Crimes/Fugitive Task Force until July 15, 1994, when he returned to the Clifton Detective Bureau. Later that year he received additional training for certification as a police academy instructor in physical and classroom training. During a Clifton Police Department awards ceremony in September 1996, Donato received an Exceptional Service Medal for his exemplary work on the Napoletano investigation and conviction.

  Of Carolyn Napoletano's antics, Donato observed, "She lies so much; she has no shame about it." He continued to hold out hope that someday a member of the Napoletano inner circle would reveal what really happened in each of the homicides.

For better or worse, Uncle Al Jiovine continued to play a significant role in the criminal investigations involving Eric and Carolyn. In the wake of Eric's trial, U.S. District Judge Garrett E. Brown, Jr., granted a motion filed by Assistant U.S. Attorney Glenn Moramarco for a reduction in Jiovine's sentence to twenty-eight months as a reward for his cooperation. Instead of remaining behind bars until March 1996, Al was rescheduled for release on November 5, 1993, less than half his original sentence. In order for New Jersey to keep its end of the bargain, Judge Hull replaced Al's three-year state sentence with three years' probation. He was given his release under the new timetable without having to testify against Carolyn as promised.

In the weeks after Eric's trial, officials in the Queens DA's office claimed they had only recently learned of Jiovine's claim that Marilyn Coludro had been murdered in their borough. But Prosecutor John Ryan from the Bronx insisted he had relayed word of Al's confession promptly in early 1991. In fact, *The Record* had reported in a 1991 story that the Coludro matter "was recently turned over to the Queens District Attorney."

Spurred on in part by a renewed letter-writing campaign from Marilyn Coludro's mother, Queens authorities finally began to investigate. After an extensive search for the dusty evidence files in Pennsylvania, a grand jury was convened. Members of the Queens team paid Eric a visit at the state prison in Trenton, but he declined to cooperate. Carolyn fainted when she was served a grand jury subpoena at the Midtown North Precinct, where she had been transferred after her unwelcome stint at the First Precinct. She then failed to appear to testify twice "because of illness." When less than a week remained in Jiovine's federal prison term, he was shipped to Queens for an interview followed by an appearance before the grand jury.

He later said that investigators from the DA's office and police department grilled him extensively on how Carolyn had been able to keep her NYPD job. "They wanted to know how she could do these things and still be walking around. They were asking me, 'Why is Carolyn still working for the police department? Come on, Al, you know what the story is. Why is she still working? Who does she know? Is she having a relationship with somebody at One Police Plaza?' I said, 'Well, don't you know?' "

In mid-December 1993, Eric was indicted for Marilyn Coludro's murder, based in large part on Jiovine's testimony. Cover-up or accomplice-type charges could not be lodged against Carolyn because of the statute of limitations. Any chance of filing murder charges against her rested in the hands of Bronx prosecutors for the murder of Gladys Matos.

A carefully crafted, seven-paragraph news release from the Queens DA's office about Eric's indictment failed to mention Carolyn Napoletano, her employment, the history between the Napoletanos and NYPD's auxiliary police force, the Matos murder, or the inexplicable failure of Marilyn Coludro's missing-persons report to be transmitted on the NCIC system in 1984. Regarding the belated identification of the corpse, the news release stated only, "Her body was identified in mid-1986 when the missing-persons report was carried on a nationwide police network." As a result of the blandness of the public relations effort, the indictment received virtually no coverage in the New York news media.

At the same time, the prospective prosecution quickly ran into serious trouble. As Al later reconstructed his "cooperation," he admitted that he had given Queens investigators one version of the Coludro murder the night before his grand jury appearance, and a different one when he finally testified. He described his first story as "a little white lie, a fib. I told them what I thought they wanted to hear," namely that he had been more involved in the murder clean-up and cover-up than he had previously admitted. The next day, however, during his sworn testimony before the grand jury, Al reverted to a version that kept him far away from any of the actual events.

If Al could now be believed, the car searched at his mother's house in New Jersey had indeed been the one used to transport Marilyn Coludro's body to the Delaware Water Gap in Pennsylvania. He also now maintained that Carolyn had made the trip with her son, and contended that as Marilyn's corpse lay in his bathtub, Eric and Carolyn had laughed about the murder.

Because the Queens DA was relying so heavily on Jiovine, a defense could easily be built around the argument that Al had been a spurned lover who murdered Marilyn in a jealous rage. Unlike with Myra's murder in New Jersey, Al easily qualified as an alternate suspect. Even in his version the killing had occurred in his apartment, one of his kitchen knives had been the murder weapon, and the body had been wrapped in his bedspread and driven to Pennsylvania in his car. Then there was the nasty note he had written ordering Marilyn to get out, and he also now admitted that when the Housing Authority police had come to his apartment looking for the girl, she had actually been hiding in his closet.

At a minimum, given that Al and Carolyn were cognizant of so many details back in 1984, the evidence demonstrated vividly that either of them could have taken action to stop Eric's killings. If they had, Wanda Matos and Myra Napoletano—and even Wendell Owens, the pedestrian apparently struck by Eric's car—could be alive today.

The Queens prosecution was beset with other pitfalls, most especially the proximity of the Coludro burial site in the Delaware Water Gap to the Georgia-Pacific plant where Al's brother-in-law and confidant Larry Knoepfler had worked. Queens authorities interviewed Larry, but, as with Al, he carefully crafted a story that protected himself.

Queens officials realized that their "easy case" was anything but. When Eric objected to being extradited to New York, that *pro forma* dispute was conveniently cited to excuse prosecutorial paralysis. As the months rolled by and Eric's indictment passed the one-year mark without a formal arrest, the question arose whether Queens officials had secured the indictment merely to save face. Clearly, the Queens team was in no hurry to arrest Eric because that event would start the clock under New York's speedy trial provisions. By putting the extradition issue on the slow track, the case could get lost in the system. Officials could point to the indictment as proof that they had done something about Eric while blaming the ensuing "delays" on legal technicalities. It was not until March 30, 1995, more than fifteen months after his indictment, that Eric was extradited and arrested in Queens. Several more months would pass before his arraignment.

The Bronx "investigation" into the murder of Gladys Matos was even less promising. With straight faces, officials maintained that their comatose case was still "active and pending." Spokesman Steven Reed insisted, "We are doing what we need to do to prosecute the case. It's a firm commitment." He refused to answer any other questions.

Prosecutor John Ryan, who retired from the Bronx DA's Office shortly after Eric's New Jersey trial, explained that the key witness, Michael Sanchez, had disappeared long ago, supposedly to the state of Texas. He also contended that Jiovine's more recent version of the Coludro slaying was of dubious value because of his guilty plea to federal obstruction of justice charges regarding the 2:44 A.M. phone call. "Essentially, he pleaded guilty to perjury. That doesn't make for a great witness," Ryan said.

Carolyn continued to insist that at the time of the shooting she and Eric had been in downtown Manhattan, inside the Park Row Gourmet coffee shop, eating the egg special, "you know, the egg, potatoes, toast, orange juice, and coffee. Eric's was sugar, mine with Sweet 'n' Low. It was all one price, like two-ten, something like that.

"Eric and I were in that coffee shop. We were there every day. That never came out. I guess that was like our alibi," she said. "We know that the detectives had to go in to ask. We knew they would break their asses to get down there. That's why he was never arrested. If we're in the coffee shop every day for a couple of years, at the same time, and this is within a half hour or whatever of her being killed, how can you blame that on Eric? And how could I help kill her if she was killed when we were in the coffee shop? Now, Al. Al was around. Where was Al?"

While Carolyn offered nothing substantial to implicate Al Jiovine in the Matos murder, it was clear he was still having a hard time telling the truth. In a follow-up interview with John Ryan, Al admitted taking the ride to Delaware to bury Myra's body. But he continued to insist to New Jersey investigators that he had not.

Jiovine also continued to lie about how Eric had selected Delaware for Myra's burial. He told Donato, Ruth, Talarico, and Purdy he had no idea how the site had been selected, continuing to keep secret the trip he had made to the car auction in Bear, Delaware, with Eric and Carolyn.

When Jiovine was contacted for an interview for this book—coincidentally the same week he testified before the Queens grand jury—the first question he asked was, "How much are you going to pay me?" Jiovine was told that like everyone else, no money would be paid to him. In the course of the discussion, Al was asked how Eric had selected Delaware as the site to bury Myra's body.

"I don't know," Jiovine said. "I think it was between him and his mother. They must have talked about it."

He was asked if he knew whether Carolyn and Eric had ever been to Delaware. Jiovine answered that they had been to Pennsylvania. He had gone with them to visit Myra's sister, Janet.

Asked to explain what the trip to Pennsylvania had to do with a question about Delaware, he responded, "I imagine it's not too far from there."

Jiovine was asked if he had ever been to Delaware. "I never went to Delaware. I've never been there," he said, insisting again that he had no idea how Eric had found the burial site. "I'm trying to put this puzzle together. He must have been down there before for some reason." He suggested that perhaps Eric had been in that area with Myra's sister.

But hadn't he gone to Delaware with Eric and Carolyn? "I don't know. I mean, the thing is— I wish I could tell you yes, but I can't tell you yes."

"To buy a car or something?" he was asked.

"No. Not in Delaware," Jiovine replied. "I was down in south Jersey to an auction. I don't recall ever being in Delaware. I don't recall it. I've been in south Jersey." He went on to explain that he had purchased a diesel-powered Oldsmobile Cutlass Ciera at an auction in south Jersey— describing the same car he had bought at the auction located several miles from where Myra's body had been found.

Again, it was suggested to Jiovine that he had actually purchased the car in Delaware. "All they gotta do is trace the vehicle identification number. It's under my name," he said. Of course, Jiovine was safe with that offer of proof. The motor-vehicle records would show that Al Jiovine of Dumont, New Jersey, had purchased the car from Thomas E. Reed of Lancaster, Pennsylvania. The Delaware auction had served only as middleman.

Jiovine said he did not recall the name of the auction but might remember if he heard it. Then he proposed that Eric had probably gone to the auction with someone else. "I was just wondering if Eric didn't go to Delaware also when I wasn't with him," he said. "I know that Myra's father went down there to buy a taxi from this auction. That might be the loophole that is missing." Now he was claiming that Eric and Pablo had gone to Delaware!

It was firmly suggested to Jiovine that the auction was located in Delaware. "Oh! Well, if the auction was in Delaware, I didn't know it. I really didn't. It's been such a long time ago, I mean. I would never lie to you—or anybody. I thought it was in Jersey."

Finally, Jiovine was confronted with the name of the auction in Bear, Delaware: Wrangle Hill. "Did you ever hear that name?"

"I don't know," he replied.

"Would that have been the auction?"

"The name rings a bell," he conceded before quickly changing the subject to the car's leaky transmission.

Carolyn's post-trial maneuverings were just as oily. Paranoia continued to pervade her daily life. With renewed vigor she continued to come up with new explanations for the damning circumstantial evidence against her. Through it all, the months rolled off the calendar; the start of her trial remained nowhere in sight.

Carolyn believed her phone was still tapped, and that she was being followed. She took to sprinkling baby powder on her kitchen floor, then claimed that "they" had left footprints while sneaking into her apartment to remove important documents.

Her conspiracy and tampering case should have been disposed of swiftly in the wake of Eric's conviction. Her attorney, Russell G. Bickert, had observed in the midst of Eric's trial, "If Eric is acquitted, they'll drop the charges. If he's convicted, she'll take a plea." The only problem was, Carolyn refused to see things that way.

In fact, Purdy did offer Carolyn a plea: If she quit her job at NYPD and admitted her guilt, the prosecutor's office would refrain from petitioning a judge to send her to prison. Purdy figured the deal would save valuable court time while guaranteeing that Carolyn would finally be out of law enforcement.

Carolyn viewed the offer as a sign of prosecutorial weakness. "Why should I take a plea?" she asked. "They don't have anything on me." Predicting that the charges would eventually be dropped, she instead went on the offensive, lambasting virtually everyone connected with her son's conviction: the judge, the "bought-off" jurors, Ernie Caposela, and witness after witness—especially "Al the lying pedophile." While condemning Jiovine's sexuality, however, she continued to maintain she was certain he had never touched her son.

Carolyn also made it clear she would not relinquish her NYPD job without a fight. Succeeding in surviving ten years with the department—meaning she now had important

vested pension rights—Carolyn set her sights on another transfer, to the office at One Police Plaza dealing with the news media. "I want to work in Public Information. I've seen the way stuff is relayed to the newspapers. The information that's given out is totally different. Totally different," she said. "From what I have seen working there, you don't see everything in your file. Things are removed before you see it. My friend and I are gonna write a book one day. We're gonna call it *Inside NYPD*."

While Carolyn harangued, Bickert kept trying to convince her to take the plea. She kept balking, though, and their relationship became argumentative and untenable. By late 1993, representation of Carolyn was reassigned to another pool attorney, Leonard Carafa of Lodi, New Jersey.

Another series of delays followed. The transcripts from Eric's trial had to be prepared. Then Carafa needed time to review the transcripts. The defense attorney also needed time to familiarize himself with the rest of the case.

Carolyn's antics also contributed to the delay. She called in sick for one pretrial hearing, claiming diarrhea. For another hearing date she said she could not get off from work. The she claimed she was out of vacation time. On another occasion, while in the courthouse waiting for her case to be called, Carafa approached to explain that Judge Hull had gone home after taking ill. "Oh, yeah?" Carolyn snapped back. "I hope he drops dead."

Somehow her case dragged on through 1994 and 1995 and into 1996. With the major pretrial motions yet to be argued, the case was transferred to a new judge. Trial dates were scheduled, then postponed. Meanwhile, missed plea-bargain deadlines were simply rescheduled, without any consequence to the defendant.

Despite the shenanigans, Bill Purdy still did not want to put the county through another Napoletano trial; he again offered Carolyn a deal with no prison time. Tired of always feeling like he was the one being forced to do NYPD's dirty work, Purdy even dropped his demand that she quit her police department job.

But the prosecutor's largesse still did not work. Carolyn became more convinced than ever that Purdy was not serious in pursuing the matter. She demanded that she be allowed entry into a pretrial intervention program, where, if she stayed clean for a year, any criminal record would be expunged.

Given the seriousness of the underlying charge, the murder of Myra Napoletano, Purdy vigorously rejected that request, and so the standoff persisted.

- 42 -

Two days after Mother's Day 1996, Eric Napoletano stood before the Honorable Thomas A. Demakos in New York State Supreme Court in Kew Gardens, Queens. For once acting like a protective son, Eric had come to court to save his mother's hide. As usual, Carolyn was nowhere to be found.

The Napoletanos had skillfully worked the clock in their favor. Carolyn's charges in New Jersey were nearly five years old; Eric's Queens prosecution had been stalled for half that time. People had begun to ask questions. The Napoletanos knew that their cases would have to be closed eventually.

Eric sent word through Kenneth Reiver, his court-appointed attorney in New York, that he had a plea-bargain idea of his own: He would consider pleading guilty to the 1984 Coludro murder in Queens if his mother was allowed to enter the pretrial intervention program in New Jersey.

Incredibly, the authorities in both states decided to consider the offer.

During the ensuing months Prosecutors Purdy and Dewey in New Jersey would claim that they had considered the deal in order to help rescue New York's faltering case. But Queens authorities, led by Assistant District Attorney Peter Reese, would contend that they had agreed to listen to Eric's offer only as a favor to their beleaguered colleagues in New Jersey. Not surprisingly, once Eric and his mother determined that both sets of prosecutors were interested, they worked the situation for all it was worth.

As always, every twist and turn focused on Carolyn's desire to retain her NYPD job. Under the New Jersey PreTrial Intervention program (PTI), defendants usually admit their misdeeds and often express remorse. But Eric and Carolyn were adamant that her entrance into the pro-

gram had to specifically preclude any admission of guilt.
There was to be no confessional, no telling of what really
happened.

Also, many times pretrial intervention candidates are
interviewed by the program director, then nominated for
admission if they qualify. But Eric and Carolyn were
adamant that they wanted the Passaic County Prosecutor's
Office to exercise its right to vouch for her automatic entry
into the program.

As the Napoletanos sought to negotiate and renegotiate,
the clock kept ticking. Then suddenly, just weeks before the
publication of this book in hardcover edition, everyone
finally signed on board. Under Eric and Carolyn's terms.

Eric looked quite different as he was brought into Criminal Term Part K-2, a beautifully paneled courtroom high
above Queens Boulevard, shortly before one o'clock that
Tuesday, May 14, 1996. He was fat, with a big potbelly.
The blue sports jacket now fit him tightly. His hair had
grown long; a rubber band held it together in a ponytail. His
face was overrun with a bushy beard. The darting eyes were
gone. He looked downright mellow.

Ken Reiver, an experienced criminal defense attorney
from Cedarhurst, New York, turned to address Judge
Demakos: "I would like the record to reflect that after many
months of negotiations and discussions with the prosecutors
in New Jersey and Mr. Reese and the Queens County District Attorney's Office, as well as with Mr. Napoletano, that
Mr. Napoletano has authorized me on his behalf to withdraw his previously entered plea of not guilty under indictment 4162 of 1993 and to enter a plea of guilty to the first
count, murder in the second degree, violation of 125.25
under the penal law, in full satisfaction of this indictment."

"Your Honor, this plea is conditioned on certain consider-
ations that were entered into between myself and Mr. Purdy
and Mr. Dewey from the Passaic Prosecutor's Office. They
are here today," Reiver continued. "The New Jersey prosecutor has assured me that as a condition of this plea that all
charges against Ms. Napoletano will be dismissed contingent on her entering a PreTrial Intervention Program."

But, Reiver said, there were a couple of additional points
he needed to stress. "The most important matter, your
Honor, is Mr. Dewey has agreed to place on the record the

statement that Ms. Napoletano's entry into this program is explicitly not conditioned on any inculpatory allocution by her before the New Jersey Court, and the New Jersey prosecutors are here now and they're prepared to put this on the record, because Mr. Napoletano's plea is expressly conditioned on these matters."

Judge Demakos said he understood what Reiver was telling him but was not quite certain that such assurances were legally enforceable. "Do you understand that even if they place this condition on the record here, I have no control whether those conditions are met in Jersey?"

"I understand that," the defense attorney replied as Eric began to fidget.

Reiver explained that Dewey had assured him the deal had been preapproved in New Jersey, that the Passaic County Prosecutor's Office had recommended it, and that the proper authorities had already been spoken to on Carolyn's behalf. "Also, Your Honor, Mr. Napoletano agrees that the plea that he's entering into is going to carry an indeterminate sentence of fifteen years to life, and that is consecutive to a thirty-years-to-life sentence that he is presently serving in New Jersey."

Appearing to grow more agitated, Eric leaned over and began whispering into Reiver's ear. That much had not changed; Eric could still jabber away when he felt the need.

As Assistant DA Reese interjected to tell the judge that Eric's New York plea would also include a waiver of appeal, the defendant's demeanor grew more animated.

Reiver listened intently as Eric expressed his feelings. Shaking his head in acknowledgment of his client's demands, the attorney then resumed his address to the bench. "Your Honor, as I indicated to the Court, this matter as you know has been very difficult, and inasmuch as Mr. Napoletano is waiving some very substantial rights here, he must be assured that his mother will be entered into this program. Otherwise he would never enter into this plea."

Judge Demakos still was not satisfied. He told Reese that he wanted New Jersey to put its commitment on the record. But even that, he continued, would not guarantee everything would go according to plan. "The plea is not conditioned on the completion of what you're doing in Jersey, because I have no control over that. If the Jersey authorities don't follow through on the promise they made here, that has no effect on the condition of this plea."

Dewey assured the judge that he had already prepared a consent order which he would have executed promptly. "It's within the prosecutor's power to accept the defendant into the pretrial program." Seeking to make the commitment official, he continued: "The Court has my word on the record today. I have Chief Assistant Prosecutor Purdy from my office here. We both have the power to bind my office, and these are my representations."

As Reiver again sought to convey his client's growing uneasiness with the plan, Judge Demakos announced that he would postpone sentencing Eric until after his mother had been enrolled in the pretrial program.

Again Eric bent over to whisper into his lawyer's ear. After listening for a bit, Reiver explained to the court that Eric wanted to be certain that he could withdraw his plea and go to trial in the event his mother was not admitted into the program.

Beginning to look frustrated, Judge Demakos observed that Dewey was now on the record that the deal would go through.

Again, Eric bent over for a private chat. "Judge, Mr. Napoletano does not trust the Jersey prosecutor," Reiver said.

"He's putting it on the record here!" the judge replied.

Dewey jumped in to assure the court that if Carolyn was not admitted into the program, the plea agreement would be void.

Finally, Eric was satisfied. "Okay, Your Honor, that's perfectly satisfactory," said Reiver.

At that point, Judge Demakos directed that Eric be sworn in.

"Do you solemnly swear to answer questions put to you by the Judge, so help you God?" the court clerk asked.

As usual, Eric was not going to go easy. "I promise to tell the truth," he replied, refusing to address the supernatural.

Judge Demakos again stepped in. "Do you affirm to tell the truth?"

"I affirm to tell the truth."

"All right," said the judge.

It was time to take the plea. "Eric Napoletano, you have been indicted for the crimes of murder in the second degree,

several counts, and your lawyer indicates to me that you're
offering to plead guilty to the first count of the indictment
which charges you with murder in the second degree in that
you on June first, 1984, in the County of Queens with intent
to cause the death of Marilyn Coludro, caused the death of
Marilyn Coludro, by slashing her throat with a knife, and
your lawyer tells me that you're going to plead guilty to
that. Is that what you wish to do?"

"I was *one* of the parties involved in the slashing, yes,
Your Honor."

"I'm sorry?" the judge asked back.

"I was one of the parties involved in the slashing," Eric
repeated.

"I understand that," Judge Demakos said. "Well, is that
what you wish to do, plead guilty to that?"

"Yes."

Judge Demakos then took Eric through the standard dis-
claimers. In response to the judge's questions, Eric said he
knew that by pleading guilty he was waiving his rights to a
trial by jury, to confront the government's witnesses, to call
his own witnesses, to testify on his own behalf, to remain
silent and not answer any questions, and to consult with his
attorney.

"You also understand that by pleading guilty not only are
you admitting that you committed the crime, but that plea is
tantamount—in other words, it has the same effect, same
consequences—as if you had gone to trial and had been
found guilty by a jury. Do you understand that?"

"Yes."

"And understanding all of this, do you still wish to plead
guilty?"

"As long as they give my mother the PTI program, yes, I
do," Eric replied.

Satisfied with Eric's commitment to the guilty plea, the
judge moved to the next obligatory aspect of the proceeding—getting Eric to provide some details of the
murder.

For starters, the defendant was asked to explain where *he*
had committed the crime.

"Albert Jiovine and I killed Marilyn Coludro in his apartment," Eric announced in a raised voice.

The statement appeared to take everyone in the courtroom
by surprise. Dewey and Purdy looked especially angry.

"How did you do that?" Judge Demakos continued.

"It started out as a verbal altercation, which escalated into a physical confrontation, which resulted in myself stabbing her several times and her attempting to flee the location. I restrained her by placing my hand over her mouth and dragging her toward the bathroom. Al Jiovine then picked up the knife and slit her throat—and she died as a result of those injuries."

Suddenly, the entire plea bargain was in danger of falling apart. It sounded as if Eric was trying to place all of the blame on Uncle Al.

The veteran judge moved in to rescue the situation. "You indicated that you stabbed her first?"

"Yes," Eric replied softly.

"So what you're telling me, you and this—who is this?"

"Albert Jiovine—"

"—Acted in concert, together, in causing the death of Marilyn Coludro?"

"Yes," said Eric.

"What were your intentions when you stabbed her, you yourself stabbed her?"

"I intended to kill her at that point."

Eric's game was over. He had said enough to make the plea stick, albeit the bare minimum. But no one seemed to care. Two felony cases, one in New York and one in New Jersey, were about to be closed.

Judge Demakos explained to Eric that the Queens DA's Office was going to recommend a sentence of fifteen years to life, to run consecutively with the thirty-plus years in New Jersey. Eric said he understood.

The judge asked Reese if he thought the plea should be accepted. The assistant DA requested permission to ask a few questions.

"After you killed Marilyn Coludro, could you tell us what you did with her body?"

Leaving his mother out of the equation, Eric claimed that he and Al Jiovine had driven the corpse to Pennsylvania.

"And what did you do with the body there?"

"We disposed of it."

Reese asked for more.

"We tossed her over an embankment."

"And that was in the Commonwealth of Pennsylvania?"

"Yes."

"And what time of day did you commit the murder?"

"Approximately six-thirty in the evening."

"And that was on June first, 1984?"

"Yes."

"Your Honor, I recommend that you accept the plea," Reese concluded.

"The plea is accepted by the Court," said the judge.

Eric was escorted out of the courtroom. He would await sentencing in the Queens House of Detention while the New Jersey authorities finalized his mother's deal.

Outside court, Bill Purdy was visibly upset that Eric had been able to control the flow of the court proceeding with his pesky demands. Purdy had been pained all along about the plea bargain. He would always feel strongly that there was no place in law enforcement for the likes of Carolyn Napoletano. But after looking at all of the circumstances—the relatively minor charges against Carolyn, the likelihood that she would avoid prison, the lack of a guarantee that she would lose her NYPD job, the chance of Eric winning his appeal in New Jersey, and the need of both states to use Jiovine's dubious testimony in any new trials—Purdy had concluded that the plea was a fair deal for the criminal justice system. For a moment, though, he sounded like a man burdened with regret.

"He's a murdering scumbag!" Purdy told several newspaper reporters. "He's going to soft-soap whatever he can. It's so typical. He and his mother manipulate everything."

As for New Jersey letting Carolyn off the hook, Purdy added, "If this were a perfect world, she would be in jail for a long time. But due to the laws in New Jersey, the chances of her doing any time were next to nil."

Walt Dewey added that Eric's plea and waiver of appeal guaranteed that he would be behind bars for many decades, possibly for the rest of his life. "You never know, what if we lost our case on appeal? At the same time we get closure for the family, and we're helping New York. They were relying on Al, and you know Al."

Also asked to defend the deal with Carolyn, Dewey now downplayed the charges against her. "Her possible exposure was five years with a presumption of non-incarceration. We would have had to bring in FBI agents from across the country to testify. Is that the way the taxpayers want us to spend their money—for a woman who would probably get probation?"

Several of the reporters turned around to look for Reese. But he was nowhere to be found. He had scampered away to attend to other business.

That left Eric's defense attorney, who was perhaps the most perplexed by the day's developments. Reiver said he thought his client was "crazy" for taking the plea. "He's doing thirty-to-life in New Jersey. What's he got to gain on this murder when this is a case he could win? I don't know why he did it, other than to save his mother."

As could be expected, the New York news media played the mother-son plea bargain to the hilt. *Newsday* headlined a story by Karen Freifeld: "Mother's Day" and "Son's Plea in Murder Spares Mom Prison." The *New York Daily News* headlined one of its stories: "A Killer's Gift to His Mother." Reporter Robert Gearty began his article with the observation: "Even serial killers have moms."

The same group of winners and losers gathered inside Judge Demakos' courtroom on June 20, 1996, for Eric's sentencing. On this occasion Marilyn Coludro's mother attended as well. To the degree that it was legally possible, Marta Rivera was finally going to get her revenge.

Events in New Jersey had transpired as Dewey had predicted: Judge Stephen H. Womack had signed the paperwork authorizing Carolyn's acceptance into the pretrial intervention program. No one had made her reveal a single detail about any of the murders.

Eric, then, was pleased.

Dressed in a green jacket and plaid skirt, Marta Rivera asked Reese if Carolyn was present in the courtroom. The prosecutor said he did not believe so. "I haven't seen her in so long, I don't know if I would recognize her," Rivera added.

As court personnel escorted Eric to the defense table, Rivera removed her chewing gum and rubbed her hands in anticipation.

Eric's appearance had deteriorated another level during the prior five weeks. He looked a mess. The top several buttons on his shirt were unbuttoned. His shirt hung out of his pants.

As Judge Demakos explained Rivera's right to speak at

the sentencing of her daughter's murderer, she rose from her front-row seat and approached the well of the courtroom.

She began softly by thanking the numerous detectives from New York and Pennsylvania who had labored on the investigation as well as the district attorney's office.

She said her life had been devastated and in turmoil for twelve long years. "But I intended to live long enough for this encounter, in which I would once again face that beast! That animal dressed up in a human suit!"

Rivera looked straight at Eric, punctuating the words "beast" and "animal." In typical fashion, Eric reacted by talking nonstop into attorney Reiver's right ear.

Her voice cracking, Rivera said Eric had "employed his evil forces to brainwash an innocent young girl to satisfy his wicked desires, then sadistically smashed her life away."

Highly critical of the way society and the system viewed "money, color, and race," Rivera lashed out at the "incomprehensible as well as shameful procedures the New York City authorities had used to handle this vicious animal. My desperation and my cries for help were never heard. Moreover, they were ignored and neglected. . . . They could have prevented this unspeakable, monstrous, and criminal act."

Instead, she continued, police and prosecutors left Eric to join forces with "his wicked mother and his so-called uncle" to kill her daughter, then "skillfully conceal the evidence and thereby ridicule the authorities." To make things worse, she added, "Two other victims paid with their lives at the hands of this monster."

"I accept the fact that nothing will bring Marilyn back. It hurts profoundly, but I am convinced that her spirit is dancing with happiness at seeing my heart rejoice," Rivera told the judge. Professing unconditional love for her daughter and the Highest Authority, Rivera then asked that the "most severe punishment there is" be imposed on Eric and his accomplices. "Their miserable lives should be terminated immediately. Our beautiful planet should be cleansed of such repulsive animals."

Eric was beginning to behave as he had throughout Carmen Acevedo's tearful address at Eric's sentencing for Myra's murder. He was smiling, laughing, and trying to chat away with his attorney.

When asked by Judge Demakos if he had anything to say

before sentencing, Eric answered no in a loud and gruff voice.

The judge then observed that he was sickened by Eric's lack of remorse for such a "ruthless and cold-blooded act. In all my years, this behavior is beyond my comprehension." He officially sentenced Eric to fifteen years to life, to begin running only if and when Eric was released by New Jersey prison authorities. But, the judge continued, "I am sure that our parole board will never parole him!"

Outside court, Marta Rivera answered reporters' questions about her charge that racism had contributed to her daughter's death. "If I was white with money, Marilyn would still be here," she contended.

She also took the opportunity to once again lambaste Carolyn. "She'll be next. I'm gonna go after her now," Rivera declared. "I'm going to bring her to justice." Asked how she planned to carry out her goal, Rivera replied forcefully, "I'll find ways."

Family members consoled her and led her away.

With the Napoletano deals completed on both sides of the Hudson River, Pete Reese was now available for questions from the news media. Pressed to explain why Carolyn had not been charged in the Coludro case, the prosecutor cited a five-year statute of limitations on felonies other than murder.

Just how deep did he think her involvement went?

"We believe Carolyn moved the body. But we cannot prove it," Reese replied.

On August 28, 1996, a three-judge panel of the Appellate Division of Superior Court in New Jersey unanimously affirmed Eric's conviction in the murder of Myra Acevedo Napoletano.

Among other things, Eric claimed that Judge Hull had improperly allowed witnesses to testify that he had been controlling, threatening, and verbally abusive to his wife.

The appeals court saw things much differently. "Viewing the state's evidence in its entirety, and giving the state the benefit of all reasonable inferences, it is clear that a reasonable jury could have found guilt beyond a reasonable doubt."

In the end, then, New Jersey had not needed to cover its

bet. But Carolyn had done quite well covering hers—at her son's expense.

More than twelve years had now passed since the blood-draining butchering of Marilyn Coludro, and the disappearance of her missing-persons report.

More than eleven years had passed since the point-blank shooting of Gladys Matos, and the supposed alibi about mother and son eating eggs and toast in a coffee shop near One Police Plaza.

And more than six years had passed since the strangulation of Myra Acevedo Napoletano, and the supposed alibi about mother and son skipping dinner at the Red Lobster to stay by the phone in midtown Manhattan.

In spite of it all, Carolyn Napoletano continued to be employed by the New York City Police Department.